Accounting Classics Series

Publication of this Classic was made possible
by a grant from Arthur Andersen & Co.

Suggestions of titles to be included in the Series are solicited and should be addressed to the Editor.

Accounting Publications of Scholars Book Co.
Robert R. Sterling, Editor

Sidney S. Alexander, et al., *Five Monographs on Business Income*
Frank Sewall Bray, *The Accounting Mission*
Raymond J. Chambers, *Accounting, Evaluation and Economic Behavior*
Henry Rand Hatfield, *Accounting: Its Principles and Problems*
Bishop Carlton Hunt (Editor), *George Oliver May: Twenty-Five Years of Accounting Responsibility*
Kenneth MacNeal, *Truth in Accounting*
George O. May, *Financial Accounting: A Distillation of Experience*
William A. Paton, *Accounting Theory*
W. Z. Ripley, *Main Street and Wall Street*
DR Scott, *The Cultural Significance of Accounts*
Charles E. Sprague, *The Philosophy of Accounts*
George Staubus, *A Theory of Accounting to Investors*
Robert R. Sterling (Editor), *Asset Valuation and Income Determination: A Consideration of the Alternatives*
Robert R. Sterling (Editor), *Institutional Issues in Public Accounting*
Robert R. Sterling (Editor), *Research Methodology in Accounting*

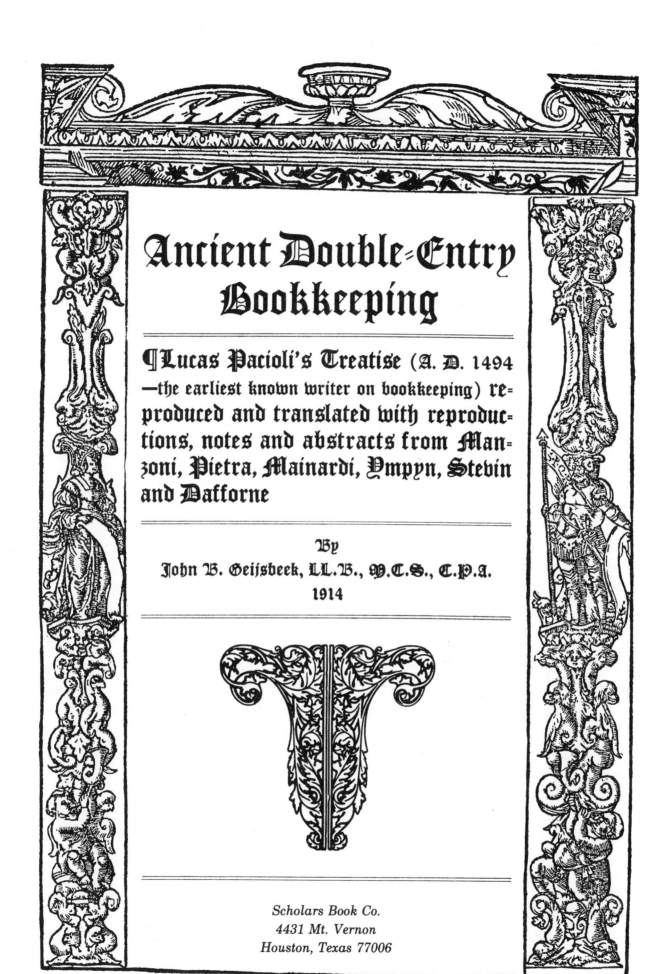

Ancient Double-Entry Bookkeeping

Lucas Pacioli's Treatise (A. D. 1494 —the earliest known writer on bookkeeping) reproduced and translated with reproductions, notes and abstracts from Manzoni, Pietra, Mainardi, Ympyn, Stevin and Dafforne

By
John B. Geijsbeek, LL.B., M.C.S., C.P.A.
1914

Scholars Book Co.
4431 Mt. Vernon
Houston, Texas 77006

Dedicated to My Wife

Marie Lillie Schmidt,

whose initials I have always loved to connect with

My Little Sweetheart,

without whose patience, kindness, help,
and indulgence, my contributions to the
educational field of the professional
accountant would not have been possible.

TABLE OF CONTENTS

INTRODUCTION

By Page Lawrence, C.P.A.

Nearly all historians, when tracing the growth of an art or science from mere empiricism to the establishment of recognized principles, are confronted with an apparent insurmountable gap or complete silence during the period known in history as the Dark Ages.

Archaeological and historical researches have convinced this civilization that in Ancient Babylon, Greece and Rome there was a high state of civilization—both industrial and social.

Today we may study Aristotle's politics with great profit in our attempts to understand the political and economic conditions confronting this generation. An acquaintance with the Greek philosophers is essential in understanding our present philosophical thought.

It would seem that, since we find so much help in consulting these ancient writers in an attempt to solve the political problems of today which are presented by this complex civilization, in a large measure at least our mentors must have been confronted with the same economic and industrial difficulties that we are attempting to solve now as accountants.

One is convinced that the ancient writers on political economy and commerce were closely allied with the scribes or accountants who recorded the business transactions of those days. This allegiance seems to have been lost after the Roman supremacy (and the consequent growth and spread of commerce), and it is only within recent years that the modern economist and accountant has acknowledged that a truer understanding of modern commerce can be had with cooperation and that the two sciences (economics and accounting) are finding so much in common that each is dependent upon the other for a full understanding of modern business conditions.

Mr. John P. Young, Editor of the San Francisco Chronicle, ably presented accounting in antiquity before the convention of the American Association of Public Accountants at San Francisco (Year Book 1911, page 153). He showed that Rome in Cicero's time was dependent upon the independent verification of accounts and statements thereof by one skilled in accountancy. The familiarity with which he mentions the accountant would seem to indicate that his place in the Roman social organization was well established.

However, after the recorded utterances of Cicero the historian finds in the pages of history no further mention of those individuals acknowledged to be skilled in accounts, which we are pleased to call accountants, until the writings of Pacioli in 1494 and Stevin in 1604.

It seems especially appropriate that one so greatly interested as the author in that work dear to the hearts of all progressive accountants, and who has done so much to place the education of the accountant on equal footing with that of law or medicine, should be the first of modern times to translate this first recorded book of the principles of debit and credit into the English language.

It is a significant fact that the rules and principles elucidated by Pacioli are contained in a book given over to mathematics. One cannot help but believe that the derivation of double-entry bookkeeping is an explanation of the algebraic equation used with such skill by the ancient Greek mathematicians, applied practically to the scientific recording of business transactions for, just as in algebra, the equation once established cannot be changed but by the addition of positive or negative quantities.

This work will give an added assurance that the apparently empirical rules of commerce are based upon an ancient scientific and mathematical foundation, to those who have attempted to instill into the commercial mind the idea that accountancy is a science, the prime requisite of a mastery of which is a thorough education in the theory of economics and allied sciences supplemented by practical experimentation in the application of formulae to practical business situations.

The accountant has to correct constantly, or at least modify, the attitude of the business man toward matters which are his dearest heirlooms handed down from the days of the Ancient Guild system, i. e., that the only way to learn how to do business is to do it along the rule-of-thumb method communicated from father to son by word of mouth.

Accountants, who remember the dearth of accountancy literature in this country up to a few short years ago, are dumbfounded at the mass of accountancy publications which are constantly flooding the market at this time. While I believe that the profession of accountancy as a whole recognizes the inestimable value of these publications, one cannot help but think in perusing their pages that they are largely influenced by the empirical methods of general business, rather than based on scientific principles. In other words, on "how" but never "why."

We are wont to look in vain through mazes of descriptions, forms and precedence of some particular business enterprise for a principle of accountancy which can be applied to the specific difficulty we have in hand. It should be the aim of some of the brilliant members of the profession of accountancy to take the great mass of historical records which have been published in the last few years of how this or that business should be kept and, with the aid of recognized authorities on economics, codify, with quotation of their source, the scattered and ill defined principles of accountancy for the benefit of accountancy education, and to this end no better examples of axiomatic principles can be had than in the books of Pacioli, Pietra and Stevin.

The author, recognizing from his experience as an educator in accountancy (coming as he did from Holland some twenty years ago without knowledge of American commercial practices or language) the lack of clearly expressed principles in accountancy, commenced researches which have finally culminated in this published translation in English of the first known writings on the subject of double entry book-keeping.

At every turn, in the preachment of the scientific principles of his profession to the commercial mind, in his successful efforts for the passage of the Certified Public Accounts law in Colorado, then in his work as secretary of the first examining board in that state, in his labors as Dean of the School of Commerce, Accounts and Finance of The University of Denver, and as an instructor on practical and theoretical accountancy subjects and, finally as Chairman of the Educational Committee of The American Association of Public Accountants, the author has ever been confronted with the dearth of practical exemplification, historical or otherwise, of the true foundation of what in modern times might be called the Art of Accountancy.

To weld together into a well balanced whole the two plans of accountancy education, as embraced in the curriculi of universities and colleges offering training to the embryo accountant, has long been the goal of his educational endeavors, i. e., to leaven the purely academic training by instructors or professors whose own knowledge of accountancy is in the main pedagogical, with the practical knowledge as imparted by the practicing accountant and the business man. (The author, in the American Association of Public Accountants Year Books for 1911-12-13 and 14, has gone into this subject extensively, showing that educational institutions of the country have chosen either the one or the other of the two methods of teaching—the academic training in pure theory, treated in much the same manner as economic subjects are presented and without the same degree of accuracy, or the practical lecturing upon accountancy subjects by practicing accountants and business men, supplemented by the best text books obtainable—and urging the while the necessity for the development together of the two accountancy educational plans, as is done in Great Britain.)

While it is true that to men of little or no practical experience in accountancy must be given the credit for producing some of the finest examples of purely theoretical accounting which the literature of accountancy has today, the first mentioned criticism that this pedagogical instruction does not teach the actual application of the theory to modern business, again applies. On the other hand, with the practical accountant as the instructor or the writer of text books, too little cannot be said of the difficulty he has in imparting to students and laymen the principles which seem exceedingly clear to him. And it was through this research, this labor to combine in accountancy education theory with practice and practice with theory, that this book was born. It is apparent in reading the ancient works of Pacioli, of Stevin and Pietra, in their exhaustive explanations and their lengthy and precise instructions that in their endeavors to systematize the recording of the transactions of commerce of their time, they encountered many of the same sort of, if not the identical, problems with which we are confronted today. The modern translations of their works, with the author's own views presented as notes, it is believed will shed some light into the darkness which has so long shrouded the actual foundation of the practice and the theory of the profession of public accountancy.

DENVER, COLORADO, August, 1914.

PREFACE

As no technical books worth while can be prepared without diligent and persistent research, it naturally follows that no such works can be produced unless there is material furnished to build upon, and the cheapest and easiest foundation is usually the writings of men who have excelled in the same line of endeavor. In other words, a library of books is absolutely essential to the advancement of thought on technical and professional subjects.

While studying to Americanize my knowledge of accountancy twenty years ago, I came to the conclusion that there were then on that subject few modern books and still fewer ancient ones. This conviction was constantly strengthened by conversation with my fellow-workers, and it remained unchanged until a few years ago.

When my duties came to include the teaching of accountancy and the direction of the thought of my students, the choice of books for their reading became a serious problem. It was then my privilege to start the collection of a considerable library of works on accountancy and its allied subjects.

However, I could learn of but few books of ancient date, and they were so scarce, difficult to get, and high priced, that most of them remain yet to be acquired. Among those which I did get is an original copy of the oldest published work on bookkeeping. The price for copies of this book ranges from $50 to $250, and it is thus not within the means of ordinary students and is even beyond the inclination of acquisition of many of the most wealthy libraries. It became my desire to have it reproduced, together with a free translation of its most important parts.

This desire increased when my research showed me that the first man to follow the teachings of this Italian book and to translate it into another language, was a fellow-countryman of mine, a Hollander named Jan Ympyn Christoffels. He translated it into the Holland, French, and English languages, and to this day we follow his lead, (as outlined in the title of his book), of calling double-entry bookkeeping by the use of day book, journal, and ledger, the Italian method of bookkeeping.

The Hollanders of ancient New Amsterdam (now New York) have left their unmistakable imprint on our American political and social life, by the introduction into this country of many things which originated in their mother-country and which were unknown even in England prior to their use in America. To this day many of these things remain unused in England, which is one reason why we are so different from the English. Among these things may be mentioned:*

The recording of deeds and mortgages in a public office; the equal distribution of property among the children of a person dying intestate; the office of a district attorney in each county; the practice of giving a prisoner the free services of a lawyer for his defense; the township system, by which each town has local self-government; the practice of making prisoners work; the turning of prisons into work houses; the system of university education; free public school system; the red, white and blue striped flag; the principles contained in our Declaration of Independence; the granting of religious freedom; the cultivation of roses; the present banking system; the use of reading and spelling books for children; the telescope; the microscope; the thermometer; the discovery of capillary circulation of the blood; the pendulum clock; measuring degrees of latitude and longitude; the compass; the wind-mill with movable cap; the glass hothouse; the use of underclothing; the bedstead; the brick; the game of golf.

It has seemed to me fitting that another Hollander should present to his American professional brethren, and put within the reach of every student of accounting, for research and study, a reproduction of that prized Italian book, which, as we shall see, has influenced us to such an extent that the principles it enunciates as of use in its day, remain the foundation of our present methods of bookkeeping.

It was not my aim to give a complete literal translation, because much of the text is reiteration and pertains to subject-matter purely local and now entirely obsolete, which would necessitate lengthy explanations of ancient methods of no present value or use. Therefore, numerous foreign terms and ancient names have been left untranslated. Furthermore, as the book was written in contemporary Italian, or, in other words, in the local dialect of Venice, which is neither Italian nor Latin, it is extremely difficult to get local talent sufficiently trained in this work to translate it all literally.

The old style of writing is unattractive and tiresome to follow. While it is customary and proper in translations to follow the original style as much as possible, and to change it no more than is necessary to make it readily understood and easily read in modern language, it was found extremely difficult to do that in this instance, and furthermore, it would have served no practical purpose. And then, who is there at the present time but a scholar of some eminence and a linguist of no mean accomplishment, who will presume to say what is correct and what is incorrect? Such authorities never agree among themselves, and it would be useless to attempt to please them all. Therefore, we are extending the translations, not so much for academic purposes as for the practical use of less pedantic people, upon the theory that they who wish to obtain knowledge of any science must first learn its history and then trace its gradual growth. There is hardly another science about which there is as much doubt and darkness as bookkeeping, and therefore we merely present this translation as a contribution to the history of bookkeeping.

---

*William Elliott Griffis in "The Ladies' Home Journal."

Criticism has been made of the title of this book, "Ancient Double-Entry Bookkeeping," in the use of the word "Ancient" as applied to the year 1493 A. D. The long obscurity of the "Dark Ages," during which there was no light whatever upon this important subject, has, in our belief, made the treatise of Pacioli ancient, and, further the abrupt "leap through the dark" from this ancient work to the works of modern times, we believe justifies the title.

The reader is further referred to the German translation of Pacioli's book by E. L. Jäger which appeared in 1876, and the Russian translation by E. G. Waldenberg which was printed in St. Petersburg in 1893.

Pacioli's book was first photographed and plates made from these photographs. Proof sheets from these plates were then sent to Rome, Italy, and there transcribed on a typewriter in modern letters, to facilitate translating. The typewritten transcript was then translated into English, which was then compared with an existing German translation by Dr. Jäger. Discrepancies were carefully noted by reference to the original book, and the best possible corrections made. This method brought to the surface obvious and glaring short-comings in the German translation, and it also demonstrated our own inability to comprehend and properly translate some of the old terms and words, which even the Italy of today has long forgotten. With it all then, we are free to admit that in numerous places our English translation is defective. However, we are not imposing on those who are better scholars than we, because we give the original Italian side by side with our English version, and any one so disposed can easily check it and correct our copy to suit his fancy.

The only object of our endeavors is to give something where there was nothing to those who heretofore could not avail themselves of the contents of this old and pioneer work on a subject now universally recognized as being the foundation of all our modern industrial and commercial problems.

We ask your indulgence for errors and omissions, and for the price of this book, as the work had to be done hastily and cheaply, for the financial success of this enterprise is exceedingly problematical, owing to the excessive cost of preparation and reproduction, and the very small possible circulation. The work therefore should be viewed largely as a labor of love, a voluntary philanthropic contribution to the profession of accountancy.

Acknowledgment is due and most gladly given to: my wife, a Certified Public Accountant of the State of Colorado, who aided with the German translation; to Mr. Robert Ferrari, LL.D. Roma, Italy, who aided with the Italian translation; to Mr. Henry Rand Hatfield, PH.D., University of California, who criticized the work; and to Mr. Page Lawrence, C.P.A., who wrote the introduction:—truly a veritable combination (trust) of formidable minds in restraint of duplication (competition) of this work, a combination of love and harmony, for without friends and without consideration for our neighbor there is neither peace nor accomplishment.

The book, therefore, is the result of a faithful compliance with the motto of the Boers of South Africa: "*Eendracht maakt macht*," which translated does not mean, as commonly stated, "In union there is strength," but rather that "United, harmonious, loving cooperation to the same lawful end tends toward power that brings just results."

J. B. Geijsbeek Molenaar.

DENVER, August, 1914.

PARTIAL BIBLIOGRAPHY

1494 to 1636.

Sixteen of the most influential books out of a possible total of 50 works.

I. ITALIAN.

Summa de Arithmetica, Geometria,
Proportioni et Proportionalita.

Part 1, Section 9, Treatise 11,
Particularis de Computis et Scripturis.

Frater Lucas de Burgo Sancti Sepulchri, Ordinis Minorum
et sacre theologie magister, in arte arithmetice et geometrie.

Venice 1494

Geijsbeek-Lawrence Library, Denver.
Harvard University Library, Cambridge, Mass.

La Scuola perfetta dei mercanti.

Fra. Paciolo di Borgo Santo Sepolcro.

Toscana 1504

Summa de Arithmetica

(see full title above, this being practically a duplicate edition of
1494, but contains less contractions and abbreviations.)

Venice 1523

Edinburgh, Chartered Accountants' Library.
Library, University of California.

Quaderno doppio col suo giornale secondo il costume di Venetia.

Domenico Manzoni.   Venice 1534

Also 1554-1564-1565-1573-1574

Edinburgh, Chartered Accountants' Library (1554 edition).

Indrizzo de gli economi.

Don Angelo Pietra de Genoa.

Mantua 1586

Geijsbeek-Lawrence Library, Denver.

La Scrittura Mercantile fatta e riordinata.

(Reprinted in 1700 under the title of "L'Economo overo La Scrittura tutelare, Scrittura Mercantile.")

Matteo Mainardi.   Bologna 1632

Geijsbeek-Lawrence Library, Denver.

II. GERMAN.

Ein Teutsch vertendig Buchhalten für Herren oder Gesellschafter inhalt
Wellischem process.

Johann Gotlieb.   Nuremberg 1531

Royal Library, Munich, Germany.

Zwifach Buchhalten.

Wolffgang Schweicker.   Nuremberg 1549

Kheil Library, Prag.
Edinburgh, Chartered Accountants' Library.

Buchhalten nach arth und weise der Italianer.

Passchier Goessens from Brussels.

Hamburg 1594

State Library, Stuttgart, Germany.

5

III. DUTCH.

Nieuwe Instructie Ende Bewijs der Looffelijcker Consten des Reken-
boeckse ende Rekeninghe te houdene nae die Italiaensche maniere.
Jan Ympyn Christoffels.

Antwerp (Dutch) 1543
Antwerp (French) 1543
Antwerp (English) 1543

City Library at Antwerp (Dutch).
Library of the Nicolai Gymnasium at Reval, Rus-
sia (English).
Fideicommiss-Bibliothek at Maihingen-Wallerstein,
Germany (French).

Verrechning van Domeine (including chapters on) Coopmans Bouck-
houding op re Italiaensche wyse and Vorstelicke Bouckhouding op de
Italiaensche wyse.
Simon Stevin.

Amsterdam 1604

Geijsbeek-Lawrence Library, Denver.

Hypomnemata Mathematica.
Simon Stevin.

Leijden 1608

IV. ENGLISH.

A briefe instruction and maner to keepe bookes of accompts after the
order of Debitor and Creditor, and as well for proper accompts parti-
ble, etc. newely augmented and set forth by John Mellis, Scholemaister.
(purporting to be a reprint of a book by Hugh Oldcastle, London,
1543.)
John Mellis.

London 1588

Library of Institute of Chartered Accountants in
England and Wales (London).

The Merchants' Mirrour or Directions for the Perfect Ordering and
Keeping of his Accounts. Framed by Way of Debitor and Creditor
after the (so-termed) Italian Manner.
Richard Dafforne.

London 1636
Also 1651-1660-1684

Geijsbeek-Lawrence Library, Denver.
Harvard University Library, Cambridge, Mass.
Library of Congress, Washington, D. C.

HISTORICAL REFERENCES

Schatzkammer Italienischen Buchhaltens.

    Christophorus Achatius Hagern.   Hamburg 1654

        State Library, Stuttgart, Germany.

Beiträge zur Geschichte der Erfindungen.

    Johann Beckmann.   Leipzig 1786

      Library of Congress, Washington, D. C.
      State Library, Stuttgart, Germany.

Origin and Progress of Bookkeeping.

    B. F. Foster.   London 1852

      Library of Institute of Chartered Accountants
      in England and Wales (London).

Die Berechtigung der einfachen Buchhaltung gegenüber der doppelten.
    Ernst Ludwig Jäger.   Stuttgart 1868

      Library, University of California.

Beiträge zur Geschichte der Doppelbuchhaltung.
    Ernst Ludwig Jäger.

                    Stuttgart 1874
      Library, University of Chicago.
      Library, University of California.

Lucas Paccioli und Simon Stevin.

    Ernst Ludwig Jäger.   Stuttgart 1876

      Library, University of Chicago.

Luca Pacciolo, considerato come ragionere, lezione tenuto alla r. scuolo di commerzio.
    Guido Brandaglia de Arezzo.

                    Venice 1882
Elenco Cronologico della opera di computisteria e ragioneira venute alla ence in Italia.

                    Rome 1886
      Library of Congress, Washington, D. C.

Ueber einige ältere Bearbeitugen der Buchhaltung—Tractates Von Luca Pacioli.
    Carl Peter Kheil.

                    Prag 1896
      Geijsbeek-Lawrence Library, Denver.

The History of Accounting and Accountants.
    Richard Brown, Editor.

                    Edinburgh 1905

HISTORICAL

Printing from blocks of wood in which the letters were carved, was known long before the Christian era, but this was cumbersome and slow and hence but few books were published in that manner. Printing from loose metal type which could be set up in the way known to us to-day did not begin to be a success until after A. D. 1462, when the German city of Maintz or Mentz (where the first well-known printer, Gutenberg, and his students lived) was sacked by Adolph of Nassau, and those who were printers were scattered far and wide through other cities.

Even during the first part of the sixteenth century, one-fourth of all the books printed came from one city only, i. e., Venice in Italy. Therefore a book produced from loose type in 1494 in Venice, must have been among the very first printed, and its subject must have been at that time of such prime importance as to make it worthy of being among the first to be published. The oldest treatise which has come down to us either printed or written on the subject of bookkeeping, is included as a part of a rather large printed volume on arithmetic and geometry. This volume was published in November, 1494, in Venice, Italy. It has been used considerably by later writers on the subject of arithmetic and geometry, and is mentioned in numerous works of bibliographers, both ancient and modern. The title is: Summa de Arithmetica Geometria Proportioni e Proportionalita.'' Bookkeeping is treated in Part One, Section 9, Treatise 11, under the chapter title of ''Particularis Computis et Scripturis,'' which translated would mean: ''Particulars of Reckonings and Their Recording.''

The exact name of the author cannot be established definitely from this work, as his full name does not appear on the title page nor anywhere else. The author calls himself in this book Frater Lucas de Burgo Sancti Sepulchri, which translated into English may be called Brother Lucas of the City of the Holy Sepulchre. The City of the Holy Sepulchre, or Sancti Sepulchri, is a city in the northern part of Italy near Venice. On page 67-2, line 5, of Frater Lucas' book ''Summa de Arithmetica,'' he states that about A. D. 1470 he dedicated a certain book to his students named Bartolo, Francesco, and Paulo, the three sons of a prominent merchant of Venice named (Antonio de) Rompiasi. From other writings and other evidence, bibliographers have come to the conclusion through their researches that the real name of this ''Frater Lucas'' was Lucas Pacioli.

The copyright of the book published in 1494 expired in 1504, and about that time a reprint of the chapter on bookkeeping appeared in Toscana, under the title of ''La Scuola perfetta dei Mercanti.'' A copy of this reprint was not in the possession of the writer, but it would appear that there the name of the author was given as Fra. Paciolo di Borgo Santo Sepolcro. In other writings he is known as Patiolus, which is supposed to be the Latin for Pacioli.

In 1509, shortly before he died, he wrote a book called ''Divina Proportione,'' in which he gives a foreword and reproduces several letters he has written. In these he signs himself as Lucas Patiolus. This book was written in Latin. On page 33-b of this book, in section 6, treatise No. 1, chapter No. 1, the author refers to his book published in 1494 in the following words: ''*in opera <u>nostra</u> grande dicta summa de arithmetica etc. impressa in Venetia nel 1494 et al Magnanimo Duca d'Urbino dicata.*'' We underscored the word ''nostra,'' which means ''our.''

Lucas Pacĭoli, as we will call him hereafter, believing that to be his proper name, was born about 1445 in the little city of Sancti Sepulchri, in the Province of Arezzo, of Tuscany, west south-west of the City of Urbino. He was a great lecturer, mathematician, writer, scholar, teacher, and traveler, a well-known and famous man, who was the first to translate into Latin the works of Euclid. Successively he was professor of mathematics at Perugia, Rome, Naples, Pesa and Venice, and was chosen for the first occupant of a professor's chair founded by Louis Sforza. He was in Milan with Leonardo da Vinci at the Court of Louis the Moor until the invasion of the French. It is not improbable that Leonardo da Vinci helped Pacioli in the writing of this work as there are indications of two distinct styles of writing. He belonged to the Order of Friars Minor of St. Francis. It is apparent that he took the cloth late in life, for protection and standing needed in his many traveling tours, during the unrest then existing in Italy. He wrote his treatise on bookkeeping when he was about 50 years old, and died near the end of the year 1509, at the age of 65.

It is but natural that bookkeeping should be always in its greatest perfection in those countries where commerce has reached its highest stage. It is well known that during the twelfth, thirteenth, fourteenth and fifteenth centuries Venice was a powerful republic, from which all European commerce radiated, until in 1498 the East Indian ocean route was discovered, from which time on the commercial power of Venice waned. It is safe to assume that the book here reproduced faithfully depicts the conditions existing at the time of its writing and the prevailing system of recording the transactions of commerce. All the world's commerce, practically speaking, was concentrated in this small territory, therefore its system of bookkeeping must have been the most perfect known in the world at that time. The existence of a well advanced system of bookkeeping in the centers of commerce must have caused considerable confusion and correspondence with the places where such a system did not exist, in order to equalize and settle accounts between the merchants residing in these various places.

It is therefore probable that a great need existed for taking advantage of the facilities which the new inventions in printing permitted, to present to the commercial world outside of these centers a systematic treatise of the most important part of commerce, namely, the recording of its transactions and results. Pacioli does not claim that he invented double-entry bookkeeping, but on the other hand mentions in his book the existence of ancient customs and numerous methods named after the places where they were used. Thus he calls the method of bookkeeping he describes, the method of Venice, as distinguished from those in use in other cities, the names of which appear in the translation we have made of his book.

While Pacioli gives in his book on arithmetic and geometry copious illustrations, as will be seen from the sample page of that portion of the book herein reproduced, he did not give examples and illustrations of the day book, the journal and ledger, which he describes. His book therefore has never become as popular as those of later writers who give these examples. Pacioli, however, was very lengthy and careful in his minute and detailed description of the various methods employed. The reading of his book will be a revelation to those who have an idea that the present high state of development of American commerce should have produced methods of bookkeeping unknown at such an early period as when Pacioli wrote. They will find that there then existed the little safeguards which are not described or explained in present books of instruction on bookkeeping, but which we accountants are always wont to preach about to those bookkeepers who come under our observation, and which we do not pass by simply as mere suggestions but upon which we insist emphatically with a "You *must* do this." Pacioli especially describes these little things with great emphasis, and in a style cunning in the extreme, fully punctuated with adages to bring the truth home so no one could forget it. He, however, on the other hand, does not spend any time in explaining the modus operandi of bookkeeping, which we learn only by practice (as he puts it), as he doubtless appreciated that he was not writing his treatise to teach bookkeeping to those who did not know anything about it, but only describing the advantage of the particular method in use in Venice in order to convert merchants to a change from their system to the best system then known.

Writers who have followed after Pacioli have practically all given full illustrations of the journal and ledger, but have rather neglected to explain the "whys" and "wherefores" of the little and valuable details upon which Pacioli has laid so much stress, taking them as matters of fact rather than as fundamental principles. As we all know, it is the little things which throw the safeguards about a proper system of bookkeeping.

It is not the writer's aim to go into detail as to the history of bookkeeping. Any one desiring to study this subject in its entirety, is referred to the most remarkable records and researches of Jäger, Kheil, and Row Fogo as edited by Brown, the title of whose books are fully described in the bibliography hereto appended.

Jäger and Kheil were prominent German scholars, who must have devoted an enormous amount of time to their researches as to the origin and growth of bookkeeping. Jäger was somewhat hasty and inaccurate; Kheil is somewhat brief, and therefore difficult to understand by those who have not read other books on the subject. Both of these books are written in German.

Happily we Americans have the aid of the recent book written in Scotland by Brown and his associates. The treatise they present is exhaustive, brief, to the point, and exceedingly accurate, fully illustrated, and is of immense value to every student of the subject of accountancy.

The writer does not wish to duplicate the work of any of these three, but by the present volume he desires to emphasize the fact that Pacioli's work is the real foundation of all books published in Germany, Holland, France, and England within the first hundred years after it was written. We will do nothing more than describe the effect of Pacioli's book on Manzoni and Pietra which appeared in Italian, Gotlieb, Schweicker, and Goessens, which appeared in German, Ympyn and Stevin in Dutch, Ympyn in French, and Ympyn, Oldcastle, Mellis, and Dafforne in English, as these books undoubtedly have been the basis for subsequent works in these various languages, most of which are at present available for comparison and study. The titles of other contemporary books can be found in the bibliography of Mr. Brown's work, for he gives an exhaustive list of over 150 books written on this subject between Pacioli's time and the beginning of the nineteenth century. Of these, 50 were written prior to the publication of Dafforne's "The Merchants' Mirrour" in 1636, which is really the first popular English work. Most of these 50 were written in Italian, Dutch, or German, with the honors about evenly divided.

As we have said, Lucas Pacioli's book appeared in Venice in 1494, with a ten-year copyright. At the expiration of that period, or in 1504, the same printers published an exact duplicate of this book, under a different title. Twenty-one years after the last date, or in 1525, there appeared in Venice a very unsatisfactory and incomplete work on bookkeeping by Giovanni Antonio Tagliente, of which the historians do not say much.

Forty years after Pacioli's book of 1494, or in the year 1534, Domenico Manzoni published in Venice his book on bookkeeping, which proved very popular, as during a period of 40 years it went through six or seven editions, which may be termed a tremendous success, considering the conditions of those times.

Manzoni dedicated his book to Alouisius Vallaressus, a rich brother of a friend of his named Petrus. It seems apparent from his preface that he commenced the book years before it was published, when all three (the author, his friend, and the latter's rich brother) were going to school in Venice. In the title he mentions "the method of Venice," but he does not tell anywhere how or where he gained his knowledge and does not give Lucas Pacioli any mention or credit.

Manzoni wrote in dialect, or what is called "patois." He says in his preface that he is not a scholar and cannot use flowery language but only the speech of his mother, which he learned by word of mouth. He states too that he is a poor man. In those days only the very rich and the clergy could attend schools. The poor were usually artisans, learning their trade from their parents.

Manzoni's book may be termed a revised reprint of Pacioli. Page after page is identical and word for word, and the remainder is merely shorn of the religious expressions, adages, and peculiar repetitions which Pacioli so freely indulged in. Much of value and many of the details given in Pacioli's book are here omitted.

This book is divided into two parts, one for the text and the other for examples of journal and ledger. While the text covers but 12 of the 36 chapters of Pacioli, the two parts combined may be said to reproduce about 18 chapters of Pacioli. At the beginning of the writer's translation of Pacioli's book herein, a comparative index is given, which illustrates just how much of Pacioli's book Manzoni copied and what he left out. The only new idea in his book as compared with that of Pacioli, is the consecutive numbering of the journal entries. In some respects, however, Manzoni is clearer than Pacioli, as for instance, he gives definite rules for the making of journal entries; tabulates six things or matters of information always contained in every journal entry; describes the form of journal better by mentioning five "standing" or "down" lines; explains the use of more than one day book; and gives a chapter to the apparent transposition of the terms "A" (our "To") and "Per" (our "By") in the ledger from its customary use in the journal.

Manzoni gives full illustrations of the journal and ledger, with its entries, which Pacioli, for reasons stated, did not deem necessary. The addition of these illustrations of course has made the book more popular, and Manzoni, while a plagiarist in other respects, must be given the credit of having really been the first to do this. The writer regrets that Manzoni's book is not accessible to him for on that account only one reproduction can here be given, namely, the last page of the journal, which is taken from Brown's history of accounting.

In 1586, nearly 100 years after Pacioli wrote, we find that Don Angelo Pietra published a work on bookkeeping fully illustrated with numerous examples. The book was printed in Mantua by Franz Osanna. Pietra was a monk, born in Genoa, stationed at the Monastery of Monte Cassino, Neapel, Province of Caserta, near Sora. He was the auditor, storekeeper, and cellarer of that monastery. He belonged to the Order of St. Benedict, and dedicated his book to Lastancius Facius, the abbot of the Benedictine monastery at Mantua. Pietra's style is very clear and concise, and his book contains some 60 short but pithy chapters. As will be seen from the comparative index heretofore mentioned, and given farther on in this book, Pietra had for his guide the books of both Pacioli and Manzoni, for he covered matters which Pacioli did, and also the items which we have just seen Manzoni mentioned in his book but which we do not find in Pacioli. Especially is this true in the enumeration of the items which always must appear in a journal entry. Pietra uses Manzoni's six items in the same order, but adds thereto two others. He also gives the definite rules for making journal entries, mentions the transposition of "A" and "Per," the five standing lines in the journal, and enumerates several day books. He gives further some 30 additional items which neither Manzoni nor Pacioli mentions. Jäger does not speak very highly of Pietra, but it seems to the writer that Pietra was an ingenious man, fully as well educated as Pacioli, and a good deal more experienced in the necessities required of a bookkeeper. He recommends several innovations, prominent among which is double entry bookkeeping for those who are not in business for profit but are capitalists or associations not organized for the making of profits, which we might call eleemosynary corporations. For this purpose he describes three different ledgers, one for merchants, one for bankers, and one for capitalists and those similarly situated. He calls the ledger for the capitalist "economic ledger."

Unlike Pacioli and Manzoni, Pietra does not begin with an inventory, but with a proprietorship account. He is exceedingly careful in the taking of his inventory, and gives in his book a large folded insert containing a tabular inventory. He gives a tabulation of entries for the ledger which do not have to go through the journal (such as closing entries). He advocates the vouchering of disbursements. He minutely explains that expense accounts can show two balances, and that they can show a profit as well as a balance to be carried forward in the nature of an inventory. The detail of some 30 items which he mentions in his book and which neither Manzoni nor Pacioli describes, we give farther on, by the side of the reproduction of some of the pages of Pietra's book.

In 1632 there appeared in Bologna a work on bookkeeping written by Matteo Mainardi. This book is of a far later date than the ones heretofore mentioned, but it is somewhat remarkable in that it attempts to describe, besides the system for the merchants, one for the keeping of executor's and trustee's accounts. In many respects this book compares favorably with that of Pietra, and Mainardi undoubtedly had all the three books just described at his command. In the reproductions herein, we are giving only the title, the preface, and two pages of the journal, the last for the purpose of indicating the method then in use of showing journal entries with more than one debit or more than one credit, and to indicate further that bookkeeping made far greater progress in Holland than in Italy, as will be apparent from the discussion of Simon Stevin's book published in 1604.

We will now pass to the German authors. We have mentioned before that Venice and other places in the northern part of Italy were the centers of commerce from which the distribution of merchandise was made to the inland. The nearest commercial city of the inland known in those days was Nuremberg, and it is therefore but natural that we should find there the first work on bookkeeping published in the German language. The author was Johann Gotlieb, and the book was published in Nuremberg in 1531, three years before Manzoni, the second Italian writer, published his book. The author states frankly that he has translated his work from the "Welsh," meaning by this term "Italian." His book is considered a brief and very poor copy of Pacioli.

Gotlieb's book, however, is not the first that we know of in Germany. Henricus Grammateus, who called himself in German Heinrich Schreiber, lived for a long while in Vienna and there wrote in 1518 a book called "Rechenbüchlin, Künstlich, behend und gewiss auf alle, Kauffmanschafft gerichtet" containing mostly a text on arithmetic, but devoting some pages to the description of a very poor system of bookkeeping, which by a stretch of the imagination may be identified as possibly covering double-entry bookkeeping. This work was printed in Erfurt in 1523, and in Frankfurt in 1572.

After Gotlieb's book we find one published in 1549 at Nuremberg entitled "Zwifach Buchhalten," by Wolfgang Schweicker. This work can not be called excellent, nor is it as exhaustive or as good as that of either Pacioli or Manzoni, but there is no doubt that he had both of these books at his command, and especially followed Manzoni. The three German books thus far mentioned were undoubtedly not good enough to have become standards, and they have exerted little influence on the methods of bookkeeping used since then in Germany.

The first writer who was able to leave an impression which is lasting to this day was Passchier Goessens, a Dutchman from Brussels. He wrote, in 1594, at Hamburg where he was then living, a book on bookkeeping. Goessens states very plainly in his preface where he had learned the art and the title indicates that he followed the Italian system. He obtained his information from some of the earlier Dutch writings, which we will soon mention. German bookkeepers therefore, have benefited more by the knowledge which the Dutch imparted to them than by that which their own countrymen brought direct from Italy.

Next in importance and period of time, we come to the influence of the Dutch writers on the German, French, and English subsequent authors on the subject of bookkeeping. The Dutch for centuries controlled the supremacy of the seas, as they were great ship-builders and navigators. They were excellent, careful and honest tradesmen, and their trade was sought far and wide. Yet the Italian cities, through their ancient relation with the eastern nations, had become the world's leaders in commerce and the Dutch people were therefore forced to trade with these Italian republics until the discovery in 1498 of an all-ocean route to the eastern countries. Thereafter the center of commerce was shifted from Venice and its surrounding republics to Holland. As the Dutch were such travelers on water, they naturally sent their young men by water to the trade centers, for education and training, and in this way the knowledge of commerce also shifted from Venice to the Dutch countries.

Jan Ympyn Christoffels was one of the Dutch merchants who visited Venice and the northern part of Italy and he remained there for twelve years. He returned evidently wise in the knowledge of the keeping of books according to the Italian manner and wrote a book on that subject. He did not, however, live to see his book published, but his widow Anna Swinters published his manuscripts in the Dutch and French languages during the year 1543. Of the Dutch edition there seems to be but one copy in existence, which is in the City Library at Antwerp. The French work, however, can be purchased. The discovery by Hugo Balg of an English copy of this book in a Russian library was reported by the German scholar Kheil, although it was so mutilated that the name of the author does not remain, and the exact date of its publication is not known. However, from the similarity of the contents Kheil established the authorship of this book. The widow of Jan Ympyn Christoffels (better known as Jan Ympyn), says very distinctly in the preface of the Dutch book that it was written by her husband and that she merely published it, which statement would indicate that the English book was written prior to 1543. The illustrations in the book bear date of 1536 and 1537.

Ympyn claims to have obtained his knowledge in Italy, and says he used Italian books for the foundation of his work. He gives credit, however, indirectly to a person who has never been known as an author on bookkeeping, and historians rather indicate that this person was merely an excellent bookkeeper from whom he gained considerable knowledge. He mentions, however, very distinctly the book of Lucas Pacioli, although he calls him Brother Lucas de Bargo. We find Lucas Pacioli's name thus quoted in a large number of books subsequently published, from which we may infer that Ympyn's work was well known and used by a good many writers, because from no other source could they have obtained this faulty version of Pacioli's name.

The next important writer in the Dutch language was Simon Stevin, who wrote in Latin a book on mathematics, which was published in Leijden in 1608, in which he includes several chapters on bookkeeping. These were a reproduction of a book published in the Dutch language on "bookkeeping for merchants and for princely governments," which appeared in Amsterdam in 1604, and was rewritten in The Hague in 1607 in the form of a letter addressed to Maximiliaen de Bethune, Duke of Seulley. This Duke was superintendent of finance of France, and had numerous other imposing titles. He had been very successful in rehabilitating the finances of France, and Stevin, knowing him through Prince Maurits of Orange, was very anxious to acquaint him with the system which he had installed and which had proven so successful. This manuscript of 1607 was published in book form by Stevin's son Hendrick "in the second year of the Dutch Peace" of Munster (1648), which ended the eighty year war with Spain; this would make the date of publication 1650. Hendrick Stevin dedicated the book to the sister of the deceased Prince Maurits, expressing the hope that she may continue with the system of municipal bookkeeping which had made her brother's stewardship of the affairs of government so successful. Stevin's book becomes very important to Americans, because he materially influenced the views of his friend Richard Dafforne, who through his book "The Merchants' Mirrour," published in 1636, became practically the English guide and pioneer writer of texts on bookkeeping.

Simon Stevin, who was born in Bruges near Antwerp in 1548, and died in The Hague in 1620, was a traveler, author, mathematician, engineer, and inventor, a highly educated man who thought bookkeeping important enough to induce Prince Maurits of Orange, the then governor of the Dutch countries, to install double-entry bookkeeping throughout his territory, thus practically putting municipal accounting on the double-entry system, the very thing we are today after more than three hundred years sighing for. Stevin wrote part of the text of his book in the form of a dialogue, consisting of questions and answers, which he says actually occurred in the arguments he had while teaching Prince Maurits the art of bookkeeping.

Simon Stevin served his apprenticeship in a mercantile office in Antwerp, where he learned bookkeeping. After that he held important public offices, such as quarter-master-general, surveyor of taxes of Bruges and, under Prince Maurits was minister of finances and chief inspector of public works. There he displayed such inventive ingenuity in engineering that he may be said to have been the founder of modern engineering. His discoveries were in dynamics and hydrostatics, and among his many other inventions may be mentioned an important improvement to the canal locks. He was the first to bring into practical use decimal fractions. His works on engineering and fortifications have remained standards until the last decade or two.

Stevin was a prolific writer on many varied subjects. Among other things, he wrote about the art of war on land as well as on sea, about the construction of buildings, residences, and fortifications, the improvement of cities and agricultural lands, about water mills, canals, the art of singing, the art of oratory, rhetoric, mathematics, geometry, and about the weighing of metals and alloys through the difference in weight above water and under water.

The writer would consider Stevin to be one of the first men of whom we have a record as performing duties equal to those of a modern accountant. We have seen that his regular work was that of superintendent of finance (secretary of the treasury) and chief engineer of fortifications and public buildings of Holland, besides being tutor and adviser to Prince Maurits of Orange. In addition to all of this, he was continually called in to settle disputes between partners, audited numerous mercantile books and drew therefrom financial statements, made up partnership books to obtain their settlements, installed systems in all departments of government, in mercantile houses, royal households, municipalities, for construction of specific fortifications and public buildings, traveled to England, France, Germany, Italy, Denmark and Belgium, in order to appear before courts to give testimony in the settlement of financial affairs, and performed numerous other duties of an accountant, which we may infer from his remarks throughout his book.

Jäger, Kheil, and Row Fogo through Brown ridicule to a considerable extent the old writers on bookkeeping, instead of describing the worthy things about them and marveling at their accuracy and ingenuity. Especially do they harangue about Stevin's Latin, but overlook entirely the many worthy suggestions from Stevin's inventive genius.

In Brown's book on the history of accounting Stevin's treatise on mercantile bookkeeping is highly spoken of but Stevin is ridiculed for his endeavor to put municipal accounting on the double-entry system. We feel this to be an injustice to Stevin, for the reason that while his descriptions on municipal accounting may at first blush appear to be faulty, we learn from the descriptions and illustrations he gives of mercantile bookkeeping that he was exceedingly brief but accurate, and that therefore in the text we should take much for granted.

Stevin did not fully illustrate municipal accounting, for three reasons: first of all the officials who were to use the system he installed received regular orders with forms attached from headquarters; therefore his book was not a full exposition of all these orders with their forms, but was merely a review of the entire system. Secondly, (as he states) he was writing an argument in favor of his system to those officials who were forced to use it and might hesitate to support it loyally. This he did in an authoritative manner, by quoting continually the friendly and close association he had with the Prince, which of course he could not make use of in his official orders. Thus he put power and dignity behind his orders. Thirdly, he fully illustrated mercantile accounting and insisted on the employment only of clerks who were well versed in the art of bookkeeping according to the Italian method. After illustrating mercantile accounting thoroughly, he then simply describes the difference between the two systems, which (he reiterates) is his only aim. He gives eight pages of journal and forty pages of ledger on municipal accounting, although they contain only opening and not closing entries. The latter he explains fully in his text by stating deviations from the system used by merchants.

Yet apparently Stevin's treatise on municipal accounting is judged only by the absence of illustrations, but no credit is given him for the ingenious devices he mentions and which we now call internal checks. Brown evidently had not read much of the text, nor his son's subsequent book and notes, which as we have seen heretofore were published in 1650, at which time his son states that while some defects were found in the previous treatise, the system had survived until that day and had been improved upon, he describing such improvements in addition to reproducing his father's works.

Stevin was very ingenious in prescribing methods for what we now are wont to call "internal checks." For instance, in order to check the pay roll of the soldiers and other public officials, he demanded that the pay roll be sent direct to the auditors (and he calls them *auditeurs*, the French for auditors), and then insisted that the cook at the mess-house where all the soldiers and officials were being fed, should report independently to the auditors the number of meals served.

Another internal check which he suggested in order to stop the making of errors and the stealing in the collection of taxes and rents, was to make the sub-treasurer's report to the general treasurer each month of not only the cash receipts and disbursements but the persons remaining delinquent in their payments. After the reported delinquents remained so for three months, he suggested the sending of the sheriff by the general treasurer (not the sub-treasurers) to sell the property of the delinquent tax-payer or to collect from him a bond. He explains that thus you can force the tax-payer to demand a receipt from the sub-treasurer when paying, and display it to the sheriff, and thus get evidence against the sub-treasurer of stealing.

Towards the end of this book we are reproducing Stevin's journal and ledger, and appended thereto we have given some further remarks describing the superiorities of Stevin's work, which will prove interesting reading. Stevin undoubtedly followed Ympyn, who in turn as we have seen, obtained his knowledge from Pacioli.

Up to this date then, we have, besides general mercantile books, records of specific systems of book-keeping for merchants, branch stores, traveling salesmen, partnerships, household accounts, bankers, capitalists, monasteries, executors, and municipalities, as we will see from the specialties enumerated by these writers.

We next will make a survey of how the knowledge of bookkeeping came to England, whence it probably came to America.

We find that a school teacher by the name of John Mellis wrote in London in 1588 a book on book-keeping, which in his preface he states to be a reprint of a book by Hugh Oldcastle, which Mellis says appeared in London in 1543 under the title of "A profitable treatyce called the Instrument or Boke to learne to knowe the good order of the kepying of the famouse reconynge called in Latyn Dare and Habere and in Englyshe Debitor and Creditor." No copy exists as far as is known of this book of Oldcastle, and it is not therefore an absolute certainty that it ever existed. It might have been a manuscript only, and again, the date may not be reliable. It may also be that the book was written by some one else, and given to John Mellis by Hugh Oldcastle. It may therefore have been Jan Ympyn's book in English, especially as the dates are so close together. However this may be, Mellis's book is nothing more than a translation of Pacioli's book, and Mellis states that he had traveled and studied in the Dutch country. Brown in his history of accounting openly says that every English writer on accounting in the early days gained his knowledge from the Dutch, because Holland was the training school for English merchants, and he gives numerous instances to support his statement.

Any one doubting that Mellis's book is a translation of Pacioli, should compare Mellis's description of the checking of the ledger, as quoted by Brown, with our translation of this same subject in Pacioli's book. That Mellis is undoubtedly a copy of Pacioli, appears from an error he made in referring in one of his chapters to a chapter previously mentioned, naming it chapter 15, the same as Pacioli stated in his chapter 16, but as Mellis left out chapter 5 of Pacioli, containing a short introduction, and also chapter 7 about the certification of books by notaries, Mellis's chapter 14 is the same as Pacioli's 16, and Mellis's chapter 13 is the same as Pacioli's 15; yet Mellis makes reference to chapter 15 the same as Pacioli, instead of using chapter 13. The discovery of this error is mentioned in Brown's history of accounting.

Next in importance, and the last book we will mention in our survey, is "The Merchants' Mirrour," by Richard Dafforne. Dafforne says that in Germany, Italy and Holland, there had existed a great many able writers on bookkeeping, and he gives a large list of authors. He attributes the existence of these books to the demand, stating that there would not be a supply unless there was a demand. He very much deplores the fact that such a demand did not exist in England, nevertheless he contributes his book, which is undoubtedly a very able treatise. He even speaks of his acquaintance with Simon Stevin, and he writes his book on the same order as Stevin, namely, in dialogue style, or questions and answers. Dafforne's book was published in London for the first time in 1636, and appeared afterwards in 1651, 1660, and 1684. Later English writers have followed Dafforne and Mellis. Therefore, directly and indirectly, Pacioli through the Dutch, has laid the foundation of our present accounting literature and our present knowledge of bookkeeping.

We are reproducing most of the text of Dafforne's book and a few pages from the daybook, journal and ledger. Anyone doubting that Dafforne followed Simon Stevin and other Dutch writers on bookkeeping will be convinced by reading his text. Numerous quotations are made from these and other Dutch authors throughout the text and even in the title page. In one place an abstract from the bible is rendered in the Dutch language. Further Dafforne states that he received his knowledge and ideas in Holland and that part of the illustrations and text was written in Holland. The mentioning of so many Dutch customs and Dutch names in the ledger accounts shows that he himself succumbed to what he feared: "They being then at Rome, will do as there is done."

While we have described thus far the oldest text books in existence on the subject of bookkeeping, the records of books of account predate these considerably, and for further information on this subject we can do no better than refer you to Brown's history of accounting, where not only detail is given but where also convincing illustrations are reproduced. However, the purpose of presenting to the reader a correct idea of what was done in this line, we might state that the books of the steward of the city of Genoa in 1340 were kept on the double-entry principle. The oldest mercantile ledger at Venice is dated 1460, and is that of the firm of Donado Soranzo & Brothers. This ledger has a profit & loss and a capital account. Specimens of this ledger are reproduced in Brown's history of accounting on pages 99 to 106, and will greatly help the reader to understand Pacioli's instructions, in respect to the year, the Roman figures in the money column, and the Arabic figures for the smallest coin or Picioli, etc.

DISCURSION IN THEORY

We find in the translations of the old treatises on bookkeeping the terms debit, credit, inventory, journal, cash, capital, balance, per (modern by), a (modern to), assets, liabilities, etc., and a definition of each of these with their use in the olden times should prove of interest.

Our word debit is put in Italian as *"debito"*, which comes from the old Latin *debita* and *debeo*, which in business and from the standpoint of the proprietor means "owe" or "he owes to the proprietor," that which was loaned or given him by the proprietor. (The old authors do not use it in ledger accounts.)

Our word credit is put in Italian as *"credito,"* coming from the old Latin word *"credo,"* which means "trust or believe," as in business our creditors were "believers" in the integrity of the proprietor, and therefore loaned or gave him something. Therefore, from the proprietor's point of view, the word should be translated as the creditor "is owed by the proprietor," that which was loaned or given to the proprietor. (The old authors do not use it in ledger accounts.)

Inventory in Italian, *"inventario,"* comes from the Latin *"invenio,"* which means to find out or discover.

Journal in Italian *"giornal"* comes from the Latin *"diurnalis"* which means daily happenings or diurnal.

Ledger comes from the Dutch *"Legger"* meaning "to lie down" and was originated probably from the necessity that the ledger, which was called the big book, became so large and cumbersome that it remained, or was lying, always in one place.

Cash in Italian, *"cassa,"* comes from case or box, which is the same as the Italian *borscia* from the Latin *bursa* or purse.

Capital, which is mentioned in Italian as *"Cavidale,"* comes from the old Latin *"capitalis,"* which means "chief" or "head," and also from the Latin *"capitali,"* which means property. Thus capital would mean "the property of the chief," i. e., proprietorship.

As to the word "balance," the following will indicate its meaning. A clear distinction is made by the old writers between (1) the difference in an account between the debit amounts and the credit amounts, (2) the reason for entering this difference in the account, and (3) the status of the account after equalizing both sides by the making of an entry and closing the account. We term all three balances and balancing, while two are distinctly opposite. In Italian they call the difference or the remainder, *"resto,"* and say they have entered this remainder in order to close (*saldo*), and then they state that the account is in balance (*bilancio*).

As to the terms "By" and "To," Manzoni says, as does Pacioli, that in the journal entries the word "Per" denotes the debtor and always precedes it, and that "A" denotes the creditor.

Manzoni then goes on to point out that the prevailing system (which Pacioli describes) in his time was to use "Per" only (and not "A") as far as it relates to the ledger. He calls it a misuse which experts do not condone, and in his examples of ledger entries he uses in the debit of the debtor's account "A" because the name following it must of necessity be the name of the creditor and, as "A" denotes the creditor, so it must here precede the name of the creditor, as well as in the journal, in spite of the fact that it is written on the debit side of the ledger. Likewise he puts on the credit side "Per" in front of the name of the debtor. Stevin, as explained, follows Pacioli.

Until the very recent present day we used in the ledger "To" on the debit side as a prefix to the name of the creditor and "By" on the credit side as a prefix to the name of the debtor.

It is difficult to say whether we can translate the Italian *"Per"* into our "By" and the Italian *"A"* into our "To," as these two expressions or words can be translated in many different ways according to the noun or verb following or preceding it, together with the consideration of the tense and case used.

If, however, we take a literal translation of the Italian ledger heading used for our debit, or *"dee dare,"* we come to "shall give." Putting this into a sentence read from a ledger we have as at the present time, "John Doe debit to Richard Roe" and in the old Italian, "John Doe *dee dare* (shall give) A (To) Richard Roe," and as to the credit, we have in our present day "Richard Roe credit by John Doe," and in the old Italian, "Richard Doe *dee havere* (shall have or receive) Per (by the hand of) John Doe."

Our version, therefore, is that today we follow Manzoni rather than Pacioli and Stevin in this respect.

As to the journal, the old necessity for being particular in designating and separating the debtor from the creditor by Per and A and the much commented upon little diagonal lines (//), has been obviated through the use of two columns in the journal—one for the debit amount, the other for the credit amount—and by the use of two lines of writing and by careful indentation. Thus, while we do not use the old expressions (Per and A) in the journal, we are more careful and systematic in separating debits from credits than the old authors were.

It would be interesting to learn when and where and under what circumstances and conditions the double column in the journal originated. From the fact that a trial balance, with total debits and total credits instead of differences between debits and credits, is called a French trial balance, we might infer that that system originated in France because a French trial balance is based upon the system that all entries are journalized and the total debits and the total credits of the journal are added to the total debits and credits of the previous trial balance in order to arrive at the totals which the present trial balance should show. Such a trial balance makes an absolute necessity for the having of two columns in the journal.

Stevin explains debit and credit as follows:

"Genomen dat ymant met naem Pieter, my schuldich vvesende, doet daer op betaling van 100 L: Enick 't gelt in een casse leggende, al of ict heur te bevvaren gave, segh dat die casse my 't selve gelt schuldich is, vvaer deur ick haer al oft een mensch vvaer, debiteur make, en Pieter crediteur, om dat hy syn schult vermindert, stellende int Iornael 't begin der partie aldus, 'Casse debet per Pieter'."

The above translated would be about as follows:

"Suppose that some one by the name of Peter owed me some money, on account of which he paid me £100, and I put the money in a cash drawer just as if I give it the money for safe keeping. I then say that that cash drawer owes me that money, for which reason (just as if it were a human being) I made it a debtor and Peter of course becomes a creditor because he reduces his debit to me. This I put in the Journal thus: 'Cash Debit Per Peter'."

From the above translation of the previous Dutch quotation it would seem that the journal entry shown is rather a hasty conclusion. The entry, in order to follow his explanations, should have been a double entry somewhat as follows: Cash Debit to Myself—Proprietor Credit—for the money I gave the cash drawer for safe keeping. To be followed by: Myself Debit to Peter Credit—he gave me money which I may have to return to him if he does not owe it to me.

As most of the entries, if made in this form would have both a debit and a credit to the proprietor for the same amount, these are simply omitted.

If we eliminate on both sides, according to algebraic formulae, the word "myself," we then have abbreviated the two entries to a real algebraic term, namely, "Cash Debit to Peter." Thus we have condensed two entries of thought to one entry written down, very much the same as in algebra $a = b$; $b = c$; hence $a = c$. In many of the old Dutch books Stevin's idea of a twofold double entry is mentioned, and is brought down to the present day, which accounts for the existence of a clear idea on this principle in Holland and in modern Dutch books on bookkeeping (see N. Brenkman, 1880, Theory of Double-Entry Bookkeeping).

It must be admitted that if we today would abolish the use of the words debit and credit in the ledger and substitute therefor the ancient terms of "shall give" and "shall have" or "shall receive," the personification of accounts in the proper way would not be difficult and, with it, bookkeeping would become more intelligent to the proprietor, the layman, and the student.

Elsewhere we have seen that Stevin insists upon testing when a journal entry in debit and credit must be made by asking the question, "When does proprietorship begin" or "When does proprietorship end," from which it is apparent that proprietorship *must* enter in the consideration of each entry and, if it is not there, it is simply eliminated by the rules of algebra. This, of course, would at once lead to the personification of the capital and profit or loss accounts into "the proprietor" as differentiated from "the business," and would then immediately show the fallacy of the statement that capital and surplus are liabilities, as well as of the absurd theory that assets must equal liabilities.

The following translation of the dialogue between Simon Stevin and the Prince Maurits of Orange on this subject fully illustrates that Stevin then understood his subject far better than do some modern text writers and theorists, and it makes certain recent so-called "discoveries" appear mere mental vagaries, as far as the credit for discovery is concerned. It merely illustrates that they are today as deep thinkers as Stevin was 300 years ago.

The Prince. I must ask another question. The entries stand in my ledger as debits and credits. Which of these two stand to my advantage and which to my disadvantage?

Stevin. Debits in the ledger are your advantage, for the more Peter owes you the more your capital is, and likewise much pepper in the warehouse, which stands as a debit, will make much money in the cash drawer. However, credits are the reverse.

The Prince. Are there no exceptions to this?

Stevin. I cannot recall any.

The Prince. Yet capital as a debit does not seem to me as an advantage, and capital as a credit being a disadvantage to me appears entirely wrong.

Stevin. I forgot that. You are right. I meant to say that capital is an exception.

The Prince. Further, expense is a debit and it, together with the debit in the profit and loss, are both disadvantages.

Stevin. Because these two are a part of the capital account they are included in the exception.

The Prince. The credits in the cloves account in the ledger are in excess of the debits by £74-4-7. This is an advantage to me because it represents a profit, yet it is in the credit.

Stevin. The reply to this would be that if the account were closed (which you can do when you please, but usually at the end of the year), the excess in the credits would be transferred to the profit and loss account and your question would not arise.

The Prince. Yet it remains that with accounts like the cloves account, where they show a profit or a loss, it is not so frequently true that at all times debit is an advantage and credit a disadvantage.

15

Stevin.	That appears to be true and in that respect it is somewhat similar to your exception, but it shows all the more positively that in all accounts of capital, or those pertaining to capital, debit is always a disadvantage and credit an advantage.
The Prince.	Why has capital more exceptions than all the others?
Stevin.	Because capital debit means as much as though the proprietor said, "I am debit to all the other accounts." It follows that the more a proprietor is debtor in this manner the more it is to his disadvantage, and the more he is creditor the more it is to his advantage, for which reason capital must be the reverse of other accounts, and it is not therefore really an exception.
The Prince.	If capital stands for the name of the proprietor, why is the proprietor's name not used instead of the word capital inasmuch as through the use of that word so many things become so difficult to understand?
Stevin.	Merchants often form partnerships with many who together put in one principal sum of money. For this reason we need one designation indicating them all at once as proprietors, and for this the word capital is used with good reasons.

Furthermore, at that time the words assets and liabilities were not known in bookkeeping. Happy days they must have been. These terms ought not to be known or used now. What we now term liabilities, and some of which some of us are almost tempted to call "near liabilities" very much the same as we define "near silk," never are and never will be liabilities, for at the time the financial statement is prepared these amounts are not supposed to be due, hence the proprietor cannot possibly be liable for them at that time. At most he is "trusted" for them by his creditors, as the old authors expressed it correctly. Neither are assets at any time, in a going, solvent business, real assets. The words assets comes from "*assez*" which means "enough." The question of whether the proprietor has enough to cover his liabilities does not come up until his ability to meet his obligations is questioned or until he is called upon to render a statement to the court wherein he is brought for this purpose to answer the question whether he has enough (*assez*—assets) to cover that for which he is liable (liabilities) or past due credits or trustings by the creditors. Those who doubt this should study from the reported court cases the difference between mercantile insolvency and legal insolvency.

In analyzing a financial statement I believe these assets and liabilities may be interpreted to mean something like this: The proprietor, in order to be permitted to continue to do business on credit, makes here a showing to those interested by which he agrees that his books show that the personifications of cash, real property, personal property, merchandise, as well as the persons owing him, are obligated to him and "shall give" him the amounts stated on the left hand side of the statement or the amounts appearing to the debit of these accounts in the ledger and to the credit of his own account, and that thereby the proprietor will be able to meet whatever obligations he contracts with those with whom he has dealings. He further states in this report that persons interested should take notice that the books show that the following persons "shall have" or "shall receive" from him the items when they become due and payable and standing on the right hand side of the statement, or the amounts appearing to the credit of these accounts in the ledger and to the debit of his own account. That these items are to be deducted from the items of cash, real property, personal property, etc., before those interested in the statement can judge as to whether they shall trust (*credito*—credit) him further. Thus it becomes at once apparent that capital, together with surplus and losses and gains, represent the ownership of the things owned less those owed, leaving a net ownership, and net ownership can never be a liability (i. e., a thing to be liable for). If surplus ever can be a liability then a minus-surplus or a deficit must of necessity become an asset, which is an absurdity.

The statement of affairs described by Stevin and elsewhere reproduced, may be considered to be merely a statement of the closing entries as they would be made in the respective individual ledger accounts in order to make both the debits and the credits even and equal. For whatever each debit account shows more in the debit than in the credit, as Stevin explained, it is given by the owner to that account for safe keeping as if it were a person—hence this person or this account owes the proprietor; therefore, the proprietor trusts these personified accounts and becomes the creditor. With the credit accounts it is the reverse; hence Stevin's statement of affairs is the capital account itemized with a preponderance of credits to represent net capital. The English follow this method of rendering a financial statement to this day. Why Americans reverse the process is difficult to perceive.

From the foregoing it will further be seen that thus with the aid of ancient terms we can read intelligently and explain the abbreviated forms used in bookkeeping so that it becomes at once apparent why accounts like the cash account, which to the uninitiated looks like proprietorship, can be shown on the debit side of the ledger and why capital account, which always represents ownership, appears on the credit side. This at first thought may seem contradictory, but the reason for this apparent inconsistency lies in the elimination (through bookkeeping) of equal terms (as per rules of algebra) brought about by the theoretical making of double entries (two entries, each with a common debit and credit) and thus abbreviating it beyond the interpretation of ordinary language. Thus we may go on and with equal ease prove, as the German scholar Jäger has done, that double-entry bookkeeping is much older than single-entry bookkeeping, the latter being a still further shortening of methods of classification by the use of the terms debit and credit. Stevin very clearly suggests this in his explanation of the rules of partnership.

It is to be regretted that in the transfer of the expositions of the theory from the Dutch language (as so plainly exemplified by the scholar Simon Stevin) to the English (by the flowery schoolmaster Richard Dafforne) should have been so badly done that all records of the scientific part of the art and theory have been so completely obscured as to suggest even in the present day an argument on theories so well known in those olden days.

16

LUCAS PACIOLI REPRODUCED

The following eight pages, from 18 to 26, and the succeeding 32 left-hand pages, numbers 28 to 80, represent photographic reproductions of the oldest extant book on double-entry bookkeeping, published in Venice, Italy, in 1494. The reproductions are of the same size as the original, and fully illustrate the make-up of the book, which is one of the oldest books ever printed from loose metal type in Roman letters, as explained at the opening of the historical chapter. The ink used was vegetable dye ink, and is today as black and as fresh as India ink, after 420 years of use and exposure. It is printed on hand-made rag paper, unsized, which after so many years of exposure to air and light is still so far superior to the very best modern paper that a comparison cannot be made.

On page 18 appears the title of this book, "Summa de Arithmetica, Geometria, Proportioni et Proportionalita," (Review on Arithmetic, Geometry, and Proportions). Below the title is a brief synopsis of the contents of the book. Part 1, Section 9, Treatise 11 of this ancient book treats of double-entry bookkeeping and begins on page 199-a of the original, or page 32 of this volume, under the title of "Particularis de computis et Scripturis" (Particulars of Reckonings and Their Recording). This can be found in the seventh line of page 32. The picture directly under the title, on page 32, is said by some to be that of the author of this book, but there is nothing in this or any other book which substantiates this assertion.

Page 19, which immediately follows the title page of the original, contains a dedicatory letter by the author, whose name appears on the second line. The lower half of this page is occupied on the right by an epigram of praise to Pacioli by a friend of his and on the left by an epigram by the author to the reader.

The first of the four last lines of this page contain, a list of the letters to be used by the printer, merely as a guide for those who are not familiar with this style of printed letters. Thereafter, on the last line, the year (1494), then the date (November 20th), and then the place (Venetia or Venice), all of these pertaining to the record of publication.

Page 20 is another dedicatory letter to the Duke of Urbino. The author's name appears here in the third line.

On page 22, in the third line of the center paragraph, the author's name is given again, this time in the genetive case, hence Fratris Luce instead of Frater Lucas.

Pages 24 and 25 are reproduced in order to show the marginal notes there given, indicating the abbreviations used in the book, and their interpretation. Page 25 is also given for the reference the author makes in line 7 to three of his pupils, Bartolo, Francesco, and Paulo, the three sons of a prominent merchant of Venice named (Antonio de) Rompiasi. The dash over the "o" in the original indicates that an "m" follows the "o."

Page 23 is given to reproduce the type of numerous marginal illustrations the author gives on nearly every page of his chapters on geometry and arithmetic, considering the many illustrations here used it seems very strange that he should not have given some in his chapter on bookkeeping.

Page 26 is given to show that our modern so-called "efficiency engineers" have nothing the best of this monk of over 400 years ago, as to "organization charts." This chart illustrates the intricacies of proportions.

Pages 28 and 30 contain the index of the chapter on double-entry bookkeeping. No translation is given of these pages, because they are merely repetitions of the headings of each chapter, and therefore their translation appears at those places. In their stead, a comparative index is given of four of the earliest writers on bookkeeping, in order to illustrate how closely they have followed each other.

On pages 32 to 80 (left-hand only) are the reproductions of the original chapter on double-entry bookkeeping. Opposite each reproduction is given the translation in modern English subject to the qualifications mentioned in the preface.

Sũma dé Arithmetica Geo metria Proportioni τ Pro portionalita.

Continentia de tutt'à lopera.

De numeri e mẽſure in tutti modi occurrenti.

Proportioni e ṗportiõalita anotitia del. 5ᵒ de Eucli de.e ve tutti li altri ſoi libri.

Chiaui ouero euidentie numero.13.ṗ le q̃tita conti nue.ṗportiõali del.6ᵒ e.7ᵒ de Euclide extratte

Tutte le pti delalgoriſmo:cioe releuare. ptir. multi plicar.ſũmare.e ſotrare cõ tutte ſue ṗue i ſani e rot ti.e radici e progreſſioni.

De la regola mercanteſca ditta del.3.e ſoi fõdamen ti con caſi exemplari per cõmᵒ 8.G.guadagni:perdi te:tranſpoztationi:e inueſtite.

Partir.multiplicar.ſummar.e ſotrar de le proportio ·ni e de tutte ſozti radici.

De le.3.regole de' catayn ditta poſitiõe e ſua ozigie.

Euidentie generali ouer concluſioni nᵒ66.abſoluere ogni caſo.che per regole.ordinarie nõ ſi podeſſe.

Tutte ſozte binomij e reciſi e altre linee irratiõali del decimo de Euclide.

Tutte regole de algebza ditte de la coſa e loz fabzi che e fondamenti.

Compagnie i tutti modi.e loz partire.

Socide de beſtiami. e loz partire

Fitti:peſciõi:cottimi:liuelli:logagiõi:e godimenti.

Baratti i tutti modi ſemplici:compoſti:e col tempo.

Cambi reali.ſecchi.fittitij.e di minuti ouer comuni.

Meriti ſemplici e a capo danno e altri termini.

Reſti.ſaldi.ſconti.de tempo eденari ela recare a un di piu partite·

Oz argẽti.e loro affinare. ecarattare.

Molti caſi e ragioni ſtraozdinarie varie e diuerſe a tutte occurentie commo nella ſeq̃uente tauola ap pare ozdinatamente de tutte.

Ozdine a ſaper tener ogni cõto e ſcripture e del qua derno ſn vinegia.

Tariffa de tutte vſanςe e coſtumi mercanteſchi in tut to el mondo.

Pratica e theozica de geometria e de li.5.cozpi regu lari e altri dependenti.

E molte altre coſe ð grandiſſimi piaceri e frutto cõ mo difuſamente per la ſequente tauola appare.

Magnifico Patritio veneto Bergomi pretori designato. D. Marco sanuto viro in omni disciplinarum genere peritissimo Frater lucas de burgo sancti sepulcri ordinis minorum ⁊ inter. Sa. Theo. professores mininus. S. P. D.

Non me preterit Magnifice senator omnes: quos aliquod virtutis specimē oblectet tibi ꝙ plurimum debere: tum nobilitate: quā preclaram a maioribus tibi traditam: indices magis illustras: tū humanitate: eruditōe: ⁊ eloquētia: quibus pauci nō dico tue ciuitatis homies: ꝗ totius italie te equauerint. Ego vero humanitate allectus: eruditionē admiratus: operā ⁊ diligentiam tuam de amicis bene merendis expertus: maxime tibi me debere cōfiteor. Sꝫ quom animo repeto qua cura ⁊ studio laboraueris: vt nostrum hoc volumē perpetuis impressorum monumentis traderetur non satis mihi ipsi sufficere videor: vt aliqua ex parte quātulacūqꝫ tibi satisfaçerem Alij pleriqꝫ multi si quippiā in aliqua doctrina profecerint: libros: quibus ad id peruenitur maxime latere cupiunt. Tu cōsumatissimus astrologus: in Arithmetica eminētissimus: in Geometria excellētissimus nostra: vt ederentur nobis solititius curasti. Profecto illud existimo: ingenij tui foecunditatem nō formidasse: si hec in manus hominū peruenirent: propterea nō tibi plurima superfutura: que alios fugerent: uerissimūqꝫ esse illud Plynianum ex te didici. Ita certe recondunt qui pauca aliqua nouere iuidētes alijs. Opus itaqꝫ ipsum te hortante ⁊ impellente impressum: qđ Illustrissimo Urbini Duci dicauimus ad te recognoscendum mitto: cui si canes nostri oblatrauerit qđ soles tuis clientibus egregiū patrocinium: mihi prestes: obsecro. Nam certus sum non defuturos qui has nostras vigilias multo studio multoqꝫ labore desudatas: rephēsuri sint: Opus certe variū: copiosū: iocūdū: vndiqꝫ mathematicis theorematibus scatens ⁊ qđ nō mediocrē fructum sit allaturum hijs qui Euclidi Astrologie ⁊ negotiationi operam sunt daturi. Sed vide queso quid nobis obtigerit: dum tibi satisfacere conor maius mihi obligationis vinculum inecto: non satis fuerat: ꝙ te auctore noster liber in lucem prodiret. tutelam etiam tuam deposcimus. Uerum quod nos efficere non possumus deum optimum maximuꝫ vna cum serafico nostro sancto Francisco adiuuantibus cōfratribus nostris frequenter orabimus: vt tibi pares gratias ingenio doctrine virtuti ⁊ nobilitati tue referant. Uale Ad uota

Fa. Pompilij epigrāma ad lectorem.

Que fuerant medijs carie consumpta latebris
 Restituit lucas lector amice tibi
Moenia si lapides quot habēt erecta subauras:
 Aut ubi phoebeos temperet annus equos:
Et que ceruleas ducat te stella per undas:
 Et que decliuo corpore signa cadant:
Linea: quid corpus: quid circus et angulus oīs:
 Que sit apellea picta tabella manu:
Ultima que terris regio. quas fluctibus urbes
 Extremus gelidis abluat occeanus.
Tempore seu certo concordem emittere uocem
 Nature mores discere seu cupies.
Demere seu numeros numeris siue addere tētas
 Solicitum medio seu iuuat esse foro:
Hunc eme: quicquid erit liber hic cōducet agēti:
 Quod non dant plures: hic feret unus opem.

Clarissimi uiri Domini Giorgij Sūmarippa veronēsis patricij Epigramma ad auctorem.

Chi douesse lodar tua nobeltate:
 La pratica: Teorica e Doctrina
 Per lopra non humana: ma diuina
 Hoggi impressa in uenetia alma citate
Luca burgense mio excellente frate
 Conuerria hauer studiato in medicina:
 Astronomia: e in liberal foccina
 De larti tutte: e in le Mechanicate.
Ma essēdo cussi ben dillucidata
 Da tua excellença in ogni loco e parte
 E a Guido Ubaldo Illustre intitulata
Sera da tutto il mondo sibramata
 Che ogni poema ogni eloquença et arte
 Di comendarla rimarra excusata.
   Pur uedendo tiagrata
Pongo sto grandi sale in tua uiuanda
Per farla saporita Acui la manda:

Tabula. a.b.c.d.e.f.g.h.i.k.l.m.n.o.p.q.r.s.t.u.x.y.ç.⁊.ɔ.ꝶ.AA. Omnes sunt quaterni preter ꝶ qui est quinternus. Et AA qui est septernus.

Registrum Geometrie: quiere in ultima carta totius operis.

M°cccc°lxliiij°xxª. Nouembris. venetijs

Ad illuftriffimū Principē Gui.Abaldū Arbini Ducē Montis feretri:ac Durantis Comitē:Grecis latinifq3 litteris Ornatiffimuʒ:ʒ Mathematice difcipline cultorē feruētiffimū:Fratris Luce de Burgo fancti Sepulchri:Ordinis minoʒ:ʒ facre Theologie Magiftri.In artē arithmetice:ʒ Geometrie. Prefatio.

A quātita Magnanimo duca
e fi nobile ʒ excellēte cofa che molti philofophi
p q̄fto lhano giudicata ala fubftātia para:e co/
meffa coeterna. Peroche hano cognofciuto p
verū modo alcuna cofa in reʒ natura.fenʒa lei
nō potere exiftere. Per la qual cofa de lei itēdo
(cō laiuto de colui che li noftri fenfi reggi)tra/
ctarne:nōche p altri prifchi e antichi phylofo/
phi nōne fia copiofamēte tractato:e i theorica
e pratica. Ma p che loʒ victi gia ali tēpi noftri
fono molto obfcuri:e da molti male aprefi:e ale
pratiche vulgari male applicati:diche in loʒo
opationi molto variano:e cō grādi elaboriofi af
fanni mettano in opa:fi de nūeri cōmo de mifu
re:vnde di lei parlādo nō intēdo fe nō quāto che ala pratica e opare fia meftiero:me
fcolādoci fecōdo iluoghi oportuni ancoʒa la theoʒica:e caufa de tale opare:fi de nu
meri cōmo de geometria.Ma pria acio meglio q̄llo che fequita fe habia apphende
re:effa quātita diuideremo fecōdo el nſo ppofito:ediuidēdola aciafcun fuo mēbro
affegnaremo fua ppria e vera diffinitiōe e defcriptiōe.E aloʒa poi fequira q̄llo che
Arift.dici in fecūdo pofter.Tūc eni maxime fcit aliqd cū habet fuuʒ qd eft ʒc.

Diffinitiones ʒ diuifio difcrete ʒ continue quantitatis:articulus primus prime
diftinctionis.

Dico adōca.La quātita effere imediate bimembre:cioe cōtinua e difcreta.
La continua e quella lechui parti fonno copulate e gionte a certo termine
cōmune:cōme fōno legni:ferro:e faxa ʒc. La difcreta oueramēte nūero:
e quella lecui parti nō fonno giōte adalcuno termine cōe:cōmo e.1.2.3.ʒc.
Diche prima dela difcreta:cioe del nūero:e poi dela continua cioe geometria:quā
to alo intento afpecta chiaramente tractaremo.

Diffinitio numeri propriiffima.articulus fecundus.

Numero e(fecōdo ciafcuno phylofophāte)vna multitudine de vnita cōpo/
fta:et effa vnita nō e numero:ma ben principio de ciafcun numero:ede q̄lla
mediāte laquale ogni cofa e ditta effere vna.E fecōdo el feuerin Boetio in
fua mufica:e la vnita ciafcū nūero i potētia:ʒ paffiʒ i fua arithmetica Regi
na e fondamēto dogni numero lapella.Laqual piu magnificāda in le cofe naturali
diffe in q̄llo che fa de vnitate ʒ vno.Omne qd eft:ideo eft:qʒ vnū nūero eft.Ene an/
coʒa el nūero in ifiniti mēbʒi diuifo:p quel che effo Arifto.dire:cioe.Sigd ifinitum
eft:nūerus eft.E p la terza petitiōe del feptio de Euclide:la fua ferie in ifinito pote/
re pcedere:et quocūq3 nūero dato:dari pōt maioʒ vnitatē addēdo.Ma noi piglia
remo quelle parti anoi piu note e accomodate.E pero dico cō glialtri alcuno effere
primo:ede quello che folo vala vnita e nūerato:e nō ha altro nūero:che itegralmē
te apōto lo parta.Altro e ditto cōpofto:ede q̄llo che da altro nūero e mefurato:oue
ro nūerato.Exēplū primi Cōmo.3.7.11.13.e.17.ʒc.Exēplū fecūdi.Cōmo.4.chel
doi lo mefura e nūera:e.8.chel.2.e.4.El.12.14.18.e fimili:tuti fōno ditti nūeri cō
pofti:nō folo che cōftino ex digito ʒ articulo(fecondo facro bufco in fuo algoʒifmo)
ma pche itegralmēte paltri nūeri fi poffano mefurare e ptire:fecōdo el fēfo de Eucli
de in feptio anche.20.30.40.che fōno meri articuli:p effo fōno ditti cōpofiti. Al/
cuni fono nūeri cōtra fe primi:ʒ fono q̄lli(cōmo e detto)che p fola vnita fono mefu/
rati e nūerati:cōme fōno.11.13.17.19.che luno a laltro eʃaltro a luno e pmo:nec
reliquū p alterū itegraliter diuidi pōt vt pʒ ituēti.De q̄li alcuno po effere cōpofto e
laltro primo e luno laltro po effer primo:cōmo p la.24.del.7°.fi dimoftra. Exēpluʒ

WHAT WAS PACIOLI'S REAL NAME ?

In the historical chapter, we have stated that the name of the author of the first book on bookkeeping was not definitely known. This is quite apparent from the different versions of the spelling of the name, which we find in the various books, and it becomes rather amusing to read how the various authors mentioning this name take delight in stating that the other fellow is wrong and they are right. Yet no two of them apparently give it alike.

Brown in his history of accounting especially ridicules Ympyn's version, and with it all Brown himself spells it Paciolo, with an "o" at the end, whereas all the authorities he quotes spell it with an "i" at the end, and he gives no explanation as to why he prefers the "o". Below we give a tabulation of the various spellings of these names by the various authors, each one being preceded by the authority from which we have taken the name. We have adhered to the spelling of Lucas Pacioli throughout, because we believe that to be the proper spelling, from the two best researchers who have written about him, namely, the two Germans Jäger and Kheil, and further, because we believe that the "li" in the old Italian was Latinized into "lus," and the "c" is the old Italian for the Latin "t" in most all cases where the Latin "t" is preceded and followed by a vowel. Furthermore, we have the author's own version of his own name, as we have seen elsewhere, in the only book that is published with his name in full, namely: "Divina Proportione," which was written in Latin and where he gives the Latin of his own name. While "*Luca*" is the Italian for the Latin "*Lucas,*" we follow the author's own spelling in his Italian as well as Latin books, namely "Lucas":

AUTHORITY.	SPELLING OF NAME.
Summa de Arithmetica (author's original)	Frater Lucas de Burgo Sancti Sepulchri

(The above name appears first on the second line of page 19 of this book, which is the second page of the original; also on the third line, page 20 of this book, which is page 3 of the original; and in the third line of the second paragraph, page 22 of this book, being page 4 of the original—here, however, it is given in the genitive, hence Fratris Luce instead of Frater Lucas).

La Scuola perfetta dei Mercanti (second edition of Summa de Arithmetica by same printers)	Fra Paciolo di Borgo Santo Sepolcro
Divina Proportione (author's original)	Lucas Patiolus (the Latin of the Italian Pacioli)
Contemporary writers	Lucas Pacciolus
Jan Ympyn Christoffels (in his French book)	Frere Lucas de Bargo Sancty Sepulcry
Guido Brandaglia	Luca Pacciolo
Ernst Ludwig Jäger	Lucas Paccioli
Carl Peter Kheil	Fra Luca Pacioli di Borgo Sansepolcro
Beckmann's History	Lucas von Borgo
Anderson's History	Lucas von Borgo
Clitofonte Bellini (Trattato Elementare Teorico—Pratico di Ragionesia Generale)	Luca Paciolo
V. Vianello (Luca Paciolo nella Storia della Ragionesia)	Luca Paciolo
Pawell Ciompa (Grundrisse einer Oekonometrie)	Luca Paciolo
L. Gomberg (Grundriss der Verrechnungswissenschaft)	Luca Paciolo
V. Gitti (De Computio—modern)	Fra Luca Pacciolo
Moritz Cantor (Geschichte der Mathematik)	Paciuolo
Sigismund Günther (Geschichte der Mathematik)	Paciolo
Catholic Encyclopedia	Lucas Pacioli
Richard Brown	Fra Luca Paciolo Da Borgo San Sepolchro
John B. Geijsbeek	Lucas Pacioli

tria.Proportiõi e Proportiõalita possi intendere.Certo nullo sia che tal laude se attribuesca .Lascio
bormai ognaltra cosa che longo seria el dire:ma solo tutte le cose create stã nostro spechio.che niuna
si trouera che sotto numero.peso e mesura non sia constituta commo e dicto da salamone:nel secondo
de la sapientia.Hanc deniq3 preoculis summus opifex in celestium terrestriumq3 rerum dispósitione
semper habuit.Dum orbium motus:cursusq3 syderum z planetarum omnium ordinatissime dispone
ret.Hec quando ethera firmabat sursum.Et appendebat fundamenta terre:z librabat fontes aqua-
rum.Et mari terminum suum circundabat legemq3 ponens aquis ne transirent fines suos:cum eo
erat cuncta componēs zc.Non sia chi temerariamcte giudicãdo dica quel che fin qua de le Mathe-
matici discorso habiamo i persuasiõi a.U.D.S.sia facto.Ala qual(siando di loro ede ognaltra Ecel-
lente)non acadeua per connumeratione de lutilita siegue in ogni doctrina e pratica per esse persuader
li infiammarla a seguirle e abraciarle.   Ma solo a suasioni e aperimento de la nobilita e utilita
grandissima(commo sopra dicemmo)de li Reuerenti di.U.D.S.quali in simili exercitandose lor vi
ta sustengano.Commo per tutte degne terre a.U.D.D.subiecte si fa chi al trafico.E altri laudabili
exercitij sonno dati.Di quali la degna.U.Cita de Urbino principalmente e piena.Lascio de la cita de
Ugobio esse ntial membro de.U.D.D.La quale de ogni trafico reluce.Lascio Fosambrone.Cagli e
Macerata altre.U.degne cita.Castel durate.Sãtagnilo .e Mercatello.E molti altri luoghi al.U.
D.D.sottoposti ne li quali,non me curo stendermie per che da se sia manifesto.Chi con poco e chi con
asai sua vita exercitando sempre insu le famose fiere per aqua e per terra.Ora avinegia.Ora a ' Roma.
E a fiorença se ritrouano.Per le qual cose non dubito la presente opera summamente esserli grata:co
cio sia che in lei a tutte occurrentie(commo habian deducto)li sia suffragatorie seruente.Non altro
e per lo presente a.U.D.S.da exponere se non che in tutti versi vie e modi lo infimo de quella figlio-
lo e seruo frate Luca dal Borgo san sepolcro de lordine de li minori humile de sacra Theologia pro
fessore deuotamente alei se ricomanda.La qual lo omnipotente dio secondo ogni suo bon desiderio li
piacci aacrescere e conseruare con tutti de la casa sua excelsa:e di quella beniuoli eaderenti.   Uale.

Ad illustrissimum Principem Gui.Ubaldum Urbini Ducem.Montis feretri: ac durantis
Comitem.Grecis latinisq3 litteris Ornatissimum:z Mathematice discipline cultorē feruentissimuz:
Fratris Luce de Burgo sancti Sepulchri:Ordinis minorum:z sacre Theologie Magistri:In arte
Arithmetice:z Geometrie.   Epistola.

Uom animaduerterēm Illustrissime Princeps imensas dulcedines:ac
maximas utilitates quas ex hiis scientijs assequimur:que greci mathe-
mata nostri disciplinas possunt appellare:si recte pratice z Theorice
animo demandentur.Constitui nouum hoc volumē pro ingenij nostri
tenuitate comPonere maxime in eorum usum ac voluptatem edere qui
virtutum celo affecti essent.In quo (ut ex subscripto indice facile perspi
ci potest)varias diuersasq3 Arithmetice Geometrie Proportionis et
proportionalitatis partes plurimum necessarias:tum in prati:tum in
Theorica collegimus:firmissimisq3 rationibus z canónibus perfectissi
mis subiecimus:et antiquis z recentibus philosophis cuiuscunq3 pra-
tis indubitata fundamenta.Quamobrem non immerito libri titulus.
Summa Arithmetice Geometrie Proportionum z Proportionalitatum dicatur. Ubi ante omnia
studuimus exactam in huiuscemodi facultatibus pratim tradere quemadmodū ex ordinatissima eius
serie haud difficulter intueri licet.Uerum quia temporibus nostris verba propria matheseos ob rari
tatem bonorum preceptorum apud latinos ferme interiere:cupiens ego usui esse hijs qui vestre ditiõi
parent(non ignarus stilo elegantiori.Eloquio Ciceroniano te salientem eloquentie undaz adiri opor
tere)quid q3 vnusquisq3 non hec caperet:si latine per scripta essent:potius vernaculo sermone descri
psimus.Litterature itaq3 peritis pariter.Et imperitis hec commodum et iocunditatem afferent:si in
eis se exercuerint vacent quibuslibet facultatibus et artibus:ob per tractata que communia vniculq3 vi
dentur z optime applicari posse.   Et primo quis non dico doctus:sed multo minus q3 mediocriter
eruditus est:qui non perspicue videat quantum hereant quantumq3 necessaria sint.Astrologie cuius
principes hac tempestate vigent auunculus tuus princeps Octauianus:vna cum Reuerendissimo for
simpronij Episcopo Paulo mindeburgensi quos in omnibus semper admiror z veneror:quorumq3
exactis iudicijs hoc ipsum opus non immerito caritate subiecimus:ut que bene scripta sint approbent

no al.q.ſia la linea.q k.catetto del triangolo.q b d.nelquale menato la linea.f.r. equediſtan
te al.i k.ſira.f.r.equale a la linea.i k.perche equediſtante e la linea.f.i.ala linea.k c.b. k.e ſia.r
k.iguale al.f i.e il triangolo.q i f.e.f r b.ſonno ſimili.Onde ſe traremo.r k.cioe.i f.del.k b.ri
marranno.b r.3.e perche eglie coſi b r.al.r ſ.coſi.f.i.ala q. Onde multiplicando.r ſ.per.f.i. e
dividendo per.br.vienne.5.per lo catetto.q i.Onde tutta.q f.e.20.che e laltezza de la pira
mide.q a b c d.

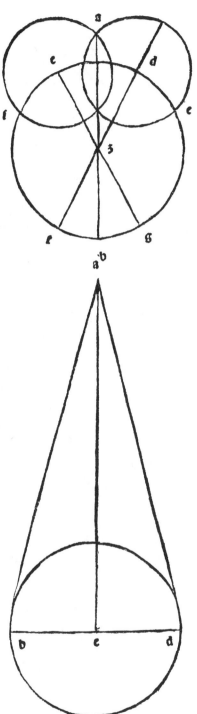

E innuna ſpera ſi piglia vn ponto dalquale.4.rette linee ſi menino infra loro
iguali e vadino ala ſuperficie de la ſpera e quelle linee nõ ſieno inuna ſuperficie
piana quel ponto ſia il centro de la ſpera. Verbi gratia ſia la ſpera.a b e in õlla
ſia il ponto.c. dalquale ſieno menate. 4.line infra loro iguali.c b.c g.c d.c e.e nõ
ſienno li ponti.b.g.d.e.inuna ſuperficie piana dico il ponto.c.eſſere centro de la ditta ſpera e
queſto euidentemente appare e po nõna biſogno de dimonſtratione.

Vando ſira menato dal ponto del capo dogni piramide colonnale al cētro õ la
baſa ſua perpendiculare ſopra la ſua baſa: aloza le linee rette che ſonno menate
dal ponto del capo ſuo al cerchio contenente la ſuperficie de la ſua baſa ſonno i
fra loro iguali. E la multiplicatõe duna di quelle linee che ſonno menate dal ca
po loro al cerchio contenente la ſua baſa:ne la mita del cerchio contenente la ditta baſa. E la
rea de la ſuperficie de ditta piramide colonnale: verbi gratia:ſia la piramide colonnale.a b g
d.delaquale la ſua ſomita ſia.a.e la ſua baſa ſia il circulo.b g d.del quale ſia il centro.e. E la li
nea.a c.oztogonalmente ſia ritta ſopra il piano del cerchio.b g d.e dal ponto.a.ala linea cir
cunferentiale contenente il circulo.b g d.de la baſa de la data piramide di colonna ſe meni
molte linee.a b.a g.a d.dico certamēte le rette.a b.a g.a d.infral loro eſſere iguali. La pua me
niſe dal centro.e.le rette.e.b e g.e d.che ſonno tutte iguali infra loro. E perche.a e.e perpen
diculare ſopra il piano del circulo.b g d.fienno gliangoli.a e b.a e g.a e d.retti. Onde li triã
goli ſonno oztogonij.a e b a e g.a e d.hano le baſe iguali che ſonno.e b.e g.e d.e il lato.a e.e
commune. Onde li lati ſubtendenti a gliangoli retti che ſonno.a b.a g.a d.ſonno infra loro
iguali. E per queſto e manifeſto che tutte le rette linee che ſi poſſono menare dal.a.ala linea
circunferente.b g d.eſſere iguali a la linea.a b.

Acoza dico che multiplicato.a b.nela mita de la linea circunferente.b g d.fara
larea de la ſuperficie de la piramide:cioe larea diſuoza de la ſuperficie.a b g d.la
quale ſuperficie e dal circulo de la baſa.b g d.infino ala ſua ſummita. E ſe nõ foſ
ſe coſt. Aloza ſia la multiplicatõe de la linea.a b.de la mita del circulo.b g d.ma
gioze o minoze quella, che facia larea de la ſuperficie dico che quella, quantita che ſe mul
tiplica per.a b.a fare larea de la ſuperficie ſua minoze ouer magioze de la mita de la linea cir
cuſerente.b g d. E ſia la quantita.i c.e il doppio del.i c.e piu chel cerchio.b g d . Adonca fa
ro ſopra il cerchio.b g d.vna figura retti linea hauente e lati e gliangoli iguali contenente
quello:e fienno li lati inſieme agionti meno che lo doppio del.i c.che ſia la figura.l k t. E me
nero la linea.a b.laquale e perpendiculare ſopra la linea.b k.in queſto modo. Menero la li
nea.e t.fienno li quadrati de le linee.e b.7.b t.iguali al quadrato de la linea.e t.e commune a
tutti ſia il quadrato de la perpendiculare.a e.ſiranno li quadrati de le linee.e b.e b a. Igua
li al quadrato de la linea.e t.e commune ſagionga il quadrato de la perpendiculare.a
e.fienno li quadrati de le linee.a e.e b.b t.cioe li quadrati de le linee.a b.e.b t.iguali al qua
drato.a t.onde langolo.a b t.e retto. Perpendiculare adonca la linea.a b.ſopra la linea.t k.
Similmente ſi moſtra la linea.a g.eſſere perpendiculare ſopra.k l.e.a d.ſopra la linea.t l. E
perche le rette.a b.a g.a d.ſonno infra loro iguali virra de la multiplicatione duna di quel
le commo del.a b.ne la mita de lati del triangolo.t k l.lembado ouer area de la ſuperficie de
la piramide.a t k l.magioze de la ſuperficie de la piramide.a b g d.concioſia coſa che la con
tenga quella:cioe quello che infral cerchio.b g d.e il ponto.a.e la mita de lati del triangolo
t k l.e minoze che la quantita.i c. Adonca gia fo la multiplicatione de la linea.a b.quello cĥ
e meno de la linea.i c.e magioze de la ſuperficie de la piramida di colonna che e impoſſibi
le. Adonca non ne poſſibile che la multiplicatione de la linea.a b.ne la linea che ſia magio
re de la mita del cerchio.b g d.ſia lembado ouer continentia de la ſuperficie.a b g d. Anco
ra pozzo la linea.i c.mioze de la mita de la circũferentia del circulo.b g d.e ſe poſſibile e cĥ õ
dutto.a b.i.i c.ne puega larea de la ſupficie õ la piramide.a b g d. A multiplicare adõca õ la
.: õ la circuferētia õ circulo.b g d.fara la ſupfi.õ ua mioze piramide õ la piramide.a b g d.

rum:e partendo soldi per.20.neuē 8̸ .Per che la lira vbiq̃ si tene soldi.20.Le 8̸ .poi farne
oro:si partano per la valuta de quel oro occurrente:secondo li luogbi.E quello cħ auança
de li ꝺ.partendoli in.12.sonno ꝺ.E cio che auança de li ɓ.partiti in.20.sono ɓ.E cio che auã
ça de le 8̸.partite in la valuta de loro occurrente sonno.8̸.Et sic in ceteris discurrendo:ver
bi gratia.Poniamo che tu babi arcdure ale magiori valute ouer magiori monete questa q̃
tita de picioli:cioe picioli numero.96598.Dico che prima facci commo festi di sopra in li pe
si ordinamente reducendo prima ala immediata moneta sequente:quale e el soldo in que
sto modo.Partendo la ditta summa de picioli per.12.neuen.8049.e sono soldi e auança.10
che son.10.picioli.E poi farne 8̸.partirai questi soldi venuti per.20.neuene.402.E que
ste sono 8̸.de valuta:e auança.9.che son.9.soldi.E poi per farne oro.Partirai le 8̸.per la
valuta del ditto oro a 8̸.E virratte loro.E quello che auançara sira 8̸.Como se volesse far
duc̄.li quali in questo bauemo posto valere 8̸.7.luno.Le ditte 8̸.venute partirai per .7. ne
uen.57.E son duc̄.e auança.3.che son 8̸.Si che de primo ad vltimum reducendo li ditti pi
cioli ala magior moneta siranno duc̄.57.8̸.3.ɓ.9.ꝺ.10.E cosi regerate in tutte valute meno
ri:reducendole ale magiori:vt in ista.

Tertium notandum.Eadem via procedens.

Vello che habiamo detto deli pesi e moneta:ancora se habia a intēdere de le q̃
tita che vadano a numero:e anche a mesura o sia colma:longa:e rasa secōdo lo
ro ingordita:si commo de sopra dicemmo.Meglio:e pegio:e longo e corto:e i
gordo diuersamente se atendano:secondo le quantita:vt supra declarauimus.
Si che bauendo tu octaui de braccio de panno numero.46595. de panni a volerli redu
re a canne:la qual communiter se tien braccia.4.Prima partirai ditti octaui per.2. e virrat
te quarte:per che sempre in ogni quātita.2.octaui fanno.ɋ.e lo remanēte sira octauo. E poi
le quarte partirai per.4.e virratte braccia per che.4.fanno braccio.1.E lauanço sira quar
te.E poi li braccci partirai per.4.e virratte cāne:e lauanço siran braccia.Si commo bauesse
li octaui preditti partili in.2.neuen.23297.E son quarti. E auança.1.che e.1.octauo. E poi
partti.23297.per.4.e virranne.5824.E sonno braccia e auāça.1.che e.1ª.quarta.E poi par
ti li braccia per.4.neuen.1456.e sonno canne:e auança nulla che son:nullo braccio.Sicħe
de primo adultimum la ditta reductione fa canne.1456.braccia o quarte.1.octaui.1. E tu i
tutte altre simili per te farai 7̸.

Quartum notandum de caratteribus praticis hoc in opere vsitatis.

Estiero e ancora da notare quello importino li caratteri per noi in questopera
vsitati acio le loro abbreuiature sien intese per chi legera bauenga che molti per
le proposte questioni per se stessi le aprendino.Non dimanco piu sonno quelli
di poca pratica(per li quali principalmente questo libro si fa)che non sonno
quelli che intendano.E impero qui sequente tutti li caratteri:e abreuiature che per noi cō
munamente in questo libro se vsaranno:dechiararemo:si in larte menore ouer mercatoria:
commo in arte magiore:ouer algebra.Le quali piu per li pesi:e monete:e mesure:che p al
tro sonno trouati:excepto in algebra che per força(differentie causa)so bisogno trouare.
Per che non si potte a tutte quantita metter nome.Ideo 7̸.

Questi caratteri e abreuiature commo vedi.Alcuni sonno che piu de vna cosa
represēntano.Perocħe ale volte peso:e ale volte valuta di monete.Si commo
questo 8̸.che dici lira a valuta de moneta:che sintende soldi.20.E libra a peso
che sintende once.12.e cosi questa.p̃.che dici piu. picioli. pecce .piedi.Per la q̃l
cosa tu nelli luogbi doue le trouerai per tuo ingēgno chiaro cognoscerai quale de luno de
questi te represēntara:secondo el suon de la materia che li se contra.Onde fra le valute.p̃.
denota picioli.Fra mesure piedi.Fra quantita de panni pecca . In operatione de algebra
piu:e cosi de ciascuna de laltre:secondo li lechi e le materie te represēntarāno luna de le co
se ditte qui al suo incontro sicħe tu per te vsarai lo ingēgno tuo:el qual bisogna sia supple
mento a quello cbio mancasse. Quia suppletio fit loco defectus. Per che non e possibile
mai ponere tutto quello che alarte se ricerca:si commo e manifesto a quelli che di compone
re volumi se delettano.Iurta illud.Dicite pierides non omnia possumus omnes:e cosi fa
rai dele sequenti che son per algebra.

Idem notādum de caratteribus algebraticis.⟨

Er loperare de larte magiore:ditta dal vulgo la regola de la cosa ouer algebra
e amucabala seruaremo noi in questo le qui da lato abreuiature ouer caratteri:

i iij

Duc̄. ducati.
8̸.Lirc. lira. libra. libre.
ɓ. Soldo. soldi.
ꝺ. Denaro. denari.
p̃. Piciolo.picioli.pecça.
⊙. Oncia. once.
q̃'.quarti. q̃°.q̃ª q̃ᶜ.
Oct. octauo. octaui.
Cħa. cāna. cāne.
ɓ. Bracio. braci.
m̃.Mina. mine. meno.
  mesetaria.
m̃³. Marca. m̃ᶜ.marcħ.
k. Caratto. caratti.
gª. grane. grani.
g°. Grossi. grossoni.
bl. Bolognino.bolognin
  bolçone.
vª. Uia.
rª. Regula. resta.r°.
Mⱥa. multiplica.
Mⱥare. multiplicare.
Mⱥato. multiplicato.
Drã. differentia.
Drē. differentie.

ꝝ. pᵃ. nᵒ. nūo.
ꝝ. 2ᵃ. co. cosa.
ꝝ. 3ᵃ. ce. censo.
ꝝ. 4ᵃ. cu. cubo.
ꝝ. 5ᵃ. ce. ce. censo decenso.
ꝝ. 6ᵃ. pᵒ. rᵒ. primo relato.
ꝝ. 7ᵃ. ce. cu. censo decubo e anche cubo decenso.
ꝝ. 8ᵃ. 2ᵒ. rᵒ. secundo relato.
ꝝ. 9ᵃ. ce. ce. ce. censodecenso de censo.
ꝝ. 10ᵃ. cu. cu. cubo decubo.
ꝝ. 11ᵃ. ce. pᵒ. rᵒ. censo de primo relato.
ꝝ. 12ᵃ. 3ᵒ. rᵒ. terço relato.
ꝝ. 13ᵃ. cu. ce. ce. cubodecenso decenso. Quoi dir econuerso.
ꝝ. 14ᵃ. 4ᵒ. rᵒ. quarto relato.
ꝝ. 15ᵃ. ce. 2ᵒ. rᵒ. censo de secundo relato.
ꝝ. 16ᵃ. cu. pᵒ. rᵒ. cubo de primo relato
ꝝ. 17ᵃ. ce. ce. ce. ce. censodeceso decenso decenso.
ꝝ. 18ᵃ. 5ᵒ. rᵒ. quinto relato.
ꝝ. 19ᵃ. cu. ce. cu. cubo decenso de cubo. Ouer ceso cubo cubo.
ꝝ. 20ᵃ. 6ᵒ. rᵒ. sexto relato.
ꝝ. 21ᵃ. ce. ce. pᵒ. rᵒ. censo deceso de primo relato.
ꝝ. 22ᵃ. cu. 2ᵒ. rᵒ. cubo de scdo rᵒ.
ꝝ. 23ᵃ. ce. 3ᵒ. rᵒ. censo de terço rᵒ.
ꝝ. 24ᵃ. 7ᵒ. rᵒ. septuno relato.
ꝝ. 25ᵃ. cu. ce. ce. ce. cubo deceso decenso deceso. Quer censo de cubo decenso deceso. Quer censo deceso decenso de cubo.

Que oia idem important.

ꝝ. 26ᵃ. 8ᵒ. rᵒ. octauo relato.
ꝝ. 27ᵃ. ce. 4ᵒ. rᵒ. censo de quarto relato.
ꝝ. 28ᵃ. cu. cu. cu. cubo decubo decubo.
ꝝ. 29ᵃ. ce. ce. 2ᵒ. rᵒ. censo deceso de secundo relato.
ꝝ. 30ᵃ. rᵒ. nono relato.

Finis.

ꝝ. Radici.
ꝝ ꝝ. Radici de radici.
ꝝ v. Radici vniuersale. Ouer radici legata. Quoi dire radici vnita.
ꝝ cu. Radici cuba.
ꝗᵃ. quantita.

si commo ancora nelli altri nostri quatro volumi de simili discipline per noi copilati hauemo vsati: cioe in quello che ali gioueni de peroscia in titulai nel.1476. Nel quale non con tanta copiosita se tratto. E anche in quello che a çara nel.1481. de casi piu sutili e forti componemo. E anche in quello che nel.1470. deriçamo ali nostri releuati discipuli ser Bart. francesco e paulo fratelli octopiasi da la çudeca: degni mercatanti in vinegia: figliuoli gia de ser Antonio. Sotto la cui ombra paterna e fraterna i lor propria casa me releuai. E a simili scientie sotto la disciplina de miser Domeneco bragadino li in vinegia da la excelsa signoria lectore de ogni scietia publico deputato. Qual fo imediate successore: al perspicacissimo e vldo doctore: e di san Marco canonico maestro paulo da la pergola suo preceptore. E ora a lui: al presente el Magnifico et eximio doctore miser Antonio cornaro nostro condiscipulo: sotto la doctrina del ditto bragadino. E questo quando erauamo al secolo. Ma da poi che labito indegnamante del seraphyco san francesco ex voto pigliamo: p diuersi paesi ce conuenuto andare peregrinando. E al presente q i peroscia per publico e molumento a satisfation comuna: a simili faculta ci retrouiamo. E sempre p ordine de li nostri Reueredi prelati: maxime del reuerendissimo.p.nostro generale prciente maestro Francesco sasone da brescia: correndo glianni del nostro segnore Jesu Christo.1487. lanno.4º. del pontificato del sanctissimo in christo.p.innocetio octauo.

Ra tornando al proposito de li caratteri questi sono marie in algebra. E bauenga che in infinitum si possa procedere non dimeno quato al proposito nostro in questo: li trenta gradi ascendenti per via et modum algebre et almucabala. Hoc est restaurationis z oppositionis sonno bastanti. E se pur tu piu ne vorrai per te stesso gradati porrai formarne. E questi sonno li gradi quasi modernamete cosi noiati hauenga che in tutte le cose li nomi sieno a placito. E se codo qualche similitudine materiale iposti si comma di sopra nella distinctione.2ª.nel trattato.3ª al articulo.9º. dechiarammo. E cosi ancora sonno a placito tutti li caratteri quali noi qui habiamo posti p che tante terre tante vsançe. Juxta illud tot capita tot sensus. Et velle suu cuiqz e: questo dico acio tu imperito non crededte necessitassero. De li quali poi in algebra trattado formaremo loro libretti si commo in questo al suo luogo vederai. E quelle figure denançe poste che començano.ꝝ.prima.ꝝ.2ª.ꝝ.3ª.7c.fin.ꝝ.30ª.sono denominationi dela pratica de algebra secondo li arabi primi inuentori de si facte pratiche operatiue. Ma del numero i genere apresso li greci foron secondo ysidoro etymologiarum: e molti altri Pictagora el prio e da poi lui Nicomaco: dal qual el piu de la sua arithmetica Boe. prese. E a presso li latini foron prima Apuleo e poi Boe. e de la geometria forono li egyptij ab inundatione nili vt ipse ibidem inducit. Ideo ipsum lege qui optime de huiusmodi materia i plerisqz locis trattat quem pluries memini me legisse vade z tu fac similiter z proderit tibi 7c.

Distinctio sexta de proportionibus z proportionalitatibus. Tra.pmus.ar.primus.

Snuno che di numeri alcuna cosa ha scripto sempre ancora in siemi co qlli de mesure al quato ha tractato: e i copagnia desse del comun lor vestimeto ditto.pportione. E qsto sia manifesto se be si leggi di molti phy lor libri: de mathematiche faculta copilati. Como de Euclide megarense: La cui opa sempre tutti li antichi ginnasij: cioe de stoyci: academici: peripatetici: platonici 7c. anc. di degna disciplina mathematica illustrati. Nella q le lui de arithmetica: cioe de numeri trattando: ancora de geometria: cioe de misure largamete disse: e con quelle a gióse (como e ditto) el lor comun velo ditto.pportióe. Unde diuise ditta opa i.15. libri partiali. De li qli.10. sono de geometria: cioe p°. 2°.3°.4°.6°.11°.12.13.14°.15°. E quattro sonno de arithmetica pncipalmete: cioe.7°.8°.9°.10°. e vno (a tutti qsti coe: cioe el qnto) so de la.pportióe. La ql (como se dira) cosi se aspecta al nuo: como ala mesura. Del seuerino Boetio ancora se ben si guarda i la sua arithmetica: trouerasse le forçe de geometria: e anche particulare metióe de le.pportiói. De thebit ancora degno pho (del ql molto Boetio exponedo Euclide fa metione: maxime nel qnto) p sue ope diffusamete o luna e di laltra isiemi co le.pportioni tratto. De Ameto figliuolo de Joseph (del qual el campano exponedo el quito de Euclide fa

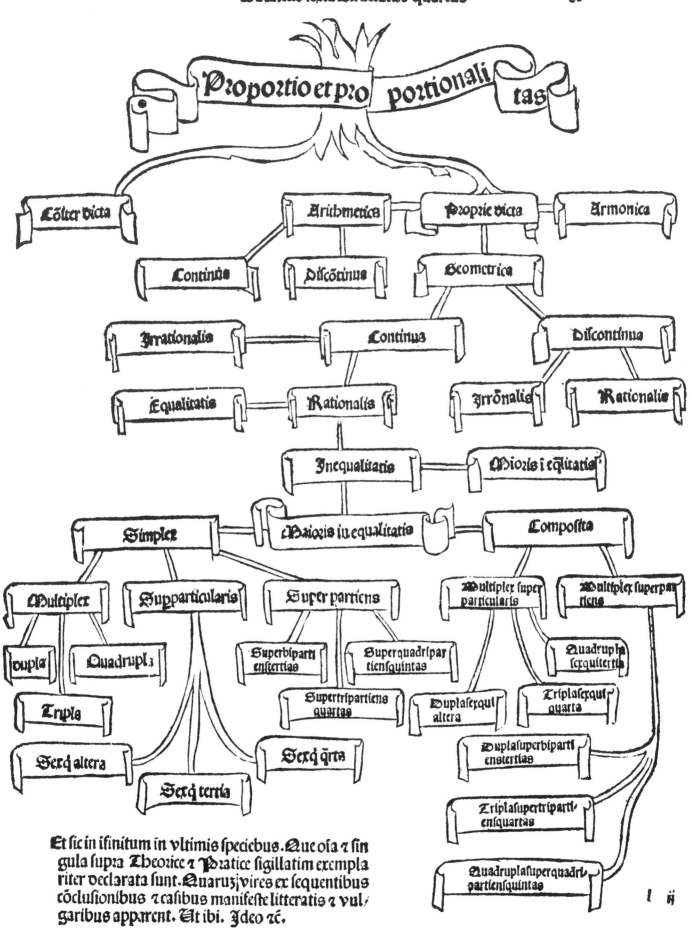

Et fic in ifinitum in vltimis fpeciebus. Que oia z fin
gula fupra Theorice z Pratice figillatim exempla
riter declarata funt. Quaruz; vires ex fequentibus
cöclufionibus z cafibus manifefte litteratis z vul-
garibus apparent. Ut ibi. Ideo zc.

PECULIAR SAYINGS OF PACIOLI

Chapter 1. "Where there is no order there is confusion."
2. "Every action is determined by the end in view."
3. "Defining diligently and truthfully so that truth will always guide you."
4. "More bridges are necessary for a good merchant than a lawyer can make."

"The merchant is like a rooster, which of all the animals is the most alert, and in winter and summer keeps his night vigils and never rests."

"Also it is said that the head of the merchant has a hundred eyes and still they are not sufficient for all he has to say or do."

"The law helps those that are awake—not those that sleep."

"Dante says:
'My son, it behooves that you quit your laziness.
God promised the crown to the watchful ones.
He who lies on feathers or under cover will never amount to anything. Such a one leaves on this earth the same trace as the smoke in the air or foam on the water'."

"Work should not seem to you strange for Mars never granted a victory to those that spent their time resting."

A sage said to the lazy man to take the ant as an example.

Apostle Paul says that no one will be worthy of the crown except he who shall fight valiantly for it.

Remember God and your neighbor.

Attend religious meditation every morning, for through this you will never lose your way.

By being charitable you will not lose your riches.

The Saviour in the book of St. Matthew admonishes, "Seek you Christians first the Kingdom of God and then the other temporal and spiritual things you will easily obtain."

18 and 31 Who does nothing makes no mistakes; who makes no mistakes learns nothing.

22 Officials do not bother about details.

23 Accounts are nothing else than the expressions in writing of the arrangement of his affairs, which the merchant keeps in his mind.

If you are in business and do not know all about it, your money will go like flies, that is, you will lose it.

29 Books should be closed each year, especially in partnership because frequent accounting makes for long friendship.

33 If the losses are in excess of the gains—from which state of affairs may God keep every one who really lives as a good Christian.

35 If you do not put the place and date on a letter, you will be made fun of, because we say the letter which does not bear the date was written during the night, and the letter which does not bear the place we say that it was written in the other world and not in this one.

no mette pegno.10.contra.15.vnaltro mette.20.contra.27.dimandase chi che
uantagio e quanto p c.   Fa cosi prima uedi quanto meritaria.20.de scontro a
rata.che.10.a.15.e dise.10.a.15.che hara.20.uirra hauer.30.donca uedi che non
ha debito scontro habiando.27 or uedi che li manca che li machera da.27.a.30.
che son 3.uedi che pte son de suo capital che e.30.che son li $\frac{1}{10}$.e tato ebbe di dano n l so ca
pitale respecto a laltro.donca arguesci che laltro habia uataragio li $\frac{3}{10}$.del suo capitale cb uol
dir.15.per.c°.che si troua anche a questo modo dicendo colui mettendo.10.tiraria.15.se me
tesse.100.che tiraraue opera tiraria 150.qual salua.Poi p laltro dirai se.20.uol.27.che uo
ra.100.che uirra a uolere.135.cb uedi che manco che.150.del p°.si che ebbe suataragio. Si sape
qto p c°.abbati.135.de.150.resta.15.e tato ebbe dano i tutto per hauer messo.100.cioe haue
danno tal parte qual son.15.de.100.che son li $\frac{3}{20}$.ut supra la'tro auanzo p u che lui.5.in tut
to che son li $\frac{3}{20}$.pur de.100.suo capitale:siche auantragio.15.p c°.fatta per che semp tal par
te quale pde luno qlla medesima preuene a nazare laltro e cosi i baratti.

Tauola del Quaderno.

COMPARATIVE INDEX OF THE EARLIEST WRITERS

The following is a schedule showing comparatively the contents of the chapters of Pacioli, Manzoni, Pietra and Ympyn, so that the reader may have a quick perception of the extent to which Manzoni, Pietra and Ympyn have followed Pacioli. Only the most important items are given. Carefully note the coincidence that even the order in which the chapter is given practically remains unchanged from that of Pacioli.

CONTENTS OF CHAPTERS.	Pacioli	Manzoni	Pietra	Ympyn
The things a merchant needs and description of system of keeping a journal and a ledger	1	Vol. I/1	1	1
Description of an inventory, movables, immovables, accounts receivable, accounts payable	2	Vol. I/2	6-8	2
Sample of an inventory in full detail by lots	3	Vol. I/3	9	......
Useful instruction to a merchant	4	Vol. I/4	10	......
Introduction to second part of the treatise covering "Disposition"	5	......	......	3
Description, etc., of the day book	6	Vol. I/5	16	4
The marking of the books and the use of the cross on them	6	......	21	......
Authentication of books by notaries	7	Vol. I/7	16	......
Sample entry for the day book	8	......	......	5-6
Nine methods of purchasing goods, as many for selling	9	Vol. I/11	26-28	7
Description of the journal	10	Vol. I/8	20-24	8
The two terms "Per" and "A" and the two little lines //	11	Vol. I/10	2	9
The term "Cash"	12	Vol. I/9	49	9
The term "Capital"	12	Vol. I/9	30-33	9
Samples of journal entries	12	Vol. I/12	......	9
One kind of money in amount column	12	Vol. I/12	30	9
Line under each entry and through money column, diagonal line through day book entry when journalized, or check off at beginning or end of entry	12	Vol. I/12	30	9
The Ledger	13	Vol. II/1	30	10
The Index	13	Vol. I/11	36	10
Four lines for money, one for ledger pages, two for dates	13	Vol. II/1	......	10
Posting from journal to ledger	14	Vol. II/5	39	11
Two diagonal lines, one on left and one on right, when entry is posted	14	Vol. II/6	......	..
Posting figures one above other, divided by a little line	14	Vol. II/7	38	11
The place for the date	15	Vol. I/11	......	12
Year in Roman figures	15	Vol. II/2	14	12
Change in year between entries	15	Vol. I/11	......	12
In personal account more detail required	15	Vol. II/4	......	......
Spacing of ledger to save transfer	15	Vol. I/12	36	12
Index	15	Vol. I/11	36	10
Further instruction about merchandise entries in the ledger	16	Vol. I/12	36	......

CONTENTS OF CHAPTERS.

CHAPTER NUMBERS.

Conmo se debiano saldare tutte le partite del quaderno vechio:e i chi:e per che e de la ſu
ma ſumarum del dare e delauere ultimo ſcontro del bilancio.　　　　　ca°.34

Del modo e ordie a ſaper tenere le ſcripture menute cōmo ſóno ſcripti de mano lře familia
ri poliçç:pceſſi:ſentêtie e altri iſtrumēti e del regiſtro de le lettere ipoztãti.　　　ca°.35

Epilogo o uero ſũmaria recolta de tutto el pzeſente tractato:acio con bzeue ſubſtãtia ſe ha
bia mandare a memozia le coſe dette.　　　　　　　　　　　　　　　ca°.36

Distinctio.nona.Tractatus.xi°.pticularis de cōputis z ſcripturis.

De quelle coſe che ſóno neceſſarie al uero mercatante:e de lozdine a ſape bē tenere vn q̃/
derno cō ſuo gioznale : vinegia e anche p ognialtro luogo.　　　　Capitolo pzimo.

A reuerenti ſubditi de.U.D.S.Magnanimo.D. acio a pieno
de tutto lozdine mercanteſco habino el biſogno:dell'ocrai.(oltr.
le coſe dinançe i q̃ſta nřa opa ditte) ancoza particular tractato
grandemête neceſſario cōpillare.E in q̃ſto ſolo lo iſerto: p che
a ogni loro occurrêça el pſente libzo li poſſa ſeruire.Si del mo /
do a conti e ſcripture:cōmo de ragioni.E per eſſo intendo dar/
li nozma ſufficiente e baſtante in tenere ordinatamente tutti lor
conti e libzi.Pero che.(cōmo ſi ſã)tre coſe maxime ſóno opoz
tune:a chi uole con debita diligêtia mercantare.De le q̃li lapotiſ
ſima e la pecunia numerata e ogni altra faculta ſu ſtantiale.Ju
rta illud phy vnũ aliquid neceſſariozũ é ſubſtantia.Sêça el cui
ſuffragio mal ſi po el manegio traficante exercitare.Auêga che
molti gia nudi cō bona fede cōmençando:de grã facêde habio fatto.E mediante lo credito
fedelmête ſeruato i magne ridecçe ſieno peruenuti.Che aſai p vtalia diſcurrêdo nabiamo
cognoſciuti.E piu gia nele grã republiche non ſi poteua dire:che la fede del bon mercatan
te.E a quella ſi fermaua loz giuramento:dicêdo.A la ſe de real mercatante.E cio nó deuef
ſere admiratione:cōcioſia che i la fede catolicamête ognuno ſi ſalui:e ſença lei ſia ipoſſibile
piacere a dio.　　La ſecōda coſa che ſi recerca al debito trafico:ſie che ſia buon ragioncri: e
pmpto cōputiſta.E p queſto cōſequire.(diſopza cōmo ſe ueduto)dal pzicipio alaſine: ha/
uemo iducto regole e canoni a ciaſcuna opatione requiſiti.In modo che da ſe:ogni dilige/
te lectoze:tutto potra ipzendere.E chi di queſta pte non foſſe bene armato:la ſequête in ua
no li ſerebbe.　　La.3.ª e vltima coſa opoztuna ſie:che cō bello ozdie tutte ſue facêde debita
mête diſponga:acio con bzeuita:poſſa de ciaſcũa hauer notitia:quanto aloz debito e anche
credito:che circa altro non ſatêde el trafico.E q̃ſta pte fra laltre e alozo utiliſſima:che i lor
facêde altramête regerſe:ſeria ipoſſibile:ſêça debito ozdine de ſcripture.E ſêça alcũ repoſo la
loz mête ſempze ſtaria in gran trauagli.E po acio con laltre q̃ſta poſſino hauere.el pſete tra
ctato ozdiai.Nel q̃le ſe da el mó a tutte ſozti de ſcripture:a ca°.p ca°.pcedêdo.E bē che nó
ſi poſſa cuſi apóto tutto el biſogno ſcriuere.Nó dimeno p q̃l che ſe dira.El pegrino igeg°a
q̃lũcaltro laplicara.　　E ſeruaremo i eſſo el mó de vinegia:q̃le certamête fra glialtri e molto
da cōmêdare.E mediante q̃llo i ogni altro ſe pozra guidare.E q̃ſto diuideremo L2.pti pn
cipali.Luna chiamaremo iuêtario.E laltra diſpóne.E p.ª de luna:e poi de laltra ſucceſſiua
mête ſe dira ſcdo lozdie i la ppoſta tauola contenuto.Per la q̃l facilmête el lectoze pozra le
occur.têtie trouare ſecondo el numero de ſuoi capitoli e carti.

Hi cō lo debito ozdie che ſaſpecta uol ſap bē tenere vn q̃derno cō lo ſuo giozna
le a q̃l che qui ſe dira con diligêtia ſtia a têto.E acio bē ſintêda el pceſſo idurre/
mo i cãpo vno che mo dinouo cōmêci a traficare cōmo p ozdie deba procedere
neltenere ſoi conti e ſcripture:aciochee ſucitamête ogni coſa poſſi ritrouare poſta
al ſuo luogo p che nó aſertando le coſe debitamête a li ſuoi luoghi uerebbe i grandiſſimi tra
uagli e cō fuſiói de tutte ſue facêde.Jurta cōe dictũ vbi nó é ozdo ibi eſt cōfuſio.E pero a p
fecto documêto dogni mercatante de tutto nřo pceſſo faremo cōmo di ſopza e ditto.2. pti
pncipali.E q̃li apramête q̃ ſequête chiariremo:acio fructo ſalutifero ſabia ipzêdere. E pzia
dimoſtrando chē coſa ſia iuêtario e cōmo ſabia far e De la p.ª pte pncipale de q̃ſto tractato
detta iuêtario.E che coſa ſia iuêtario:e cōme fra mercatanti ſabia fare.　ca°.2　　Cōuienſe
adonca p.ªmête pſupponere e imaginare che ogni opante e moſſo dalfine. E p poter q̃llo
debitamête cōſeqre ſa o ẕni ſuo sfozo nel ſuo pceſſo.vnde el fine de q̃lũche traficante e de
cōſequire licito e cōpetête guadagno p ſua ſubſtêtariōe .E po ſempze con lo nome de meſer
domenedio:debiano cōmençare lozo facende.Ei nel pů°.dogni loz ſcripture:el ſuo ſancto

COMPLETE TRANSLATION OF PACIOLI

SECTION NINE—TREATISE XI.

PARTICULARS OF RECKONINGS AND THEIR RECORDING.

CHAPTER 1.

THINGS THAT ARE NECESSARY TO THE GOOD MERCHANT AND THE METHOD OF KEEPING A LEDGER WITH ITS JOURNAL, IN VENICE AND ELSEWHERE.

In order that the subjects of His Illustrious Highness, the most honorable and magnanimous Duke of Urbino (D. U. D. S.—*Docis Urbini Domini Serenissimi*), may have all the rules that a good merchant needs, I decided to compile, in addition to the subjects already treated in this work, a special treatise which is much needed. I have compiled it for this purpose only, *i. e.*, that they (the subjects) may whenever necessary find in it everything with regard to accounts and their keeping. And thereby I wish to give them enough rules to enable them to keep all their accounts and books in an orderly way. For, as we know, there are three things needed by any one who wishes to carry on business carefully. The most important of these is cash or any equivalent, according to that saying, *Unum aliquid necessarium est substantia*. Without this, business can hardly be carried on.

It has happened that many without capital of their own but whose credit was good, carried on big transactions and by means of their credit, which they faithfully kept, became very wealthy. We became acquainted with many of these throughout Italy. In the great republics nothing was considered superior to the word of the good merchant, and oaths were taken on the word of a good merchant. On this confidence rested the faith they had in the trustworthiness of an upright merchant. And this is not strange, because, according to the Christian religion, we are saved by faith, and without it it is impossible to please God.

The second thing necessary in business is to be a good bookkeeper and ready mathematician. To become such we have given above (in the foregoing sections of the book) the rules and canons necessary to each transaction, so that any diligent reader can understand it all by himself. If one has not understood this first part well, it will be useless for him to read the following.

The third and last thing is to arrange all the transactions in such a systematic way that one may understand each one of them at a glance, *i. e.*, by the debit (*debito*—owed to) and credit (*credito*—owed by) method. This is very essential to merchants, because, without making the entries systematically it would be impossible to conduct their business, for they would have no rest and their minds would always be troubled. For this purpose I have written this treatise, in which, step by step, the method is given of making all sorts of entries. Although one cannot write out every essential detail for all cases, nevertheless a careful mind will be able, from what is given, to make the application to any particular case.

This treatise will adopt the system used in Venice, which is certainly to be recommended above all the others, for by means of this, one can find his way in any other. We shall divide this treatise in two principal parts. The one we shall call the Inventory, and the other, Disposition (arrangement). We shall talk first of the one and then of the other, according to the order contained in the accompanying Table of Contents, from which the reader may take what he needs in his special case.

He who wants to know how to keep a ledger and its journal in due order must pay strict attention to what I shall say. To understand the procedure well, we will take the case of one who is just starting in business, and tell how he must proceed in keeping his accounts and books so that at a glance he may find each thing in its place. For, if he does not put each thing in its own place, he will find himself in great trouble and confusion as to all his affairs, according to the familiar saying, *Ubi non est ordo, ibi est confusio* (Where there is no order, there is confusion). In order to give a perfect model to every merchant, we will divide the whole system, as we have said, in two principal parts, and we will arrange these so clearly that one can get good results from them. First, we will describe what the inventory is and how to make it.

CHAPTER 2.

FIRST PART OF THIS TREATISE, WHICH IS CALLED INVENTORY—WHAT INVENTORY IS, AND HOW TO MAKE IT.

First, we must assume that every action is determined by the end in view, and in order to pursue this end properly, we must use every effort. The purpose of every merchant is to make a lawful and reasonable profit so as to keep up his business. Therefore, the merchants should begin their business with the name of God at the beginning of every book and have His holy

NOTE—The words in parentheses are the author's, as also the punctuation and paragraphing, as the original is extremely deficient in these. The words in italics are copied exact from the original.

nome hauera mēte zc. E po p°.cōuen che facia suo diligente iuētario:i q̄sto modo.che sem
pre p°.scriua in vn foglio o uero libro da pte.Cioche se ritroua hauer al mōdo:oe mobile:e
dest abile.Cōmençando semp da le cose che sōno in piu pgio e piu labili al perdere. Cōmo
sō li ō.cōtanti.Bioc. Argenti zc. Per che le stabili.Cōmo sōno.Casi.Terreni.Lacune val
le.Peschiere e simili nō si possano sinarire:cōmo le cose mobili. E succesiuamēte poi de ma
no i mano.scriuase laltre.Ponendo sēpre p'el di:e milesimo:el luogo, el nome suo nel ditto
iuētario.e tutto ditto iuētario si deue tenere in vn medesimo giozno:p che altramēte darebe
trauaglio nel māegio futuro. E po a tuo exēplo:porre q vn pr n".cōmo se debia fare.Perlo
q̄l tu pte porrai i ogni luogo el ppolito sequire zc.vz.

Forma exēplare cō tutte sue solennita in lo inuentario requisite.   ca°.;
Al nome de dio.1493.a di.8.nouembre in vinegia.

Questo se quēte si e lo iuēta: io de mi. A.da vine°.De la cōtrada de scō apostolo.
El q̄le ordenatamēte io de mia mano ho scripto:o ho fatto scruere dai tale zc.
De tutti li miei beni:Mobili: e Stabili:Debiti:e Crediti che al mōdo mi ritro
uo:sin q̄sto psēte giozno sopra ditto.p°.prima. In p°.mi trouo de cōtāti fra ozo
e moneta:duc.tanti zc.Di q̄li tāti sōno dozo venitiani.E tāti dozo ongari.E tāti fio. larghi
fra papali:senese fiorētini zc.Lauāço moēte dargēto e rame de piu sorti:cioc. Trōi. Mar
celli.Carlini de re.E de papa. E grossi fiorētini.Testoni milanesi zc.2ª Itē mi trouo i go
ie ligate e desligate.Pecci n°.tāti zc.De li q̄li tanti sōno balassi i tauola ligati:i ozo ancili pe
sano.5.e caratri grani zc.luno o uero i suma.Qui poi dire a tuo mō zc. E tanti sōno safili
pur a tauola ifozmagli da dōna. Pesano zc. E tāti sōno rubi cocu legni desligadi pesano zc.
lialtri sōno diamāti grecci a tauola:e pōtidi zc.Narrādo le sorti e pesi a tua uoglia.3ª Itē
mi trouo veste de piu sorte.tāte de la tale e tante de la tale zc. Narrādo suoi cōditiōi. Colo
ri:fodre e fogie zc.4ª Itē mi trouo argēti lauorati de.p. sorti.Cōmo tacce bacili.R āini.
Cosileri. Pironi zc.E q narra tutto le sorti a vna p vna zc. E pesa ciascuna lozta dapse so
tilmēte. E tiē cōto de pecci de pesi zc. E de le legibe.O venetiana.O ragusea zc.E anche
stāpo.o uero segno che hauessero farne mentiōe zc.5ª Itē mi trouo i massaria ō panni li
ni:cioe Lēçoli.Touagli.Camise.Façali zc.Capi n°tāti zc.lēçuoli de.3.teli.Odi.2 ½.zc.tele
padouane o altre zc.nuoui o vsati lōghi tanti bz.zc. E camise tante zc.touagle de rese zc.fa
çuoli grandi n°tanti zc. E piccoli tanti zc.noui vsati zc.a tuo mō narra".le sorti. 6ª Itē
mi trouo lecti ō piūa.n°.tanti zc.cō soi caueçali de piu noua o ho vsata zc.federa noua zc.
q̄li pesano i tutto.o ho vno p vno.8.tante zc.E eḡte del mio seg°.o dalt°.cōmo si costu
ma zc. 7ª Itē mi trouo de mercantie i casa ouer i magaçeni.zc.de piu sorti.p°.Colli tan
ti de çēçari. michini pesano. 8.tanc.zc.Segnati del tal seg°.zc. E cosi andarai narran".a sor
ta p sor.ditte mercantie cō tutti cōtrasegni sia possibile.e cō q̄ta.piu chiarecca si possa.de pe
so n°.e misura zc. 8ª Itē mi trouo colli tanti de çēçari bellidi zc. E carchi tāti de pip zc.
pip lōgo.o uer pip tōdo scdo che sira zc. E fardi tanti di canelle zc.pesa°.zc. E colli tanti
garo°.zc pesa°.zc.cō fusti poluere e capelleti.o ho seça zc.E pecci tāti.de ançini zc.pesa°.zc.
e pecci tanti sani.rossi o bianchi pesa°.zc.E cosi andarai mettēdo p ordie v".sotto laltro zc.
9ª Itē mi tr°.pelami da fodre:cioe agnelie.bia.e albertōi pugliesi o marchiani zc.n°.tan
ti de la tal sor.zc.e volpe mar.n°tante cōçe zc.e n°.tante crude zc.E camoçe cōçe e tru
de zc.n°.tante zc. 10ª Itē mi trouo pelle si.fo.arme.dossi.vari.çebelini zc.n°.tanti de
la tal sorte.E n°.tanti de la tale zc.Cosi destiguēdo a v°.a v°.diligētemēte con tutta verita:
acio el uero te habia a guidare zc. Auendo sēp auertēça a le cose che uāno a n°. E a q̄le che
uāno a peso.E a q̄le ch vāno a misura.po ch di q̄ste.3.sor'. si costūa fare el trafico p tutto.
e alcune si mercatio a.M°. Altre a.c°.altre a.8.altre a.5.altre a n°.cioe a cōto cōmo pella
mi zc.altre a pecci.cōmo gioie:e perle fine zc. Si che di tutte sa ben nota a cosa per cosa zc.
E queste te bastino a tua guida.L altre per te poi sequirai sempre zc.   11ª. Item
mi trouo destabile priam.vna casa a tanti sulari zc:a tante camere.Corte. Pozzo.Orto zc.
posta in la contra de sancto apostolo:fora canale zc.apresso el tale:e tale zc.Nominando
li cōfini:e referēdoti ali instri se ui sōno ātichi piu veri zc. E cosi se piu nauesse de le cale i di
uer si luoghi:notarle a simili zc.12ª. Itē mi trouo terreni lauoranui cāpi.o uero staioze.o
o uero panora zc.Nominādoli scdo luso del paese doue te trou.o uero doue sōno situua
ti zc.n°tāti zc.Intrēdēdo el cāpo o uero staioza de tauole tāte o cāne o priche o beuolche zc.
posti in la tal villa de padouana o altrōde zc.Apresso li beni del tale zc.Chiamādo li cō
fini zc.E instrumēti.o uero prita de catasti.p li q̄li paghile fationi i cōmuno zc.Quali lela
uora el tale zc.rēdano lāno de fitto cōmūo:stara tāti e.ō.tāti zc.E cosi pte ua narādo tu
tuoi possessiōze.Bestiami soci.13ª Itē mi tro° ba'ala came°.ō ipsti°.ouer alt°.mōte iv"

34

name in their minds. To begin with, the merchant must make his inventory (*inventario*) in this way: He must always put down on a sheet of paper or in a separate book whatever he has in this world, personal property or real estate, beginning with the things that are most valuable and most likely to be lost, such as cash, jewels, silver, etc., for the real estate, such as houses, lands, lakes, meadows, ponds, etc., cannot be lost as personal property. Then all the other things must be put down one after another. In the said inventory give always first the day, the year, the place and your name. This whole inventory must be completed in one day, otherwise there will be trouble in the future in the management of the business.

As an example for you, I will give you, now, an idea as to how the inventory is to be made, so that you may use it as a guide in any particular case.

CHAPTER 3.

EXAMPLE OF AN INVENTORY WITH ALL ITS FORMAL REQUIREMENTS.

In the name of God, November 8th, 1493, Venice.

The following is the inventory of myself, N. N., of Venice, Street of the Holy Apostles.

I have written down systematically, or had written by Mr. So-and-So, this inventory of all my property, personal and real, what is owed to me (*debiti*), and what is owed by me (*crediti*), of which I on this said day find myself possessed in this world.

First Item: First I find myself possessed in cash, in gold and coin of so many ducats, of which so many are Venetian, and so many gold Hungarian; of so many large florins made up of Papal, Siennese and Florentine, etc. The rest consists of many different kinds of silver and copper coins, *i. e., troni, marcelli,* papal and royal *carlini* and Florentine *grossi,* and Milanese *testoni,* etc.

Second Item: I also possess, in set and unset jewels, so-and-so many pieces, among which are many *balassi* set in gold, rings weighing so-and-so-many ounces, carats, grains, etc., per piece or in bulk, etc., which you can express in any manner you wish. There are so-and-so-many sapphires set on clamps for women; they weigh so much. And there are so-and-so-many rubies, unset, weighing so much. The rest consists of unpolished pointed diamonds, etc. Here you may give such descriptions and weight as you desire.

Third Item: I have clothes of many kinds; so many of such kind; and so many of such-and-such kind, etc., describing their condition, colors, linings, styles, etc.

Fourth Item: I have several kinds of silverware, as cups, basins, rammi, cosileri, piromi, etc. Here describe all the different kinds one by one, etc., and weigh each kind diligently. Keep an account of pieces and weights, and of the alloy, whether the Venetian or the one used at Ragusa, etc. Also mention the stamp or mark that they might have.

Fifth Item: I have so much *massaria dei lini*—that is, bed sheets, table cloths, shirts, handkerchiefs, etc., so many of each. Of the bed sheets, so many are made three-piece sheets, and so many are three and one-half, etc., mentioning whether the linen is Padua linen or some other kind, new or used; length so many *braccia,* etc.; so many shirts, etc.; table cloths of so many threads; so many big handkerchiefs and so many small, mentioning whether new or used, giving the different kind in your own way.

Sixth Item: I have so many feather beds and their respective pillows, mentioning whether the feathers are new or used, whether the pillow-cases are new or used, etc., which altogether or one by one weigh so much, marked with my mark or with some other mark, as the custom is.

Seventh Item: I have at home or in the store so much goods of different kinds: First, so many cases of ginger *michino,* weighing so many pounds, marked with such-and-such mark, and so on, describing each kind of said goods with all their marks that you might possibly give and with all the possible accuracy as to weight, number, measurement, etc.

Eighth Item: I have so many cases of ginger *bellidi,* etc., and so many sacks of pepper, long pepper or round pepper, depending on what it is; so many packages of cinnamon, etc., that weigh so much; so many packages of cloves, etc., that weigh so much, with *fusti polvere* and *cappelletti* or without, etc., and so many pieces of *verzini* weighing so much, and so much sandalwood, red or white, weighing so much, and so on, entering one item after another.

Ninth Item: I have so many skins for coverings, that is, so many white kids and so many *albertoni* or *marchiani,* etc., so many of such-and-such kind, etc., so many fox skins, so many tanned and so many raw, so many chamois skins tanned, and so many raw.

Tenth Item: I have so many fine skins, *fore armenti, dossi varii, zebelini,* etc., so many of such-and-such kind, and so many of such-and-such kind—defining diligently and truthfully each time so that truth will always guide you, etc., distinguishing the things that ought to be entered by pieces from those that ought to be entered by weight, and those that ought to be entered by measurement, because in these three ways business is conducted everywhere; certain things are reckoned by the bushel, others by the hundreds, others by the pound, others by the ounce, others by number, others by a *conto* (by single numbers) as leather goods or skins, others by the piece, as precious stones and fine pearls, etc.; so you will make a notation of each thing. These examples will serve as a guide for all the rest, etc.

Eleventh Item: I have in real estate: first, a house with so many stories, so many rooms, court yard, wells, garden, etc., situated in St. Apostle Street over the Canal, etc., adjoining such-and-such parties, etc., giving the names of the boundary line properties, making reference to the oldest and most reliable deeds, if there are any; and so, if you have more houses in different localities, you will enter them in a similar way.

ducati tanti de capedale nel sextier de canareggio ʒc. O uero pte i vno sextierle e pte i vnal
tro. Narrando ancora i nome de chi sonno scripti. E chiamando el libro de quello officio
El numero de le carti doue e la tua partita. El nome del scriuano che tien ditto libro: acio cō
piu tua facilita qdo vai a scotere li possi trouar. Pero che in tali officij bisogna hauere mol
ti scontri alcuolte per la gran multitudine che ci interuiene ʒc. E nota el milesimo che respō
dano a tépo p tépo acio sappia quádo uengano li so pro. e quáto per cēto respōdino ʒc. 14

Item mi trouo debitori numero tanti ʒc. luno e s' tale del tale ʒc. che me deue dare duca
ti tanti ʒc. L'altro e el tale del tale ʒc. E cosi narrali a vno:a vno con boni contra segni: e co
gnomi: e luoghi: e quanto te debano dare: e p che. E cosi se ui son scripti de mā o instrumē
ti de nodari fra uoi fáne mētione ʒc. In summa debo scotere ducati táti ʒc. De boni ō. Se si-
rá persone da bene ʒc. altraméti dirai de tristi ō. ʒc. 15   Item mi trouo essere debito i tut
to ducati tanti ʒc. tanti a al tale. e tanti al tale ʒc. Nominádo li toi creditori a uno a vno: E
se ui sōno chiarecce fra uoi. o de scripti o de instrumenti nominarli. E chi. E commo. el di el
luogo per molti casi poteriéno occorrere in iudicio e for de iudicio ʒc.

Utilissima exortatione: e salutiferi documéti al bō mercatāte ptinéti.   ca°.4
Cosi discorso cō diligéça tutte le cose che te ritroui imobile e stabile: cōme e dec-
to a una per una: se fosser ben diecimilia di che condiuoni e faculta si sia e banchi
e imprestiti ʒc. tutte al buono ordine cōuiense nominarle in ditto cuétario cō tut
ti cōtrasegni nomi: e cognomi qto sia piu possibile. Per ch al mercatáte nō possa
no mai le cose essere troppo chiare. Per l'infiniti casi che nel trafico possano occorrere: com
mo ala giornata sa chi in esso se exercita. E pero bé dici el prouerbio che bisogna piu ponti
a fare vn bō mercatáte. che a fare vn doctore de leggi. Chi e colui che possa nūerare li prīti:
e casi che ale mani uengono ali mercatanti. Ora p mare. Ora p terra. Ora a tempi de pace e
dabondantia. Ora a tempi de guerre e carestie. Ora a tempi de sanita e morbi. Ne quali té
pic occurrece li conuiene saper prendere soi partiti. Si p li mercati: cōmo p le fieri che ora i
una patria e cita si fáno. E ora in l'altra ʒc. E pero ben se figura e asimiglia el mercatante al
gallo. Quale e fragl'altri el piu uigilante animale che sia: e diuerno e di state fa le sue notur
ne uigilie. che mai per alcū tempo resta. Auenga che de filomena se dica: cioe del rosignuo
lo che tutta la nocte canti: non dimeno questo si pō de state al caldo tempo uerificare: ma
non diuerno: cōmo la experiencia e impronto adimostrarlo. E ancho sia simigliata la sua
testa a vna che habia cēto ochi. che anchora nō li sōno bastáti: ne in dir ne i fare. Le qual co
se solole dica chi le pua. Marinolo. Uenitiani. Forētini. Genouesi. Napolitani. Milanesi. Ancoitá. Bressini. Bergamaschi. Adlani. Senesi Luchesi. Perusini. Urbiati. Forosin
proniani Caglesi. E Ugubini. Castellani. Borghesi. e Fulignati cō Pisái. Bolognesi. e Fe
raresi. Mátouái. Ueroesi. Uigéti. e Padouái. Trani. Lecia. Bari. cō Uerōta Leql rpu' tra
l'altre i italia del trafico tengano el principato. Marie la excelsa cita de venetia cō fioréça.
Norma e regola d'ogni partito. chal bisogno aprender sabia. Si che bé dicáo le leggi muni
cipali vz. uigilantibus ʒ non dormientibus Jura subueniunt: cioe a chi ueggbia e nō a chi
dorme le leggi souengáo. E cosi neli diuini officij si canta da la sancta chiesa. che idio ali vi
gilanti a promesso la corona. E pero questo fo el documéto di virgilio dato a Dante: cōmo
a suo figliuolo. Quando nel cáto. 24°. de lo iferno li dici exortandolo a la fatiga: per laqle
al monte de le uirtu se peruiene. O ʒ mai conuien figliuolo che tu te spoltri. Disse el mae
stro mio che pur in piuma. In fama nō si uiene ne sotto coltre. Sotto la qual chi sua uita
cōsuma. E tal uestigio dise in terra lascia. Qual fume i aire e i aqua la schiuma ʒc. E vn al
tro uulgar poeta al medesimo ci cōforta dicédo. Nō te para strania la fatiga ch marte nō
concesse mai batagl a A quelli che possando se nutrica ʒc. Lo exemplo anchora del sapiéte
molto fo acto conueniéte. Dicédo al pigro che si spechiasse nella formicha. E paulo apolto
lo dici che niū sira degno di corona saluo che chi hara legitimaméte combattuto ʒc. Que
sti recordi li o uoluti adure per tua utilita: acio non te para graue la cotidiana solicitudine
in tue facende. marime in tenere la péna in carta: e tutte scriuere a di per di: qnel che te oc
corre: cōmo se dira nel seqnte. Ma sép sopra tutto p' idio el prio te sia auáti gliochi e mai
nō manchi da ludire la messa la matia. Recordádote che p lci mai si pde camio. Ne p la ca
rita si scema ri ebcce cōmo p qsto sctō uerso te dici. Nec caritas opes: nec missa miuit uer ʒc
E a qsto ci exorta el saluator i sā matheo qdo dici. Primū qrite regnū dei: ʒ hec oia adiicie
tur uobis. Cercate xpiani pmaméte el reame ō li cieli e pot l'altre cose téporali e spūali facil

36

Twelfth Item: I have so many pieces of land under cultivation (fields or *staiore* or *panora*) etc., entering them by the name according to the usage of the country where you are, saying where they are situated, etc., as, for instance, a field of so many *tavole*, or *canne*, or *pertiche*, or *bevolche*, etc., situated in such-and-such town in the Province of Padua or somewhere else, adjoining the land of so-and-so, giving all the boundary lines and referring to deeds or the description from the recorder's office, for which land you pay taxes in such-and-such municipality, which are worked by so-and-so with a yearly income of so much, and so on; you will enter all your possessions, etc., cattle, etc.

Thirteenth Item: I have in deposit with the Camera de l'Impresti (a bank), or with another bank in Venice, so many ducats; or with the parish of Canareggio, etc., or part in one parish and part in another, giving the names under which they have been deposited, mentioning the book of the bank, the number of the page where your account is, and the name of the clerk who keeps said book, so that you can easily find your account when you go to get money, because in such offices they must keep very many accounts on account of the big crowd that sometimes goes there, and you must also see that dates are put down precisely so that you know when everything falls due and what the per cent. is.

Fourteenth Item: I have so many debtors (*debitori*): one is so-and-so, who owes me (*me dee dare*—shall give me) so many ducats, and so on, giving the names of each one, putting down all annotations as to the names, their family names, and how much they owe you (*te debbono dore*—shall have to give you) and why; also whether there are any written papers or notarial instruments. In total I have so many ducats to collect, you will say, of good money, if the money is due from good people, otherwise you will say of bad money.

Fifteenth Item: I am debtor in total to the extent of so many ducats, etc. I owe so many to so-and-so. Here mention your creditors (*creditori*) one by one, writing down whether there are any documents or writings or instruments; if possible, mention the persons present when the debt was incurred, the reason, the time and the place, for any case that might arise in court or out of court.

CHAPTER 4.

VERY USEFUL ADMONITION AND GOOD ADVICE TO THE GOOD MERCHANT.

And so, as we have said, you shall enter diligently every thing that you have, whether personal property or real estate, one by one, even if there were ten thousand items, putting down the condition and nature, whether deposited or loaned, etc. You will have to mention each thing in proper order in the said Inventory with all marks, names, surnames—as far as possible—for things are never too clear to a merchant on account of the different things that may happen in business, as anybody in business knows. Right is the proverb which says: More bridges are necessary to make a good merchant than a lawyer can make. Who is the person that can count all the things that can happen to a merchant—on the sea, on land, in times of peace and abundance and times of war and famine, in times of health or pestilence? In these crises he must know what to do, in the marketplaces and in the fairs which are held now in one place and now in another. For this reason it is right to say that the merchant is like a rooster, which of all the animals (*animale*) is the most alert and in winter and summer keeps his night vigils and never rests. And they say of the nightingale that it sings throughout the whole night; however, this may be in the summer during the hot weather, but not during the winter, as experience shows. Also it is said that the head of the merchant has a hundred eyes, and still they are not sufficient for all he has to say or to do. These things are told by people who have had experience in them, such as the Venetians, Florentines, Genoans, Neapolitans, Milanese, people of Ancona, Brescia, Bragama, Aquila, Sienna, Lucca, Perugia, Urbino, Forosempronio, Cagli, Ugubio, Castello, Brogo, Fuligno, Pisa, Bologna, Ferrara, Mantua, Verona, Vincenza, Padua, Trani, Lecce, Bitonto, which are among the first cities of Italy and have the first place in commerce—especially the cities of Venice and Florence, which adopt rules that respond to any need. And well say the municipal laws: *Vigilantibus et non dormientibus jura subveniunt*—which means, The law helps those that are awake, not those that sleep. So in the divine functions of the Holy Church they sing that God promised the crown to the watchful ones, and this was the instruction that Virgil gave to Dante as to his son, in Canto 24 of the Inferno, where he exhorts him to the work by which one can reach the hill of virtue: Now, my son, it behooves that you quit your laziness, said my master, for he who lies on feathers or under covers will never amount to anything. Whoever spends his life in this way, he said, will leave on this earth the same trace as the smoke in the air or foam on the water, etc.; and another Italian poet admonishes us in the same way, saying: Work should not seem to you strange, for Mars never granted a victory to those that spent their time resting. And it is also very good to quote that sage who said to the lazy man to take the ant as an example; and the Apostle Paul says that no one will be worthy of the crown except he who shall fight valiantly for it.

I wanted to bring in these reminders for your own good, so that the daily care about your business would not seem heavy to you, especially the writing down everything and putting down every day everything that happens to you, as we shall unfold in the next chapters. But above all, remember God and your neighbor; never forget to attend to religious meditation every morning, for through this you will never lose your way, and by being charitable, you will not lose your riches, as the poet says: *Nec caritas, nec Missa minuit iter,* etc. And to this our Savior exhorts us in the book of St. Matthew, when he says: *Primum quaerite regulum dei, et haec omnia adiicietur vobis,* which means: Seek you, Christians, first the kingdom of God and then the other temporal and spiritual things

mente confequirete. Pero chel padre voftro celeftiale fa molto bene voftro bifecmo zc.E q̃
fto uoglio te fia baftãte a tuo amaeftrameto diuetario zc.e altri boni vocũmti albenfare zc

De la. :ª.parte pricipale del pfente tractato ditta difpõne:cõme la fabia a intendere e in
che cõfifte:circa al trafico:e de li.3.libri pricipali del corpo mecãtefco.   cº.5

Equita ora la fecõda parte principale del pfente tractato laqual ricemo effere
la difpofitione di laquale alquãto piu longo cõuie chio fia:che i lapcedête a ben
chiarirla. E pero di lei faremo doi pti. Luna ditta corpo o uero monte de tutto el
trafico. Laltra ditta corpo o vero monte de botega. E prima diremo del cor po
generale de tutto el manegio le fue erigête. Al quale dico prima imediate doppo fuo iuen
tario bifognare.3.libri p piu fua deftreça e cõmodita. Luno ditto memoriale. E laltro detto
Giornale. Laltro dėtto. Quaderno. Auėga che molti p le poche lor facende facino folo cõ
li doi fecõdi:cioe giornale e quaderno. E pero prima diremo di luno cioe memoriale. E poi
fufequêtemête de lialtri doi delor modi:uerfi e vie cõmo debiano effere tenuti. E prima da/
remo fua diffinitione.

Del primo libro ditto memoriale o vero fquartafoglio o vachetta q̃l che fenten
da e commo in effo fe habia a fcriuere:e p chi.   caº 6

Ade memoriale o vero fe cõdo alcuni vachetta o fqrtafoglio e vn libro nel q̃le
tutte le facêde fue el mercatãte piccole e grãdi che amã li vegano.a giorno p gior
no e ora p ora ifcriue. Nel q̃le difufamête ogni cofa di uêdere e cõprare (e altri
manegi)fcriuêdo fe dichiara nõ lafando vn iota El chi. El che. El quãdo. El do
ue:cõ tutte fue chiareççe:e mêtioni:cõmo a pieno di fopra in lo enuentario te diffi:fença piu
oltra te le replichi. E i quefto tal libro molti coftumano ponere loro iuêtario. Ma p che el
puere a molte mani e ochi nõ laudo te li mobili e ftabili foi a pieno porre. E quefto li zo
fol fi fa p la furia de le facêde che fi feffe.nel quale deue fcriuere el Patrone,li Fattori Gar/
çõni :le dõne(fe fãno)in abfêça lũ de laltro. Pero chel grã mercatãte nõ terra fempre fermi
li garçoni ne factori. Ma ora li manda in qua:ora li manda in la:i modo che alcuolte lui cõ
loro fõno fora. Chi a fiere chi a mercati zc. E folo le dõne o altri garçoni reftano a cafa che
forfe a pena fãno fcriuere. E pure loro p non eruiare li auentori conuengano vendere:e fco/
tere:pagare:e cõprare fecõdo lordine che dal principale li fia ipofto. E loro fecõdo loro po
tere ogni cofa debono fcriuere i ditto memoriale nominãdo femplicimête le mõnete e pefi
che fãno:e trar fore a tutte forte de monette che vendano e cõprano o uero pagano e fcota
no po che i̇ quefto tale non fa cafo a che moneta fi caui fore.cõmo nel giornale e quader
no:cõ difotto fe dira zc.e quadernieri a fã tta tutto poi lui quãdo veli põe i giornale. Dich
tornando poi lo principale vede tutte fue facende e rafettale fe li pare altramête zc. E pero e
neceffario ditto libro a chi fa afai facêde. Per che ferebe fatiga belleçiare:e per ordine ogni
cofa la prima uolta mettere i li libri auctentici e con diligêça tenuti. E i q̃efto e in tutti al
tri prima ponere el fegno difora i fula copt:acio nel fucceffo de le facêde fiãdo pieno ⅃ fcri
ptura o uero fornito certo têpo p la qual cofa tu vorrai vnaltro libro prendere:o uero de ne
ceffita te cõuerra quãdo quefto foffe pieno. Ma ale uolte molti coftumano fdiuerfe pti: b̃
che nõ fia pieno anoualmête far faldi e anche li libri nuoui cõmo defotto itederai. E i ditto
fecondo libro per debito ordine bifogna renouare fegnale diferente dal primo:acio detem
po in têpo fi poffa cõ prefteça trouare loro facêde. Per tal uie ancora millefimo. E pero be/
ne fi coftuma fra li ueri catolici fegnare li primi loro libri:de quel gloriofo fegno dalq̃l fug
gi ogni noftro fpiritual nemico:e la caterua tutta infernal meritamête trema del fegno:
cioe de la fancta croci dal q̃ale ancora neli teneri anni a iparar de legere lalfabeto cõmen
çafti. E poi li fequêti libri fegnarai per ordine dalfabeto:cioe de. A. E poi li terçi del.B.zc.
difcorrendo per ordine dalfabeto. E chiãmafe poi libri croci cioe   Memorial croci.
Giornal croci:cioe   Quaderno croci:cioe   Alfabero o uero extratto croci. cioe.   zc.
E poi ati fcõi libri fe dira Memorial. A. Giornal. A. Quaderno. A. zc. E de tutti quefti li/
bri el numero de lor carti fi conuen fegnare per molti refpecti e caurele che aloperante fan
no de bifogno. Auega che molti dichino nel giornale e memoriale non bifognare p che
le cofe fe guidano ifilcate a di p di:vna fotto laltra che fia baftante a lor ritronare.   Que
fti tali dirchono el uero fe le facende de vna giornata non paffaffero vna carta. Ma noi ve
demo che molti groffi traficanti non che una carta ma doi e tre nepirano in vn giorno de
le qual poi(chi uoleffe far male)nepotrebbe tagliare e cauare una. La qual fraude nõ fi po/
trebe poi per uia d li giorni cognofcere ne difcernere. Per che li di fon quelli che fêça dubio

you will easily obtain, because your Heavenly Father knows very well your needs, etc.

And this I hope will be sufficient as an instruction for you to make the Inventory, etc., and to do other things well.

CHAPTER 5.

SECOND PRINCIPAL PART OF THIS TREATISE NAMED DISPOSITION (ARRANGE-MENT)—WHAT IS UNDERSTOOD BY IT—WHAT IT CONSISTS OF IN BUSINESS, AND THE THREE PRINCIPAL BOOKS OF THE MERCHANT.

Comes now the second principal part of this treatise, which is called disposition, and of this I have to talk more at length than of the first part, in order to make it very clear. I will divide it in two parts. We shall call the one, *Corpo overo monte de sutto el trafico;* the other, *Corpor overo monte de botega* (Commerce in general, and Your store in particular).

First, we shall speak of commerce in general and its requirements. Immediately after the Inventory, you need three books to make the work proper and easy. One is called Memorandum (*Memoriale*), the second Journal (*Giornale*), and the third Ledger (*Quaderno*). Many, on account of their small business, use only the last two, that is, the journal and the ledger.

We shall speak about the first—that is, of the memorandum book, and thereafter of the other two, about their makeup, and how they should be kept. First of all, we will give the definition of the memorandum book.

CHAPTER 6.

OF THE FIRST BOOK, WHICH IS CALLED MEMORANDUM BOOK (*MEMORIALE*), OR SCRAP BOOK (*SQUARTA LOGLIO*), OR BLOTTER (*VACHETTA*). WHAT IS UNDERSTOOD BY IT AND HOW ENTRIES SHOULD BE MADE IN IT AND BY WHOM.

The memorandum book, or, according to others, scrap book or blotter, is a book in which the merchant shall put down all his transactions, small or big, as they take place, day by day, hour by hour. In this book he will put down in detail everything that he sells or buys, and every other transaction without leaving out a jot; who, what, when, where, mentioning everything to make it fully as clear as I have already said in talking about the Inventory, so that there is no necessity of saying it over again in detail. Many are accustomed to enter their inventory in this book, but it is not wise to let people see and know what you possess. It is not wise to enter all your personal property and real property in this book. This book is kept on account of volume of business, and in it entries should be made in the absence of the owner by his servants, or his women if there are any, for a big merchant never keeps his assistants idle; they are now here, now there, and at times both he and they are out, some at the market place and some attending a fair, leaving perhaps at home only the servants or the women who, perhaps, can barely write. These latter, in order not to send customers away, must sell, collect or buy, according to the orders left by the boss or owner, and they, as well as they can, must enter every transaction in this memorandum book, naming simply the money and weights which they know; they should note the various kinds of money that they may collect or take in or that they may give in exchange. As far as this book is concerned, it is not as important to transfer to standards the various kinds of coin handled as it is with the journal and ledger, as we will see hereafter.

The bookkeeper will put everything in order before he transcribes a transaction in the journal. In this way, when the owner comes back he will see all the transactions, and he may put them in a better order if he thinks necessary. Therefore, this book is very necessary to those who have a big business. It would be too much trouble to put down in a beautiful and orderly way every transaction immediately after it take place, in books which are authentic and kept neat with care. You must make a mark on the cover of this book, as well as on all the others, so that you can distinguish them when, in the process of the business, the book is filled or has served for a certain period of time and you take another book. You must take another book when the first one has been used entirely, yet many are accustomed in different localities to balance annually these books although they are not full; and they do likewise with the other books not yet mentioned, as you will see hereafter.

On the second book you should put another mark different from the first, so that at any time you can trace your transaction easily. For this purpose we use the date. Among true Christians there is the good custom to mark their first books with that glorious sign from which every enemy of the spiritual flees and before which all the infernal spirits justly tremble—that is, the holy cross, by which in our tender years we begin to learn to read. The books that follow, you may mark in alphabetical order, calling A the second, and B the third, etc. So that we call the first books with the Cross, or Memorandum with Cross, and the second Memorandum A, Journal A, Ledger A. The pages of each of these books ought to be marked for several reasons known to the merchant, although many say that this is not necessary for the Journal and Memorandum books. The transactions are entered day by day, one under the other, in such way that it may be easy to trace them. This would be all right if all the transactions of one day would not take more than one page; but, as we have seen, for many of the bigger merchants, not one, but several pages have to be used in one day. If some one would wish to do something crooked, he could tear out one of the pages and this fraud could not be discovered, as far as the dates are concerned, for the days would

possano successiuamente sequire:non dimanco el mancamento.sira fatto.Si che per qsto
e altri asai respecti sempre e buono numerare e signare in tutti li libri mercanteschi.E di ca
sa e di botega tutte le carti 7c.   ca°.7

Del mo como i molti luoghi se babio aucteticare tutti li libri mercateschi e p che e dachi.

Questi tali libri conuegosi secondo l'usance bone de diuersi paesi:neli quali luo
ghi miso retrouato portarli: e apresentarli a certo officio de mercaranti como son
no consoli nela cita de perosa e a loro narrare como questi sono li toi libri i ligli
tu intendi scriuere o uero far scriuere de ma del tale.7c.ogni tua facenda ordina
tamete.E dire a che monete tu li uoli tenere:cioe a.§.de picioli:o uero a.§.de grossi:o uero
a duc.e.§.7c.O vero a fio.e.s.o vo a.g.tari grani.o.7c.Le ql cose sepre el real mercatate
nelpricipio dogni suo libro deue potere nella p° carta.E qdo mano se mutasse nella scriptu
ra daltri che nel pricipio se dicesse:conuense p uia del ditto officio chiarirlo.El scriua poi o
tutto cio fa metioe i registri de ditto officio como i tal di mi presentasti tali e tali libri segna
ti del tal segno 7c.E biamato lu cosi e laltro cosi 7c.Di qli el tale a tante carti el tale tate 7c.
li quali disse douere essere tenuti p ma sua o del tale 7c.Ma i vno (ditto memoriale.O vo
uachetta.o secondo alcuni ditto squartafacio).ciascuno di suoi familiari de casa a la gior
nata poteua scriuere per le ragioni sopra asegnate.E alora ditto scriua de sua propria mano
jn nome de lofficio scriuara el medesimo nella prima carta de li tuoi libri:e fara fede de tut
to 7c.E boleralli del segno del ditto officio i fede autentica per tutti li iudicii che acadesse p
durli.E questa tal usanca merita sumamete essere comedata 7c.E cosi li luoghi che la obser
uano.Pero che molti tegano li loro libri dopii.Uno ne mostrano al conpratore e laltro al
uenditore.e che pegio e secondo quello. giurano e spgiurano 7c.che malissio fano.E po p
tal uia dofficio degno andando:no possano cosi de facili dir buscie:ne fraudare el primo 7c.

Li quali poi con diligenca segnari e ordinatamente disposti tu teneuai co lo nome o dio
a casa agomecare a scriuere tue facede.E prima nel giornale ponere per ordine tutte le pate
de lo inuentario nel modo che sequente intenderai.Ma prima intendi come nel memoriale
se costuma dire 7c.

Como se debino dittare le partite i onto memoriale co crepli   ca°.8

Ja e ditto se bene ai amente como i ditto memoriale:o uero uachetta:o vero sqr
tafacio secondo altri che ogniuno di tuoi li po scriuere.E pero del dittare tal ptie
i esso no si po dare piena doctrina.Pero che chi intedera :e chi non di toi di ca
sa.Ma el comu costume e questo cioe.Metamo che tu habi coprato alquante
pecce de pano(vtpura.20.bianchi bresani)p duc.12.luna basta che semplicimete ponga la
prita cosi dicedo cioe.Jn questo di habiamo o uero io o coprato das felipo de rufoi dabres
sa pani n°.20.blachi bressai posti i su lauolta di 6 stesao raglia pietra 7c.Loga lua o le pecce
di coueto br.tati 7c.Per duc.tant luna 7c.segnare del tal n° 7c.nominado se sono atre lici
o uero a la piana bassi o alti fini o mecai bergamaschi o uigetini o verosi padoani fiorctini
o matoai 7c.E similiter nominar secifosse sensale e narrar sel mercato so a cotati tutto:o vo
parte cotati e pte termene:e dir quato tepo.O uero noiar se fosse pte o cotati e parte robbe
E specificare che robbe.o de numero peso e misura.E a che pregio el.Mo°.o etc°: o uero .§.
o uero a raso de conto 7c.O uero se fossero tutti a tepo e narrare che termie.O de galie o
barutto.o de galie de fiadra o de retorni de naui 7c.E specificare la muta de ditte galie.O
de naui 7c.o se fosse termine de fiere:o altre solenita: commo per lasensa proxima futura
7c.o uero p la pasqua denadal 7c.o uero de resureri.o uero carleuale 7c.Piu e maco scdo
che uoi cocludeste el mercato.E finaliter i ditto memoriale no si conuerria lassare poto alcu
no.E se possibile fosse dir quate parolle uesinterposero p che(como nelinuentario sopra so
detto)al mercante le chiarecce mai soro troppo 7c.

De li.9.modi p li quali comunamete si costuma fra li mercati coprare edelemercatie qua
li al piu o le uolte de necessita atempo si comprano.   ca°.9

Poi che al comprare siamo nota che quello che tu compri po acadere comuna
mente i.9.modi:cioe a denari.contanti.o uero a termine.o uero alincontro dar
robba.Qual ecto comunamente editto baratto.o uero a pte o.e parte termie.o
vero a parte comdti e parte robbe.ouero a pte robbe.e pte termine. o uero p ase
gnatione de ditta.o uero parte i ditta e pte termie a tc.o ueropte ditta e parte robba.Jn li
qli.9.modi el piu de lenolte se costuma comprare.E se per altro uerso facesse in uesita:i ql

40

follow properly one after the other, and yet the fraud may have been committed. Therefore, for this and other reasons, it is always good to number and mark each single page in all the books of the merchants; the books kept in the house or kept in the store.

CHAPTER 7.

OF THE MANNER IN WHICH IN MANY PLACES MERCANTILE BOOKS ARE AUTHENTICATED, WHY AND BY WHOM.

All these books, according to the good customs of several countries where I have been, should be taken and shown to a certain mercantile officer such as the Consuls in the City of Perosa employ, and to him you should state that those are the books in which you intend to write down, or somebody else write down for you, all your transactions in an orderly way; and also state in what kind of money the transactions therein should be entered—that is, whether in *lire di Picioli*, or in *lire di Grossi*, or in *ducats* and *lire*, etc., or in *florins* and *denari*, or in ounces, *tari*, *grani*, *denari*, etc. The good merchant should put down these things always on the first page of his book, and if afterwards the handwriting should be done by somebody else than the one stated at the beginning of the book, this should be recorded at the office of the said officer. The clerk should mention all this in the records of the said officer—that is, on such and such a day you presented such and such books, marked with such and such mark, which books are named, one so-and-so, the other so-and-so, etc.; of which books one has so many pages, another so many, etc., which books you said would be kept by you or by so-and-so; but that it may be that in said Memorandum Book or Scrap Book or Blotter, some person of your family might enter said transaction, as explained before. In this case, the said clerk shall write down on the first page of your books, in his own handwriting, the name of the said officer, and will attest to the truth of everything and shall attach the seal of that office to make the books authentic for any case in court when they might be produced.

This custom ought to be commended exceedingly; also the places where the custom is followed. Many keep their books in duplicate. They show one to the buyer and one to the seller, and this is very bad, because in this way they commit perjury. By presenting books to the said officer, one cannot easily lie or defraud. These books, after they have been carefully marked and authenticated, shall be kept in the name of God in your own place, and you are then ready to start your business. But first you shall enter in an orderly way in your Journal all the different items of the Inventory in the way that I will tell you later. But first you must understand how entries should be made in this Memorandum Book.

CHAPTER 8.

HOW ENTRIES SHOULD BE MADE IN THE SAID MEMORANDUM BOOK, AND EXAMPLES OF THE SAME.

We have said already, if you will remember, that any one in your family can make entries in the said Memorandum Book, or Scrap Book or Blotter. Therefore, it cannot be fully stated how the entries should be made, because some members of your family will understand and some will not. But the common custom is this: Let us say, for instance, that you bought several pieces of cloth—for instance, 20 white *bresciani*, at 12 ducats apiece. It will be enough simply to make the entry in this way: On this day we have or I have bought from Mr. Filippo d'Rufoni of Brescia, 20 pieces of white *bresciani*. These goods are at Mr. Stefano Tagliapietra's place; one piece is so long, according to the agreement, and paid for at so many ducats, etc., marked with such and such number, etc. You mention whether the cloth is *a trelici*, or *a la piana*, wide or narrow, fine or medium, whether the Bergamo kind, or Vincenza, or Verona, or Padua, or Florence, or Mantua. Also you have to state here whether the transaction was made through a broker and whether it was made in cash entirely or part only in cash and part on time, stating the time, or whether it was part in cash and part in trade. In this case you must specify the things that were given in exchange, number, weight, measurement, and the price of the bushel or of the piece, or of the pound, etc., or whether the transaction was all by payment on time, stating the time when the payment should be made, whether on *Galia de Barutto*, or on *Galia de Fiandra*, or on the return day of a ship, or on the date of some fair, or other festivity, as for instance, on the next harvest day or on next Easter, or on next Christmas, or on Resurrection day or Carnival day, etc., according to what was understood in the transaction. Finally, I must say that in this memorandum book nothing should be omitted. If it were possible, it should be noted what many others had said during the transaction because, as we have said about the Inventory, the merchant never can be too plain.

CHAPTER 9.

OF NINE WAYS IN WHICH THE MERCHANT USUALLY BUYS, AND THE GOODS WHICH IT IS MORE OR LESS NECESSARY TO BUY ON TIME.

Since we are talking about buying, you must know that usually you can make your purchase in nine ways—that is: either in cash or on time; or by exchanging something, which is usually called a trade; or partly in cash and partly on time; or partly in cash and partly by trading and partly on time; or by draft (*assegnatione de ditta*); or partly by draft and partly on time, or partly by draft and partly by trading. In these nine ways it is customary to make purchases. If you would make your purchases in some other way

modo propzio fa che tu e glialtri per te nel memoziale la narri aponto con uerita e farai be
ne zc. E cofi quando tu faceffe le tue compze a tempo. Como fe coftuma ale volte tarfi de
guati. O vero biade. vini. fali E curami dabecari. E fegli. che fi obliga eluenditoze. al cópza
tore. de dar tutto el guato che per quel tempo hara. E cofi el becaro te uende e promette tut
ti li cozi. pelle. fego. che per qllo anno in fua becarria. fara zc. La tal foza. per tanto la .5. zc.
E latale per tanto zc. E cofi de li feghi de manzo. caftroni zc. E le pelle motonine nere: p
tanto el c°. acóto. E tanto le montonine bianche zc. E cofi de liguati. O biade fpecificar tan
to el M°. E tanto lo ftaro. o el moggio. o la cozba. dele biade: cómo inful chiuli de perofcia
fi coftuma. E de guati. al Bozgo falepolcro noftro. Mercatello. Santagnlo. Cita o caftel
lo. Furli zc. Siche de ponto in ponto. far mentione di tutto a pieno in ditto memoziale. o
per te: o per altri che fi fcriua. E narra la cofa femplicimente. commo tenafcuta zc. E dipoi
el bon quadernieri. i capo de. 4. o. 5. o vero. 8. giozni. Piu e manco che fteffe del ditto meino
riale metarle in gioz. nale. a di per di tutte comme le fonno nafcute. Ma folo in quefto diffe
rente: che non bifogna che in ditto giozonale fe diftenda. con tante filaltocch de parolle. com
mo fe fatto in ditto memoziale. Pero che bafta alui vna uolta hauere lacofa ben dizefta in
ditto memoziale. Al qual poi el giozonale fempze fa a referire. Pero che quelli che coftuma
no tenere. 3. libri (a modo ditto) mai debano ponere cofa in giozonale. che pzima non lauino
in ditto memoziale zc. E quefto bafti quanto alozdine de ditto memoziale. O per te o p al
tri tofia tenuto zc.   E nota che per quanti modi tu da altri poi compzare. cofi tu per tan
ti poi vendere. E per confequente altri po comprare da te. Del qual vendere non mi ftedo
altra mente. Pero che tu per te habiando quefta foma de compazare. pozrai a fetarlo zc.

Del fo libzo principale mercantefco. ditto giozonale: quel chel fia: e comme fe debia difpo/
nere ozdinatamente.   Capitolo   10

EL fo libro ozdinario mercantefco. e ditto giozonale. Hel quale. (comme e ditto)
deue effere el medefimo fegno che in lomemoziale: E carti fegnate zc. Como
difopza del memorial e ditto. Per le ditte cagioni. E fempre nel pzincipio de ca
duna carta: fe deue mettere el Maldefimo. e di. E dipoi demano in mano ponere
pzima le partite tutte del tuo euentario. Del qual giozonale. (per effere tuo libro fecreto) poz
rai a pieno narrare e dire tutto quello che di mobile e ftabile te ritroui. Referendote fepre
al ditto foglio che per te. o per altri foffe fcritto. el quale in qlche caffa. o fcatola. o filza. o maz
zo. o tafca : che cofi fe ufa el feruarai. Commo te diro de le lettere. E fcripture menute. ma
le partite del ditto giozonale: fi conuengono fozmare e dittare per altro modo piu ligiadro:
non fuperfluo. ne anche tropo diminuto : commo qui feguente de alquante partite te daro
exemplo. Ma pzima e danotare el bifogno di doi termini. che in ditto giozonale fi coftuma
vfare. nela cita maxime excella de Uinegia. Di qualli immediate diremo.

De li. 2. termini nel ditto giozonale vfitati. maxie i Uenegia. Luno ditto. Per. e laltro dit
to. A. e quello che per lozo fe habia a denotare.   Capitolo. 11.

DI fonno (commo e ditto) li termini vfitati i ditto giornale. Luno e ditto. Per.
E laltro e ditto. A. Liqli hano loro fignificati. ciafcuno feparato. Per lo. Per.
fempre fe dinota el debitore. o vno o piu che fe fieno. E per lo. A. fe dinota lo
creditore. o vno o piu che fe fieno. E mai fi mette pzita ordinaria i giornale (che
al libro grade fabia apozre) che nó fe dinori p°. p liditti doi termini. Deli qli fepze nel pzin
cipio de ciafcuna pzita fi mette el. Per. Pero ch° p°. fi deue fpecificare eldebitoze. e di poi iine
diate elfuo creditoze. diuifo lu dalaltro p doi vgolette cofi. Il. Como nelo ex° difotto te fira
noto zc.   Del modo a fap ponere e dittare le pzite i lo giozonale del dare e de lauere có
molti exepli. E deli doi altri termini nel qderno vfitati luno detto Caffa. e laltro Cauedale
E quello che per effi fe habia intendere.   Capitolo. 12.

ADóca có lo nome de dio comézarai apócre nel tuo giozonale. La p°. pzita del tuo
iuetario. cioe la p°. deli d. cótari: che te ritroui. E p fape ponere ditto iuetario
allibro. e giornale. bifogna ch tu imagini doi altri termini. luno ditto. Caffa e lal
tro ditto Cauedale. Per la caffa. fintéde la tua p°. overo borfcia. Per locouedale. fe itéde tut
to el tuo móte e cozpo de faculta pñte. Elqle cauedale. i tutti lipzincipii de qderni: e giornali
mercatefchi: fepre deueffere pofto creditore. E la ditta caffa fepre deuefter pofta debitrici.
t'mai p nullo tpo nel manegio mercatefco. lacaffa po cére creditrici. ma folo debitrici overo
para. Pero ch° qñ nel bilacio del libro fi trouaffe creditrici denotarebe errore nel libr° cómo
difotto a fuo loco te daro fumaria recozdanza. Ora nel giozanale ditta pzita de contanti fi
deue mettere e dittare in quefto modo. v3.   Z

you must state in your memorandum book with precision the way that you have made the purchase, or have somebody else do it for you, and you will do well.

You buy on time usually when you buy *guati* or oats, wines, salt, remnants from a butcher shop, and fats. In these cases, the seller promises to the buyer to give all the *guati* that he will have in that season. The butcher will sell you and promises to give you all the hearts, skins, fat, etc., that he will have during that year. This kind for so much a pound, that kind for so much a pound, etc., and similarly for the fat of beef, of mutton, etc.; the black skins of mutton at so much apiece; and the white mutton skins, etc., and so with the oats, or *guati*; you must specify the price for each bushel or other measure and the kind of oats as is the custom at Chiusi de Perugia. In buying *guati* you must see whether they are of our city San Sepolcro, or Mercatello, or Sant' Angelo, or Citta de Costello, or Forli, etc.

In this memorandum book, whether kept by you or by others, you must mention every single point. You state the things in a simple way as they happened, and then the skillful bookkeeper, after four or five days, or eight days, may enter all these transactions from the said memorandum book into the Journal, day by day; with this difference, though, that it is not necessary for him to put down in the Journal all the long lines of words that were used in the memorandum book, because it is sufficient to put them down in an abridged way, and besides, references should always be made from one book to the other. Those that are used to keeping these three books in the way we have said never must enter one thing in Journal if they have not first entered it in the memorandum book. This will be enough as to the arrangement of the said memorandum book, whether it is kept by you or others. Remember that there are as many ways to buy as to sell; therefore, I need not explain the ways of selling, because you knowing of the ways of buying can understand the selling.

CHAPTER 10.

THE SECOND IMPORTANT MERCANTILE BOOK WHICH IS CALLED JOURNAL; WHAT IT IS, AND HOW IT SHOULD BE KEPT IN AN ORDERLY WAY.

The second common mercantile book is called the Journal (*Giornale*) which, as we have said, must have the same mark that is on the memorandum book and the pages marked as we have said in talking of the memorandum book.

Always at the beginning of each page you must put down the date, and then, one after another, enter all the different items of your inventory.

In this Journal, which is your private book, you may fully state all that you own in personal or real property, always making reference to the inventory papers which you or others may have written and which are kept in some box, or chest, or *filza*, or *mazzo*, or pouch, as is customary and as is usually done with letters and other instruments of writing.

The different items entered in the said Journal ought to be entered there in a neater and more systematic way, not too many or too few words, as I will show in the few following examples. But first of all you must know that there are two words or expressions (*termini*) necessary in the keeping of a Journal, used according to the custom of the great City of Venice, and of these I will now speak.

CHAPTER 11.

THE TWO EXPRESSIONS USED IN THE JOURNAL, ESPECIALLY IN VENICE, THE ONE CALLED "PER," AND THE OTHER "A," AND WHAT IS UNDERSTOOD BY THEM.

As we have said, there are two expressions (*termini*) used in the said Journal; the one is called "per," and the other is called "a," each of which has a meaning of its own. "Per" indicates the debtor (*debitore*) one or more as the case may be, and "a," creditor (*creditore*), one or more as the case may be. Never is any item entered in the Journal which also is to be entered in the Ledger, without preceding it by one of the two expressions. At the beginning of each entry, we always provide "per," because, first, the debtor must be given, and immediately after the creditor, the one separated from the other by two little slanting parallels (*virgolette*), thus, //, as the example below will show.

CHAPTER 12.

HOW THE ENTRY SHOULD BE MADE INTO THE JOURNAL BY MEANS OF THE DEBIT AND THE CREDIT, WITH MANY EXAMPLES. THE TWO OTHER EXPRESSIONS USED IN THE LEDGER, THE ONE CALLED "CASH," AND THE OTHER "CAPITAL," AND WHAT SHOULD BE UNDERSTOOD BY THEM.

With the name of God you shall begin to enter into your Journal the first item of your Inventory, that is, the quantity of cash that you possess, and in order to know how to enter this Inventory into the Ledger and Journal, you must make use of the two other expressions (*termini*); the one called "cash" (*cassa*) and the other "capital" (*cavedale*). By cash is understood your property or pocketbook (*borscia*: from *bursa*, or bag); by capital is understood the entire amount of what you now possess.

This capital must always be placed as creditor (*creditore*) in all the principal mercantile Ledgers and Journals and the cash always debtor. Never at any time in the management of your business may cash be creditor, but only debtor unless it balances. For if, in balancing your book, you find that cash is in the credit, it would denote a mistake in the book, as I will remind you hereafter at its proper place. Now this entry ought to be made in the Journal, and ought to be arranged in this way:

Debitore   1
Creditore   2

Poi pla 2ª ptite dirai cosi

Linea del dedare

Forma ō metter i giornale.   Mº.cccc°.Lxxxxiiii.a dì.8.nouēbre i venegia.   prī°

Per cassa de cōtanti. A cauedal de mi tale ᵹ.p cōtanti mi trouo i qlla al prūte.fra oro e mo
nete.arzēto e ramo ō diuersi cogni.cōe ape i lo foglio delo iuētario posto i cassa.ᵹ. i tutto
duc.tāri doro.E monete duc.tantival i tutto al modo nr̄o venitiano.a oro.cioe a grossi.24
per duc.e picioli.32.per grosso a 8.a oro.   2ª.   8   ᵹ   p

Per gioie ligate e disligate de piu sorti: A cauedal ditto. per balassi tanti. ligati ᵹ. pesano
ᵹ.E safili tanti ᵹ.e rubini e diamāti ᵹ.Cōe ape al sopraditto iuētario.Quali metto tu
lere a comū corso. libalassi tanto. ᵹ. E cosi dirai de ciascuna sorta.suo pgio cōuno. mon
tano in tutto ducati tanti ᵹ. vagliano.   8   ᵹ   p

E hauēdo tu nominato vnauolta el dì. E ancora el debitore.e ancora.el creditore.nō trame
çandose altra ptita poi dire. A dì ditto.Per ditto.E al ditto ᵹ.per piu breuita.   3ª.

Per argenti lauorati: Al ditto che sintēde pur el cauedal p piu sorte argēti cal prūte mi trouo
cioe Bacili tanti ᵹ.E rami tanti ᵹ.E taçe tante ᵹ.E piron tanti ᵹ.E cosilier tāte ᵹ.
pesano in tutto tanto ᵹ.val   8   ᵹ

Destinguēdo.bene di pōto p q̄ste prime ptite ogni cosa cōe festi in lo inuētario. Ponēdoli
tu p te vn comun pgio. E fallo grasso.piu presto che magro.cioe Se ti pare che vaglino.
20.e tu di.24.ᵹ.Acio che meglio te habia reuscire el guadagno.E cosi de mano in mano
porrai tutte laltre cose.con suoi pesi n°.e valute.ᵹ.   4ª.

Per panni de lana de dosso: Al ditto.p veste tante di tal colore ᵹ.E a tal foggia ᵹ. Fode
rate ᵹ.vsate o vero noue ᵹ.a mio dosso.o vero de la mia dona.o uero de figlioli ᵹ.Met
to valere a comune stima.luna p laltra.in tutto duc tanti ᵹ.E p mantelli tāti de tal colore
ᵹ.Cōe dicesti ᵹle veste e cosi dirai de tutti ditti pāni p tutto.   5ª.   8   ᵹ   p

Per pāni lini: Al ditto p lençoli tanti ᵹ. E tutto narra comme sta in lo inuentario, monta
no E vagliano.ᵹ.   6ª.   8   ᵹ   a

Per letti de piuma: Al ditto ᵹ.p piume tāte ᵹ.E qui narra commo sta in lo inuentario.
montano o vagliano.   7ª.   8   ᵹ   p

Per çençer mechini: Al ditto.p colli tanti ᵹ.narra cōmo i inuētario.si contene.montano e
vagliano a comune stima ᵹ.duc.tanti ᵹ.   8   ᵹ   p

E cosi poi tu p te stesso seqrai di porre tutte laltre ptite de q̄laltre robbe.deciascuna facie
do sua ptita.sepata.cōmo q̄ ō çeçer se ditto. Ponēdoli pgio de comū corso.commo disopra
e ditto.El or n° segnl.e pesi.commo de ponto stāno i ditto foglio diuētario.Chiamādo den
tro laptira.cō moneta cō tuvoli.E nel trar fora.conuē poi cō sieno a vna sorta.Perch non
staria bene.a cauar fora.a diuerse sorte ᵹ. E tutte ditte ptite ō giornale sererai a i ª.avna ti
rando la riga.de q̄to dura tua scriptura. narratiua. fin al termine che si tra fora. El mede
simo modo seruarai ale ptite del memoriale ᵹ.E so che tu del memoriale mettarai i giorna
le.cosi a vna a vna.andarai depēnando i lo memoriale.con vna sola.riga.a trauerso cosi /.
cō denotara qlla tale ptita.eēr posta i lo giornale ᵹ.E se tu non volessi trauersare la ptiª.cō
vna linea.e tu lāciarai la pª.lfa del prīcipio dela ptita.o uero lultia.commo al capo di q̄sta.E
fatto. O vero farate tu da te q̄lcō alt°.segno.tale cō tu itēda.p qllo ditta ptira eēr stata mes
sa iḡiornale ᵹ.E aūēga cō tu da te possi usare molti varii e diuersi termini e segni.nō dime
no te debi sēpre studiare de usare li comuni.che p li altri traficāti i tal paese si costuma di fa
re. Acio non para tu sia discrepante dalusitato modo mercātesco ᵹ.

Del 3°.euīn°.libr° prīcipale mercātesco.detto el q̄derno cōmo deba eēr fatto e d'l suo alfa
beto commo se debia ordinare. vgnolo e dopio.   Cap° 13.   E poste che tu ha
rai ordinataṁēte tutte le tuoi ptite al giornale.poi bisogna che di qllo.le caui. E poetle in lo
3°.libro ditto q̄derno grāde.El q̄l communamēte i costuma fare de doi tāte carti ch'l giorna
le.In sogle conuerra eēr vno Alfabeto.overo Reptorio o voi dir Trouarello ō alcuni. ala
fiorētina se dici lo stratto. Nel q̄l porrai tutti debitori.e creditori. Per le lre che comēçano
con lo n°.dele sue carti.cioe quelli che comēça p. a. i. a.ᵹc. E del dopio alfabeto.E q̄sto
similmēte commo sopra dicemo conuiē ch̄ sia segnato del medemo segno ch'l giornale e me
moriale.Postoui el n°.dele sue carti. E disopra i margine. da luna bāda e laltra. et milesimo
E in la prima. sua carta.dentro porrai debitrici la cassa.sicommo ella e la pª. nel giornale.
cosi deue eēre pª.nel q̄derno. E tutta qlla faciata.si costuma lasarla stare per ditta cassa. E in
dar ne i hauere non si pone altro.E q̄sto p che la cassa se manegia piu che ptita ch̄ sio.i ora
p ora.i metter e cauar dinari. E po lse lassa el cāpo largo. E q̄sto q̄derno cōuiē che sia riga
gato.de tāte righe.q̄te che sorte monete volitrar fore. Se trarai. 8 ᵹ ō p. Farai.4.righe.
e dināçe ale 8.farane vnaltra.p metarui el n°.dele carti de le ptite che isiemi de dare. E ha

FIRST. November 8, MCCCCLXXXXIII in Venice.

Debit 1.

Credit 2.

Line of the debit.

Per cash // A—Capital of myself so and so, etc. In cash I have at present, in gold and coin, silver and copper of different coinage as it appears in the first sheet of the Inventory in cash, etc., in total so many gold ducats and so many silver ducats. All this is our Venetian money; that is counting 24 *grossi* per ducat and 32 *picioli* per *grosso* in gold is worth: L............(*Lire*), S............ (*Soldi*), G............ (*Grossi*), P............ (*Picioli*).

For the second item you shall say this way:

SECOND. Per mounted and unmounted precious stones of several kinds //. A capital ditto for so many mounted *belassi*, etc., weighing, etc., and so many sapphires, etc., and rubies and diamonds, etc., as the said Inventory shows to which, according to current prices I give these values: *Belassi* worth, etc.; and so you shall state a price for each kind in total that are worth so many ducats. Their value is
L............, S............, G............, P............ .

After you have once named the day, the debtor and the creditor, you may say for brevity—if you don't make any other entry in between: On the day ditto, per ditto, // a ditto.

THIRD. Per silver //. A ditto—by which capital is understood—for several kinds of silver which at present I possess—that is, wash basins so many, so many coppers, so many cups, so many *pironi*, and so many *cosilier,* etc., weighing in total so much. Their value is: L............, S............, G............, P............ .

You shall give all the details in entering these items for everything as you have them in the Inventory, giving to each thing a customary price. Make the prices rather higher than lower; for instance, if it seems to you that they are worth 20, you put down 24, so that you can make a larger profit; and so you will enter everything, putting down for each thing its weight, number, value, etc.

FOURTH. Per woolen clothes //. A ditto, for so many clothes of such and such color, etc., of such and such style, etc., lined, etc., new or used, etc., for myself or for my wife or for my children, I give the total value, according to the current price, so many ducats. And for cloaks, so many of such and such color, etc., and so on, for all the other clothes: L............, S............, G............, P............ .

FIFTH. Per linen //. A ditto, for so many bed sheets, etc., and put down their number and value as the Inventory shows: L............, S............, G............, P............ .

SIXTH. Per feather beds //. A ditto, etc., for so many feathers—and here put down all that the Inventory shows, number and value: L............, S............, G............, P............ .

SEVENTH. Per ginger //. A ditto, for so many packages, etc., giving all the details that are contained in the Inventory, number, value, according to common prices, etc., so many ducats: L............, S............, G............, P............ .

In this way you can continue to enter all the other items, making a separate entry for each different lot, and as we have said before, giving the current prices, number, marks, weights, as the Inventory shows. Indicate only one kind of money, to which you reduce the estimated values. In the column for the amounts, only one kind of money should appear, as it would not be proper to have appear in this column different kinds of money.

You shall close each entry in the Journal by drawing a line from the end of the last word of your descriptive narrative (explanation) up to the column of the figures. You shall do the same in the memorandum book, and as you transfer an entry into the Journal from the memorandum book, you shall draw a single diagonal line (*una sola riga a traverso*) through it in this way /; this will show that this item has been entered (*posta*) in the Journal.

If you should not draw this line through the entry, you shall check off (*lanciarai*) the first letter of the beginning of the entry, or the last letter, as we have done at the beginning of this; or otherwise you shall use some other sign by which you will understand that the said item has been transferred into the Journal. Although you may use many various and divers expressions or marks, nevertheless you must try to use the common ones which are used by the other merchants, so that it will not look as if you would deviate from the usual mercantile custom.

CHAPTER 13.

THIRD AND LAST PRINCIPAL MERCANTILE BOOK CALLED THE LEDGER. HOW IT IS TO BE KEPT. ITS ALPHABET (INDEX), AND HOW THIS CAN BE KEPT SINGLE AND DOUBLE.

After you have made all your entries in the Journal in an orderly way, you must transfer them to the third book, called Ledger (*Quaderno Grande, i. e.,* big book). This Ledger contains usually twice as many pages as the Journal. In it there must be an alphabet or repertory or "*trovarello*" (finding key) according to some; the Florentines call it "*Stratto.*" In this index you shall write down all the debtors and creditors in the order of their initial letter, together with the number of their respective pages. You shall put the names that begin with A in the A page, etc.

This Ledger, as we have said before, must bear the same sign or mark that is on the Journal and memorandum book; its pages should be numbered; and at the top at the right margin as well as at the left margin, you shall put down the date. On the first page you shall enter cash as debtor. As in the Journal, so in the Ledger, cash should be entered on the first page. It is customary to reserve the whole of the first page to cash, and not to enter anything else either under the debit (*in dare*) or the credit (*in havere*). This because the cash entries are more numerous than all others on account of almost continuously paying out and receiving money; therefore, it needs much space. This Ledger must be ruled, and should have as many lines as there are kinds of money that you want to enter. If you enter *lire, soldi, denari* and *picioli,* you shall draw four lines, and in front of *lire* you shall draw another line in order to put in the number of the pages of the Ledger debit and credit entries.

ucre fe fcatenano.E dinãçe farai.2.righe.p potere metteze.li di õ mano i mano. commo ne
li altri q̃derni hai vifto che piu non miftédo i q̃fto 2c.p poter trouar p̃fto leprite 2c. E pur
fira fegnato croci commo li altri.

Del modo a poztar le ptite de gioznale in quaderno.e pche de una in gioznale fene facia
doi in quaderno:e del modo a depennare le ptite in gioznale e de li doi numeri dele carti
del quaderno che in le fue margine fi pone e pche.   Cap° 14.

Er laqual cofa.fappi che di tutte le ptite che tu harai pofte in logioznale.al qua
derno grãde.te ne cóuẽ fẽpze fare doi.cioe vna in dare e laltra in hauere pche lifi
chiama debitoze p lo. Per. E lo creditoze p lo. A. cómo difopza dicémo chõ
luno e de laltro.fi deue da pfe fare 1ª.ptita:q̃lla del debitoze. ponere ala man fini
ftra. E q̃lla del creditoze.ala man dextra.E in q̃lla del debitoze.chiamare lacarta. doue fia
q̃lla del fuo'creditoze. E cofi'in q̃lla del creditoze.chiamare la carta di q̃lla doue fia. El fuo
debitoze.E in q̃fto modo fẽpze uẽgano incattenate tutte le ptite del ditto q̃derno grãde. nel
q̃l mai fi deue metteze cofa in dare che q̃lla ancoza non fi ponga in haueze.E cofi'mai fi de
ue mettere cofa in hauete che ancoza.q̃lla medefima có fuo amõtare nõ fi metta in dare. E
di qua nafci'poi.albilancio che del lib°.fi fa.nel fuo faldo tãto cóuiẽ che fia el dare.q̃to laue
re.Cioe fũmate tutte le ptite che firãno pofte in dare fe foffero bene. 10000. da pte in fu vn
foglio. E di poi fũmate fimilmẽte tntte q̃lle che in hauere fi trouano. tanto debbe fare luna
fumma q̃to laltra.altramẽte demoftrarebbe eẽre erroze nel ditto q̃derno.cõe nel modo del
far fuobilancio fe dira apieno 2c.E cofi cóe dvna de giornale ne fai.2.al q̃derno.cofi a q̃lla
ptita che del gioznale leui farai doi righe a trauerfo fo cõ'vai leuando.cioe fe p³.tu la metti i
dare. Pzia farai 1ª.riga atrauerfo.verfo al prin°.dela ptita.che dinota eẽr pofta in dare al q̃
derno. E fe la metti in hauere.o pzima.o poi cõe acade ale uolte fare al q̃dernieri q̃'do li aca
de fcriuere i luogo.ch l'in q̃lla carta li nandera.2.o.3. p nõ ui'hauere a toznare.fene fpaça di
metterle li aloza.E po fo che mette cofi deue depennare p hauerla meffa in hauere.farai lal
tra depẽnatura.verfo man dextra.dal canto doue finefci la ptita che õnotara eẽr meffa i ha
uere.leq̃l linee ftaranno cõe difopza in q̃fto uedi figurato a laptita.p³.dela caffa. luno ditta
linea.de dare.e lalt³.de hauere. E cofi dalato i margine dinãçe alpzincipio bifogna che pó
ghi.2.nu'.luno fotto laltro.q̃l di fopza che denoti la ptita.del debitoze.a q̃te carti che la fia
pofta in lo q̃derno E q̃llo de fotto che denoti le carti de ditto q̃derno.'doue fia pofto el cre
ditoz.cõe vedi li ala ptita dela caffa difopza i q̃fto.che fta cofi.¦. feça tramẽço. E ancoza al
cuni coftumano cofi có tramẽço.¦. a guifa de rotti.che nõ fa cafo.Ma e piu bello feça tra
meçço. Acio achi vede nõ pareffero fpeççati.O vero rotti 2c.E vol dire q̃llo.1°.di fopza che
la caffa. E nella p³.carta del q̃derno.El cauedale. E nella fa carta de ditto q̃derno.i hauere.
e q̃lla in dare 2c.E nota che fẽpze q̃to piu p̃fto tu pozrai mettere elcreditoze al fuo debitoze.
fera piu liçadro.auẽga che pofto doue fiuoglia tanto mõti.Ma p rifpetto del milefimo.che
ale uolte fe iterpõe fra 1ª.ptï³.e lalt³ refpõde male.E có fatiga.nõ poca.fe ritrouano loz tpi
cõe fa chi .pua ch' ogni cofa cofi apieno nõ fi po dire.Ma bũo³.ch ãcoza tu alq̃to có tuo na
turale ingegno ta iuti.E po fẽpze ftudia dafettar ditto creditore immediate a p̃fto el fuo de
bitoze in la medema faciata.o vero ila imediate feq̃nte.nõ interponẽdoui fra luno e laltro.al
tra ptita. Peroche nel .ppzio giozno che nafci eldebitoze in q̃llo medemo nafci el creditoze
E p q̃fto rifpetto fẽpze fe deue acoftar luno a lalt° 2c.

Del modo a fape dittare'le ptite de lacaffa e cauedale nel quaderno in dare e hauere:e õl
milefimo che difopza nel pzincipio dela carta a lanti co fi mette in effo:e dela fua mutatione
e'del cõptir lifpacij dele carti fo le ptite piccole e grãdi fo elbifogno dele facéde.   Cap°. 15.

Oz q̃fte cofe difcozfe.a tuo amaeftramẽto.ozmai ditamo la p³.ptira de la coffa i
dare e poi q̃lla del cauedal in hauere in lo libzo grãde.Ma cõc e ditto p³. defo
pza nel quaderno pozrai el milefimo alabacco antico. cioe per alfabeto cofi.

M cccc.Lxxxiiii.2c.El di nõ fe coftuma mettarlo difopra in loquaderno cõe in
lo gioznale.pche 1ª.ptita in quaderno.hara diuerfi di.E po nõ fi pozra feruar ozdine deli
di.difopra cõe apieno nel feq̃nt cap°.fe dira.Ma dẽtro dela ptita cõe intẽderai la p³.uolta
E poicofi dalato in lo fpacio che difopra dicémo dinance ala ptita.q̃'do tal partita nafceffe
daltro milefimo che difopra nel principio dela carta foffe fcritto che fole auenire achi de an
no in anno nõ ripozta e falda fuoi'libri ficbe tal milefimo fi pozra difuora.nndo in margine
ripetto a põto a q̃lla ptita li nata cõc uedi pofto qui difotto.q̃fto folo auene in lib° grande
che in li altri nõ po auenire.Dõca ciaai cofi.tzaẽdola fore pure alabacco ãtico p piu belleça

P ii

Before these lines you shall draw two more lines wherein to mark the dates as you go on, as you have seen in the other books, so that you may find each item quickly. This book shall also bear the sign of the cross as the others.

CHAPTER 14.

HOW THE ENTRIES SHOULD BE TRANSFERRED FROM THE JOURNAL INTO THE LEDGER AND WHY, FOR EACH ENTRY OF THE JOURNAL, YOU HAVE TO MAKE TWO IN THE LEDGER; HOW ENTRIES IN THE JOURNAL SHOULD BE CANCELLED. THE TWO NUMBERS OF THE PAGES OF THE LEDGER WHICH ARE PLACED IN THE MARGIN OF EACH ENTRY AND WHY.

For each one of all the entries that you have made in the Journal you will have to make two in the Ledger. That is, one in the debit (*in dare*) and one in the credit (*in havere*). In the Journal the debtor is indicated by per, the creditor by a, as we have said. In the Ledger you must have an entry for each of them. The debitor entry must be at the left, the creditor one at the right; and in the debitor entry you must indicate the number of the page of the respective creditor. In this way all the entries of the Ledger are chained together and you must never make a credit entry without making the same entry with its respective amount in the debit. Upon this depends the obtaining of a trial balance (*bilancio*) of the Ledger.

There can not be a closing (*saldo*) because there must be as much in credit as there is in debit. In other words, you shall add together all the debit entries, even if there are ten thousand, on a separate sheet, and then add together in the same way all the credit entries; the totals of the one should be the same as the totals of the other; otherwise it would show that some mistake has been made in the Ledger. We will speak at length about this when we talk about the way of making the trial balance (*bilancio*). And since for one entry of the Journal you make two in the Ledger, you shall draw two diagonal lines as you make the transfer—that is, if you first transfer the debit entry, you shall first draw a diagonal line (*riga a traverso*) at the beginning of the entry in the Journal which shows that the entry has been posted (*posta*) to the debit into the Ledger. If you transfer the credit entry, either at this time or later, as it often happens that the bookkeeper can make two or three entries on the same page in order to prevent his coming back to write on that same page—in which case he should draw a line at the right side where the entry terminates. This will show that the entry has been transferred to the credit of the Ledger. These two lines, you may see in the preceding diagram, drawn in the margin by the first cash entry; the one is called debit line, and the other credit line. At the side, in the marginal part, you shall write down two numbers before the beginning of the entry, the one under the other. The upper indicates at what page of the Ledger the debit entry is, and the lower indicates the page of the Ledger where the credit is, as you will see at the cash entry in the above example, like this $\frac{1}{2}$, without a line between them. Some are accustomed to draw a line in between, like this, $\frac{1}{2}$. This does not matter, but it looks nicer without the line between, so that the figures will not appear to the reader as if they were fractions. The upper figure, 1, means cash was entered in the first page of the Ledger, and capital was entered in the second page of the said Ledger; the cash on the debit, and the capital on the credit side. You should know that the closer to the debtor you can place the creditor, the nicer it will look. It is just the same, however, no matter where it is; but it may look bad on account of the date which at times must be put between entries, and it makes it difficult then to find the dates. We can not tell you everything fully, but you with your natural ingenuity must guide yourself. Therefore you always try to put the said creditor immediately after its debtor on the same line or on the line immediately following without entering anything else in between, for whenever there is a debit item there must exist at the same time a credit item. For this reason, get the one as near as possible to the other.

CHAPTER 15.

THE WAY IN WHICH THE CASH AND CAPITAL ENTRIES SHOULD BE POSTED IN THE LEDGER IN THE DEBIT AND THE CREDIT. THE DATE WHICH AT THE TOP OF THE PAGE IS WRITTEN DOWN ACCORDING TO THE ANCIENT USE. CHANGING OF THE SAME. HOW TO DIVIDE THE SPACE ON THE PAGES FOR SMALL AND LARGE ACCOUNTS AS THE BUSINESS REQUIRES.

After having told you these things for your instruction, we write now the first entry of the cash in the debit column, and then the first entry of the capital in the credit column, in the Ledger. But, as we have said, you shall write down in the Ledger the year in the old way by using the alphabet, thus: MCCCCLXXXXIII, etc. It is not customary to put the day at the top in the Ledger as in the Journal, because one account in the Ledger may have several dates, and therefore you can not keep the dates in order by putting them at the top; but you shall put the days in the body of the entry, as you will understand hereafter.

We put the day to one side, in the space of which I have spoken, just before the entry. If an item refers to a transaction which happened in a different year than that written at the top of the page, which happens when one does not balance and transfer his books at the end of each year, then this year shall be put on the side, in the margin near the entry of the item to which it refers. This only happens in the Ledger, and can not happen in the other books. In making this entry for the year, use the antique letters, which are neater,

non dimeno aqual che tu te caui non fa caſo τc. Donca dirai coſi.

yhs.   M.cccc Lxxxiiij.

Caſſa de cõtanti die dare a di.8.nouẽbre.per cauedal per contanti de piu ſorte fra oro e mo
nete me trouo hauere in quella in queſto preſente di in tutto ca.2.   8. x^m. ſ   g   p̄

E qui nõ biſogna che troppo te ſtẽda.p hauer bẽ gia ſteſo in giornale. Ma ſempre ſtudia
dir breue. La prima nel comẽçare ſe dici alquanto:ale ſequẽti in la medema ſol ſe dici.e a
di ditto τc.per lo tale. car.   8   ſ   g   p̄

L aqual coſi poſta che lharai.depẽnarai in giornale in dare comme ſopra te diſſi. E poi i ha
uer per lo cauedal dirai coſi.vʒ.

yhs   M.cccc°.Lxxxiiij.

Cauedal de mi tale τc. die hauere a di.8.nouembre.per caſſa.per contanti me trouo in quel
la fin al di preſente in ori e monete de piu ſorte in tutto. car.1.   8. x^m.ſ o g o p̄ o

E coſi ancora.i qſta baſta ſucciniamẽte dire per lacagion ſopra ditta.:altre poi che q ſotto
ala medema prita.ſe haueranno aporre fin che la ſia piena baſtara adire. E a di tanti τc.per
latal coſa τc. Cõe uedi acẽnato qui da canto. e anco in fin di qſto barat exemplo. coſi ſequi
rai con breuita in tutte.maxime in quelle partite che a te ſolo aſpettano.cioe che non hai a
rendere conto adal cuno. Ma in qlle che tu hauerai a rendere cõto adaltri.alqto piu ti cõ
uerra dire.auenga che ſempre ſe recorre.per le chiareçe al giornale τc. E poi darai laltra de
pẽnatura.a qlla del giornale in hauere.cõe ſopra ti diſſi in.12°.cap° E in lamargine dauan
ti.ala prita.porrai li doi numeri cõe diſſi pur in ditto loco dele carti doue ſono. El debitore
el creditore.cioe qllo del debitore deſopra.E qllo del creditore de ſotto cõe facemo diſopra.
ala prita de lacaſſa. E poi ſubito porrai in lo tuo alfabeto.cioe reprtorio. qſto debitore e credi
tore.ognuno ala ſua lra cõe ſai che diſopra diſſi.Cioe la caſſa.al la lra.C. dicẽdo dẽtro in q
ſto modo.cioe.Caſſa de cõtanti.   k. 1.   E ancora el cauedal porrai al. E dicendo. Ca
uedal de mi pprio.   k. 2.   E coſi p tuo ingegno adarai aſcuando. tutte le prite. e li nõl
de li debitori perſõe e robbe τc. E coſi de creditori.porrai nel ditto repertorio. a leſue lettere
acio poi con facilita poſſi ſubito retrouarli in ditto quaderno grande τ cetera.

E nota che hauendo tu pduto el tuo qderno p alcun caſo ocrobaria.o incẽdio di foco.o
naufragii τc. E hauẽdo tu luno de li altri doi libri.Cioe memoriale.o vero giornale. cõ eſſo
porrai ſempre refare vnaltro qderno.cõ le medeſime prite a di p di. E ponerle al numero de
le medeſime che i ql pſo ſi retrouauano.Maxime hauẽdo tu el giornale.doue qdo ne leua
ſti le prite. E põeſti al lib°.tu imargie põeſti li doi nui.Oli debitori e creditori.ſuo ſoura lal
tro che chiamauano le carti. del qderno doperano ſituati.e di põto atante carti li porrai fa
re ritornar cõ tuo ingegno τc. E qſto baſti qto a vna prita poſta τc.   Poi la ſa prita ch
fo dele çoie al qderno ponẽdola a ſuo cõdecẽte luogo dittarai coſi. E pri°. ſempre ſença piu
te replichi .porrai diſopra nel principio dela carta.el mileſimo ſe nõ vi foſſe poſto p altra pti
ta. p°. poche ale uolte in vna medema facia el quaderniex aſettara.2.o.3.ptite ſo che cogno
ſcera lo ſpatio eẽr baſtãte al manegio di qlla. pche forſe uedara qlla tale prita hauerſi chia
re fiade adoperar. E p qſto li dara vn luoco piu anguſto. che a quelle che ſpeſſo li acade. a
dopare:ala giornata cõe di ſopra.al cap° 13°. de la caſſa e cauedal ſo detto ql ſi coſtumaua
laſarli tutta lafaciara del lib°. pche ſpeſſiſſime fiade.p eẽre grãdi le facẽde ſi conuẽgano ma
negiare. E qſto ſol ſi fa p nõ hauer tãto ſpeſſo afar reporo inãçe τc.ora al ppoſito trouato
li el loco cõe ſe dici.dirai coſi in dare.cioe verſo man ſiniſtra.coſi ſempre ſa aporre el debito.
Dioe de piu ſorte. dienno dare a di.8.nouẽbre.p cauedale. p pecci n° tanti τc.peſano tanto
τc.dequali tanti ſonno balaſſi legati τc. E tanti ſafili τc. E tãti rubini coculegni τc. E tanti
diamanti creçi τc. lequali in tutto.o vero a ſorta per ſorta metto valere a comun pgio.de cõ
tanti duc.tant τc.val car. 2   8 40.ſ o.g o.p̄ o.

E coſi depennerai.la prita in giornale.nel dare tirando la linea comme de ſopra al.12° cap°
te diſſi. E poi andarai al cauedal. E porrai qſta medema con mãco parolle per leragion gia
diſopra adutte in queſto capitolo e porrala in hauere ſotto quella p°.ch gia li hai poſto dela
caſſa. E dirai coſi.vʒ.

a di o   detto.per çoie de piu ſorte commo li apare τc. car.3.   8.40.ſ o.g o.p̄ o.

E coſi poſta farai laltra depẽnatura.al giornale i hauer.cõe te mõſtrai diſopra al.12°.ca°.
E porrai i margine li numeri dle carti. doue tal prite al quaderno poneſti cõmo dicemmo
vno ſopra laltro.comme qui denançe apare che metto habi poſta la prita in dar a carti.3.E
qlla del cauedal ſta pure alogo ſuo a carti.2.pfin tanto chella non e piena.che dipoi innãçe

although it does not matter very much.

Thus, you shall put it this way:

JESUS .... MCCCCLXXXXIII.

Cash is debtor (*dee dare*—shall give) on November 8, "per" capital. On this day I have in moneys of different kinds, gold and other coins; page 2: L.X^m, S.................., G.................., P.................. .

Here you do not need to be very lengthy if you have already given the description in the Journal. Try to be very brief.

At the beginning of the page we say more, but in the entries following it is enough to say: on ditto, "per" such and such; page, etc., L.................., S.................., G.................., P.................. .

After you have made the entry in this way, you shall cancel in the Journal as I have explained to you. Then in the credit side you shall write down this way:

JESUS .... MCCCCLXXXXIII.

Capital of myself, so and so, is creditor (*dee havere*—shall have) on November 8, "per" cash. On this day I have in cash, in gold and other kinds of money; page 1:

This entry is also sufficient; express yourself briefly for the reason above said. If there are other items to be entered in the same account, it will be enough to say, on ditto, "per" such and such, etc., as has just been shown. At the end of this treatise, I will give you an example, and thus you will go on expressing yourself briefly especially in those things which are private—that is, of which you do not have to give an account to any one. But as to other things for which you have to give an account to other people, it will be better for you to be more explicit, although for explanations we always rely on the Journal. Then you will cancel, by drawing a line, the credit entry in the Journal as I have said above in Chapter 12. In the margin, just opposite the entry, you shall write down the two numbers of the pages where the debit and credit entries are. That is, you should put the number of the debit page above, and the number of the credit page below, as we have done above in the cash entry. Then you shall at once enter in the alphabet or repertory (index) this debtor and this creditor, each one under its own letter as I have told you before. That is, cash at the letter C, by saying in this way: Cash, page 1. And capital also at the letter C, saying: Capital belonging to me, page 2. And so on, you shall enter (in this repertory) all the creditors under their respective letters, so that you may find them easily in the Ledger mentioned.

Take notice, that if by any chance you should lose this Ledger through robbery, or fire, or shipwreck, etc., if you have either of the other two books, that is, the memorandum book or Journal, you can, by means of this book always make up another Ledger with the same entries, day by day, and enter them on the same pages on which they were in the last book; especially so, if you have the Journal in which, when you transferred the different entries into the Ledger, you wrote down at the margin the two numbers of the debit entry page, and the credit entry page, the one above the other, which two numbers indicated the pages of the ledger where the two entries had been entered. In this way you can duplicate your Ledger. This is enough said for the posting of one entry.

For the second entries, which pertains to precious stones, you shall enter in the Ledger as follows:

FIRST, without my telling it to you over again, you shall write down at the top of the page the date, if there has been no date written before because of another account, for at times on the same page two or three accounts are made. Sometimes you won't give much space to one special account because you know that you will not have to use that account over again. Therefore you will give to this account a smaller space than the space you give to other accounts which you had to use more, as we have said above in Chapter 13, when talking about cash and capital, to which we give the whole page, as we have to use these two accounts very often because of the many transactions. This is done in order to lessen transfers.

Now then, after you have found the proper place (in the ledger), you shall write down on the left— because the debtor must always be at the left: Precious stones of many kinds debit (*dienno dare*—shall give), on November 8, per capital, for so many pieces, etc., weighing so much, so many are counted *balassi*, etc., and so many sapphires, etc., and so many rubies, etc., and so many unpolished diamonds in bulk (or divide the different kinds), for a value of so many ducats; page 2: L40; S0; G0; P0.

You shall cancel this item in the Journal on the debit side by drawing a line as I have told you in Chapter 12. And then you will go to capital, and you shall enter this entry with fewer words, for the reasons above expressed in this chapter, writing it down on the credit side under the first entry that you have already made, and you shall express yourself this way:

On the day, or ditto, for precious stones of several kinds, as it appears at page 3: L40; S0; G0; P0.

After which you shall draw another line on the credit side of the Journal, as I have shown in Chapter 12; you shall put down in the margin the two numbers of the pages of the Ledger in which you have made these entries, one above the other, as I have told you. We shall say, for instance, that you have entered the debit entry at page 3; the capital entry will still appear at page 2, as long as that page is not filled.

a tutte laltr̄ le poztarai.cóme diſotto ne repozti intēderai apieno.E q̄ſto p q̄ſta.e a ſue ſim̄
lie ua baſtāte z̄c.E poſta che larai al ditto q̄derno. E aſettata in gioznale.e tu ſubito lapor
rai al reptorio o vero alfabeto.cóe diſopza i q̄ſto cap° fo detto. Cioe ala ſua lr̄a. S. o vero.
3. fo.pchē lr̄a la .pferirai.cóe idiuerſi paeſi acade.che qui i uinegia molto ſi coſtuma pone
re el. 3. doue noi in toſcana ponemo el ḡ.ſiche acozdarala tu a tuo Judicio z̄c.

Cōe ſe debino dittare ſeptite delemercantie che per inuentario o altro modo lhomo ſe ri
trona:nel quaderno'in dare e in hauere. Cap° 16°.

E altre. 4.ptite poi ſu ſequēti del tuo mobile.cioe argēti.pāni.lini.letti de piuma
E veſte de doſſo z̄c.Poi p te ſteſſo facilmēte mettarai del iuētario in gioznale de
póto cóe li le poneſti.denotate.pche cóe dicēmo diſopza cap°.6° q̄ſto tal inuenta
rio nõ ſi caua del memoziale.p la ragiõe li aſegnata.E po ſuo dittare in gioznale
E ancoza nel grã lib° i dare e hauere. e di pozre alalfabeto.laſciaro oz mai ſeq̄re al tuo pegri
no ingegno del q̄l moltome'cõfido E ſolo la.7ª.ptita de cēcer mechini che ti troui aſettare
mo igioznale.E ancoza al q̄derno laq̄l te fia baſtāte e ſufficiēte amaeſtramēto a tutte le altre
che dimercātia alcun̄ ſe ritronaſte.hauēdo ſēpze tu ua te inãe glioclhi loz n°.peſi.e miſure e
valute i tutti li modi che tal mercātie ſe coſtumaſſe vēdere.e cõpzare fra mercāti i rialto o fo
ra.fo li'paeſi.dele q̄li coſe q̄ apieno nõ e poſſibile ponere erēpli.ma cõ facilita. da q̄ſti pochi
q̄ cõpēdioſamēte poſti pozrai di q̄lūcaltri iprēdere a tua ſufficiēca.po che ſe noi volēmo dar
te erēplo del modo verſo e via.di mercare atrani.lecia.bari.E berõta.cioe aloz nomi ōpeſi lo
ro.E miſure loro z̄c.E coſi dela marca.E anche dela nr̄a toſcana.troppo ſerebbe grāde el
volume.che cõ bzeuita' itendo concludere E p q̄lla. 7°.de cēcer nel gioznale. dirē coſi. v̄z.
Per cēceri mechini i mõte a refuſo.o i colli dirai cóe a te pare z̄c. Al ditto che ſintēde caue
dal.pche li diſopza imediate larai p.ozdiñe de ditto iuētario.cóe dicēmo diſopza cap°. 12°.
in la ptita ſa de le coie.p colli tanti peſano. z̄c. E p.8.tante q̄do foſſero arefuſſo i mõte z̄c.
q̄li me retrouo hauere in lemani al dl pñte metto di comū corſo valere el c°.o vero la 8.z̄c.
duc̄.tanti z̄c.mõtano in tutto netti duc̄.tanti z̄c.val   8   ß   ḡ   p̄

E coſi poſta cb larai nel gioznale.E tu al memoziale.o vero inuētario.la dipēna.e lãca.al
modo ditto ſopª.al.12°.cap° z̄c.E coſi obfuarai p tutte lalt̄ z̄c.Di q̄ſta cóe ſo detto e de q̄lū
che altra che i gioznale ſi metta.ſēpre al gran ltb°.ſi fanno doppie.cioe 1ª.i dare e laltra i ha
nere cóe diſopza dicēmo cap.14°.La qual poi nel quaderno in dare.ponendola dittarala i
q̄ſto modo.Poſto pª.ſēpre el mileſimo ſe nõ ui foſſe in capo de la carta.ſēca mettarui el gioz
no diſopza po che cóe dicēmo diſopza cap.15° El di nõ ſi coſtuma pozre ſopza nel pzin° de
lacarta del quaderno p riſpetto che in q̄lla medeſima facia potrebono eere piu ptite õ diuer
ſi debitozi e creditozi.lequali bēche lenaſchino ſotto vn mileſimo.Ma ſiranno in diuerſi me
ſi e corni.cóe diſcozrēdo p tutto poi aprendere.E q̄do bene ancoza in ditta facia del libzo
grande nõ vi foſſe altro che 1ª.ſola ptita di caſſa.o daltro ancoza el cozno poſto diſopza nel
quaderno.nõ ſipotrebbe ſeruare.pche in ditta ptita.ocozira di mettere caſi ocoſi in diuerſi
meſi.E di e p q̄ſto e che li antichi diſopza nel quaderno nõ hano i libri mercāteſchi vſitato
mettere el giozno.pche non hano ueduto verſo ne via ne modo che con uerita ſi poſſa aſet
tarcilo z̄c.Laqual partita in dare coſi pozrai dicēdo z̄c.

Cēceri me chini.in monte.o uero colli z̄c.dien dare a di.8.nonembze per cauedal.per colli
tanti z̄c.peſano. 8.tante z̄c.quali mi trouo hauere in caſa. o ucro magacen al pzeſente qual
de comun corſo ſtimo valere el cento z̄c.duc̄.tanti z̄c.E per tutti monta duc̄. ḡ. p̄.z̄c.val
carti. 2.   8   ß   ḡ°   p̄

E coſi depennarai la partita del coz11ale in dare.cioe a man ſeneſtra cóme piu uolte to dit
to E poi in hauere aſettarala in q̄ſto modo al cauedal comme te moñſtrai ponere quella
dele coie ſopza a cap°.15° coſi v̄z.

a di o detto.per cēceri mechini in monte o vero colli z̄c.car. 3.   8   ß   ḡ°   p̄.

E coſi poſta che lharai depennarai la partita del gioznale in hauere. cioe verſo mande
ſtra.cóe dinãce vedi fatto.E poni li numeri dele carti dinãce alei in margine vno ſopza lal
tro.Cioe el.3.diſopza el.2.diſotto pche tu hai meſſo el debitoze a carti.3.nel quaderno. el cre
ditoze e a.2.Cioe el capital.e ſubito poi la metti in alfabeto.o vero reptorio ala ſua lr̄a. Cioe
al.3.ſe p.3.la cõpiti.o vero al.S.p la raſõ ditta in lo pcedēte ca°.a q̄lla ptita ſa dele coie z̄c.

Del modo a tenere conto con li officii publici:e perche:e de lacamera delimpzeſti in ve /
netia che ſe gouerna per via de ſeſtieri. Cap° 17°.

                                   p iii

This example will guide you in other cases.

After you have made the entries in the Ledger and marked it in the Journal, you shall put it at once in the index as I have told you above in this chapter—that is, under the letter G or Z, according as to how *Gioie* (stone) is pronounced. In Venice the custom is to pronounce it with Z; in Tuscany, with G. Guide yourself according to your own understanding.

CHAPTER 16.

HOW THE ENTRIES RELATIVE TO THE MERCHANDISE OF WHICH ONE IS POSSESSED ACCORDING TO HIS INVENTORY, OR OTHERWISE, SHOULD BE MADE IN THE LEDGER BOTH IN THE DEBIT AND THE CREDIT.

You will be able to transfer easily by yourself from the Inventory to the Journal the four items of your personal goods—that is, silver, linen, feather beds, clothes, etc., exactly as you write them in the Inventory, as we explained in Chapter 6. This Inventory was not contained in the memorandum book, for the reasons therein expressed.

And as to how to make these entries in the Journal and the Ledger, and as to how to record them in the Index, I will leave to your ability, on which I count very much.

We shall proceed to enter in the Journal, as well as in the Ledger, the seventh item (of the Inventory), which pertains to Ginger. This must be a sufficient instruction for you by which to make any other entry relative to your merchandise. You should always have in mind their number, weights, measurements and values according to the different ways in which it is customary to make purchases or sales among merchants in the Rialto, or elsewhere. It is not possible to give here full examples for all these operations, but from those few that we give here you will be able to understand how to go ahead in any other case. For if we wanted to give you an example of all the ways in which merchants do business in Trani, Lecce, Bari and Bitonto—that is, to give you the names of their weights, measurements, etc., and also to tell you about the ways that they use them in Marca and in our Tuscany, this would make our treatise very long, which, on the contrary, I intend to make short.

As to this seventh item to be entered in the Journal, we shall proceed thus: Per Ginger in bulk or package—you shall express yourself as you like— // a ditto—by which capital is understood, because you have already mentioned it in the entry immediately preceding, when you entered your second item from the inventory, that is, precious stones—as we said in Chapter 12—I possess on this day so many packages weighing so much, or I possess so many pounds, if in bulk, according to the current prices, of a value by the hundred or by the pound, of so many ducats; in total I give them the value of so many ducats.

L⸺, S⸺, G⸺, P⸺.

After you have entered it in the Journal in this way, you shall cancel it in the memorandum book or inventory, as we have said in Chapter 12, and you shall do the same for the other items. Of this entry, as we have said, as well as of any entry made in the Journal, you shall make two different entries in the Ledger; that is, one in the debit and the other in the credit.—See Chapter 14. In making the entry in the Ledger in the debit, you shall proceed in this way: First you shall put the year, in case there is none, at the top of the page, without there putting down the day, for, as we have said in Chapter 15, it is not customary to put down the day at the beginning of the page of the Ledger because on that same page several entries may be made under the debit and credit which, while belonging to the same year, refer to transactions made in different months and days. Even if on that page of the Ledger there was only one cash entry or other entry, the day put at the top of the page could not be very well kept because, under the said entry, it would be necessary to write down transactions which happened in different months and days. For this reason the ancient people never put the day at the top of the pages in mercantile ledgers, as they saw that there was no justification for it, etc.

You shall make this entry in the debit (in the Ledger) in the following manner: Ginger in bulk, or so many packages, debit (*dee dare*—shall give) on November 8 per capital, for so many pieces, weighing so many pounds, which I on this day have in my store, or at home in my house, and which according to current prices are worth so many ducats and in total so many *ducats, grossi, picioli*, etc.; Page 2:

L⸺, S⸺, G⸺, P⸺.

Then you shall cancel this entry on the debit side of the Journal—that is, at the left, as I have told you often, and then you shall enter it on the credit side under Capital, as I have shown you in entering the precious stones item in Chapter 15, that is:

On ditto per Ginger in bulk or packages, etc.; Page 3: L⸺, S⸺, G⸺, P⸺.

After you have entered it in this way, you shall cancel the entry on the credit side of the Journal— that is, at the right—as I have shown you before, and you shall also write down at the margin the numbers of the respective pages of the Ledger one above the other—that is, three above and two below, as you have made the debit entry at Page 3 and the credit entry at Page 2, and you shall thereafter enter it in the alphabet or repertory under its respective letter, which may be Z or G, for the reasons given in the preceding chapter.

CHAPTER 17.

HOW TO KEEP ACCOUNTS WITH PUBLIC OFFICES, AND WHY. THE CAMERA DE L'IMPRESTI (MUNICIPAL LOAN BANK) IN VENICE, WHICH IS MANAGED BY *SESTIERI* (DISTRICTS).

Ora de laltre nõ te ne do.altra norma.cioe di q̃lla de pellami.da fodre cõçe e cru
de.e fine 7c.dele quali a 1ª.p 1ª.formarai la ptita in giornale e quaderno p ordie
depẽnando.e ſegnando in tutti li lochi che non teſcordi perche al mercante biſogna altro ceruello.che de beccaria 7c.   Quella dela camera dipreſti o daltro mõte cõe in firença.elmõte dele dote i genoa li lochi o uero altri officii che ſi foſſero cõ
liquali tu haueſſe a fare.per alcuna cagione fa che ſempre con loro tu habia buono ſcõtro.
de dare e de hauere in tutti li modi con qualche chiarecça ſe poſſibile e de man deli ſcriuani
di q̃lli luochi q̃l tiẽ ſotto bona cuſtodia al modo che dele ſcritture e lettere te diro.pche a q̃
ſti tali officii ſpeſſo ſe ſogliano mutare ſcriuant.liqli ognuno a ſua fantaſia uole guidare libi
bri delo officio.biaſimãdo ſempre li ſcriuan paſſati.che non tenuan bon ordine 7c. E ſempre ognuno pſuade elſuo ordine migliore deli altri.imodo che ale volte incrociano le ptite.
de tali officii.che non ſene tien 1ª.cõ laltra.Eguai chi cõtali a afare.E po fa che ſia a caſa.E
col capo abotega.cõ q̃ſti tali.E certamẽte forſi el fãno a bon fine nõ dimeno moſtrão igno
rãça. E coſi tirrai cõto.cõ li gabellari.e datiari de robbe che tu uẽdi e cõpri.caui e metti nele
terre 7c.Cõe ſi coſtuma fare in vinegia.che ſi tiene p li piu dela terra.cõto lõgo cõ lo officio
dela meſſetaria.chi a.2.p.c° E chi a 1ª.p c°. E chi a.4.p c°.7c.Chiamando el libro. del ſen-
ſaro.che viſinterpone. e notare al tuo libro.E anche la mare.in ſu cõ fa. cioe el lib° doue va
in nota li mercati al ditto officio che coſi lo chiamano in venetia po che ciaſcuno ſenſaro a
vno libro.o uero luogo in qualche libro al ditto officio doue lui va a dare in nota li mercati
che fa.ſi cõterrieri.cõe foreſtieri altramẽte caçano in pena.ſaltramẽte faceſſaro. E ſonno pri
uati.E bene q̃lla ercelſa.S.licaſtiga e loro.e ſcriuani cõ mal ſi portaſſero cõe de molti me ri
cordo.gia neli tp̃i paſſati eẽre puniti ſtraniamẽte.E po ſantamente fanno a conſtituire vno
elq̃le a ſolo q̃ſta cura.in renedere tutti lioofficii.cioe ſe liloro libi ſono bñ.o⨍o male tenuti 7c.

Comme ſe debia tener conto con lo officio dela meſſetaria in venetia e del dittare le ſue
partite in memoriale.çornale.e quaderno.e ancora deli impreſti.   Cap°.   18.

Ji che q̃do vorai cõ tali offitii tener conto.la camera deimpreſtiti.farai debitrici
de tutta laſorte de cauedali a tanto el c°.7c. Noiando li ſeſtieri doue ſon poſti.E
ſimilmente ſe piu aſa giornata.necõpraſſe che molti ſe ne vendano p te o p altri
cõe ſa chi realto vſa. Nota bñ inchi ſõno ſcritti e luoghi.7c. E coſi nel ſcotere li
loro .p.ſẽpre farala creditrici.a di p di.E ſeſtier p ſeſtieri 7c. E coſi cõloffitio dela meſſetaria
El cõto tirrai i q̃ſto modo.cioe q̃do tu comprarai alcuna mercantia p meçço õ ſeſari.alora
de tutto lo amõtare.a raſone de.2.o de.3.o de.4.7c.p c°.farane creditore eloitto officio dela
meſſetaria.E debitrici q̃lla tale mercantia.plaq̃l cagione tu paghi 7c.E po conuene chel cõ
pratore ſempre ritẽga al uẽditore nel pagamẽto.de contanti.o vero p altro modo che labia
aſatiſſare non fa caſo.pchel ditto officio.non vol andar cercando altro ſenon larata che li
aſpetta.auenga che liſenſari reportino el mercato in nota.cõmo.e cõ.e cho.leſtato fatto. per
chiarecçe euidẽte de contraẽti q̃do fra loro.naſceſſe differença alcuna cõe acade. El comun
puerbio dici.chi non fa non falla.e chi non falla non impara 7c.deleq̃li dfe volendoſe le pti
chiarire hano regreſſo almercato notato.plo ſenſaro.al quale fo li decreti publici li ſi pſta
fede cõe a publico inſtrumento denotaro.E fo la forma di q̃llo . elpiu dele volte. El degno
offitio deconſoli demercanti.formano le loro iuridiche ſentençe 7c. Dico adonca compran-
do tu alcuna robba.tu dic ſape.q̃llo che la paga de m̃.E p lamita retieni.al uenditore. Cioe
ſe la robba paga.4.p c°.a q̃llo officio p õcreto.publico del dominio.E tu alui retieni.2. p c°
E tanto manco liconta.E hara el ſuo douere.E tu poi del tutto reſti obligato al ditto offi-
tio.E del tutto larai afar creditore al tuo libro contado cõlui.E q̃lla tal mercantia farai õbi
trici.cõe dicẽmo 7c.pche el ditto offitio non vol cercare.chi vende.ma chi compra.E po poi
a tal cõpratori li e conceſſo.di cauare tanto di q̃lla mercantia.p q̃to a pagato la m̃.fora õ
la terra.in loro bolette.ala tauola.de luſcita.o per mare o p terra che la uogliono cauare ala
giornata.E po conuẽgano li mercanti tenere beu conto con lo ditto officio.acio ſempre ſa
pino q̃to poſſino cauare.pche non ſi laſſano cauar.per piu che ſi comprino ſe di nouo non
paghinõ la m̃.de contanu 7c.delequali compre q̃ ſequente ti pongo erẽplo.e coſi.del ditto
officio.comme ſe habino a dittare in giornale. E anche in libro grande. E diro coſi.   pri
ma.in memoriale.ſemplicimente. Jo o vero noi in queſto di poſto diſopra o comprato da ß
Guan antonio da meſina.çucari palermini caſſi n°.tante.pani n°.tanti.peſanõ in tutto. netti.
de panelle.caſſi.corde.e paglie. § tante per duc. tãti. el c°.montano duc.tãti 7c.abatto per la
ſua parte dela m̃.a ragion de tanto per c°.duc.g.p̃.tanti 7c.lenſaro ß quan de gagliardi.vale
netti ducati.g.p̃.tanti 7c.pagammo contanti.

I shall not give you any more rules for the other items—that is, leather goods for coverings, tanned or raw, etc., for each of which you shall make entries in the Journal and Ledger, carefully writing down everything and checking off, etc., without forgetting anything, because the merchant must have a much better understanding of things than a butcher.

If you have accounts with the Camera de L'Impresti, or with other banks, as in Florence, or with the Monte de La Dote, in Genoa, as well as similar offices or bureaux with which you have business, see that you keep these accounts very clearly and obtain good written evidence as to debits and credits in the handwriting of the clerks in those institutions. This advice you will carefully follow, for reasons to be explained in chapter on documents and letters. Because in these offices they often change their clerks, and as each one of these clerks likes to keep the books in his own way, he is always blaming the previous clerks, saying that they did not keep the books in good order, and they are always trying to make you believe that their way is better than all the others, so that at times they mix up the accounts in the books of these offices in such way that they do not correspond with anything. Woe to you if you have anything to do with these people. Therefore, be very careful when dealing with them, and be observant at home and keep your head in the store. Maybe they mean well, nevertheless they may show ignorance. In this way you shall keep accounts with the *Gabellari* and *Datiarii* (revenue officers) as to the things that you might sell or buy, things that you grow, things that you plant, etc., as it is the custom in Venice where people are used to keeping an account through the office of the *Messetaria* (market master or exchange), some at 2%, some at 1%, some at 4%. You should mention the book of the broker through whom the transaction was made, and also mention the special mark that the broker has in this book—that is, the book in which he makes a record of the market transaction at said office which they call *"Chiamans"* in Venice. For each broker has a book in the said office, or a place in some book in the said office, in which he has to make a record of all the transactions which he has with the citizens of the town or with outsiders. If the broker should not do that he would be fined and dismissed.

And justly the glorious republic of Venice punishes them and their clerks who should misbehave. I know of many who in the past years have been heavily punished, and right they are in having one officer whose only duty is to oversee all these officers and their books whether they are well kept or not, etc.

CHAPTER 18.

HOW YOU SHOULD KEEP YOUR ACCOUNTS WITH THE OFFICE OF THE *MESSETARIA* IN VENICE. HOW TO MAKE ENTRIES PERTAINING THERETO IN THE MEMORANDUM BOOK, JOURNAL AND LEDGER, AND ABOUT LOANS.

When you want to do business with the said offices, you shall always charge to the Camera de L'Impresti (municipal loan bank) so many per cent. on all your funds or capital, naming the district where one resides. Likewise, for the amount of the daily sales for many are the sales made for you or for others, as those people know who are familiar with the Rialto. Be careful to put down the name of the party that buys and his place of business, etc. When you withdraw said funds, you shall always credit the said bank, day by day and district by district.

In doing business with the office of the *Messetaria* (exchange), you shall keep the account in this way: When you buy any merchandise through brokers, you shall credit the said office of the *Messetari* with the 2% or 3% or 4% of the whole amount, and shall charge it to that specific merchandise, for you are thus paying for it, etc. Therefore the buyer, when he makes his payments to the seller, should always retain that percentage, no matter whether the payments are made in cash or otherwise, as the said office does not concern itself about anything except the rate (%) to which it is entitled. The brokers make a report of the transaction, how and what for and with whom made, in order to have things clear in case any question should arise, which may happen.

A common proverb says: Who does nothing, makes no mistakes; who makes no mistakes learns nothing, etc.

If any question should arise and the parties wish to settle it, they would go and examine the records of the transaction made by the broker, to which records, according to the public decrees, as full faith is given as to a public notarial document, and according to these records very often the office of the Consuls of the merchants issues its judgment.

I say, then, when you buy anything, you must always know what is due to the *Messetaria*, and you withhold half of this from what you pay to the seller; that is, if the particular thing that you buy is subject to a 4% payment to that office, as per public decrees of the Republic, you withhold 2% of what you give to the seller. You give him that much less in order that he receives what is due him. You then will become a debtor for the whole amount which is due the said office, and you shall credit the said office with it in your Ledger when you keep an account with that office and charge it to the goods that you have bought, as we have said, because that office does not interest itself in the party who sells out, but in the party who buys. In accordance with this, the buyer will be allowed to take out of the official warehouses merchandise in proportion to the brokerage paid and according to their books kept at the shipping counter, whether it came by land or sea. Therefore, the merchants should keep a careful account with the said office so that they know how much merchandise they can take out. They are not allowed to take out more than they have bought unless they have paid the extra brokerage.

Of these purchases, I will give you here an example and how the transaction with the said office must be recorded in the Journal and in the Ledger. First, you shall express yourself in the memorandum book in the following manner:

I (or we), on this day above mentioned, have bought of Mr. Zuan Antonio, of Messina, so many boxes of Palermo sugar and so many loaves of the net weight—that is, without the boxes, wrappers, ropes and straw—so many pounds at so many ducats per hundred; I deduct for what is due to the *Messetaria* at the rate of so much per cent., so many *ducats, grossi, picioli*, etc. The broker was Mr. Zuan de Gaiardi; net value, so many *ducats, grossi, picioli*, paid in cash.

La medeſima in giornale dira coſi   acontanti.

Per çucari depalermo. A caſſa contati a ſ cuan de antonio damefina.per caſſi n°.tante pani n°.tanti. peſano nettti.de caſſi.panelle. corde.e paglie. §.tante.a duc.ranti el c° motano duc. tanti ꝛc.abatto.p la ſua parte dela m̄.a raſon de tanti per c°. ꝛc. duc.tanti ꝛc. reſtanonetti. duc.tanti ꝛc. ſenſar ſ.cuan de gaiardi.   §   ſ   ꝗ   p̄

La medeſima in quaderno dira coſi.

Zucari de palermo.die dare.adi tale.p caſſa contati a ſ cuan dantonio de meſina. per panni numero tanti peſano netti.§.tante per duc.ranti el cento.montano netti in tutto a carti 1ª.

E farai creditrici la caſſa di quel tanto ꝛc.   §   ſ   ꝗ   p̄

E ſempre farai loffitio dela m̄.creditore del doppio che tu retenefti alu編ditore. cioe p la ſua e p̄latua pte. ꝛc.E ſempe ſubito notato la robba imediate i vnalt°.ptita ſotto farai credi tore ditto officio per ditto çucaro cōe harai diſotto.E dibitrici ditta robba. Per exemplo du na pagata a contanti.Or prendine vna pte a cōtanti e parte. a tpo p̄ª.imemoriale coſi dirai.

A contanti e tempo.a di tanti ꝛc.

Jo o comprato a di detto.Da ſ cuan dantonio.damefina. cucari de palermo pani n°.tanti. peſano netti. §.tante.per duc.tanti el c°.montano duc.ranti.abatto per ſua parte de m̄.a raſo de tanti per c°.duc.tanti ꝛc.de quali al preſente.li no contati duc. tati p parte e del reſto mi fa tpo ſin tutto agoſto .pri°.che vien ꝛc.ſenſar ſ cuan de gaiardi v.l.   duc.   ꝗ   p̄

E ſappi che de qlle coſe che ſe ſcriue mercato per loſenſaro.a loffitio non biſogna far ſcrit to de man .perche el mercato baſta.ma pure a cautela ale uolte ſi fa ꝛc.

In giornale la medema dira coſi.prima quel tal de tutto creditore.E poi debitore de ql la parte de d̄. che lui haue.

yꝰ.   1493.a di tanti del tal meſe ꝛc.

Per çucari palermini: A ſ cuan dantonio de meſina per pani numero tanti peſano netti in tutto §.tante.a duc.tanti el c° montano duc.tanti ꝛc.abatto per la ſua pte de meſſetaria a ra ſon de tanti per c°.duc.tanti ꝛc.reſta netto duc.tanti ꝛc.de quali alpreſente li nedebo contar tanti ꝛc. E del reſto. mi fa termine fin tutto agoſto proximo che vien. ſenſaro ſer cuan de gaiardi.val.   §   ſ   ꝗ   p̄

Fanne creditore ſubito lofficio dela m̄.dela ſua rata.

Per li ditti:a lofficio dela m̄.per lamontar ſoura ditto.cioe de duc.tati ꝛc a raſo de tati p c°. p lamia parte e qlla del debitore i tutto monta duc.ꝗ.p̄.ranti val.   §   ſ   ꝗ   p̄

La parte de contanti. debitor luſ.E creditore la caſſa. coſi.

Per ſ cuan dátonio.de miſina: A caſſa cōtati alui p pte peli ſoura ditti çucari ſo la forma d̄l mercato.duc.tati ꝛc.ape del receuere ſcritto de ſua mano val. '   §   ſ   ꝗ   p̄

La medema in quaderno dira coſi.

Zucari de palermo.dien dare a di tal dinouembre . per ſ cuan dantonio damefina. per pani n°.tati peſano netti § tante ꝛc.p duc.tanti el c°.mōtano netti de m̄.K.4. §   ſ   ꝗ   p̄

Quando uoleſſe farne partita nuoua.Ma uolendo ſequitare la prepoſta baſtaua dire a di. tanti ꝛc.per ſ cuan dant° damefina p pani n° tati peſano §.tate ꝛc.mota.K.4.§   ſ   ꝗ   p̄

La medema in hauere dira coſi.

Ser cuan dátonio demefina.die hauere a di tanti de nouembre.per cucari de palermo. pa ni n°.tanti peſan netti §.tante per duc.tanti el c°.montano.netti de m̄.duc.tanti.de quali al preſente li ne debio dar contanti duc.tanti ꝛc.delauanço.mi fa tpo per tutto agoſto .prio ſu turo.ſenſar ſ cuan de gagliardi.val   K.4.   §   ſ   ꝗ   p̄

In dare lamedema. Per la parte deli contanti.dira coſi.

Ser cuan alincontro.die dare a di tale ꝛc.p caſſa . cōtati alui p pte de çucari.hebi dalui ſo nri patti duc.tanti ꝛc.ape p ſuo ſcritto de man in libreto.val.   K.1ª. §   ſ   ꝗ   p̄

La medema.ala m̄.e anche per la precedente i quaderno coſi.

Offo.dela m̄.die hauer.a di tal p çucari de palermo cōprai da ſ cuan danto° de meſina p la montare de duc.tati.a tati p c°.ſenſar ſ cuan de gaiardi monta. K.ꝛc §   ſ   ꝗ   p̄

Commo ſe debia ordinare el pagamento che haueſſe a fare per ditta e banco d̄ ſcrita ne li tuoi libri principali: Cap° 19.

Coſi p tal copre.qſta ti baſta a guidarte.o ſia a tutti cōtanti.o a pte cōtanti.E p re tpo. o cōtati e ditta o tutti in banco.o cōtanti e banco.o cōtati.E robbe.o rob ba.e ditta.o tutta ditta o robbe.e tpo.o robba e banco.o baſico e tpo.o baco e dit ta.o banco.cōtanti. ditta.e robbe. ꝛc.poche i tutti qſti modi ſe coſtuma coprare. le qli tu per te.al ſeſo dela precedéte metterale imemoriale.e dricarale i giornale.equaderno.

                    ꝗ iiij

The same should be entered in the Journal in the following manner:

Per Palermo sugar // A cash. Cash paid to Mr. Zuan Antonio of Messina for so many boxes and so many loaves, of the net weight—that is, without the boxes, wrappers, ropes and straw—so many pounds; at so many ducats per hundred, it amounts to so many ducats; I deduct what is due to the *Messetaria* at so much per cent., so many ducats, etc.; net residue, so many ducats, etc. The broker was Mr. Zuan de Gaiardi. L............, S............, G............, P.............

In the Ledger you shall make the entries as follows:

Palermo sugar debit (*dee dare* or shall give) cash. Cash paid to Mr. Zuan Antonio of Messina for so many boxes and so many loaves, weighing, net, so many pounds, at so many ducats per hundred, which amounts to—Page 1: L............, S............, G............, P.............

And you shall credit cash with the same amount, and shall always credit the *Messetaria* with twice the amount which you withhold from the price paid to the seller—that is, for the commission due by the seller and by you.

Immediately after, you shall make another entry crediting the said office with the said sugar and charging the said merchandise. This will do for a purchase by cash. Now we shall consider one made partly in cash and partly on time.

First, in the memorandum book you shall say as follows: By cash and on time on such and such day, I have bought on the said date of Mr. Zuan Antonio of Messina so many loaves of Palermo sugar, weighing net so many pounds, at so many ducats per hundred, making a total of so many ducats. This is in part payment; for the rest I shall have time to pay until the whole month of August next, etc. The broker was Mr. Zuan Gaiardi. D............, G............, P.............

You must understand that you do not need to have a written paper containing the terms of the transaction, for the broker shall record that in the said Office. This record is enough for you, but as a precaution, sometimes people require a contract.

You will make the entry in the Journal as follows: First you shall credit Mr. So-and-So for the total amount, and then charge him for the money that he has received.

JESUS 1493

On such and such a day of such and such month, etc., per Palermo sugar // A Mr. Zuan Antonio, of Messina, for so many loaves, weighing net so many pounds at so many ducats per hundred, making a total of so many ducats; deducting for his share of the brokerage at so much per cent., so many ducats, leaving a net balance of so many ducats, of which now I have to pay so many, and as to the rest I have time until the end of next August. The broker was Mr. Zuan de Gaiardi; value L............, S............, G............, P.............

Immediately after, credit the office of the *Messetaria* with the commission due to it: Per ditto // A Office of the *Messetaria*. For the amount above mentioned—that is, so many ducats at the rate of so much per cent. for my share and for the share of the debtor (seller), in all amounting to so many *ducats, grossi, picioli*: value: L............, S............, G............, P.............

For the cash payment, you shall charge him and credit cash in the following manner:

Per Mr. Zuan Antonio of Messina // A cash. By cash paid him for part payment of said sugar according to the terms of the transaction, so many ducats, as it appears from his receipt written in his own handwriting. Value: L............, S............, G............, P.............

In the Ledger you shall write down as follows:

Palermo sugar debit (*dee dare*—shall give) on such and such a day of November, per Zuan Antonio of Messina, for so many loaves, weighing net so many pounds, etc., at so many ducats per hundred, making a total, net of the brokerage; Page 4: L............, S............, G............, P.............

These items shall be entered in the credit column as follows:

Mr. Zuan Antonio of Messina, credit (*dee havere*—shall have), per Palermo sugar so many loaves, weighing net so many pounds, at so many ducats per hundred, amounting, net of the brokerage, so many ducats, of which I must now pay so many ducats, and for the rest I have time until the end of next August. Broker, Mr. Zuan de Gaiardi; Page 4; value: L............, S............, G............, P.............

For the cash payment you shall put in the debit column:

Mr. Zuan, debit (*dee dare*—shall give), on such and such a day, etc., per cash to him paid for part payment on sugar—I received from him according to our agreement—so many ducats, as it is shown by his own handwriting in his book; page 1: L............, S............, G............, P.............

The account of the *Messetaria* in the Ledger shall be as follows:

Office of the *Messetaria*, credit (*dee havere*—shall have), on such and such day, per Palermo sugar bought from Mr. Zuan Antonio, of Messina, for the amount of so many ducats, at so many ducats per hundred. Broker, Mr. Zuan de Gaiardi; Page, etc.: L............, S............, G............, P.............

CHAPTER 19.

HOW WE SHOULD MAKE THE ENTRIES IN OUR PRINCIPAL BOOKS OF THE PAYMENTS THAT WE HAVE TO MAKE EITHER BY DRAFT OR THROUGH THE BANK.

And as to the purchases, this should be sufficient to guide you, whether the payment of the purchase should be made all in cash or part in cash and part on time; or part in cash or part by bill of exchange or draft (*ditta*); or all through the bank; or part in cash and part through the bank; or part through the bank and part on time; or part through the bank and part by bill of exchange; or part through the bank, part in cash, part by bill of exchange and part by merchandise, etc.

For in all these ways it is customary to make purchases, and in each case you shall make entries, first in the Day Book, then in the Journal, then in the Ledger, taking as a guide the foregoing example.

Mà q̃do haì à far pagamẽto a pte bãco e ditta. Fa cõ pª. cõſegni la ditta. e poi p re°. ſcriuì l
banco. p piu figurta. vnde ancora q̃ſta cautella ſuſa p molti e bene. q̃do ben pagaſſero á con
tantu. de far per reſto in bancho. E p cõpito pagamẽto ꝝc̃. E pagandolo pte. banco pte. rob
ba. parte ditta. e parte cõtanti. de tutte q̃ſte faralo debitore. E q̃lle tal coſe farale creditrici
ognuna al ſuo luogo ꝝc̃. E ſe per altri modi te acadeſſe cõprare. per ſimili te gouerna. ꝝc̃

E hauẽdo inteſo eluerſo ðl cõprare p.tanti uerſi prẽderai el vẽdere tuo ad altri. facẽdoſi
debitori. e creditrici le tue robbe. E debitrici la caſſa. ſe ti da contanti. e ðbitrici le ditte. ſe te le
cõſegna in pagamẽto. E creditore. el banco. ſe tel da. E coſi di tutto p ordine cõe diſopra e
ditto ðl cõprare. E lui de tutto q̃llo ti da. in pagamẽto faralo creditore ꝝc̃. e q̃ſto ti baſti e q̃
ſta materia a tua inſtructiõe ꝝc̃.   Dele ptite famoſe e pticulari nel maneggio traficãte cõe
ſono baratti cõpagnie ꝝc̃. cõe le ſe habbino a ſettare e ordinare neli libri mercãteſchi. e pª. ð
li baratti ſẽplici cõpoſti e coltpo cõ aptí e rẽpli ð tutti i memoriale.çornale e q̃der°. Ca.20.

E q̃ta. douer dar modo. cõe ſe habino aſettar alcũe ptite famoſe pticulari. cõ ne
li maneggij traficãti ſi ſogliano el piu dele volte. ſolẽiçare. E metterle dapſe. acio
di q̃lle diſtintte dalaltre. ſene poſſa cognoſcere. el p dãno che di q̃lle ſeq̃ſſe. cõe
ſono li baratti. e le cõpagᶜ. viaggi recomãdati. viaggi i ſua mano. cõmiſſiõe haui
te p altri. banchi de ſcritta. o vero ditta. Cabi reali. ð un cõto de botega ꝝc̃. delcq̃li q̃ ſeq̃te
ſuccitamẽte a tua baſtança. te daro notitia. cõe le debi guidare. e reggere nell tuoi libri ordi
natamẽte. acio nõ te abagli in tue facẽde. E pª. moſtraremo cõe ſe debia aſettare i°. baratto.
Sõno li baratti cõmunamẽte de.3. ſorte cõe diſopra in leraciõ ſo detto. Diſtictio.9ª. Ꙇ. 3°.
carti.161.fin in.167. a pieno ſich̃ li recorri a itenderli.   Dico adõca che in tutti i uerſi che te
acadeſſe ſcriuere i lib° el baratto. ſẽpre puramẽte. pª. in lo memoriale debi narrarlo ad lͬfam.
dẽt°. dela ptita cõ tutti ſuo modi e conditiõi ch̃el ſira ſtato fatto. e cõcluſo. o comẽcani. o fra
voi ſoli. E q̃do l'arai coſi narrato. E tu poi alafine riduralo i ſu li cõtanti. E ſo che q̃lle tal
robbe ueder a i ualere. a cõtanti p tãto tirarai fora la priª. a che moneta ſi voglia i memoriale.
che non fa caſo. poiche poi el q̃dernieri la redura tutta a 1ª. ſorta al autẽtico. cioe q̃do la met
tara al giornale. E al q̃derno grãde ꝝc̃. E q̃ſto ſi fa pche cauãdo tu fori le valure dele robbe
a q̃l che ti ſtanno abaratto. nõ potreſti neli tuoi cõti. e ſcripture. cognoſcere ſeça grãdiſſima
difficulta. tuo vtile. o vero p ditta ſequita. Leq̃li ſẽpre cõuiẽſi redure a cõtanti. p volerle ben
cognoſcere. ꝝc̃.   E ſe di tali mercãtie hauute p baratti: voleſſi da pte pticularmẽte tenerne
cõto. p poder veder il ſuo retratto. ſeparatamẽte da laltͬe. robbe che dital ſorta haueſſe. pª. in ca
ſa. o che da poi cõpraſſe. p cognoſcere qual ſia ſtata megliore icepta. lo poi fare. E ãcora acu
mulare tutte mercãtie inſieme. cõe ſe haueſſe. pª. çençeri da te. E hora q̃ſti receueſſi del barat
to li quali voler metter con li altri. nel çornal dirai coſſ. cioe.

Per çençeri bellidi i mõte. o vero in colli: A çucari de la tal ſorta ꝝc̃. p colli tanti. peſano. § tã
te haui dal tal abaratto de çucari fatto i q̃ſta forma. cioe che mi li miſi el c°. de çucari ouc̃.
24. ꝝc̃. cõ q̃ſto che mi deſſe el c° de contanti ꝝc̃. E metteſe el c° di çẽçerí ouc̃. tanti. p liquali
çençeri. li cõti çucari. pani. n° tanti. peſan § tante che a contanti el c° val ouc̃.20. E p li ditti
çençari nebbe § tante ꝝc̃. pani n°. tanti ꝝc̃. vagliano ciaſcuno.   §   ᶠ   ᵖ

E pche ale volte nõ ſapraì. a põto lo n°. deli pani. che p ditti çençeri intraſſe nõ fa caſo. po cõ
poi nela ptita ſeq̃nte. ſi ſupleſci q̃l che li mancaſſe. e q̃l che li foſſe piu i q̃lla dela caſſa. mãca
ra nõ dimeno. alincõtro de çucari ſẽpre. harai el douere aponto. pche tutte dua. vãno a çu
cari i modo che laptita de çucari non pde el n° de pani. ne dil peſo. pche nõ e ſẽpre poſſibi
le d'ogni fraſchetta. da pſe tener cõto. ꝝc̃. Ora di q̃lla pte de cõtanti che vi ſono corſi. fara
ne debitrici la caſſa. E pure el ſimile. creditori ditti çucari. dicendo coſi. cioe.

Per caſſa: A li ditti ꝝc̃. Per contanti hebine l ditto baratto. dal ditto ꝝc̃. per pani n°. tan
ti ꝝc̃. peſano § tante val.   §   ᶠ   ᵖ

E ſimili ptite ſubito q̃lli mettano i mediate nel giornale a p̃ſſo q̃lla del baratto. nel q̃l hauẽ
ſti li conti ꝝc̃. ſi che a q̃ſto modo ditta reſti. non volendone tener ſeparato conto. Ma ſe ſe
parato l'ouoi tener nel giornale dirai coſi. cioe.

Per çençeri bellidi. per conto di baratto ſebbero dal tale ꝝc̃: A çucari ꝝc̃. narrando tutto.
poi a ponto commo diſopra. E in lo quaderno. poi harano loro partita. diſtincta ꝝc̃. E
queſto uo glio che ti baſti. per tutti li altri baratti che ſo per te ſença piu mi ſtenda. ti ſapa
rai guidare ꝝc̃.

De laltra partita famoſa ditta Compagnie: comme ſe debino ordinare. e dittare in tutti
li modi occurenti iu ciaſcuno libro.   Cap°. 21.

But when you make a payment part through the bank and part by bill of exchange, deliver first the bill of exchange and then settle through the bank, which is safer. Many observe this precaution on good grounds, whenever they have to make payments part in cash to settle this balance through the bank, etc. If you make payments part through the bank, part by trading something or part by a bill of exchange and part in cash, you shall charge the seller for all these things and you shall credit each of the said things, each thing in its own place.

Now that you know how to go ahead whenever you make purchases, you will also know what you have to do when you sell. In this case, you shall charge the different buyers and shall credit the different goods that you sell and shall charge cash if you get money for the same, and you shall charge bills of exchange if you get a bill of exchange in payment, and credit the latter when the bank pays the exchange.

Therefore, referring again to the purchase, you shall credit the purchaser with all that he gives you in payment, etc.

This will be enough for your instruction on this subject.

CHAPTER 20.

ENTRIES FOR THE WELL-KNOWN AND PECULIAR MERCANTILE CUSTOMS OF TRADING AND PARTNERSHIP, ETC. HOW THEY SHOULD BE ENTERED IN THE MERCANTILE BOOKS. FIRST: SIMPLE TRADINGS, THEN COMPLEX TRADINGS AND EXAMPLES OF ENTRIES FOR THEM IN THE MEMORANDUM BOOK, JOURNAL AND LEDGER.

Now we shall speak of how certain well-known and peculiar entries should be made which are of the highest importance in commerce, and which usually are kept separate from the others so that they can show their respective profits and losses (*pro e danno*). They cover tradings, partnerships, suggested business trips, trips on your own ventures, commissions from others, drafts (*ditta*) or bills of exchange (*bancha descritta*), actual trades, store accounts, etc. I will tell you briefly about these accounts, how you should make the entries in your books so that you don't get mixed up in your affairs.

First, we shall show how to enter a trade (*barato*). Trades are usually of three kinds, as we said in Section 9 of Treatise III, Pages 161 to 167, where it is stated fully and you can refer to it.

I say, therefore, that no matter how you make a record of the trade in your books, you shall first enter it in the memorandum book, stating in detail all about it, its terms and conditions and whether it was made through a broker. After you have so described it, you then at the end shall put a money value on it; and you shall put down such price in accordance with the current value which the things that you have traded have; reckoning in any kind of money in the memorandum book. Afterwards the bookkeeper, when he transfers the entry to the Journal and Ledger, will reduce that money to the standard money that you have adopted.

This is done because, without entering the value of the things that you have traded, you could not, from your books and accounts, learn, except with great difficulty, what your profit or loss is. The merchandise must always be reduced to actual money value in order to take care of it (in the books).

You may keep a separate account of the goods received in trade, if you wish to do that, in order to know how much you make out of them separate from those of the same kind that you might already have at home, or separate from those that you might get after that, in order to know which was the best transaction. You also may keep only one account of all the goods—for instance, if you have already some ginger, and you get some more ginger through a trade. In this case you shall make the entries in the Journal as follows:

Per Ginger in bulk or in packages // A sugar, such and such kind, so many packages, weighing so many pounds. Received from a trade for sugar in this manner: I valued the sugar 24 ducats per hundred, of which I should receive one-third in cash, and I valued the ginger at so many ducats per hundred. The said sugar is in so many loaves weighing so many pounds, worth 20 ducats per hundred, and for the said ginger I received so many pounds of sugar and so many loaves, and their value is:

L............, S............, G............, P............

And if you do not know exactly how many loaves of sugar you have received for the said ginger, it does not matter, because you may correct the mistake in the following entry, whether the mistake was made plus or minus, or correct it through the cash entry. On the contrary, you know exactly the weight and money value, and you lose nothing in either by not knowing the number of loaves. It is not always possible to keep an account of all small details.

Now you will debit cash for whatever cash you received, and you shall credit sugar in the following manner:

Per Cash // A ditto. In the said trade I received cash from so and so for so many loaves of sugar weighing so many pounds; value:

L............, S............, G............, P............

You shall record in the Journal direct all these different items soon after the trade is made, and should take the name of the merchandise if you do not want to keep a separate account; but if you want to keep them in a separate account, you will write this way in the Journal:

Per ginger *bellidi* received by trade from so and so, etc. // A sugar, etc., stating everything as shown above. In the Ledger then they will have separate accounts.

This will be sufficient for you for all kinds of trades.

CHAPTER 21.

THE OTHER WELL-KNOWN ENTRY CALLED PARTNERSHIP. HOW IT SHOULD BE WRITTEN IN EACH BOOK IN THE PROPER MANNER.

Altra partita famofa e la cōp².ch̄ cō alcūo faceffe p ragiōe di q̄lūdxe cofa fi fa
ceffe o di panni o de fete o de fpetiarie o de gottōi e de tētoria o de cābi ꝝc.Que
fte talifimili fēpze uogliāo fua pꝛita fepata i tutti li.z.libzi detti Del p:cioe me/
moziale pofto che tu harai el di di fopza narraralā fēplicimēte tutta con modi e
cōditiōi ch̄ lauete fatta alegan:fcripto ouer altro ift̄o ch̄ fra uoi foffe e noiando el tp̄o q̄to
lā fintēde:e di che faculta fi fa eli fattori e garçoni che faueffe a tenere ꝝc.e quello che mette
ciafcū perfe o de robba o de ō.ꝝc.o debitozi o creditozi e di tutto a vno a vno farane credi
tozi li cōp¹.ognū di q̄l tanto che mette da pfe e debitrici la caffa ō la dc̄a cōp².fe da perfe la
tiēi ch̄meg:fe reggi el trafico tēnēdola fepata dala caffa tua pꝛticular q̄tu foffe q̄l ch̄ talcō².
guidaffe p la q̄l te cōuē fare lib¹.dapfe cō q̄llo:die mō evia ch̄ di fop e dco:ō tutto el tuo ma
neggio p mē bziga:nō dimēo potrefti tutta tenerla nelli medēi toi lib¹. uericado noue pꝛite
cōmo al pꝛfite dicemo ch̄ fi chiamāo famofe p eēr fepate da tutte talt̄.ō le q̄li q̄ te vo el mō
fuccito cōmo fabi adittare i tuo mēoziale e di poi i gioznale e q̄derno ꝝc.Ma tenēdo di lei
lib¹.fepati nō ti vo alt̄:documēto fenō ch̄ liguidi fi cōmo ō tutto el tuo trafico e dco.Dirolla
cofi ime.　In q̄fto di biamo fco cōp² cō li tali e tali alarte ō la lana ꝝc.cō pacti e cōditio
ni ꝝc.cōmo ape p fcripto o ift̄o ꝝc.p āni tāti ꝝc.onde el tal octte cōtāri tāti ꝝc.Lalt̄: balle
tāte lana frāc².pefa netta §.tāte ꝝc.meffacōto duc.tāti el m°:ꝝc.elalt̄: afeg°tāti veri debito
ri.cioe el tal de duc.tāti.el tal de tanti ꝝc.e cofi io fbozfai ō pfēte duc.tāti ꝝc.e fo i fūma: tut
to ćcor.duc.tāti ꝝc.Poi in tuo gioznale dirai i q̄fto modo afettādo tutte cofe a fuo luogo
imagina v².caffa ō compagnia.cvn cauedal di cō²c.ecofi a tutte le pꝛite ch̄ tu metterai dirai
fēpze p cōto ō ꝺp².acio fabi acognofcere dalt̄.toi pꝛite pꝛiculari ꝝc.e p².ꝑmo fefti da la caf
fa comēçarai e poi fucceffiuamente afettarai laltre.　Per caffa de compagnia.al tale de ra/
giōn de compagnia acio fe haueffe altri conti con teco non fimpacino ꝝc.per contanti mi/
fēi q̄fto di p la fua rata.2°li nr̄i pacti cōmo apare p fcripto ouer ift̄o ꝝc.val §.ꝗ.g°.p̄.
Poi fimilmēte dirai de le robbe che hano meffe cofi.　Per lana franca.de la cōp².al tale p
balle tante pefano nette itutto §.tante fo cōta dacozdo con tutti ducati tanti el m°fecondo
la foz². del cōtratto ouer fcripto fra noi ꝝc.mōta itutto duc.ꝝc.val §.ꝗ.g°.p̄.E cofi an
darai ponēdo tutte.pꝛli debitozi cōfegnati dirai cofi.　Per lo tale de ragiō de cōp².Al tale
q̄l fecōdo nr̄i pacti ci cōfegno p vero debitoze de duc.tanti val §.ꝗ.g°.p̄.Oz mai
che alq̄to fei itrodutto nō mi curo fēderme piu fi cōmo in lo pꝛnci°di q̄fto trattato feci che
troppo feria auolerte ogni cofa di nuouo replicare.E po del modo de metterle al q̄deruo
grande nō ne dico perche fo te fia facile cognofcēdo gia tu in lo gioznale q̄l ua debitoze eq̄l
creditoze.fiche afettarale tu i dare e hauere in quelmodo che di fopza i quefto te ifegnai a
ca°.15°e depēnarale i gioznale cōmo diffi di fopza al ca°12°ponēdo fēpze denançe i margine
li nūcri del debitoze e creditoze:a q̄te carti li harai pofti al libro.e cofi cōmo tu li metti al li
bzo grande:cofi li afetta i alfabeto cōmo di fopza piu fiade hauemo moftro ꝝc.

De lozdine de le pꝛite de ciafcūa fpefa:cōmo de cafa ozdinarie:ftraozdinarie:e di mer/
cantie:falarij de garçoni e factozi cōmo fabino a fcriuere:e dittare nelli libzi.　ca°22.

Oltra tutte le cofe ditte te auiene hauere i tutti toi libzi q̄fte pꝛite.cioe fpefi ō mer
ātia fpefi de cafa ozdiarie fpefe ftraozdiarie vna de itrata e vfcita e vna de pzo e
dāno o uoi dire auançi e difauāçi o utile e dāno o guadagno e pdita che tāto va
le le q̄li pꝛite fōno fūmamēte neceffarie i ogni cozpo mercātefco p potere fempze
cognofcere fuo capitale.e ala fine nel faldo cōmo getta el trafico ꝝc.le q̄li q̄ feq̄nte abaftan/
ça chiariremo cōmo fe debino guidare nelli libzi.　Unde q̄lla de fpefe mercātefche fi tene
p rifpecto che nō fēpze ogni peluço fi po mettere fubito i la pꝛita de la robba che tu uendi o
cōpzi cōmo acade che da poi piu di p q̄lla ti cōuerra pagare fachini e pefadozi e ligadozi e
barca.ebaftagi.e fimili a chi vn foldo.achz.2.ꝝc.de le q̄li volēdone fare pꝛticular pꝛita fereb
be lōgo e nō meritano la fpefa poche de minimis nō curat ptoz ꝝc.E ācoza acade che tu a/
dopzarai q̄lli medefimi baftagi.fachini.barca.e legatozi i vn pōto p piu diuerfe cofe cōmo
ittruene.ch̄ i ū pōto fcarcādo o carcādo diuerfe foze mercātie li a fattigara e tu li paghi p
tutte a vn tratto che nō potrefti a ogni mercātia carattare la fua fpefa.E po nafci q̄fta pꝛi/
ta chiamata fpefe de mercātia la q̄l fēpze fta accefa i dare cōmo tutte laltre fpefi fāno Sala
rij ancoza de factozi e garçoni de botega fi mettano i q̄fte e alcuni ne fa pꝛita afo pofta p fa
pere i ditti che fpēdano lāno ꝝc.e poi i q̄fta.la faldano:che p niū mō nō poffano effere cre
ditrici:e q̄ndo cofi le trouaffi feria erroze nel libzo.E pero i memoziale el dirai cofi.

In quefto di habian pagato abaftafi barcaroli ligadozi.pefadozi ꝝc.ch̄ carcaro e fcarca
ro ꝝc.le tali e tali cofe ꝝc.duc.tanti ꝝc.

The other well-known entry is the buying of anything in partnership (*compra* or *compagnie*—may also mean joint venture but not corporation) with other people, such as silks, spices, cotton, dyes, or money exchanges, etc. These accounts must all be entered in all three books separately from your own. In the first, that is, the memorandum book, after writing down the date at the top, you shall state in a simple way all the purchases with terms and conditions, referring to papers or other instruments that you might have made, stating for how long it was made and what were its objects, mentioning the employes and apprentices that you should keep, etc., and the share, and how much each of you puts in the business, whether in goods or cash, etc., who are the debtors and who are the creditors. You should credit the partners (*compratori*) for the amount which each of them contributes, and you shall debit cash with the same if you keep the account with your own. But it is better for the business if you keep this cash account separate from your private one when you are the one at the head of the business, in which case you should have a separate set of books in the same order and way we have shown previously. This will facilitate things for you. However, you might keep all these accounts in your own personal books opening new accounts which, as we have said, are referred to as well-known accounts because they are kept separate from all the others, and I will show here how to enter them in your Day Book and then in the Journal and Ledger—but if you keep separate books, I will not give you any further instruction, because what I have said so far will be sufficient for you—you shall do as follows: On this day we have made a contract with so and so, and so and so, jointly, to buy (*facto compra*) wool, etc., under terms and conditions, etc., as appears from such and such paper or such and such instrument, for so many years, etc. So and so put in as his share, so much in cash; the other put so many bales of French wool, weighing net so many pounds, etc., estimated at so many ducats per, etc. The third, so and so, put in so many credits, namely, one for so many ducats, etc.

Then, in the Journal, putting everything in its own place, you shall imagine that you have a partnership's cash (*cassa de compagnia*) and a partnership's capital (*cavedale de compagnia*); so that in each entry you make, you shall always name the accounts of the partnership so that you can distinguish them from your own entries. First, you make the cash entry, and then follow it systematically by the other entries:

Per Partnership cash // A such and such partner's account—so that if you have other accounts, you will not get confused—so and so put in on this day as his share according to our agreement as appears from the contract, etc.; value: L........., S........., G........., P..........

Then you shall mention the other things that they have contributed:

Per French wool // A partner's account, for so many bales weighing in total, net, so many pounds, as examined by all of us, at so many ducats per bushel, according to the terms of the contract we have made, etc., worth in total so many ducats; value: L........., S........., G........., P..........

And so on for the other different items, and as to the due bills which have been put in the Company, you shall state this way:

Per Mr. So and So, Partnership's account // A so and so, according to our agreement, which so and so transferred to the Partnership as a good due bill of so many ducats: L........., S........., G........., P..........

Now that I have given you a kind of introduction to these new entries, I won't go any further, as it would be a very tiresome thing to repeat all I have said.

And I will not say anything as to the way in which to make these entries in the Ledger, as I know it will be easy for you to know what should be entered as debit and what as credit from the Journal. You shall enter them accordingly as I have told you at Chapter 15, and shall cancel these entries in the Journal as I told you at Chapter 12, always writing in the margin just opposite them the number of the debit and credit pages of the Ledger, and as you enter them in the Ledger you shall also enter them in the index, as I have told you repeatedly before.

CHAPTER 22.

REGARDING THE ENTRIES OF EVERY KIND OF EXPENSE, AS FOR INSTANCE HOUSEHOLD EXPENSES, ORDINARY OR EXTRAORDINARY, MERCANTILE EXPENSES, WAGES OF CLERKS AND APPRENTICES. HOW THEY SHOULD BE ENTERED IN THE BOOKS.

Besides the entries so far mentioned, you shall open these accounts in your books: that is, mercantile expenses, ordinary household expenses, extraordinary expenses, and account for what is cashed in (*entrata*) and what is paid out (*uscita*); one for profits and loss (*pro e danno*—favor and damages) or (*avanzi e desavanzi*—increase and deficit), or (*utile e danno*—profit and damage) or (*guadagno e perdita*—gain and loss), which accounts are very necessary at any time so that the merchant can always know what is his capital and at the end when he figures up the closing (*saldo*), how his business is going.

I will show here clearly enough how these accounts should be kept in the books. The account named "small business expenses" is kept because we can not enter every little thing in the account of the merchandise that you sell or buy. For instance, it may happen that after a few days, for these goods that you sell or buy, you will have to pay the porter, the weigher, the packer, the shipper and the driver, and others, paying to this one one penny, to the other one two pennies, etc.; if you want to keep a separate account for each of these different transactions, it would be too long and too expensive. As the proverb says:

De minimis non curat Praetor (Officials do not bother with details). And it may be that you will have to employ those same people—drivers, porters, shippers and packers—for different things, as, for instance, you may need them for loading the several merchandises in a seaport, and you will employ them and will have to pay them for all these services at one time, and you could not charge the several kinds of merchandise with its proportion of these expenses. Therefore you open this account which is called "small business expenses," which is always used in the debit as are all the other expenses. You enter in this account the salaries of your store employes, although some keep a separate account of the salaries that they pay so that they know how much they pay for salaries every year, etc. This should also always appear as a debit. If the account should be in credit, this would show that there is a mistake. Therefore you shall say as follows in the memorandum book:

On this day we have paid to drivers, shippers, packers, weighers, etc., who loaded and unloaded such and such goods, so many ducats, etc.;

Poi in lo giornale couerra dir coſi. Per ſpeſe de mercãtie: a caſſa contati: per barche e baſtagi corde e ligatori de le tal coſe in tutto duc.tãti zc.val ꝑ. In lo qderno dirai coſi. Speſi ꝏ mercãtia dié dare adi tãti p caſſa zc.val k. ꝑ. Quella ꝏ le ſpeſi di caſa ordinarie nõ ſi po far ſença.E itendanſe ſpeſi di caſa ordinarie:cõmo formenti: vini: legne: ogli: ſale: carne: ſcarpe: copelli facture de veſte: giupponi: calçe: e ſartori zc.be ueraggi: beueſtite: mancce: ouer bonemani zc.barbieri: fornaro: aquaruoli: lauature de panni zc.maſarie de cocina vaſi.bicbieri.e uetri: tutti ſeccbi.maſtelli.botti zc.bauéga che molti de ſimili maſarie vſino tener conto ſeparato per poter preſto trouar ſuo cõto e fano prita noua.cõmo ãcora tu poi fare nõ cbe di qſte ma di qualũdbe altra ti parra.ma io te amaeſtro di quelle ebel trafico nõ po far ſença zc.e tal prita di ſpeſi di caſa dittarala ſi cõmo e ditto de quella de la mercãtia.e ſecõdo cbe tu vai facédo ſpeſe groſſe adi p di metti in li libri commo del formento e vini legne zc.de le quali ancora molti coſtumano fare prita daperſe per poter poi alafine de lanno o a tépo p tpo facilmente ſapere quãto de tali cõſumano zc. ma per le ſpeſi piccole cõmo ſono amenuto cõprar carne e peſci: barbieri e tragbetti ſi uol torre o vno ouer doi duc.a un tratto e tenerli da parte in vno ſacbetto e di quelli andar ſpédédo a menuto.Percbe nõ ſeria poſſibili a vna a vna di tali tener conto.E coſi dicano per li contanti in giornale. Per ſpeſi di caſa.a caſſa qli traſſi per ſpendere amenuto in vno ſacbetto duc.tanti zc.val.ꝑ. ꝑ. ꝑ. E poi ſe ti pare ancora con queſte ſpeſi de caſa meterui le ſpeſi ſtraordinarie cbe non fa caſo.cõmo quãdo ſpendeſſe per andare aſolaçço: e p tracere alarco o baleſtro e altri giocbi o perdite cbe ti caſcaſſero e pdeſſe robbe o denari o cb te foſſero tolte o perdeſſe in mare o per fuocbi zc.cbe tutti ſimili ſintendano ſpeſe ſtraordinarie. Le quali ancora ſe le voli tenere da parte ſimilmente lo poi fare e molti luſano per ſaper netto aſafin delanno quanto bano ſpeſo de ſtraordinario per le quali anco ſintende doni e preſenti cbe tu faceſſe adalcuno per alcuna cagione zc.ꝏ le quali ſpeſe non mi curo piu oltra ſtenderme perocbe ſo certo cbe tu per te meglio ormai bauendo amente le coſe dette diſtance aſettarai cbe prima non bareſti facto ſicbe queſte laſciando diremo del modo da ſettare le partite de vna botega ſi nel tuo'quaderno e libri ordinarij: cõmo ſe tu la voleſſe tener tu da te cõmo lareſti a tenere cbe ſia bella coſa a ſapere ſicbe notale.

De lordine e mõ a ſap tener vn cõto de botega i tua mão o adaltri recõmãdata e cõmo ſe debino nelli libri autentici del patrone e ancbe in quelli de botega ſeparatamente ſcrivere e dittare.   capi.23.

Ico adonca quãdo baueſſe vna botega la ql teneſſe fornita ala giornata for de caſa tua e fore del tuo corpo di caſa.alora p bono ordine tirrai qſto mõ:cioe de tutte le robbe cbe tu ui metterai adi p di farala debitrici ali toi libri e creditrici qlle tal robbe cb'vi metti.a vna p vna e fa tua imagiatiõe cb qſta bote°.ſia vna pſona.tua debitrici di ql tãto cbe li dai e p lei ſpédi i tutti li modi.E coſi p lauerſo de tutto ql lo cbne caui e receui farala creditrici cõmo ſe foſſe vn dbitore cbti pagaſſe apte apte.E poi ogni uolta cbe tu voli con lei cõtare tu porrai vedere cõmo ella te butta.o bene o male zc.E coſi poi ſaprai qllo arai afare e i cb mõ larai a gouernarc zc.E molti ſono cb ali ſoi libri fãno debitore el pncipale cbe ſi atéde a ditta botega bécbe qſto nõ ſi poſſa debitamente ſéça volũta di ql tale.pocb mai ſi deue mettere ne ãcora de ragiõ ſi puo porre vn debitore allibo ſéça ſua ſaputa ne ãcb creditore cõ cõditiõi alcũe ſéça ſua uolũta le ql coſe facédole tu ſereſti mãco cbe da bene.E li toi libri ſeriéno reputati falſi.e coſi ꝏ le maſarie cb i qlla meteſſe e ordegni neceſſarii al a ditta botega ſecõdo ſua occuréça:cõmo ſe foſſe ſpeciaria ti conuerra formirla ꝏ uaſi.caldieri.ramini.da lauorare zc.di qli tutti farala debitrici o colui cbe li attéde cõmo ditto.e p bello iuétario li le aſegna ſcripto ꝏ ſua mão odaltri ꝏ ſua uolũta zc. acio de tutto ſia bé cbiaro.e qſto voglio ſia baſtãte qdo la botega baueſſe conſegnata a vnaltro cb p te la faceſſe o foſſe tuo cõmeſſo zc.Ma ſe la déa botega vorrai tenere a tuoi mãi qſto or die fuarai e ſtara bene: e metiamo cb cõpri e trafichi tutto p la ditta botega e nõ baui altro maneggio alora formarai li libri commo e ditto.E di cio cbe vendi e compri farai creditori cbi te da le robbe per tanto tempo ſe compri a tempo e creditrici la caſſa ſe compri a contanti e debitrici la botega.E quando tu vendeſſe a menuto.cioe cbe non ariuaſſe a.4.o.6.ducati zc.alora tutti ditti denari reporrai in vna caſſetta.ouer ſalua denaro dõde i capo ꝏ.8.o 10.giorni line cauarai.e alora farãe debitrici la caſſa e creditrici la bo°.di ql tãto:e i la prita dirai p piu robbe uédute de le qli gia bauerai tenuto el cõto e molte altre coſe in le qli nõ mi

then in the Journal you shall say as follows:

Per small business expenses // A cash. Cash paid for boats, ropes, etc., for such and such goods in total, so many ducats; value:

L............, S............, G............, P.............

In the Ledger, you shall state as follows:

Small business expenses (*dee dare*—shall give) debit per cash on this day, etc., value; page, etc.

L............, S............, G............, P.............

We can not do without the account of ordinary household expenses. By these expenses we mean expenses for grains, wine, wood, oil, salt, meat, shoes, hats, stockings, cloths, tips, expenses for tailors, barbers, bakers, cleaners, etc., kitchen utensils, vases, glasses, casks, etc.

Many keep different accounts for all these different things, so that they can see at a glance how each account stands, and you may do so and open all these different accounts, and any accounts that you like, but I am talking to you about what the merchant can not do without. And you shall keep this account in the way I have told you to keep the small business expense account, and make each entry day by day as you have such expenses, as for grain, wine, wool, etc. Many open special accounts for these different things so that at the end of the year or at any time they may know how much they are paying out; but for the small accounts, as meat, fish, boat fares, etc., you shall set aside in a little bag one or two ducats and make small payments out of this amount. It will be impossible to keep an account of all these small things.

In the Journal you shall state so:

Per household expenses // A cash. Cash set aside in a little bag for small expenses, so many ducats, value:

L............, S............, G............, P.............

If you wish, you can include in the household expenses the extraordinary expenses, as those that you make for amusements or that you lose in some game, or for things or money that you might lose, or that might be stolen or lost in a wreck or through fire, etc., for all are classified as extraordinary expenses. If you want to keep a separate account for them, you may do so, as many do, in order to know at the end of the year how much you have expended for extraordinary expenses, under which title you should include also gifts and presents that you might make to any one for any reason. Of these expenses, I will not speak any longer, because I am sure that you, keeping in mind what we have said so far, will know how to manage yourself. And leaving this subject, I will tell you of the way to open your store accounts in the Ledger and in the other books as if you wanted to conduct a store for your own account. I shall tell you that you must pay good attention, for it is a very nice thing for you to know.

CHAPTER 23.

IN WHAT MANNER THE ACCOUNTS OF A STORE SHOULD BE KEPT. WHETHER THE STORE IS UNDER YOUR CARE OR UNDER THE CARE OF OTHER PEOPLE. HOW THE ACCOUNTS SHOULD BE ENTERED IN THE AUTHENTIC BOOKS OF THE OWNER SEPARATE FROM THOSE OF THE STORE ITSELF.

I say then that if you should have a store outside of your house (branch store) and not in the same building with your house, but which you have fully equipped, then for the sake of order you should keep the accounts in this way: You should charge it in your books with all the different things that you put into it, day by day, and should credit all the different merchandise that you put in it also each one by itself, and you must imagine that this store is just like a person who should be your debtor for all the things that you may give (*dai*) it or spend for it for any reason. And so on the contrary you shall credit it with all that you take out of it and receive from it (*cavi e recevi*) as if it were a debtor who would pay you gradually. Thus at any time that you so desire, you may see how the store is running—that is, at a profit or at a loss— so you will know what you will have to do and how you will have to manage it. There are many who in their books charge everything to the manager of the store. This, however, can not be done properly without the consent of that person, because you can never enter in your books as a debtor any person without his knowing it, nor put him as a creditor under certain conditions without his consent. If you should do these things, it would not be right and your books would be considered wrong.

As to all the fixtures which you might put in said store necessary to the running of it according to the circumstances—if you had for instance a drug-store, you would have to furnish it with vases, boiling pots, copper utensils, with which to work—you shall charge your store with all this furniture. So all of these things you shall charge, and he who is at the head of the store shall make a proper inventory of all these things in his own handwriting or in the handwriting of somebody else, at his pleasure, so that everything should be clear. And this will be sufficient for a store whose management you may have turned over to somebody or to some of your employes. But if you want to run the store yourself, you shall do as I will tell you and it will be all right. Let us suppose that you buy and do all of your business through the said store and do not have to take care of any other business, then you shall keep the books as I have said before, whether you buy or sell. You shall credit all those that sell goods to you on time, if you buy on time, or credit cash if you buy for cash, and charge the store; and if you should sell at retail, as when the sale should not amount to four or six ducats, and so on, then you shall keep all these moneys in a small drawer or box from which you shall take it after eight or ten days, and then you shall charge this amount to cash and shall credit the store; and you shall make this entry as follows:

Per various merchandise sold—for which you shall have kept an account—and so on. I shall not talk at length about this because

uoglio troppo diftendere.p che fo como difopza diffufaméteihabião dcó ozmai fapzai perte
itcderle cóciofia che cóti non fono altro che vn debito ozdine dc la fantafia che fi fa el mer/
catante per el qual unifozme feruato puene ala notitia de tutte fue facéde e cognofc facil/
mére p qllo fe le fue cofe uáno bene o male.p che el pzouerbio dici chi fa mercátia e nó la co/
gnofca li foi denari douétan mofca ƶc.e fecódo le occurrençe li fa remedio. E pero piu e mã
co li fipo fempre agiongere in numero e i multitudine de ptite. E po de qîto tacótéta.

Cómo fe habino alettrare nel gioznale e quaderno le paratte de li bächi de fcritta:eqlî fe ĩ
tédino e doue ne fiazo de cábi:tu cólozo ftandomercatáte:e tu có áltri qdo foffe bächieri:
e de le quie tàçe che p li cábi fe fáno.e p che fene facia doi de medefimo tenoze   ca ,24

Ora per li banchi de fcripta ò quali fe ne trouá oggi di invinctia i bruggia iauer
fa e barçelóa e certi altrituogbi famofi e traficáti u cóuié fap çó lozo libzi fcótra/
re có gradiffima diligétia.¹E peroe da notar che có lobancho te poi cómunamé
te impaciare da te ponédoui denari per piu tua figureçça:o uero p modo de di/
pofito a la gioznata poter con quelfi far tuoi pagamenti chiari apiero gioâni e martino per
che la ditta del bancho e comme publico iftruméto de notaro p che fon per li dominij afc
gurati.onde ponédoui tu da te.ò.farai debitoze ditto bancho nominaudo patroni o uero
cópagni del bácho e creditrici la tua caffa cofi dicédo i gioznale   Per bancho de li pama/
ni: A caffa per cótanti li mifi có tali.io o altri che per me foffe in queîto di de mio conto fra
oro e moneta ƶc.i tutto ducati ƶc. Val. 8.ƒ.g.p. E farate fare dal banchieri doi uerfi i funo
foglio p piu cautela. E cofi giongédogline tu ala gioznata farai el fimile:cauandone tu lui
te fara fcriuere a te el receuere:e cofi le cofe fi uengano fempze a mátener chiare: Uero e che
aleuolte tal fcritte nó fi coftumano p che cómo e ditto li libri del bancho fempze fóno publi
chi e autentichiz. ma pur e buono la cautela p che cómo difopza fo detto al mercante le cofe
mai fozò. troppo chiare. Ma fe tu uoleffe tal prita tenerla con li patroni:o uero cópagni del
bancho ancoza lo poi fare che tanto uale po che noiando tu el bácho a modo difopza finté
de li patrói e cóp°.de quello:per li patróni direfti cofi.   Per mifer Girolimo lipamani dal
bancho e cópagni qdo foffero piu. A caffa ut fupza fequita tutto. E fempze farai neli tuoi li
bzi mentione de le chiareçe:patti:e códitioni che fra uoi nafceffero cómo de fcripti de mã: e
del luogo doue li reponi ifilça:fcatola:tafcha:o caffa acio poffi facilméte retrouarle:po che
có bona diligéça fimili fcripture fi debono feruare. ad ppetuam rei memoziã:p li picoli dc
cozano ƶc. E p che aleuolte có lo bächieri pozrefti hauerui piu facéde e maneggi i mercã
tia p te o per altri cómo cómeffo ƶc.po fempze cũ lui ti cóuié tener cóti diuerfi p non itriga
re lance có ronchoni che nafcieriá grã confuffione:e dire i le tue ptite p cóto de la tal cofa:o
p cóto del tal o p ragió de mercantia o p ragion de contanti depofitati i tuo nome o daltri
cómo e ditto:le quali cofe fo p tuo igegno ozmai reggerai ƶc. E fimilmte te reggerai faltri te
aconciaffe d.a te pche cóto fi uoleffe:faralo debitoze altuo libro p ql tal cóto:cioe ò pagamé
to noiando p pte o p reftoƶc.e ql tale farài creditoze p lo medefimo cóto e ftara bene. E q
do tu de dcó bancho cauaffe.ò.i cótáti o p paga méti che adaltri faceffe p pte o refto o uero
p remetter a daltri i altri paefi ƶc.aloza farai el cótrario de ql che finoza e dcó:cioe fe caui
cótanti farai debitrici la tua caffa:e creditoze el bancho o uer patrói di quel tanto che ne ca
uafti. E fe tu li fcriueffe adaltri farai debitoze ql tale e creditoze detto bancho o patrói di ql
tanto noiando el pche dicédo i gioznale p li cótanti cofi.   Per caffa albancho o uer mi
fer girolimo li pamani p contanti i tal di.o i qîto di ne traffi a mio bifogno ƶc.i tutto.duc.
táti ƶc.ual. 8.ƒ.g.p. E fe adaltri li fcriueffe urpura amartio di ríti cofi.   Per mart° del ta
le. Al ditto ut fupza per duc.táti ƶc.li fcriffi p pte o p prefto o abó cóto o.p ipzefto ƶc. i qîto
di.ual. 8.ƒ.g.p. E cofi leuádo ditte ptitte dl gioznale fépre a fuo luogo i qderno afertarale:e
i alfabeto cómodi difopza dati e depénandole cómo to moftro in memoziale e gioznale.p.e
mancho per te fteffo giógnédoli parolle. po che non e poffibile q de ttutto a pieno narrare
fi che conuié dal tuo cáto fia uigiláte ƶc.   El medefimo mó te cóuerra obferuare p remette
re li cábi altroue.cóme lon°:brugia:ro°:lió ƶc.e per ritrar daltro ƶc.nominando líc termi/
ni ƶc.o ala uifta o aladata o al fuo piacere:cómo fe coftuma facédo méttóe de p°.2°.e.3°. ƶc.
acio non nafca errrore fra te el tuo refpondente e de le monete che tu trai e rimetti e le lor
ualutc e ,puifiói e fpefi dáni e itereffi che có li pzotefti poderebono nafcere ƶc.fi che di tutto
fi uol far méttóe el p che e cóme. E cóme o meffo che tu habi afare con bácho:cofi uerfa uice
prédi fe foffe tu el banchieri mutatis mutandis che quando paghi fa debitore quel tale e la
tua caffa creditrici e fel tuo creditoze fença cauare.ò.adaltri li fcriueffe dirai nel tuo giozni

I have given you sufficient explanation previously and you know how to go ahead by this time. For accounts are nothing else than the expression in writing of the arrangement of his affairs, which the merchant keeps in his mind, and if he follow this system always he will know all about his business and will know exactly whether his business goes well or not. Therefore the proverb: If you are in business and do not know all about it, your money will go like flies—That is, you will lose it. And according to the circumstances you can remedy what is to be remedied; for instance, if necessary, you might open other accounts. And this will be sufficient for you.

CHAPTER 24.

HOW YOU SHOULD KEEP IN THE JOURNAL AND LEDGER. THE ACCOUNTS WITH THE BANK. WHAT IS UNDERSTOOD BY THEM. BILLS OF EXCHANGE—WHETHER YOU DEAL WITH A BANK OR YOURSELF ARE A BANKER. RECEIPTS FOR DRAFTS—WHAT IS UNDERSTOOD BY THEM AND WHY THEY ARE MADE OUT IN DUPLICATE.

In respect to banks, which you can find nowadays in Venice, in Bruges, in Antwerp, Barcelona, and other places well known to the commercial world, you must keep your accounts with them with the greatest diligence.

You can generally establish connections with a bank. For instance, you may leave your money with the bank as a place of greater safety, or you may keep your money in the bank as a deposit in order to make therefrom your daily payments to Peter, John and Martin, for a bank draft is like a public notarial instrument, because they are controlled by the state.

If you put money in the bank, then you shall charge the bank or the owner or partners of the bank and shall credit your cash and make the entries in the Journal as follows:

For Bank of Lipamani // A cash. Cash deposited with so and so by me, or others, for my account, on this day counting gold and other money, etc., in all so many ducats; value:

L_____, S_____, G_____, P_____.

And you will have the banker give you some kind of a written record for your surety; if you make other deposits you shall do the same. In case you should withdraw money, the banker shall have you write a receipt; in this way, things will be kept always clear.

It is true that at times this kind of receipt is not given, because, as we said, the books of the bank are always public and authentic; but it is better to require this writing, because, as I have told you, things can't be too clear for the merchant.

If you want to keep this account in the name of the owners or partners of the bank, you may do so, as it is the same thing, because, if you open the account under the name of the bank, by the bank you mean the owners or the partners. If you keep it under the name of the owners, you shall say this way:

Per Mr. Girolimo Lipamani, banker, and associates—if there are many— // A cash—and here you write as above. In your books you shall always mention all agreements, terms, conditions that there might be; also instruments of writing and places where you keep them, whether file box, pouch or trunk, so that you may easily find them, as these papers should be diligently kept for an everlasting memorial of the transaction (*ad perpetuam memoriam*) on account of dangers.

As you may have several different business relations with the bankers for yourself, or for others, you must keep various accounts with them so that you won't mix one thing with another, and avoid confusion, and in your entries you shall say: On account of such and such thing, or on account of so and so, or on account of goods, or on account of cash deposited in your name or in the name of others, as we have said. You will know yourself how to make these entries. In the same way you will proceed in case others should turn money over to you for some account; you shall charge that account in your book—that is, you shall charge the bank, stating whether it was in part payment or in full, etc., and you shall credit the person that gave you the money. This will be all right.

When you should withdraw money from a bank either to pay somebody else as part payment or payment in full, or to make a remittance to parties in other countries, you shall do in this case just the opposite of what we just said—that is, if you withdraw money you shall charge your cash and credit the bank or owners of the bank for the amount withdrawn; and if you should give an order on the bank for somebody else, you shall charge this party and credit the bank or owners of the bank for that much, stating the reasons. You shall enter the cash item in your Journal as follows:

Per cash // A bank, or Mr. Girolimo Lipamani, for cash which on this day or on such and such day I withdrew for my need, in all so many ducats, value: L_____, S_____, G_____, P_____.

And if you should issue an order in favor of Mr. Martino, for instance, you shall say thus:

Per Martino on such and such a day // A ditto for ditto for cash, etc., for so many ducats, for which I gave an order, in part payment or in full payment, or for a loan, etc., on this day; value:

L_____, S_____, G_____, P_____.

Every time you transfer these entries from the Journal into the Ledger, you shall also record them in the index and cancel them, as I have shown you, adding more or less words according to the facts in the case.

You must do the same in case you want to send drafts elsewhere, as to London, Bruges, Rome, Lyons, etc. You shall mention in the letter the terms, conditions, etc., whether these drafts are at sight or at a certain date or at pleasure of the payor, as it is customary, mentioning also whether it is a first, second, third draft, etc., so that no misunderstanding can occur between you and your correspondent, mentioning also the kind of money in which you draw or transmit, their value, the commission, the costs and interest that might follow a protest—in a word, everything must be mentioned, why and how.

I have told you how you have to proceed in dealing with a bank. If on the contrary you are the banker you have to do in the opposite way (*mutatis mutandis*); when you pay you charge the man to whom you pay and credit cash. If one of your creditors, without withdrawing money, should issue a draft to somebody else, you shall say in the journal

le per quel tale tuo creditore a quel tale achi lui li acocia.e cosi vieni a far comutatione da vno
creditore a unaltro e tu rimani pure debitore e uieni in qsto atto essere persona meçana e co
muna.como testimonio e factore de le parti a tuo inchiostro carta fitto fatiga e tempo siche
di qua si caua la honesta puisiõe nel cambio essere sepre licita qdo mai nõ ui corrisse pico
lo de uiaggio altre remesse in mano de terce psone zc.como nelli cambi reali in qsto a suo
luogho estato apieno detto zc.Ma siandobachieri ricordate nell isaldi cõ toi creditori far
te tornare fogli pulice o altri scripti che di tua mano hauesse de leqli quando ne fai sepre fan
ne nel tuo libro mentiõe acio te recordia fartele tornare e straçarli:acio nõ ueniffe a tepo cõ
qlli altri a domandarte e fatte fare sepre bone quietançe cõmo costumano fare chi attede al
cãbio.po che lusança e che se tu vieni.verbi gra da gineuera con vna di cãbio q in vi°.a mis
giouãnifresco baldi da fiorª.e cõpª.ch alauista o data:o a tuo piacere te douesse pagare metia
mo duc. 100.p altre tanti che dila haueffe nele man de chi li scriue cõ segnati:aloza el ditto
mis. giouãni e cõpª.acceprãdo la lra:e sborsciãdote ditti.õ.re fara scriuere õ tua mano doi qe
tançe de vn medesimo tenore:e se tu nõ sapeffe scriuere le far vn terço pte o vo notaro:
nõ sa cõ tentara duna p che luna cõuie che rimandi a ql banchieri a gineuera:chè li scriue
che a te p suo cõto paghi li ditti duc.100.i sarli sede cõmo cortescmete a fatto ql tanto che
li scriffe i cui fede in una sua li mãda laquietaça di tua mano:e laltra tene i silça apresso di se:
acio qdo cõtaffe cõ lui non poteffe negarlilo:e di la ancora tu tornãdo nõ poteffe.lametarte
di lui ne de mis giouãni po che se tu lo feffe el te mostraria detta quietança di tua mano e re
maresti confuso:si che tutte qste cose sonno cautele che si conuengano de necessita fare p la
poca fede si troua oggi di Del quale atto ne nascano doi prite i lo qderno loro.vna in ql di
mes giouãni facedo õbitore ql che li scriue p vigore de la dicãbio:e laltra i qllo del respõde
te a gineuera facedo creditore mis giouãni di quelli duc.100.per virtu de ditta tua quietaça
receuuta.e questo e el debito modo e ordine de cambiatori p tutto el mõdo: acio le lor cose
vadino cõ chiareçce:si che dal tuo lato alquãto affatigandote porrai ogni cosa con summa
diligença asettare.zc.

De unaltra partita che ale uolte se costuma nel qderno tenere detta entrata e uscita e ale
uolte senefa libro particulare:e per che.   ca.25.

Onno alcuni che ne lor libri usano tenere vna prita detta entrata e vscita i la ql
põgano cose straordinarie o altre cõmo ala. fantasia pare. Altri ne tirra una õ
spese straordinarie e i simili mettano cõmo i qlla dintrata isita pseri che li fosser
fatti.vo.gra.e cosi scdo che riceuano e dãno e tegano cõto i dare e hauere e poi a
la fine cõ laltre le saldãno i p e dãno e cauedale cõmo itenderai nel bilancio zc.Ma i uero
qlla detta di sopra spese di casa p tutte e bastãte se nõ chi uoleffe per sua curiosita tener cõ
to da p se fiã a vn potale de strega che lo porria fare ma ach fine:epo si oba a le cose cõ bre
uita asettarle.Altri luoghi costuma de litrata euscita tener vn libro a sua posta:e poi quello
saldano a tepo del bilacio nel vltimo autetico isiemi cõ le altre facede:laql cosa non e dabias
mare auega sia de piu fatiga.

Cõmo se habino asettare neli libri le prite de li uiaggi i sua mano:e quelle de li uiagdi re
comandati:e cõmo di necessita de tali nascono doi quaderni   ca.26.

J uiaggi si costumano fare i doi modi:cioe i sua mano e recomandato.'vnde na
scano diuersi modi i tener lor cõti po che sepre si prosupõgano libri doppi:o sia
i tua mano o sia recõmandato .Perche luqderno resta i casa e laltro ti cõue fare
i uiaggio.vnde sel ditto viagio fia i tua mano p bõ ordie de ciocbe tu porti forma
tuo iuctario qdernetto:giornaletto zc.tutto cõmo di sopra se detto:e uededo cõprãdo ba
ratãdo zc.de tutto fa debitori e creditori psone:robbe: caffa:cauedal:de uiaggio:e p e dan
no de uiaggio zc.e qsto e lo piu schietto e dica ch si uoglia altri. Auega ch porresti tener cõ
to cõ la casa dalaql tu togli la faculta che al ditto uiaggio porti facedola nel libretto del tuo
uiaggio creditrici:e le robbe debitrici a una p vª:cosi formaresti tua caffa:tuo cauedale zc.
ordenatamete cõmo nel tuo famoso.E tornãdo a saluameto redaresti alacasa altre robbe ali
contro.o uero.õ.e cõ lei saldaresti cõto e lutile o dãno seqto asetaresti a suo luogho nel qua
derno grãde.siche aqsto modo ancora le tue facede uercbono chiare.Ma sel viaggio recõ
mãdaffe adaltri:aloza faresti de tutto nel tuo libro debitore ql tale achi larecomãdi dicedo
per uiaggio recomãdato al tale zc.e cõ lui terresti conto cõme se foffe vn tuo auetore de tut
te robbe:e õ.a prita per partita zc.E lui dal cãto suo formara suo qdernetto:e i qllo te cõ
uerra fare creditore de tutto.E retornãdo saldara conteco.E sel tuo cõmeffo foffe i le bãde

64

as follows: Per that special creditor of yours // A the man to whom the money was assigned. In this way you just make the transfer from one creditor to another and you still remain as debtor and act as a go-between, as witness or agent of the two parties. For ink, paper, rent, trouble and time you get a commission, which is always lawful, even though through a draft there is no risk of travel, or the risk when money should be transferred to third parties, etc., as in actual exchanges, of which we have spoken in its place. If you are a banker, whenever you close an account with your creditors always remember to get back all the papers, documents or other writings in your own handwriting that they might have. When you issue any such paper always mention it in your books so that when the time comes you will remember to ask for them and to destroy them so that nobody else should appear with these papers and ask money for the second time. You must always require good receipts as those do who are accustomed to this kind of business. For the custom is this: If you, for instance, come from Geneva to Venice with a draft on Messrs. Giovanni Frescobaldi & Co., of Florence, which draft might be at sight or on a certain date or at your pleasure, and the amount were for a hundred ducats, that is, for as many ducats as you have paid to the drawer of the draft, then the said Messrs. Giovanni & Co., when they honor the draft and give you the cash will require you to give two receipts written in your own handwriting, and if you should not know how to write, a third party or a notary public will make them out. He will not be satisfied with one because he has to send one to the banker at Geneva, who wrote him to pay the hundred ducats to you for his account just to show that he honored his request, and for this purpose he will send to the other banker a letter enclosing your receipt written in your handwriting. The other receipt he will keep for himself on file so that in balancing with the other banker, the banker could not deny the transaction, and if you should go to Geneva you could not complain of him or of Mr. Giovanni for if you should complain he would show you your receipt written by yourself and you would not play a beautiful part in it. All these precautions ought to be taken by necessity on account of the bad faith of the present times. Out of these transactions two entries ought to be made in the Ledger, one entry in the account with Mr. Giovanni, in which you shall charge the drawer of the draft, (letter de cambio) the other entry in the account of your correspondent at Geneva, crediting Mr. Giovanni with that hundred ducats paid through a draft. This is the method that the bankers of all the world keep so that their transaction may appear clear; therefore you will have to take some trouble on your part and try to enter everything in its own place with great care.

CHAPTER 25.

ANOTHER ACCOUNT WHICH IS USUALLY KEPT IN THE LEDGER, CALLED INCOME AND EXPENSES, FOR WHICH OFTEN A SEPARATE BOOK IS USED, AND WHY.

There are some who, in their books, are accustomed to keep an account called Income and Expenses (Entrata e uscita), in which they enter extraordinary things, or any other thing that they deem proper; others keep an account called extraordinary expenses and in it they record gifts, which they receive or give. They keep it as a credit and debit account, and then at the end of the year they ascertain the remainder (resto) which is either a profit or a loss and transfer it to capital as you will understand when we talk about the balance. But really the account we have called "household expenses" is sufficient for all this unless someone should like to keep a separate account for his own curiosity, but it would be of no great value because things should be arranged as briefly as possible. In other places it is customary to keep the income and expense account in a separate book which is balanced when they balance the authenticated books and all other affairs. This custom is not to be criticized but it requires more work.

CHAPTER 26.

HOW ENTRIES SHOULD BE MADE IN MERCANTILE BOOKS RELATIVE TO TRIPS WHICH YOU CONDUCT YOURSELF OR YOU ENTRUST TO OTHER PEOPLE, AND THE TWO LEDGERS RESULTING THEREFROM.

Trips are made usually in two ways, either personally or through somebody else; therefore two are the ways to keep their accounts and the book always ought to be in duplicate whether the trip is made by you personally or it is in charge of somebody else. One ledger is kept at home and the other one is taken along and kept on the trip. If you conduct the trip yourself, for the sake of order and system, you must take a new inventory also a small Ledger and small Journal among the things you take with you and follow the instruction above given. If you sell or buy or exchange, you must charge and credit according to the facts, persons, goods, cash, traveling capital, traveling profit and loss, etc. This is the best way, no matter what other people may say. You might keep an account with the mercantile house which furnishes you with the goods which you take on the trip. In this case you shall credit the said house in your little Ledger and charge the different goods one by one. In this way you would open your mercantile house accounts, capital account, etc., as in your main books, and coming back safe and sound you would return to the mercantile house either other goods in exchange for those that you took or money, and you would close the accounts with the entering in your big Ledger the respective profit or loss item. In this way your business will be clear. If, however, you entrust the trip to some other party, then you should charge this party with all the goods that you entrust with him, saying: Per trip entrusted to so and so, etc., and you should keep an account with him, as if he were one of your customers, for all goods and moneys, keeping separate accounts, etc., and he on his part will set up a little Ledger in which he makes you creditor for everything. When he comes back he will balance with you; and if your traveling salesman were in fetters (sentence remains unfinished in the original)

De 1ª.prita famofa ditta .p e dáno o vero auanci e defauanci.cõe lafabía a tenere vel qder-
no.e pche ella nõ fi metta nel çornale cõme le altre ptite.   Cap°. 27

S Eqta doppo ognialtª ptiª.1ª.chiamata de .p e dáno ovoi dire vtile e dáno feqtr-
o vero auanci e defauaçi fo alcũo paefe ilaqle tutte laltᵉ.del tuo qder² fáp fe bano a faldare cõe nel bilãcio fe dira.E qfta nõ bifogna fimetta i giornale. ma bafta folo nel qder° pch lanafci i qllo dle cofe auáçate o vero mãcate i dare e bére
p laqle dirai .p e danno die dare. E .p e dáno die bére.cioe qdo dalcũa robba bauefe pdu-
to.lacui ptiª.piu nel tuo qderno reftafe i dare cb i bére.aloza aiutarai el fuo bére p pegiar
la al dare acio fe faldi.de ql tanto che li mancafe.dicedo. e die bére p .p e dáno ql q metto
p faldo de qfta.p danno feqto zc.e fegnarai lecarti dl .p e danno nel traz fuoza laptiª.E al
.p e dáno andarai i dare.dicedo .p e dáno die dare a di zc.p latal robba.p danno feqto tanto zc.pofto i qlla.aldie bére p fuo faldo ape acarti zc.E fe la fofe piu i bére ditta robba cb
i dare.aloza farefti plo aduerfo..E cofi andarai facedo a 1ª.p 1ª.de tutte robbe finite. o male o bñ cb fieno andate acio fépze.eltuo qderno fe ritroui paro de ptiᵉ.cioe cb tante fene troui i dare qte i bére.pch cofi fedeue ritrouare a ftar bñ çoe fe dtra nel bilancio. E cofi fuccin-
ta mére vedarai fe guadagni o zo pdi e qto.E qfta ptita. poi ancoza lei fi cõuerra faldare
i qlla del cauedale.laqle e vltia de tutti li qderni.e p cõfeqnte receptaculo d tutte le altᵉ. cõe
itéderai zc.   Comme fe debino repoztare innançe le ptite dl quaderno.qñ foffero pie-
ne e in che luoco fabia poztare el refto.a cio nõ fia pfa malitia nel quaderno. Cap°.   28.

A ncoza e danotare qdo 1ª.ptita e piena.o i dare o i bére che nõ uifinipo metter
piu bifogna poztarla innãçe imediate a tutte laltᵉ.nõ lafciádo fpacio nel qderno
fra el ditto repozto.e laltᵉ.ptiᵉ.cb fe reputaria fraude nel libᵒ.E deuefe repoztare
i qfto modo.cõe difopª.dicémo d faldarle i .p e dáno.cofi neli repozti.iloz mede-
fime cõuiéfe obfuare i dare e i bére feça metterle in çornale pch li repozti nõ bifogna poner-
li i çornale bécb fi potrebbe achi volefe e verria a refpõdere ancoz bñ.ma nõ fa bifogᵒ.pch
fe bería qlla fatica.piu feça frutto.fiche bifogna aiutar la minor qª.cioe fele.piu in dare cb i
bére ditta ptiª.di ql tanto aiuta el fuo bére zc.E p exᵒ.chiaro tenemettaro q 1ª. e mettiamo
che Martino babia fatto cõ teco.cõto lõgo de piu ptiᵉ.i modo.che lafua pofta fia.darepoz-
tare.efia nel tuo qder°.a carti.30.e lultiª.ptitª.de tutto el qder° .fia a carti.60.i çima.e ala medefima façata fia luogo dapoterui ancoza locare qlla de Martᵒ.E fiate dbito el ditto 8. 80
f 15.g.15 p.24.deliqli in tutto te nabía dato.8 72.f 9.g.3.p.17.dico che batta el fuo bére dl
fuo dare.cioe. 72.9.3.17.refta. 8 8 f 6 g.5 p 7.E de tanto lo deui poztar debitoze auanti. E
de qllo medefimo deui aiutare laprita in bére.e dirai cofi.adi zc.p lui medéo ql pozto auanti in qfto aldia dare p refto ql põgo q p faldo.8 8 f 6 g 5 p 7. val a carti.60.8 f g.p.E dpéne-
rai laptiª. in dare e in bére cõ 1ª.linea diametraliter.E fatto qfto andarai a carti.60.in dai
Epozrai ditto refto ponédo fépze difopª.pª.fenõ ci fofe el Mᵒ. cõe dinançe fo ditto.E dirai cofi.Martino die dare a di zc.p lui medemo p refto tratto da dzieto in qfto pofto aldie
bére p faldo d qlla.val acarti.30.8 8 f 6 g 5 p 7.E qfto medefi² modo obfuarai in tutte ptiᵉ
che bauefe a repoztare auanti incatenandole al modo ditto e feça interuallo alcũo.po cb fépze le ptiᵉ.fi vogliano ponere cõe nafcano d luogo.fito.di.e milefi² acio nifũ te pofi calu-
niare.zc.   Del modo a fapere mutare el milefimo nel quaderno fra le partite che ala çor-
nata acafcano.quando ogni anno nõn fi faldafi li libzi.   Capitolo. 29.

P Orria efb aleuolte che nele tue ptite in quaderno. tu bauefi a mutar milefi² E
nõ,bauefe faldato.aloza ditto milefi°.deui ponere in margine ariperto ditra ptita cb cofi e nata.cõe fo detto fopza in cap.15² E tutte laltre che la feqteranno fe
intéderanno al ditto mile² Ma fépze e buono defaldare ognanno.maxime chi
e in cõpª.pche el .puerbio dici ragion fpefa amifta lõga.E cofi farai a tutte fimili.

Comme fe debía leuare vn conto al debitoze chelo domandafe.e ancoza al fuo patrõe
fiando fatoze e commefo de tutta la aminiftratione de le robbe   Capitolo. 30.

B Ifogna oltra li dati documéti.fape leuare vncõtó al tuo debitoze cb te lo domã-
dafe.El qle nõ fi po de ragion negare.pftim qdo cõ teco bauefe tenuto conto
lõgo. de piu anni e mefi zc.aloza farate da prin² cb inficmi bauefe afare.o da altro termine cb lui el volefe qdo fra voi fofero ftati altri faldi da ql tpõ cb lovo-
le per vna volta volentieri li le leua. E de tutto farai vna partita in vn foglio che ui capa.
E qdo in.1ª. facia non capife faldarai tutto quello che li bauerai pofto. e poztcrai cl refto
dalaltro lato del foglio in dare.overo bauere commo nel capitolo.28° fo detto.E va con-
tinuando .E a lultimo.redulo in refto netto duna fola partita in dare. o bauer fecondo
che lanafcera. E quefti tali conti fi vogliano leuare con grandifima diligentía.

CHAPTER 27.

ANOTHER WELL-KNOWN ACCOUNT NAMED PROFIT AND LOSS, OR PROFIT AND DEFICIT. HOW IT SHOULD BE KEPT IN THE LEDGER AND WHY IT IS NOT KEPT IN THE JOURNAL AS THE OTHER ACCOUNTS.

After the other accounts, there must follow one which is named variously, according to different localities, Favor and Damage (*Pro a Danno*), or Profit and Damage (*Utile a Danno*), or Increase and Deficit (*Avanzi e Desavanzi*). Into this other accounts in the Ledger have their remainders, as we will show when we speak of the trial balance. You should not put these entries in the Journal, but only in the Ledger, as they originate from overs or shorts in the debits and credits, and not from actual transactions. You shall open the account this way:

Profit and Loss debit (*dee dare*—shall give), and Profit and Loss credit (*dee havere*—shall have).

That is, if you had sustained a loss in a special line of merchandise and in this account in your Ledger would show less in the credit than the debit, then you will add the difference (*saldo*) to the credit so as to make it balance, and you shall enter as follows:

Credit (*dee havere*—shall have), per Profit and Loss, so much, which I enter here in order to balance on account of loss sustained—and so on, and you will mark the page of the Profit and Loss account where you write down the entry. Then you go to the Profit and Loss account and in the debit column you shall enter as follows:

Profit and Loss debit (*dee dare*—shall give), on this day, to such and such loss sustained, so much—which has been entered in the credit of said merchandise account in order to balance it at page so and so. If the account of this special merchandise would show a profit instead of loss—that is, more in the credit than in the debit—then you will proceed in the opposite way. The same you shall do one by one for all accounts with merchandise or different things, whether they show good or bad results, so that your Ledger always shows the accounts in balance—that is, as much in the debit as in the credit. This is the condition the Ledger will be in if it is correct, as I will explain to you when I am talking of the balance. In this way you will see at a glance whether you are gaining or losing, and how much. And this account must then be transferred for its closing (*saldo*) into the capital account, which is always the last in all the ledgers and is consequently the receptacle of all other accounts, as you will understand.

CHAPTER 28.

HOW FULL ACCOUNTS IN THE LEDGER SHOULD BE CARRIED FORWARD AND THE PLACE TO WHICH THEY MUST BE TRANSFERRED SO THAT NO CROOKEDNESS CAN BE PRACTICED IN THE LEDGER.

You should know that when an account has been filled out, either in the debit or in the credit, and you cannot make any more entries in the space reserved for such an account, you must at once carry this account forward to a page after all your other accounts, so that there is no space left in the Ledger between this transferred account and the last of the other accounts. Otherwise it would be considered a fraud. It must be carried forward in the manner which we have given above when writing about the balancing of profit and loss. In making the transfers, you should make entries on the debit and credit sides only, without making any entry in the Journal. Transfers are not made in the Journal; still, if you so desired, you might do that and it would be all right; but it is not necessary, because it would be that much more trouble without any necessity. All that need be done is to increase the smaller quantity— that is, if the account shows more in the debit than in the credit, you ought to add the difference to the credit. I will give you, now, an example of one of these transfers:

Let us suppose that Martino has had a long account with you of several transactions, so that his account should be transferred from ledger page 30. Suppose further that the last account of your book is at page 60, and is at the top of said page, so that on the same page there is space enough to transfer the Martino account. Suppose that there is on debit side, L 80, S 15, G 15, P 24; and the credit shows that he has given you, L 72, S 9, G 3, P 17. Deducting the credit from the debit, there is a remainder (*resta*) of: L 8, S 6, G 5, P 7. This is the amount that you should bring forward to the debit side of the new page, and on the old page you must add the same amount in the credit column to make it balance, saying as follows:

On such and such day, etc., per himself, I bring forward (*porta avanti*) this amount to the debit side as a remainder (*resta*), and the same amount I enter here per closing (*saldo*), that is: L 8, S 6, G 5, P 7. see at page 60:

L..............., S..............., G..............., P...............

And you shall cancel the account both on the debit and credit side with a diagonal line. After that, you will go to page 60 and shall enter in the debit column the said remainder, always writing down at the top of the page the year, if none already has been mentioned, as has been said above. You shall enter there as follows:

Martino debit on such and such day per himself, as per remainder (*resta*) taken from the page of his old account and therein entered per closing (*saldo*), see page 30:

L 8, S 6, G 5, P 7.

This is the way for you to proceed with all occounts that you should transfer: Place them, as I have told you, without leaving any space in between. The accounts should be opened in the order in which they originate in such place and at such time, so that nobody can speak evil of you.

CHAPTER 29.

HOW TO CHANGE THE YEAR IN THE LEDGER BETWEEN TWO SUCCESSIVE ENTRIES IN CASE THE BOOKS ARE NOT CLOSED EVERY YEAR.

It might be that you must change the year in your ledger accounts before you balance it. In this case, you should write the year in the margin before the first entry of the new year, as has been previously said at Chapter 15; all the following entries should be understood as having occurred during that year.

But it is always good to close the books each year, especially if you are in partnership with others. The proverb says: Frequent accounting makes for long friendship. Thus you will do in similar cases.

CHAPTER 30.

HOW AN ABSTRACT OR STATEMENT OF AN ACCOUNT SHOULD BE MADE TO A DEBTOR WHO MIGHT REQUEST IT, OR FOR YOUR EMPLOYER IN CASE YOU ARE MANAGER OR COMMISSIONER OF THE ADMINISTRATION OF HIS PROPERTY.

In addition, you must know how to make an abstract or a statement of an account if your debtor requests it. This is a favor that cannot be refused, especially if your debtor has had an account with you for years or months, etc. In this case you should go away back to the time when you began to have transactions with him, or back to the time from which he desires to have his statement, in case you have had previous settlements. And you should do this willingly. You should copy all his account on a sheet of paper large enough to contain it all. If it should not be large enough, you will draw a balance at the end of the page and shall carry the latter, in debit or credit, forward to the other side of the sheet, as I told you at Chapter 28. And so on, until the end of the account, and at the end you must reduce the whole account to the net remainder in a single entry in debit or credit, according to the facts. These statements must be made out very carefully.

E qsto modo obfuarai neli fatti tuoi ꝓprij.e tuoi auctori. Ma se tu amiſtraſſe ꝑ altri. ꝑ uia
de acomāde.o de cōmiſiōi.alora ſimilmēte coſi lo leuarai al patrōe cōe q̃ ꝓto lharai poſto
al libro.facēdote creditore de tꝑo i tꝑo dele tuoi ꝓuiſiōi fo vñ patti. E poi i fiñe ꝑ reſto net
to.del ritratto.farate ſuo debitore.o vero creditore q̃do del tuo lihaueſſe meſſo.e lui poi lo re
uedara.pótādolo. cō liſuoi. E trouãdolo ſtar bene.te vorra meglio. E piu te fidara.ꝑ che bi
ſogna che de tutto qllo te a dato o mandato che del reccucre a lſe di tua mano li ne aſegni
amiñiſtrationi ordinatamēte. E po nota bene. E ꝑ lauerſo farai tu leuarlo a tuoi fattori. o
vero cōmeſſi ſimiliter. Ma ꝑ q̃.che foza ſe dieno li conti ſi uogliano ben pontare cō tutte lo
ro ꝑtire i qderno i gioznale e memoriale. E con tutti luoghi che laueſſe ſcritte acio nō naſceſ
ſe errore fra le pti.   Del modo e ordine a ſape retrattare.o vero iſtoznare i ꝑ.o piu ꝑtire
che ꝑ errore haueſſe poſte i altro luogo che doueſſero ādare cōe auene ꝑ ſméoragie. Capo. 21.

Ancoza neceſſario al bon quadernieri ſapere retrattare . o voi dire ſtozna
re ala fiorentina vna partita che per errore hauſſe poſta in altro luogo che el
la doueſſe andare . comme ſe laueſſe meſſa in dare. E douiala ponere in hauere
Et econtra. E quando douia ꝑorla acōto de Martino E lui la miſſe a conto
de guani.et ecōtra.ꝑero che ale volte non ſi po tanto eſſere arento che non ſi falli comme el
pzouerbio ſona. Cioe chi non fa non falla. E chi non falla non impara. E pero inretrat
tarla.tirrai qſto modo. Cioe q̃do haueſſe meſſa laꝑtita.poniamo i dare e douia andare in
haucre ꝑ retrala pozraine i ꝑ.altra.alicontro deſſa i hauere deql tanto de ponto. E dirai in q
ſto modo a di.7c.ꝑ altretanto poſto dincontro al die dare. E doula metterla q i haucre vol
a carti 7c. E tra foza qlle mdeſime.ſ.ſ.g.ꝑ.che poneſti ꝑ erro. E denãçe a ditta ꝑtita farai
i ꝑ.croci.o altro ſegno. acio leuando tu elcóto lauēghi alaſſare. E ſubito poſta qſta ꝑ retrat
to.ch e q̃to ſenulla haueſſe ſcritto del deuere. E tu poi la reponi i ditto hauere cōe douia an
dare eſtara bñ.   Comme ſe debbia fare elbilancio del libro e del modo a repoztare vn
libro in laltzo.cioe elqderno vecchio nel quaderno nuouo e del modo a pontarlo con lo ſuo
gioznale e memoriale e altri ſcontri détro e difuoze del ditto quaderno.   Capo. 22.

Ueſte coſe finoza bé notate biſogna hoza dar modo al repozto de vn libzo in lal
tro.q̃do uoleſſe mutar libro.ꝑ cagione che foſſe pieno o vero ꝑ ordine annuale
de mileſimo cóe el piu ſi coſtuma fare ꝑ luochi famoſi che ogni anno. marime
amileſimi nuoui li gran mercatanti ſépze lo obſuano. E qſto atto inſiemi con li
ſeqñti. E detto elbilancio del libro. Laql coſa voler ſeqre.biſogna grandiſſima diligétia.e ꝑ
ordine tirrai qſto modo.cioe ꝑa.farai de hauere vn cōpagno.che mal pozreſti ꝑ te ſolo far
lo. E alui darai in mano el gioznale ꝑ piu tua cautella. E tu tirrai el qderno grande e dirai
alui gomēçando dala ꝑa.ꝑtita del gioznale che chiami le carti del tuo qderno. doue qlla
ſia poſta.ꝑa.i dare e poi i hauere. E coſi tu lubbidirai. E trouerai ſépze doue te manda. E ql
te dira la ꝑtita de ch o de chi la ſira. E q̃to ſia elſuo tratto foze. E coſi tu vedarai i ql tal luo
go doue te manda.ſe hauerai ql ch.o ql chi. E ql tanto apoato trattto foze. E trouodādola
ſtare aponto cōe i gioznale lancarala.cioe pontazala. overo farai qlche ſegno alibito i ſu le
ſ.o altroue che non te abagliaſſe. E ql tal ſegno o vero lançata che coſi in altri luochi ſi co
ſtuma dir.dirai che faça.elcōpagno nel gioznale.ala medeſima pti ꝑ. E guarda che mai tu ſé
ça lui ne lui ſença te pótaſſe.overo lãçaſſe ꝑtita alcūa pdxe pozrebe naſcere grãdi errozi.po
che la ꝑtita pótata che ſia vol dire ſtar bñ.col debito modo. E qſto ancoza ſe obſua i leuaſ
de contia debitori nançe che li le daghi in mano haueslo ſcōtrato e pontato cō li luochi dl
qderno e del gioznale o daltri luochi che aueſſe notaté ditteꝑtire cōe ſopra al.30.caꝓ fo dt
to. E fatto qſto ꝑ ordine a tutto el qderno e gioznale. E trouando tu aponto cóc lui i dare e
hauere le ꝑtire ſiran giuſte e ben poſte. Nota ch lui nel gioznale ꝑbona memoria fara doi
lançate o vero póti a i ꝑ.ſola ꝑtita. E tu nel qderno uſéi ſolo afarne i ꝑ.ꝑ pti ꝑ. ſi cōe duma pti ꝑ
de gioznale in qderno ſene fa doi coſi ſi fa doi ponti. E po nel pontare del bilancio i giona
le ach e buono far doi póti ſuo ſotto lalt°.ale ſ.o uero doi lãcate i ꝑ.ſotto lalt ꝑ.ch dinoza dit
ta pti ꝑ.ſtar bñ i dare e bére al qderꝓ. Alcūi nel gioznale ꝑ lodare pótano dauãti al.ꝑ. E plo
hauere dzieto ale ſ.cōe ſe ſia lūo e lalt°. ſta bñ. Nō dimeno ſi pozria far ācoza cō i ꝑ.pótatu
ra ſola i gioznale.cioe ſolo ꝑ lo dare.pche tu poi per teſteſſo pozreſti pontare lhauere a qual
partita che hai in dare nel quaderno ſempze te manda per che ſubito tu hai quiui el numero
dele carti doue ſta lhauere quando bene quel del gioznale non te mandaſſe ſiche ſcontran
dote tu con lui ſolo indare per te ſteſſo pozreſti ſequire lo hauere ma piu commodo te ſia cō
lo compagno a modo ditto. Ma ſe fornito el gioznale de pótare a te auancaſe in quaderno
ꝑtita alcūa che non ueniſſe pótata in dare o in hauere denotaria nel quaderno eſſer erroſ.
cioe che qlla ſeraue poſta ſupflua in ql dare o vero hauere.elqual errore tu ſubito retratta

The following is the way you have to proceed in adjusting your own business with the business of your employer. But if you should act for others as an agent or commissioner, then you will make out a statement for your employer just as it appears in the ledger, crediting yourself from time to time with your commissions according to your agreements. Then at the end you shall charge yourself with the net remainder, or you shall credit yourself if you had to put in any money of your own. Your employer will then go through this statement, compare it with his own book, and if he finds it correct, he will like you better and trust you more. For this reason, of all the things that he gave or sent you, you should with your own handwriting keep an orderly account when you receive them. Observe this carefully.

On the contrary, if you are the employer, you may have your managers or commissioners make out these statements for you. But before these statements are delivered they ought to be compared carefully with each entry in the Ledger, Journal and Memorandum Book, or with any other paper relative thereto, so that no mistake could be made between the parties.

CHAPTER 31.

HOW TO TAKE OUT ONE OR MORE ENTRIES WHICH BY MISTAKE YOU MIGHT HAVE ENTERED IN A DIFFERENT PLACE FROM THE RIGHT ONE, WHICH MAY HAPPEN THROUGH ABSENTMINDEDNESS.

The good bookkeeper should also know how to take out—or as they call it in Florence *"stornare"*— an entry which by mistake you might have written down in the wrong place as, for instance, if you had entered it as a debit instead of a credit entry; or when you have to enter it in the account of Mr. Martino and you put it in the account of Mr. Giovanni.

For at times you cannot be so diligent that you are unable to make mistakes. The proverb says: He who does nothing, makes no mistakes: he who makes no mistakes, learns nothing.

And you shall correct this entry as follows: If you had placed this entry in the debit column while you should have put it in the credit column, in order to correct this, you shall make another entry opposite this one in the credit for the same amount. And you shall say thus: On such and such day for the amount which has been entered opposite here under the debit and should have been put in the credit, see page, etc., and you shall write down in the column of figures: L..........S..........G..........P.......... which you wrote down by mistake in the other column. In front of these two entries you shall mark a cross or any other mark so that when you make out an abstract or statement of the account you should leave these entries out. After you have made this correction it is just as if you had written nothing in the debit column. You then make the entry in the credit column as it should have been and everything will be as it should have been.

CHAPTER 32.

HOW THE BALANCE OF THE LEDGER IS MADE AND HOW THE ACCOUNTS OF AN OLD LEDGER ARE TRANSFERRED TO A NEW ONE.

After all we have said you must know now how to carry forward the accounts from one Ledger to another if you want to have a new Ledger for the reason that the old one is all filled up or because another year begins, as is customary in the best known places, especially at Milan where the big merchants renew every year their Ledgers.

This operation, together with the operations of which we will speak, is called the balancing (*bilancio*) of the Ledger, and if you want to do this well you shall do it with great diligence and order. That is, first you shall get a helper as you could hardly do it alone. You give him the Journal for greater precaution and you shall keep the Ledger. Then you tell him, beginning with the first entry in the Journal, to call the numbers of the pages of your Ledger where that entry has been made, first in debit and then in credit. Accordingly in turn you shall obey him and shall always find the page in the Ledger that he calls and you shall ask him what kind of an entry it is, that is, for what and for whom, and you shall look at the pages to which he refers to see if you find that item and that account. If the amount is the same, call it out. If you find it there the same as in the journal, check it (*lanzarala*—mark it with a lance Λ or V) or dot it (*pontarala*), or any proper mark over the lire mark, or in some other place, so that you can readily see it. You ask your helper to make a similar mark or check—as we are used to call it in some places—in the Journal at the same entry. Care must be taken that no entry will be dotted (*pontata*) either by you without him, or by him without you, as great mistakes might be made otherwise, for once the entry is dotted it means that it is correct. The same is done in making out statements of accounts for your debtors before you deliver them. They should have been compared with the Ledger and Journal, or with any other writing in which the entries of the transaction have been recorded, as we have said at Chapter 30.

After you have proceeded in this way through all the accounts of the Ledger and Journal and found that the two books correspond in debit and credit, it will mean that all the accounts are correct and the entries entered correctly. Take care that your helper shall mark each entry in the Journal with two dots or little lances; in the ledger you mark down only one for each entry because you know that for each entry in the journal there are two made in the Ledger, therefore, the two dots or lances.

In making this balance it is good if you mark in the Journal two dots or lances under the lire, one under the other. This will mean that the entry is correct in debit and credit in the Ledger. Some use these marks in the Journal: They put a mark before the per for the debit and after the lire for the credit. Any way both customs are good, however, one single mark in the Journal might be enough, that is, only the debit mark, because you can then mark yourself the credit side on the page of the Ledger where that entry is as this page is mentioned in the debit entry in your ledger. It will then not be necessary for your helper to call to you this credit page. So that by comparing only the debit side with him you could yourself check the credit side. But it would be more convenient for you if you proceed with your helper in the manner above said.

After you have finished checking off the Journal, if you find in the Ledger some account or entry which has not been checked off in debit or credit, this would indicate that there has been some mistake in the Ledger, that is, that that entry is superfluous whether in the debit or credit, and you shall correct this error

rai vaedo lamedefima q̃°.alincontro.cioe fe la fira de piu in dare. Et tu altre tanto porrai in
hauere. Et ecõtra. laq̃lcofa cõe fabia adittare difopra te fo detto al cap°. p̃cedẽte. E cofi ha
rai medicato tutto. El medefimo feria q̃do lui haueffe in giornale ptita fupflua. che a te nel
quaderno mãcaffe in dare o in hauere che pur fallo nel quaderno denotarebbe. El quale fi
deue repare al modo contrario del fupfluo. Cioe che tu aloza ditta ptita fubito lapongbi i
dare e in hauere in quaderno. facendo mẽtione dela varieta del corno. pche lanafcera inol'
to piu tarda in quaderno che nõ douia. Dele quali uarieta.fẽpre elbõ quaderniero deue far
ne mẽtione pche lenafchino p leuar ilfufpetto del lib°. amodo el bon notaro neli fuoi inftru
mẽti. nequali non po ne giongnere ne fminuire fença pticulare mẽtione de tal augumẽto. o
vero decremento. cofi fẽpre tal refpetto cõtie che fia nel bon quadernieri. acio la rialita mer
cantefca. debitamẽte fe venga amantenere. Ma fe la ditta ptita. folo mancaffe dal dare o da
lhauere. aloza bafta la pongbi i°. fola volta. da q̃l tal lato doue lamancaffe. con ditte mentio
ni. Cioe cõe p errore lai fatto ʒc. E cofi harai tutte cuftate tue ptire. lequali trouandole a fol
fcontri cõe e difcorfo denota eltuo quaderno eẽr giufto e ben tenuto. Unde nota che nel dit
to quaderno firãno aleuolte molte ptite non pontate con lo fcontro del giozrnale p chenon
fi bano aritrouare ineffo. E q̃fte firanno li refti pofti al die dare. o in hauere p faldi dele p /
tite nel portarle hauanti cõe dicẽmo in lo cap°.28. aloza da te fteffo di q̃lli tali refti trouerai
i. ditto q̃derno fuoi fcontri. cioe in dare. E in hauere. recẽdote p lo n°. de le carti cb ila ditta
ptita notate firãno. E trouãdo fcontro a fuoi luogbi cudica fimilmẽte elq̃derno ftar bñ ʒc.
E q̃llo che finoza fe detto del fcõtro del quaderno con lo giozrnale. el fimile intẽdi p°. douerfi
fare del memoriale ó uero fquartafoglió cõ logiozrnale a di p di. q̃do vfaffi tener memoria
le a modo che in principio di q̃fto trattato de lui te dixi. e cofi cõ tutti altri libri teneffe. Ma
lultimo conuen effere elquaderno. elo penultimo el giozrnale. Ideo ʒc.

Del modo e ordine afcriuere lefacende che occureffero nel tempo che fi fa elbilancio. cioe
che fi faldano li libri. e comme neli libri uechi nõ fi debia fcriuere ne innouare cofa alcuna
in ditto tempo e lacagione perche.   Cap°.   33.

⟦T⟧Utte q̃fte cofe ordinatamente fatte e obferuate. guarda non innouaffe piu pti°
in alcũ libro antiano al quaderno. cioe immemoziale. E giozrnale. perche el faldo
tutto de tutti li libri fẽpre fi deue intendere fatto in i°. medefimo corno Ma fe fa
cende te acadeffe in q̃l mecço che fai el tuo faldo o vero bilancio. porrale in libri
nuoui nequali intẽdi fare reporto. cioe in lomemoziale o vero giozrnale. ma nõ in quaderno
p fin tanto che non li hai portati li refti del p° quaderno. E fe ancoza non haueffe ordinati
libri nuoui porraile facẽde con li fuoi corni dapte in i°. ffoglio p fin firan fatti ditti libri. E
aloza li leporrai. fignati che firan tutti de nuouo fegno. Cioe fe q̃lli che faldi firã fegnati. cro
ci q̃fti fegna de. A. ʒc.   Cõme fe debiano faldare tutte leptite del q̃derno vecbio. e i chi
e pche: e de la ffima fũmarũ del dare e delauere vltio fcontro del bilãcio.   Cap°. 34.

⟦F⟧Atto cb harai q̃fto cõ dilegẽtia. E tu date faldarai tutto eltuo q̃derno aptita p
pti°. i q̃fto modo. cb p°. comẽçarai dalacaffa debitori. robbe e auentori. E quelle
portarai in libro. A. cioe in quaderno nuouo che non bifogna cõe fo detto difo
pra lirefti ponere ingiozrnale. fummarai tutte loz ptite in dare e hauere aiutãdo
fẽpre lamenoze cõe te diti. fopra del portare auãti. che q̃fto atto de i° quaderno in laltro. E
de põto fimile aq̃llo e fra lozo non e altra differentia fenon che in q̃llo elrefto fi porta auan
ti nel medefimo quaderno. E in q̃fto de i° libro in laltro. E doue in q̃llo chiamati le carti ð
q̃l libro. pprio in q̃fto fichiama lecarti del libro fequẽte in modo che nel reporto de vn libro
in laltro. folo i°. uolta p ciafciõ quaderno fe mette laptita. E q̃fta progatiua a lultima ptita
fempre deli quaderni che nullaltra mai po hauere cõe nel pceffo dato hai notato. E deueffe
tal riporto cofi ditare. cioe mettiamo che tu habia. Martino debitore p refto nello tuo qua
dernó. croci. a carti. 60. de. 8 12. f 15. g 10. p 26. E habilo a portare in quaderno. A. a carti. 8:
in dare te conuen nel libro croci. aiutare lhauere. doue dirai cofi defotto a tutte laltre partite
E a di ʒc. ponẽdo fempre el medefimo di. che fai elbilancio. p lui medemo porto in quader
no. A. aldie dare per refto qual q̃ põgo per faldo de questa val acarti. 8. 8 12. f 15. g 10. p 26
E depennarai la ditta partita in dare e hauere diametraliter cõe nel reporto te infegnai po
nẽdo laffima de tutta laptita fotto nel cãpo de ditta ptita in dare e in hẽre. cioe tãto da lũo
lato q̃to da lalt°. acio pa a lochio fubito ftar bñ e iq̃le cõe fe recerca al bõ faldo. ponẽdo nel
trar foza. el numero dele carti del quaderno. A. doue tal refto porti. E poi in lo quaderno.
A. in dare dirai cofi prima ponendo fopra incima de la carta. el fuo milefimo. El giorno ne
la partita per lacafone detta fopra iu lo cap. 15°. cioe Martino deltale ʒc. die dare a di. ʒc. p

by making an entry for the same amount in the opposite side—that is, if the superfluous entry was in the debit, you make an entry on the credit side, or *vice versa*. And how you should proceed to correct the error I have told you in the preceding chapter. The same would be done in case your helper finds some entry which your ledger did not show whether in the debit or credit column, which also would indicate an error in the ledger and should be corrected in a different way. That is, you should make that entry or open that account in the debit or credit, mentioning the different dates, as the entry would be made later than it should have been. A good bookkeeper should always mention why such differences arise, so that the books are above suspicion; thus the notary public in his instruments need not mention what has been added or omitted. Thus the good bookkeeper must act so that the mercantile reputation be kept up.

But if the said entry should have been entered on only one side, debit or credit, then it would be sufficient for you to put it where it is missing, mentioning how it happened through mistake, etc. So you will go on through all your accounts and, if they agree, you know that your Ledger is right and well kept.

You must know that there may be found in the Ledger some entries which are not in the Journal and cannot be found in the Journal. These are the difference between the debit and credit placed there to close (*per saldi*) the different accounts when they are carried forward, as we have said in Chapter 28. Of these balances or remainders, you will find their correlative entries in the Ledger, whether in debit or credit, on the page indicated in these accounts. When you find each correlative entry in its proper place, you may conclude that your Ledger is in proper order.

What we have said so far about comparing the Ledger with the Journal, should be observed also in comparing the memorandum book or scrap book with the Journal, day by day, if you use the memorandum book, in the manner I spoke about at the beginning of this treatise. If you have other books, you should do the same. The last book to be compared should be the Ledger, the next to the last the Journal.

CHAPTER 33.

HOW THE TRANSACTIONS WHICH MIGHT OCCUR WHILE YOU BALANCE YOUR BOOKS SHOULD BE RECORDED, AND HOW IN THE OLD BOOKS NO ENTRY SHOULD BE MADE OR CHANGED DURING THAT TIME, AND REASONS WHY.

After you have regularly done and observed all these things, see that no new entry is made in any book which comes before the Ledger—that is, in the memorandum book and Journal—because the equalizing or closing (*el saldo*) of all the books should be understood to take place on the same day. But if, while you are balancing you books, some transactions should occur, you shall enter them in the new books to which you intend to carry forward the old ones—that is, in the memorandum book or Journal, but not in the Ledger, until you have carried forward all the different accounts of the old Ledger. If you have not yet a new set of books, then you will record these transactions and their respective explanations on a separate sheet of paper until the books are ready. When the new books are ready, you enter them in these books which shall bear new marks—that is, if the old ones that you are balancing now were marked with a cross, then you should mark these new ones with the capital letter A.

CHAPTER 34.

HOW ALL THE ACCOUNTS OF THE OLD LEDGER SHOULD BE CLOSED AND WHY. ABOUT THE GRAND TOTALS OF THE DEBITS AND CREDITS, WHICH IS THE PREPARATION OF THE TRIAL BALANCE.

After you have done this carefully, you shall close your Ledger accounts in this way: You should commence first with cash account, then the different debtors, then the merchandise, and then your customers. Transfer the remainders in Ledger A, that is, in the new Ledger. You should not, as I have said above, transfer the remainders in the new Journal.

You shall add all the different entries in debit and in credit, always adding to the smaller side the difference, as I have told you above when explaining the carrying forward of the remainder. These two accounts are practically the same thing; the only difference is that in the first case the remainder was carried forward to another page of the same Ledger, while in this instance it is carried forward from one Ledger to another. While in the first instance you would mark down the new page of the same Ledger, in this case you mark down the page of the new Ledger; making the transfer from one ledger to another, any account should appear only once in each ledger. This is a peculiarity of the last entry of the accounts of the Ledgers.

In making the transfer, you should proceed as follows: Let us suppose that the account of Mr. Martino has a debit remainder (*resto*) in your "Cross" Ledger at page 60 of   L 12, S. 15, G 10. P. 26, and you want to transfer it to Ledger A at page 8 in debit; in the "Cross" Ledger you have to add to the credit column and you shall put the following at the end of all the other entries: On such and such day—putting down always the same day in which you do the balancing (*bilancio*)—per himself as posted to Ledger A to the debit, per remainder (*resto*), which amount I add here in order to close (*saldo*)— value; see page 8:   L 12, S 15, G 10, P 26.

And then you shall cancel the account in the debit and credit diagonally, as I have told you in talking about the bringing forward of the accounts. Then put down the total of all the entries, in the debit as well as in the credit, so that the eye can see at a glance that it is all even. You shall also write down at the new page in Ledger A, in the debit column, as follows: First you put down at the top of the page the year, and you put the day in front of the place where you make the entry for the reason mentioned in Chapter 15, then you say, Mr. Martino so and so, debit (*dee dare*—shall give) on such and such day

lui medemo p̄ resto tratto del libro.croci.posto al die hauere per saldo de q̄lla.val a car. 60.
8 12.ß 15.g̃° 10.p̄ 26.E cosi andarai saldãdo tutte le prtite nel lib°.croci.cb̃ tu intẽdi portare
i q̄derno. A. de cassa.cauedal.robbe mobili. e stabil.debitori.creditori.officii.sensarie. pesa̅
dori de comun 7c. con liquali se vsa ale uolte andare aconto lõgo 7c. Ma quelle partite
che non uolesse portare in ditto quaderno. A. che porriẽno eẽre q̄lle che solo a te sapregga̅
no. E nõ se obligato a segnarne cõto ad alcu? cõe son spesi de mercãtia.spesi de casa intrata
isita.e tutte spese straordinarie.fitti.pescõi.feudi. o liuelli 7c.q̄ste simili conuẽgonse saldare
in lo medesimo libro.croci.nela prita del p̄ e danno o vero anãçi e desauãçi o voi dire vti̅
le e dãno.i q̄sto modo che loro dare portarai i dare cb̃ raro si possano hauere i credito q̄lle
de le spesi dicẽdo.nel saldo aiutando cõe piu volte e ditto sẽpre la menore quantita in dare
o i hauere p̄ p̄ c dãno i q̄sto a carti tãte 7c. E cosi tutte le hauerai saldate i q̄sta del p̄ e dan
no doue subito poi sũmando suo dare e hauere porrai cognescere tuo guadag̃°.e pdita p̄ cb̃
sira i tal bilancio fatto la parita.cioc cb̃ le cose cb̃ se douiã diffalcare siran diffalcate q̄lle che
se douiano agiongnere sirã pporzionatamẽte a suoi luochi agiõte.E se de q̄sta prtita.sira p̄
el dare cb̃ lauere tu hauera pdutto q̄l tanto i tuo trafico dache lo gomẽçasti. E se sia piu lo
hauere aloza dirai che q̄l tanto habia i ditto tpo guadagnato 7c. E veduto cb̃ harai p̄ q̄sta
lutile.e danno tuo seq̄to.aloza q̄sta saldarai i laprita del cauedale.doue nel prici pio del tuo
manegio ponesti lo iuẽtario de tutta la tua faculta. E saldarala i q̄sto modo chesel dãno se
q̄to sira piu che dio ne guardi ciascuno che realmẽte fo buon xp̄iano se adopa aloza aiuta̅
rai lohauere amodo vsato dicẽdo e a di 7c. p̄ cauedal i q̄stop̄ danno seq̄to a carti 7c.val 7c.
E depẽnerai laprtita diametraliter i dare e hauere.vt su³.ponẽdo pure la sũma nel cãpo i da
re e hauere che deue battere para.E poi ala prtita del cauedale i dare dirai.cauedale die dar
a di 7c.p̄ p̄ e danno. p̄ danno seq̄to posto in quella al die hauere p̄ saldo suo val a carti 7c.
8.ß.g̃° p̄.7c. E cosi sene fosse seq̄to vtile.cb̃ serebbe q̄do q̄lla del p̄ e danno se retrouasse piu
i hauere che i dare aloza sugiõgiaresti al dare p̄ saldo q̄l tanto chiamãdo elcauedale ale car
ti suoi 7c.e alui la porresti i hauere isiemi cõ laltre robbe mobili e stabili.e di nuouo i q̄sto ca
uedal q̄le cõuiẽ eẽre sẽpre lulti³.prtita o tutti liq̄derni.porrai sẽpre cognoscere tutta tua facul
ta.giõgnẽdo li debiti e crediti che in lib°. A. portasti 7c. E q̄sta del cauedal del q̄derno. cro
ci saldarai ancora. E portarala cõe laltre nel q̄derno. A. in resto e sũma o voi a prtita p̄ pri
ta che lo poi anche fare.ma si costuma farla in sũma pche i³.volta tutto tuo iuẽtario ape. E
recordate chiamai sue carti.7c. E affetarai poi tutte leprite ol q̄derno. A.ne lalfabeto ognu
na al suo luogo cõe disopra te dissi.cap? 5°. Acio sẽpre possi cõ facilita trouare le tue facẽde
secondo loro occurenze e cosi fia saldo tutto el primo quaderno con suo giornale e memori
ale. E acio sia piu chiaro de ditto saldo.farai questo altro scontro. Cioe summarai in vn fo̅
glio tutto eldare del quaderno.croci. E ponlo a man sinistra.E summarai tutto suo hauere
E põlo aman dextra. E poi queste vltime summe resummarai. E farane de tutte quelle
del darvna sũma che si chiamara sũma sũmarũ. E cosi farai vna sũma o tutte q̄lle dalauer
che si chiamara ancora lei vna sũmasũmarũ. Ma lap³.sira sũma summarũ.del dare e la fa̅
si chiama summasũmarũ de lo hauere. Or se q̄ste doi sũme summarũ sirã pare.cioe che tan
to sia luna q̄to laltra.vz q̄lla del dare.e q̄lla delo hauere.arguirai el tuo q̄derno eẽre bẽ gui
dato tenuto e saldato p̄ la cagiõe cb̃ disopra nel cap? 14.fo detto. Ma se luna o ditte sum
me summarũ auançasse laltra denotarebbe erro nel tuo quaderno.el qual poi con diligẽtia
ti cõuerra trouarlo cõ la industria olo irelletto che dio teha dato.e cõ lartefitio dele ragio
ni che harai bene inparato.laqual prte cõe nel prici pio del pñte dicemoe summamẽte neces
sarià albon mercatante altramente non siando bon ragioneri neli soi fatti andara a rastõi
cõe ciecho. E poralline seq̄re molto dãno.adonca cõ ogni studio e cura sforçarati sopra tut
to eẽre buõ ragioneri chel modo a tua cõmodita in q̄sta sublima opa a pieno a tua bastan
ça.te lo dato con tutte sue regole a tutti suo luoghi debitamente poste.si cõe tutto facilmẽte
per la tauola nel principio di q̄sta opera posta porraitrouare. E ancora p̄ le cose dette q̄ se
quente cõme disopra nel cap?.12° te pmisi a piu tuo recordo faro 1°.epilogo.cioe sumaria
recolta cẽntiale de tutto el pñte trattato.che molto sença dubio te fia vtile. E p̄ me recorda
rati laltrissimo p̄gare che a sue laude e gloria. Io possa de bene i meglio opãdo p̄cedere 7c.

Del modo e ordine a sap tener le scripture menute cõe sõno scritti de mano lettere fami̅
liari.poliçe.pceffi snie e altri istrumẽti e del registro de le lre.iportãi. Ca? 35

E quita el modo e ordine de saper tener le scripture e chiarecçe menute comme
sonno scritti de mano de pagamenti facti quietançe de cambi.de robbe date.let
tere familiari.quali cose sonno fra mercanti de grãdissima stima.e molta impoz

per himself as per remainder (*resto*) carried from "Cross" Ledger, which has been added in the credit column in order to close (*saldo*), see page 60, value: L 12, S 15, G 10, P 26.

Thus you will proceed with all the accounts of the Cross Ledger which you want to transfer to Ledger A: cash account, capital account, merchandise, personal property, real property, debtors, creditors, public officers, brokers, public weighmen, etc., with whom we have sometimes very long accounts. But as to those accounts which you should not care to transfer to Ledger A, as, for instance, your own personal accounts of which you are not obliged to give an account to another, as, for instance, small mercantile expenses, household expenses, income and expenses and all extraordinary expenses—rentals, *pescioni, feudi* or *livelli*, etc. All these accounts should be closed (*saldore*) in the Cross Ledger into the favor and damage account, or increase and deficit, or profit and damage account, as it is sometimes called. You shall enter them in the debit column, as it is rare that these expense accounts should show anything in the credit side. As I often have told you, add the difference to the column, either debit or credit, which shows a smaller total, saying: Per profit and loss in this account, see page, etc. By doing so, you shall have closed (*saldore*) all these different accounts in the profit and loss account through which then, by adding all the debit and all the credit entries, you will be able to know what is your gain or loss, for with this balance all entries are equalized; the things that had to be deducted were deducted, and the things that had to be added were added proportionately in their respective places. If this account shows more in the debit than in the credit, that means that you have lost that much in your business since you began. If the credit is more than the debit, that means that in the same period of time you have gained.

After you know by the closing (*saldorai*) of this account what your profit or loss is, then you shall close this account into the capital account in which, at the beginning of your management of your business, you entered the inventory of all your worldly goods. You shall close the account in this way: If the losses are in excess—from which state of affairs may God keep every one who really lives as a good Christian— then you have to add to the credit in the usual manner, saying: On such and such day, Per capital on account of losses in this account, see page so and so, value, etc. Then you shall cancel the account with a diagonal line in debit and credit, and put in the total amount of all the debit entries, as well as of the credit entries, which should be equal. And then in the capital account, you shall write in the debit column: Capital debit (*dee dare*—shall give) on such and such day, per profit and loss account on account of losses as marked down in the credit column of said account in order to close (*per saldo*), value, etc.:

L............, S............, G............, P............

If instead there should be a profit, which will happen when the profit and loss account would show more in the credit than in the debit, then you should add the difference to the debit side to make the equalization, referring to the capital account and respective page. You should credit the same amount to the capital account, making the entry on the credit side where all the other goods of yours have been entered, personal or real. Therefore, from the capital account, which always must be the last account in the entire Ledger, you may always learn what your fortune is, by adding together all the debits and all the credits, which you have transferred in Ledger A.

Then this capital account should be closed and carried forward with the other accounts to Ledger A, either in total or entry by entry. You can do either way, but it is customary to transfer only the total amount, so that the entire value of your inventory (*inventario*) is shown at a glance. Don't forget to number the pages, after which you will enter all the different accounts in the alphabet of Ledger A, each at its own place, as I have said at Chapter 5, so that you may find very easily the account you want. In this way the entire first Ledger, and with it the Journal and memorandum book, are closed and closed up.

In order that it may be clearer that the books were correct before the said closing, you shall summarize on a sheet of paper all the debit totals that appear in the Cross Ledger and place them at the left, then you shall write down all the credit totals at the right. Of all these debit totals you make one sum total which is called grand total (*summa summarum*), and likewise you shall make a sum total of all the credit totals, which is also called grand total (*summa summarum*). *The* first is the grand total of the debits, and the second is the grand total of the credits. Now, if these two grand totals are equal—that is, if one is just as much as the other—that is, if those of the debit and those of the credit are alike—then you shall conclude that your Ledger was very well kept and closed, for the reason that I gave you in Chapter 14. But if one of the grand totals is bigger than the other, that would indicate a mistake in your Ledger, which mistake you will have to look for diligently with the industry and the intelligence God gave you and with the help of what you have learned. This part of the work, as we said at the beginning, is highly necessary to the good merchant, for, if you are not a good bookkeeper in your business, you will go on groping like a blind man and may meet great losses.

Therefore, take good care and make all efforts to be a good bookkeeper, such as I have shown you fully in this sublime work how to become one. I have given you all the rules and indicated the places where everything can be found, in the table of contents which I have placed at the beginning of this work.

Of all the things thus far treated, as I promised you in Chapter 12, I will now give you a summary of the most essential things for your own recollection, which no doubt will be very useful to you.

And remember to pray God for me so that to His praise and glory I may always go on doing good.

CHAPTER 35.

HOW AND IN WHAT ORDER PAPERS SHOULD BE KEPT, SUCH AS MANUSCRIPTS, FAMILY LETTERS, POLICIES, PROCESSES, JUDGMENTS AND OTHER INSTRUMENTS OF WRITING AND THE RECORD BOOK OF IMPORTANT LETTERS.

Here follow the manner and rules for keeping documents and manuscripts, such as papers relative to payments made, receipts for drafts, or gifts of merchandise, confidential letters, which things are very important for merchants

tança.e de gran pericolo in perderle e smarrirle.E prima. dele lettere familiari quali spesso fra te e li toi auetori possano acadere. queste sepre stendi e serba in vn banchetto ala fin del mese.E finito elmese legale invn maço.e ripolle daparte segnando ognuna defore cioe che la receui el di che li respondi.E cosi si fa amese p mese.E poi ala fin de lanno de tutti qlti maç di farai vn maço grade e luoga e segna suo ano? E qdo voi alcuna lra a ql ricorri. hauerai i tuo studio overo scritoio vna tasca.nela ql reporrai lre cb li amici te deskero.cb tu co letuoi mandasse aloza.fedici che lamandi a roma. mettila in tasca di roma.e se a firença in qlla defi rença ꝛc.E poi nel spaciare del fante pigliale con le tuoi al tuo respódente in quel tal luogo lemanda.pcbe el scriure sempre e buono e anche susa dar suo beueragio per cer seruito ꝛc. atorno esso cinta côprita côe si fa i piu taschette.cioe in tante ꝗte sonno le terre e luogbi in le quali fai le toe facéde côe diciamo. Roma. Firéçe: Napoli.Milano. Zenoa. Lion. Londra Bruça ꝛc.E sopra ditte taschette p ordine scriuerai ilsuo nome.cioe a luna dirai Roma.alal tra. Firéça ꝛc.in le quali poi reporrai le lre che p qlli luogbi te fossero mandate da qualcb aico che lamandasse.E fatta che li harai resposta e mandata.pure in ditta lra de sora. côe fe sti del suo receuere.e p cbi.Cosi similiter porrai mentione de la respesta. E pcbi la mandasti con lo suo giorno.El qual di mai in alcu².tua facenda fa che màcbi. o piccola o grade cb la sia maxime in lre in le qli sepre si deue porre ilmilesimo el di.e luogo.el nome tuo elqual no me si costuma mettarlo da pede aman dextra de la lra in vn câtone.el di°. cô lo di e luogo fra mercatantise usa ponere disopra nel principio dela lra.Lra p².a modo bon xpiano ha rai sepre amete de ponere el glorioso nome de nra salute.cioe el doci nome de yhu.overo in suo scâbio la figura de la sca croci.nel cui nome sep tutte le nre orationi debano eer princi piate.E farai cosi croci. 1494.a di.17.aprile i vinegia.E poi seqta tuo dire. cioe carissimo ꝛc. ma li studiâti e altre genti côe sonno religiosi ꝛc.che non traficano. vsano nel luogo do ue lalettera e fatta poner di sotto con lo di e ano°.E li mercáti costumano disopra a modô ditro alt².mente non vi ponendo el di scrbe confusione. E di te scria fatto beffe pcbe seoid la lra che non ha el di notato cbe le fatta de notte.E qlla che non a notato el luogo se dici che le fatta i lalt°.môdo.e non in qsto.e oltra le beffe cbe pegio e ne seque scondalo ut dira. Expedita che harai sua resposta.poscia al deputato luogo la poni côe hai iteso.E qsto che ditto habiamo de v.sola itédilo p tutte. Unde e ancora danotare cbe qdo le lre cbe tu mâ di fossero de ipoztança.qlle tale se vogliano p² registrarle in vn libzo da pte solo a qsto depu tato.nel ql registro si deue ponere la lra de verbo ad verbü sella sia ò grande iportâça côe sonno lre de cambio.o de robe mandate o ò. ꝛc.o vero re gistrare solo la substança.côe me moriale dicédo i qsto di ꝛc.habiamo scritto altal ꝛc.côe p lo tale ꝛc.limandamo le tal co se ꝛc.Fo p iꝝ.sua de di tanti ꝛc.ci cômise e richiese ꝛc.la qual ponémo in tasca ꝛc. E di fuoze sigilata cbe harai la tua cbe mâdi e fatto la sopra scritta susa. p molti ponerui el suo segno di fuoze.acio si cognosca cbe fia de mercanti.a iquali molto se deue hauere riguardo.p cbe son qlli côe i pricipio di qsto trattato dicemo che mantégano le repub. E a qsto fine dereue uerentia el simile li Rmi.Cardinali.pongano defore ellozo distito nome.acio nisü se possi scu sare de non sape de cbi.la fosse. E molto piu aptamete el sancto padre fa le sue patetemete apte côe sono bolle breuilegi ꝛc. Auega che alcune cose piu itrisecbe.póga sotto el sigillo di pescatoze ꝛc.Legli lre poi a mese p mese o vero anno p anno recorrai i maçgi. overo filçe e da pte le poni ordinatamete i vno armaro.o sularetto.securo.E côe nascano ala çoznata co si la setta.acio possi piu psto a tue occurece retrouarle ò laqlcosa.nô curo piu dire pcb lo aba stança mai inteso ꝛc.   Scritti de mano nô pagati de tuoi debitozi côme te acénai disopra nel cap°.17.seruarai in vn altro luogo piu secreto côe son cassi e scatole priuate ꝛc.E leqetâ çe similiter.serua in luogo securo p ogni respetto.Ma qdo tu pagasse tu ad altri elriceure faralo scriuere iꝓ libretto de pagaméti côe in pricipio te dixi.acio nô si possa cosi facilméte smartre e pdere.E cosi obseruarai de le pollice che iportano. côe sôno notole de sensaria ò mercati.o de pesadozi o bolette ò robbe messe o tratte de dogane damare o da terra e setéçe o cartuline de côsoli o altri officii o altri istruméti de notari i pgamena qli se debano repoz re i vn luogo da pte.E cosi copie scritture e pcessi delite de pcuratori.E auocati. E similme te e buono hauere vn lib°.sepato pli recordi.cbe si chiami recordâçe nel ql ala çoznata farai le tue memozie dele cose.cbe dubitasse nô recordarte.cbe te pozie toznar dâno.nel ql ogni o al manco la sera nançe vadi adozmire darai ochio.se cosa fosse daspedire o dafare cbe non fusse expedita ꝛc.alaql spaçata darai de pêna. E cosi ꝗ farai memozia de cose cbe al vicino e amico p vno o doi di pstasse côe sonno vasa de botegga caldare e altri ozdegna ꝛc.E quest

and, if they are lost, may cause great danger.

First, we shall talk of confidential letters which you may write to or receive from your customers. You should always keep these in a little desk until the end of the month. At the end of the month tie them together in a bunch and put them away and write on the outside of each the date of receipt and the date of reply, and do this month by month, then, at the end of the year, of all these papers make one big bundle and write on it the year, and put it away. Any time you need a letter, go to these bundles.

Keep in your desk pouches in which to place the letters that your friends may give you to be sent away with your own letters. If the letter should be sent to Rome, put it in the Rome pouch, and if to Florence, put it in the Florence pouch, etc. And then when you send your messenger, put these letters with yours and send them to your correspondent in that particular town. To be of service is always a good thing, and it is customary also to give a gratuity for that good service.

You should have several little compartments, or little bags, as many as there are places or cities in which you do business, as, for instance, Rome, Florence, Naples, Milan, Genoa, Lyon, London, Bruges, and on each little bag you shall write its proper name—that is, you will write on one "Rome," on another "Florence," etc., and in these bags you shall put the letters that somebody might send you to be forwarded to those places.

When you have answered a letter and sent the answer away, you shall mention on the outside of the said letter the answer, by whom you sent it and the day, just as you did when you received the letter.

As to the day, you shall never forget to mark it in any of your transactions, whether small or large, and especially in writing letters in which these things must be mentioned, namely: the year, the day, the place, and your name. It is customary to put the name at the end of the right side in a corner. It is customary among merchants to write the year and the day and the place at the top at the beginning of the letter. But first, like a good Christian, you shall always remember to write down the glorious name of our Savior—that is, the name of Jesus, or in its place the sign of the Holy Cross, in whose name our transactions must always be made, and you shall do as follows: Cross 1494. On this 17th day of April in Venice.

And then go on with what you want to say—that is, "My very dear," etc. But the students and other people, like the monks or priests, etc., who are not in business, are used to writing the day and year at the end after writing the letter. The merchants are accustomed to put at the top as we have said. If you should do otherwise and not write the day, there will be confusion and you will be made fun of because we say the letter which does not bear the day was written during the night, and the letter which does not bear the place we say that it was written in the other world, not in this one; and besides the fun made of you, there would be vexations, which is worse, as I have said.

After you have sent your answer away, you put your letter in its proper place; and what we have said of one letter will apply to all the other letters. It must be observed that when the letters you send away are of importance, you should first make a record of them in a book which is kept for this special purpose. In this book the letter should be copied, word for word, if it is of great importance—as, for instance, the letters of exchange, or letters of goods sent, etc., otherwise only a record of the substantial part should be made similarly as we do in the memorandum book, saying: On this day, etc., we have written to so and so, etc., and we send him the following things, etc., as per his letter of such and such date he requested or gave commission for, etc., which letter we have placed in such and such pouch.

After you have sealed the letter on the outside and addressed it, it is the custom of many to mark on the outside your special mark, so that they may know that it is correspondence of a merchant, because great attention is given to merchants, for they are the ones, as we said at the beginning of this treatise, who support our republics.

For this purpose, the Most Reverend Cardinals do likewise, by writing their name on the outside of their correspondence so that nobody could claim as an excuse that he did not know from whom it was. The correspondence of the Holy Father remains open so that its contents may be known, like bulls, privileges, etc., although for things which are more personal or confidential the seal representing the Fisherman (*Pescatore*—St. Peter) is used to seal them.

All these letters, then, month by month, year by year, you shall put together in a bundle and you will keep them in an orderly way in a chest, wardrobe or cupboard. As you receive them during the day, put them aside in the same order, so that if necessary you might find them more easily; and I won't talk any longer about this, as I know that you have understood it.

You shall keep in a more secret place, as private boxes and chests, all manuscripts of your debtors who have not paid you, as I said in Chapter 17. Likewise keep the receipts in a safe place for any emergency. But when you should pay others, have the other party write the receipt in a receipt book, as I told you at the beginning, so that a receipt cannot be easily lost or go astray.

You shall do the same as to important writing, as, for instance, memoranda of the brokers, or of merchants, or of weighmen, or relative to goods placed in or taken out of the custom house, either land or sea custom houses, and judgments or decrees of the consuls or of other public officials, or all kinds of notarial instruments written on parchments which ought to be kept in a place apart. The same should be said of the copies of instruments and papers of attorneys or counselors at law relative to lawsuits.

It is also wise to have a separate book for memoranda, which we call memoranda book, in which day by day you shall keep a record of the things that you might be afraid of forgetting and, if you forget them, may prove to be dangerous to you. Every day, the last thing in the evening, just before going to bed, you shall glance over this book to see whether everything which should have been done has been done, etc., and you shall cancel with your pen the things that have been done, and in this book you shall make a record of the things that you have lent to your neighbor or friend for one or two days, as, for instance, store vases, caldrons, or any other thing.

ſimili documēti con gli altri vtiliſſimi ſopra dati reporrai ʒč.piu e māco çonçando eſiminu
endo ſo luogbi e tpi a te per tuo.ingegno parera.pero cB non e poſſibile apieno de tutto a
ponto per ponto i mercātia dare norma.e notitia pocB cōme altre uolte ſe dittovol piu pōti
afare 1°. mercatāte cbe un dottore deleggi.Jdeo ʒč.Coſe cB finora ſōno dette.ſe bñ laprēdø
rai ſon certo i tutte tue facéde bñ te reggiarai.mediāte el tuo peregrino ingegno ʒč.

Summario de regole E modi ſopra il tenere vno libro di mercanti.   Cap°. 36.

   Tutti li creditori ſi debono mettere al libro dala tua mano deſtra.E li debitori dala tua
mano ſiniſtra. Tutte le prite cbe ſe metteno allib° bano a eēre doppie:cioe ſe tu fai vno cre
ditore al ſi fare 1°.debitore.Ciaſcūa prita coſi i dare cōe i bēre Obbe cōtenere iſe.3.coſe cioe
ilgiorno del pagamēto.La ſōma del pagamēto.E la cagiōe del pagamēto.   Lultimo
nome dela prita del debito debbe eēre il prio della prita del credito.   Jn qllo medeſimo
giorno cbe e ſcritta la prita del debito. i qllo medeſimo giorno debbe eēre qlla del credito.

   Lo bilancio del lib° ſintēde 1° foglio piegato p lo lōgo ſul qle dala mano deſtra ſi copiāo
li creditori del lib°.e dala ſiniſtra li debitori.E vedeſe ſe laſūma del dare e qʒtō qlla de laue
re.E alloza il lib°.ſta bene.   El bilaucio del libro debbe eēre pari.cioe cbe tanto debbe eēr
la ſūma non dico de creditori.ne debitori.QĐa dico la ſūma del credito qʒto la ſūma del de
bito.E nō eēndo ſaria errore nel libro.   El conto di caſſa conuiene cbe ſepre ſia debitrice.
overamēte pari. E ſe altrimēte fuſſe ſaria errore nellibro.   Aon ſi debbe e non ſipuo fare
1°.debitore al libro ſença liceça e uolūta di qllo tale cba aeēre debitore e ſe pure ſi faceſſe ql
la ſcrittura ſeria falſa He ſimilmēte non ſi puo porre neppati ne conditioni a. 1° credito ſē
ça liceça e volonta del creditore.E ſe pure ſi faceſſe qllaſcrittura ſaria falſa. El lib°.conuie
ne cbe ſia tutto tratto fuori a 1ª.medeſima mōeta.QĐa dētro poi bñ noiare qllo cB a cadeſ
ſe o duč.o ß.o fiorini.o ſcudi doro.o qllo cbe fuſſi QĐa nel trarre fuori conuiene cbe ſia tut
to a 1ª.medeſima moneta cōe principiaſti illib°.coſi conuiene ſeguire.   La prita del debito.
o del credito cbe ſi fa i conto de caſſa ſi puo abreuiare cbi vuole.cioe ſença dire lacagione ſo
lamēte dire da tale di tale.ó a tale di tale.pcbe la cagione ſi uiene a dicbiarar nella prita op
poſita. Ibauēdo a fare 1°.cōto nuouo ſi debbe ſcriuere i carta noua ſença tornare adietro an
cora cB a drietro vi trouaſſi ſpacio da metterla.Aon ſi die ſcriuere idrietro.QĐa ſepre auā
ti per ordine cōevanno li giorni delʼtpo cbe mai non ritornano indrieto.E ſe pure ſi faceſſe
ſaria da reputare qllo libro falſo.   Se 1ª.partita foſſe alibro meſſa per errore cbe non do
ueſſi eēre cōe aduiene ale volte per iſmemorogine e tu la uoleſſi iſtornare farai coſi ſengna
qlla tale partita in margine duna croci o duna. Ib. E dipoi ſcriui 1ª.prita alincontro.cioe a
lo oppoſito di qlla nel medeſimo conto.cioe ſela partita errata fuſſe creditrice.poniamo di
ß 50.ß 10 ð 6.E tu la farai debitrice.E dirai.de dare. ß 50.ß 10 ð 6.ſonno per la partita di
ȝtro ſegnata croci cbe ſi ſtorna percbe era errata e non baueua a eēre.E qſta partita ſegna
la. croci cōe e laltra e ð fatta.   Quando loſpacio duno cōto fuſſe pieno.in modo cB nō ui
poteſſe mettere piu prite.E tu voleſſi tirare qllo conto innançi.Fa coſi guarda qllo cB e il re
ſto del ditto conto.cioe ſeli reſta bauere o a dare Ora poniamo cbe qllo conto reſti bauere
ß 28 ß 4 ð 2.Dicò cbe tu debbi fare 1°.verſo ſoletto dala parte oppoſita ſença mettere gior
no.e dirai coſi.E de dare. ß 28 ß 4 ð 2.per reſto di qſto conto poſto bauere in qſto a car.e ð
fatto.E lo detto verſo ſi debe ſegnare in margine dauanti coſi.cioe Ṝ°. cbe ſignifica reſto
cioe cbel detto uerſo non ne debitrice ancor cbe ſia dala banda del debitore.QĐa uiene a eſ
ſere traſportato qllo credito per la via del debito.Ora ti cōuiene uolgere carta e andare tā
tó auanti cbe truoui 1ª.carta nuoua.E qui fare creditore il detto conto.E nominarlo e fa
re prita nuoua ſēça metterui il giorno.E dirai coſi tale di tale ó tali de bēre. ß 18.ß 4 .ð 2.ſō
no per reſto duno ſuo conto leuato in qſto a ca. E qſta partita ſi debbi ſegnare in margine
coſi. cioe Ṝ°. cbe ſignifica reſto E e ſatta.E coſi comme io to moſtro quando ilconto reſta
a bauere coſi ancora bai afare quando reſtaſſi adare.cioe quello cai meſſo dala banda del
credito metter dala banda del debito.

   Uando el lib° fuſſe tutto pieno o uecbio e tu uoleſſi ridullo a 1° alt° li°.nuouo
   fa coſi p°.ti cōuiene vedere cbe ſe il tuo lib°.vecbio e ſegnato i ſu lacouerta poni
   amo p caſo. A. biſogna cB i ſul lib° nuouo doue lo voi ridurre ſia ſegnato in ſu
   la couerta. B. pcbe li libi.de mercanti vāno p ordic luno doppo laltº.Fo le lře
delo.a b c ʒč.E dipoi leuare ilbilancio del lib° vecbio cbe ſia giuſto e pari cōe debba eſſere
e da qllo bilancio copiare tutti li creditori e debitori i ſul lib°.nuouo tutti p ordine cōe elli
ſtāno i ſul bilācio.E fare tutti li debitori e creditori ciaſcūo da pſe.e laſcia aciaſcº tāto ſpatio

These rules, and the other very useful rules of which I have spoken before, you shall follow and, according to the localities and times, you shall be more or less particular, adding or omitting as it seems best to you, because it is impossible to give rules for every little thing in the mercantile business, as we have already said. The proverb says that we need more bridges to make a merchant than a doctor of laws can make.

If you understand well all the things that I have spoken of so far, I am sure you with your intelligence will carry on your business well.

CHAPTER 36.

SUMMARY OF THE RULES AND WAYS FOR KEEPING A LEDGER.

All the creditors must appear in the Ledger at the right hand side, and all the debtors at the left.

All entries made in the ledger have to be double entries—that is, if you make one creditor, you must make some one debtor.

Each debit (shall give—*dee dare*) and credit (shall have—*dee havere*) entry must contain three things, namely: the day, the amount and the reason for the entry.

The last name in the entry of the debit (in the Ledger) must be the first name in the entry of the credit. On the same day that you make the debit entry, you should make the credit entry.

By a trial balance (*bilancio*) of the Ledger we mean a sheet of paper folded lengthwise in the middle, on which we write down all the creditors of the Ledger at the right side and the debtors at the left side. We see whether the total of the debits is equal to that of the credits, and if so, the Ledger is in order.

The trial balance of the Ledger should be equal—that is, the total of the credits—I do not say creditors—should be equal to the total of the debits—I do not say debtors. If they were not equal there would be a mistake in the Ledger.

The cash account should always be a debtor or equal. If it were different, there would be a mistake in the ledger.

You must not and cannot make any one debtor in your book without permission or consent of the person that has to appear as debtor; if you should, that account would be considered false. Likewise you cannot add terms or conditions to a credit without permission and consent of the creditor. If you should, that statement would be untrue.

The values in the Ledger must be reckoned in one kind of money. In the explanation of the entries, you may name all sorts of money, either *ducats*, or *lire*, or *Florence*, or gold *scudi*, or anything else; but in writing the amount in the column, you should always use the same kind of money throughout—that is, the money that you reckon by at the beginning should be the same all through the Ledger.

The debit or credit entries of the cash account may be shortened, if you desire, by not giving the reason for the entry; you may simply say from so and so, for so and so, because the reason for the entry is stated in the opposite entry.

If a new account should be opened, you must use a new page and must not go back even if there was room enough to place the new account. You should not write backward, but always forward—that is, go forward as the days go, which never come back. If you do otherwise, the book would be untrue.

If you should make an entry in the Ledger by mistake which should not have been made, as it happens at times through absentmindedness, and if you wanted to correct it, you shall do as follows: Mark with a cross or with an "H" that special entry, and then make an entry on the opposite side under the same account. That is, if the erroneous entry was on the credit side—say, for instance, for L 50, S 10, D 6—you make an entry in the debit side, saying: Debit (*dee dare*) L 50, S 10, D 6, for the opposite entry cross marked which is hereby corrected, because it was put in through a mistake and should not have been made. Then mark with a cross this new entry. This is all.

When the spaces given to any particular account are all filled so that no more entries can be made and you want to carry forward that account, do in this way: Figure out the remainder of the said account—that is, whether it is debit or credit remainder. Now let us say that there is a credit remainder of L 20, S 4, D 2. You should write on the opposite side, without mentioning any date, as follows: Debit L 28, S 4, D 2, per remainder (*per resto*) of this account carried forward in the credit at page so and so. And it is done. The said entry is to be marked in the margin so, namely: *Ro*, which means "*resto*" (remainder), but this does not mean that it is a true debit entry although it is on the debit side. It is rather the credit which is transferred through the debit side. Now you must turn the pages and keep on turning them until you find a new page where you shall credit that account by naming the account and making a new entry without putting down any day. And you shall say in the following manner: So and so is credit (*dee havere*) L 28, S 4, D 2, per remainder (*per resto*) of account transferred from page so and so, and you should mark this entry in the margin by *Ro*, which means "*resto*" remainder, and that is done.

In the same way, as I have shown you, you shall proceed if the account has a debit remainder—that is, what you enter on the credit side you should transfer to the debit side.

When the ledger is all filled up, or old, and you want to transfer it into a new one, you proceed in the following manner: First you must see whether your old book bears a mark on its cover—for instance, an A. In this case you must mark the new Ledger in which you want to transfer the old one by B, because the books of the merchants go by order, one after the other, according to the letters of the alphabet. Then you have to take the trial balance of the old book and see that it is equal. From the trial balance sheet you must copy in the new Ledger all the creditors and debtors all in order just as they appear in the trial balance sheet, but make a separate account for each amount;

q̃to tu arbitri bēre a trauagliare cō ſeco. E i ciaſcūa prīa del debitore bai a dire p tāti reſta
adare al lib°. uecbio ſegnato. B. a car. E i ciaſcūa prīa del creditore bai a dire　p tanti reſta
a bauere al lib° vecbio ſegnato. B. a car. E coſi e ridutto al libro nuouo. Ora p cancellar
il libro uecbio ti cōuiene a ciaſcūo cōto acceſo iſpēgnerlo cō lo bilancio ſopra ditto. cioe ſe
vno cōto del libro uecbio ſara creditore cbe louedrai p lo bilancio faralo debitore e dirai p
tanti reſta bauere a q̃ſto cōto poſto debbi bauere al lib°. nouo ſegnato. B. a car. E coſi ba
rai iſpēto tutto il lib°. uecbio. e acceſo al lib°. nuouo. E coſi cōmo io to moſtro duno credito
re coſi bai afare duno debitore. Saluo cbe doue al creditore ſi fa debitore poſto debbi ba
uere. E tu bai a fare creditore poſto debbi dare z e fatto .

　　Caſi cbe aptiene amettere al libro de mercanti .

　Tutti li ð. cōtanti cbe tu ti trouaſſi cbe fuſſino tuoi. pprii. cioe cbe baueſſi guadagnati i
diuerſi tpi pel paſſato o cbe ti fuſſino ſtati laſſati da tuoi parēti morti. o donati da q̃lcbe prī
cipe farai creditore te medēmo. E debitore caſſa. 　Tutte le gioie e mercantie cbe fuſſino
tue. pprie cbe tu baueſſi guadagnate. o cb ti fuſſino ſtate laſſate p teſtamēto. o cbe ti fuſſino
ſtate donate. E q̃ſte tale coſe ſi vogliono ſtimare da p ſe luna da l'alt°. q̃llo cbe vagliano a ð.
cōtanti. E tante q̃te coſe elle ſono tante ptite fare al lib°. e fare ciaſcuna debitrice e dire p tā
te mi trouo ſtimate q̃ſto di tanti ð. zc. Poſto medeſimo creditore i q̃ſto a car. E farai credi
tore il tuo cōto. cioe te medeſimo di ciaſcūa prita. Ma nota cbe q̃ſte prite ſintēde cb nō ſiē
no māco di dieci duc. luna po cbe le coſe minute di poco valore non ſimettano al libro.

　Tutte le coſe ſtabile cbe tu ti trouaſſi cbe fuſſino tue. pprie cōe ſono caſe poſſeſſiōi botte
gbe bai afare debitore detta caſa e ſtimare q̃llo cbe la uale a tua diſcretiōe a ð. cōtanti. E fa
ne creditore te medēmo al tuo ſopra detto cōto. E dipoi fare debitore la poſſeſſiōe da pſe e
ſtimarla cōe e ditto e fane creditore te medēmo al tuo ſopradetto cōto. e cōe nelle regole to
ditto tutte le prite vogliono bēre i loro tre coſe. cioe il giorno e la q̃°. dela pecūia e lacagiōe.

　Cōpre cbe tu faceſſi di mercātie. o di cbe coſa ſi fuſſe p li ð. cōtati debbi fare debitore q̃lla
tale mercantia o q̃lla tale coſa e creditore la caſſa. E ſe tu diceſſi. io lacōprai a ð. cōtati cōe e
ditto. Ma vno banco gli pago p me. o veramēte vno mio amico gli pago p me. Riſpodoti
cbe a ogni modo bai afare debitore q̃lla tale mercantia cōe diſopra. o ditto. Ma doue io t i
diſſi farai creditor la caſſa tu bai afare creditor q̃l banco. o q̃llo tuo amico cb p te glia pagati.

　Cōpre cbe tu faceſſi di mercantie. o dicbe coſa ſi ſia a termine dalcuno tpo debi fare de
bitore q̃lla tale mercancia e creditore colui da cui tu lai cōpata p q̃llo tpo　　.Cōpre cbe tu
faceſſi di mercantia. o dicbe coſa ſi ſia a pte ð. e pte tpo debbi fare debitore q̃lla tale mercan
cia E creditore colui da cui tu lai cōpata p q̃llo tpo cō q̃ſti patti cbe li babbi bauere diciamo
il terço di ð. cōtāti E loreſto fra ſei meſi. primi futuri: E doppo q̃ſto fare unaltra prita. cioe
debitore colui da cui tu lai cōpata di q̃lla q̃°. di ð. cōtanti cbe mōta q̃lla terça parte cbe fu di
parto dicōtanti E creditore la caſſa o q̃llo bancho cbe gli pagaſſe pte. 　Tutte le vēdite cb
tu faceſſi di mercantie o daltre coſe bai a fare tutto cōme diſopra ſaluo cbai a mettere p lo op
poſito. cioe cbe doue diſopra ti diſſi cbe ſēpre faceſſi debitore lamercantia: q̃ nelle vēdite bai
a fare ſēpre creditore la mercantia E debitore caſſa ſe e uēduta a ð. cōtanti o debitore q̃l banc
co cbe te li baueſſe. pmeſſi E ſe e vēduta a termine. bai a fare debitore colui acui tu lbai uēdu
ta p q̃llo termine e ſe fuſſe uēduta a pte ð. e pte tpo bai a fare cōe diſopra ti moſtrai nelle cō
pre q̃lle due prite.. 　Se tu vēdeſſi una mercātia abaratto diciamo. Jo bo vēduto libbre mil
le dilana dingbliterra abaratto di peucre cioe a libre dumilia di peucre domando comme
ſa a cōtare q̃ſta ſcrittura al lib°. coſi iſtima q̃llo cbe vale ilpipe a tua diſcretiōe a ð. cōtā
ti. Or poniamo cbe tu lo ſtimi duc. dodici ilceto adōq̃ le dumilia libbre vagliono duc. 2 40.
cōtāti. e po farai creditore lalana ð duc. 2 40. p q̃to lai venduta E q̃ſto modo obſua ſēpre i
leptire tutte gli baratti de gli ſene bauto §. duamilia dipeucre ſtimato. 2 40. duc. poſto det
to peucre debbi dare i q̃ſto a car. E fane debitore ilpeucre. 　Danari cōtanti cbe tu pſtaſſi
a q̃lcbe tuo amico bai a fare debitore lamico acbi tu gli bai pſtati e creditore caſſa. 　Se tu
riceueſſi ð. cōtanti in pſtança da q̃lcbe amico bai afare debitore caſſa e creditore lamico.

　Se tu baueſſi pſo otto. o dieci. o vēti duc. p aſſicurare naue o galee o altra coſa debbi fa
re creditore ſicurta di nauilii. cbiarire cbe e cōe e q̃do e doue e q̃to p ceto. E debitore cōto
di caſſa. 　Mercantie cbe ti fuſſino mandate da altri cō cōmiſſione diuēderle o barattarle
delquali tu baueſſi bauer la tua. puiſiōe. Dico cbe tu debbi fare debitore al libro q̃lla tale mer
cantia attenēte al tale di tale p lo porto. o p gabella. o p nolo o p mettere i magaçino E cre
ditore cōto di caſſa. 　Tutte le ſpeſe di mercantie di ð. cōtanti cbe tu farai. o p nolo. o p ga
belle. o vetture o ſenſerie. o portature fa creditore la caſſa. E debitore quella tale mercantia
per laq̃le tu gli bai iſpeſt

and leave to each account all the space that you think you may need. And in each debit account you shall say: Per so much as per debit remainder (*resta a dare*) in the old book marked A, at page so and so. And in each credit account you shall say: Per so much as per credit remainder (*resta a havere*) in the old book marked A, at page so and so. In this way you transfer the old Ledger into the new one. Now, in order to cancel the old book, you must cancel each account by making it balance, of which we have spoken—that is, if an account of the old Ledger shows a credit remainder as the trial balance would show you, you shall debit this account for the same amount, saying, so much remains in the credit of this account, carried forward in the credit in the new Ledger marked B, at page so and so. In this way you shall have closed the old Ledger and opened the new one for, as I have shown you how to do for a creditor, the same you shall do for a debtor, with this difference, that while you debit an account, which may show a credit remainder, you shall credit the account which may show a debit remainder. This is all.

THINGS WHICH SHOULD BE ENTERED IN THE BOOKS OF THE MERCHANTS.

Of all the cash that you might have, if it is your own—that is, that you might have earned at different times in the past, or which might have been bequeathed to you by your dead relatives or given you as a gift from some Prince, you shall make yourself creditor (*creditore te medesima*), and make cash debitor. As to all jewelry or goods which might be your own—that is, that you may have got through business or that might have been left you through a will or given to you as a present, you must value them in cash and make as many accounts as there are things and make each debitor by saying: For so many, etc., of which I find myself possessed on this day, so many *denari*, posted credit entry at such and such page; and then you make creditor your account (*tuo conto*), that is yourself (*medesimo*), with the amount of each of these entries. But remember these entries should not be for less than ten ducats each, as small things of little value are not entered in the Ledger.

Of all the real property that you might own, as houses, lands, stores, you make the cash debitor and estimate their value at your discretion in cash, and you make creditor yourself or your personal account (*tuo sopradette conto*). Then you make debitor an account of that special property by giving the value, as I have said above, and make yourself creditor because, as I have told you, all entries must have three things: The date, the value in cash, and the reason.

If you should buy merchandise or anything else for cash, you should make a debtor of that special merchandise or thing and like creditor cash, and if you should say, I bought that merchandise for cash, but a bank will furnish the cash, or a friend of mine will do so, I will answer you that any way, you must make a debitor of that special merchandise; but where I told you to credit cash, you should, instead, credit that special bank, or that special friend who furnished the money.

If you should buy merchandise or anything else, partly for cash and partly on time, you shall make that special merchandise debitor, and make a creditor of the party from whom you bought it on time and under the conditions that you might have agreed upon; as, for instance, one-third in cash and the rest in six months. After this you will have to make another entry—that is, make a debitor of the party from whom you bought it for the amount of the cash that you have given him for that one-third, and make creditor cash or the bank which might have paid that much for you.

If you should sell any merchandise or anything else, you should proceed as above with the exception that you should proceed in the opposite way—that is, where I told you that when you bought you should make the merchandise debitor, when you sell you will have to make your merchandise a creditor and charge the cash account if it is sold for cash, or charge the bank that might have promised the payment. And if you make a sale on time, you will have to charge the party to whom you sold it on time, and if you make the sale partly for cash and partly on time, you shall proceed as I have shown you in explaining about the buying.

If you should give merchandise in exchange, for instance, let us say I have sold 1,000 pounds of English wool in exchange for pepper—that is, for 2,000 pounds of pepper—I ask, how shall we make this entry in the Ledger? You shall do as follows: Estimate what the value of the pepper is, at your discretion, in cash. Now let us say that you estimated 12 ducats per hundred; the 2,000 pounds would be worth 240 ducats. Therefore, you shall make the wool a creditor with 240 ducats, for which amount you have sold it. This is the manner that you should follow in all the trade entries. If you have received 2,000 pounds of pepper valued at 240 ducats, you shall make the pepper a debitor and say: Said pepper debtor on this day, see page, etc., etc.

If you should loan cash to some of your friends, you shall charge the friend to whom you have given it and credit cash. If you should borrow cash from some friend, you will have to debit cash and credit your friend.

If you have received 8 or 10 or 20 ducats in order to insure a ship or a galley, or anything else, you should credit the account "ship insurance," and explain all about it—how, when and where, and how much per cent.; and shall charge the cash account.

If anybody should send you any goods with instructions to sell them or exchange them on commission, I say that you have to charge in the Ledger that special merchandise belonging to so and so with the freight, or duty, or for storage, and credit the cash account. You shall credit the cash for all cash that you have to pay on account of goods: for instance, cash paid for transportation or duty, or brokerage, etc., and charge the account of that special goods for that which you have paid in money.

Casi che acade mettere ale recordançe del mercante.

Utte lemasseritie di casa o di bottega che tu ti truoui. Ma vogliono essere per ordine.cioe tutte le cose di ferro da perse con spatio da potere agiongnere se bisognasse.E cosi da segnare in margine quelle che fussino perdutte o vendute o donate o guaste.Ma non si intende masseritie minute dipoco valore. E fare ricordo di tutte le cose dottone da perse comme e detto. E simile tutte le cose distagno. E simile tutte lecose dilengno.E cosi tutte le cose dirame.E cosi tutte le cose dariento e doro ze. Sempre con spatio di qualche carta da potere arrogere se bisognasse.e cosi vadare notitia di quello che mancasse. Tutte lemalleuerie o obbrighi o promesse che promettessi per qualche amico. e chiarire bene che e comme. Tutte lemercantie o altre cose che ti fosseno lassate i guardia o a serbo di prestança da qlche amico.e cosi tutte lecose ch tu prestassi'a altri tuoi amici. Tutti limercati conditionati cioe compre ovedite come p ereplo vno cotrato cioe ch tu mi mandi con leprossime galee che torneranno dingbliterra tanti cantara di lane dilimistri a caso che le sieno buone e recipienti.Jo ti varo tanto del cantaro o del cento o veramente ti mandaro alincontro tanti cantara di cottoni. Tutte le case o possessioni o botteghe o gioie che tu affitassi a tanti duc.o a tante lire lanno.E quando tu riscoterai ilfitto aloza gli lidinari sanno a mettere al libro comme disopra ti dissi.Prestando qualche gioia o vasellamenti dariento o doro a qualche tuo amico per otto o quidici giorni diqueste tale cose nó si mettono al libro.ma sene fa ricordo ale ricordançe.perche fra pochi giorni lai bariauere. E cosi per contra se a te fossi prestato simili cose non li debbi mettere al libro.Ma farne memoria alericordançe perche presto lai a rendere.

Comme si scriuono lire e soldi e danari picioli e altre abreuiature.

Lire soldi danari picioli libbre once danarpesi grani carati ducati fiorin larghi.
£ ß ₰ p̄ libbre ʒ ꝺp̄ g° ₭ duc̄ fio.lar

<table>
<tr><td colspan="4">

Come si debbe dettare le ptite de debitori.
Mcccc° Lxxxxiij°.

Lodouico dipiero forestai devdare a di.xiiii.nouembre.1493.ß.44.f.1:ꝺ.8.porto contati in prestaça.posto cassa auere.a car. 2
</td><td>£</td><td>44</td><td>ß 8.</td></tr>
</table>

Come si debbe dettare le ptite de debitori.
Mcccc° Lxxxxiij°.

Lodouico dipiero forestai devdare a di.xiiii.nouembre.1493.ß.44.f.1:ꝺ.8.porto contati in prestaça.posto cassa auere.a car. 2 — £ 44 ß 8.

E a di.18.detto ß.18.f.11.ꝺ. 6.promettemo p lui a martino dipiero foraboschi asuo piacer posto bere i qsto.a c.2. £ 18 ß11 ꝺ6.

Cassa i mano di simone dalesso bobeni de dar adi.14. nouebre 1493.ß.62.f.13. ꝺ.2.da francesco vantonio caualcanti in qsto a c.2 £ 62 ß13 ꝺ6.

Martino di piero fora boschi de dare a di.20.nouembre.1493.ß.18.f.11.ꝺ.6.porto luimedesimo contati posto cassa a car. 2. £ 18 ß11 ꝺ6.

Francesco dantonio caual cati de dare a di.12.di noue bre.1493.ß.20.f.4.ꝺ.2.ch p misse anostro piacer p lodouico di pieroforestai a c.2. £ 20 ß4 ꝺ2.

Come si debbe dittare leptite di creditori.
Mcccc° Lxxxxiii.

Lodouico dipiero forestai de bauere a di.22.nouebre 1493.ß.20.f.4.ꝺ.2.sono p parte di pagamento.E per lui celia promissi a nostro piacere fracescho datonio. caualcanti posto dare a c.2.£ 20 ß4 ꝺ2.

Cassa in mano di simone dalesso bobeni de bauere a di.14.nouebre.1493.ß.44. f.1.ꝺ.8.alo douico di piero forestani in qsto. a car. 2. £ 44 ß1 ꝺ8.

E a di.22.nouembre.1493 ß.18.f.11.ꝺ.6.a martino di piero foraboschi.a ca.2. £ 18 ß11 ꝺ6.

Martino di piero fora bo schidi bauere a di.18.noue bre.1493.ß.18.f.11.ꝺ.6.gli pmettemo a suo piacere p lodouico di piero forestani posto obbi bere i qsto a c.2.£ 18 ß11 ꝺ6

Francescho datonio caual canti de bauere a di.14.no uebre.1493.ß.62.f.13.ꝺ.6. reco lui medesimo ptati po sto cassa dare a.car.2. £ 62 ß13 ꝺ6.

THINGS THAT SHOULD BE RECORDED IN A RECORD BOOK (*RECORDANZE*) OF THE MERCHANT.

All the house and store goods that you may find yourself possessed of—these should be put down in order—that is, all the things made of iron by itself, leaving space enough to make additions if necessary; also leaving room to mark in the margin the things that might be lost or sold or given as presents or spoiled. But I don't mean small things of little value.

Make a record of all the brass things separately, as I have said, and then a record of the tin things, and then the wooden things, and copper things, and then the silver things and gold things, always leaving enough space between each class so that you may add something if necessary, and to put down a memorandum of any object that might be missing.

All sureties or obligations or promises of payment that you might make for some friend, explaining clearly everything.

All goods or other things that might be left with you in custody, or that you might borrow from some friend, as well as all the things that other friends of yours might borrow from you.

All conditional transactions—that is, purchases and sales, as, for instance, a contract that you shall send me by the next ship coming from England, so many *cantara* of *woll di li mistri*, on condition that it is good; and when I receive it I will pay you so much per *cantara* or by the hundred, or otherwise; I will send you in exchange so many *cantara* of cotton.

All houses, lands, stores or jewels that you might rent at so many ducats and so many lire per year. And when you collect the rent, then that money should be entered in the Ledger, as I have told you.

If you should lend some jewels, silver or gold vase to some friend, say, for instance, for eight or fifteen days, things like this should not be entered in the Ledger, but should be recorded in this record book, because in a few days, you will get them back. In the same way, if somebody should lend you something like the things mentioned, you should not make any entry in the Ledger, but put down a little memorandum in the record book, because in a short time you will have to give it back.

How *Lire, Soldi, Denari* and *Picioli*, etc., should be written down as abbreviations.

Lire; Soldi; Denari; Picioli; Libbre; Once; Danarpesi; Grani; Carati; Ducati; Florin larghi.

(See other side for their abbreviations.)

HOW THE DEBIT (LEDGER) ENTRIES ARE MADE.

MCCCCLXXXXIII. Lodovico, son of Piero Forestani, shall give on the 14th day of November, 1493, L 44, S 1, D 8, for cash loaned, posted cash shall have at page 2:

L 44, S 1, D 8

And on the 18th ditto, L 18, S 11, D 6, which we promised to pay for him to Martino, son of Piero Foraboschi at his pleasure, posted said shall have at page 2:

L 18, S 11, D 6

Cash in hands of Simone, son of Alessio Bombeni, shall give on Nov. 14, 1493, for L 62, S 13, D 2, for Francesco, son of Antonio Cavalcanti, page 2:

L 62, S 13, D 6

Martino, son of Piero Foraboschi, shall give on Nov. 20, 1493, for L 18, S 11, D 6, taken by him in cash, posted Cash at page 2:

L 18, S 11, D 6

Francesco, son of Antonio Cavalcanti, shall give, on Nov. 12, 1493, L 20, S 4, D 2, which he promised to pay to us at our pleasure for Lodovico, son of Pietro Forestani; page 2:

L 20, S 4, D 2

HOW THE CREDIT (LEDGER) ENTRIES ARE MADE.

MCCCCLXXXXIII. Lodovico, son of Piero Forestani, shall have, on Nov. 22, 1493, for L 20, S 4, D 2, for part payment. And for him Francesco, son of Antonio Cavalcanti, promised to pay it to us at our pleasure; posted shall give at page 2:

L 20, S 4, D 2

Cash in hands of Simone, son of Alessio Bombeni, shall have, on Nov. 14, 1493, for L 44, S 1, D 8, from Lodovico Pietro Forestani, L 44, S 1, D 8; and on Nov. 22, 1493, L 18, S 11, D 6, to Martino, son of Piero Forbaschi, page 2:

L 18, S 11, D 6

Martino, son of Piero Foraboschi, shall have on Nov. 18, 1493, for L 18, S 11, D 6, which we promised to pay him at his pleasure for Lodovico, son of Pietro Forestani; posted shall give entry at p. 8:

L 18, S 11, D 6

Francesco, son of Antonio Cavalcanti, shall have on Nov. 14, 1493, for L 62, S 13, D 6, which he brought himself in cash; posted cash shall give at page 2:

L 62, S 13, D 6

294 $\frac{4}{3}\frac{4}{0}$ ♇ Pro & danno // A doni uarij, per danno feguido, tratto in refto, per faldo di quello ℔ 1 — — — ual ♉

Di faldar la partida de li doni, ponendo il refto di quelli in pro & danno.
ß 2 ℊ — ℘

295 $\frac{4}{3}\frac{4}{1}$ ♇ Pro & danno // A Spefe de uiuer di cafa, per piu fpefe fatte, come in effe appar, per faldo di quelle ℔ 154 ℊ 20 ℘ 14 — — — ual ♉

Di faldar le fpefe di veftir in ditto pro & danno.
15 ß 9 ℊ 8 ℘ — 14

296 $\frac{3}{4}\frac{4}{4}$ ♇ Fitti della poffeffion da Moian // A Pro & danno per fitto di quella per l'anno prefente, finira de Luio 1541, per faldo de quelli ℔ 45 ℊ — ual ♉

Di faldar li fiiti della poffeffion, in pro & danno.
4 ß 10 ℊ — ℘

297 $\frac{4}{3}\frac{4}{3}$ ♇ Pro & danno // A Spefe diuerfe per piu fpefe fatte l'anno prefente, come in effe appar, per faldo fuo ℔ 399 ℊ 12 ℘ — — ual ♉

Di faldar le fpefe diuerfe, in ditto pro & danno.
33 ß 19 ℊ — ℘

298 $\frac{4}{4}\frac{4}{0}$ ♇ Pro & danno // A Spefe de falariadi in monte, per piu fpefe fatte l'anno prefente, come in effe appar, per faldo di quelle ℔ 48 ℊ 12 ℘ — ual ♉

Di faldar le fpefe de falariadi, in ditto pro & danno.
4 ß 17 ℊ — ℘

299 $\frac{4}{4}\frac{0}{4}$ ♇ Pro de zeccha in monte // A Pro & danno, per utilita feguida, come in quello appar, per faldo fuo, ℔ 150 ℊ — ℘ — ual ♉

Di faldar in pro de zeccha, in lo ditto pro & danno.
15 ß — ℊ — ℘

300 $\frac{4}{3}\frac{4}{3}$ ♇ Pro et danno // A Cauedal de mi Aluife Vallareffo, per utilita feguida de l'anno 1540, tratto in refto, per faldo di quello, ℔ 900 ℊ 22 ℘ 17 — ual ♉

Di faldar poi il pro & danno nel tuo cauedal, per vltima conclufione.
90 ß 1 ℊ 10 ℘ — 17

Fine dil prefente Giornale, tenuto per mi Aluife Va
lareffo, per conto d'ogni traffico, & negotio à me oc
corfo, da di primo Marzo 1540, fin adi ultimo Fe-
braro del ditto millefimo, nel qual ordinatamente de
giorno in giorno, ho fcritto di mia mano, ne
in effo piu intendo fcriuere, per hauer
quello conclufo & faldato in
12 partide, lequal ho
reportate nel li-
bro nouo fe
gnato
A

MANZONI'S JOURNAL REPRODUCED

On the opposite page is given an enlarged reproduction of the last page of Domenico Manzoni's journal. As stated before, the writer has not an original copy of Manzoni's book at hand, therefore only this page can be given which was enlarged from a reproduction appearing on page 121 of Brown's History of Accounting.

As we have seen in the historical chapter, Manzoni wrote forty years after Pacioli, but he was the first author to give illustrations of the journal and ledger, although in the text he practically copied Pacioli verbatim. Therefore, in Manzoni's book we have the first expressions in examples and illustrations of the writings of Pacioli.

The page here reproduced is the last page of the journal and contains the journal entries covering the closing of the profit and loss account (*Pro et danno.*)

We will note that the date is in the middle at the top of the page; that the name of the debtor account is separated from the name of the creditor account by two slanting lines, thus: //; that each entry is separated by a line in the explanation column only (not in the money column); that immediately to the left of each entry we find two figures, separated by a short horizontal line or dash; these are the pages of the ledger to which the debit and credit are posted, the top figure representing the debit and the lower one the credit. Immediately before these two figures, we find two slanting lines or dashes; they are the checking marks. We will see that Pietra uses a dot in this place and that Pacioli prefers a dot but mentions a check mark or any other mark. They are not the two slanting lines which are drawn through an entry when it has been posted. These two we find represented in the two little diagonal dashes at the beginning and end, as well as on the under and upper side, of the lines separating the journal entries. The writer believes from the descriptions he has read and illustrations he has seen, that these dashes are the beginning and end of the much described "diagonal lines" and illustrates his idea by the two lines he added to the reproduction in the last journal entry. The omission of these lines like that of the standing lines in the money column, is probably due to lack of printing facilities. You will recall that Pacioli mentions these lines to be made at the beginning of the entry and at the end of the entry, just before the *lire* sign.

The numbers from 294 to 300 in the left-hand margin, are the consecutive numbers of the journal entries, which Manzoni alone and no other writer herein referred to mentions.

On the right we find the four signs of the various denominations, *lire, soldi, denari,* and *picioli.* A dash is provided wherever a cypher should appear in the money column.

The two lines of printing above the money in the money columns are merely directions which Manzoni as textwriter gave to his reader. They are not a part of the journal entry. You will note that he prints them in different type. The difference in coin between the uniform one used in bookkeeping and the one used locally is also apparent, as the local coin is given as a part of the explanation to the journal entry. The "p" to the left of the journal entry and to the right of the figures in the margin stands for "per" (our by), and immediately after the slanting dashes "//" in front of the name of the credit account is used "A" (our to).

Elsewhere we have stated that except as to numbering the journal entries Manzoni mentioned nothing that Pacioli did not describe. While he copies whole chapters word for word, in some of them, however, he was clearer, more brief and more systematic than Pacioli. We give one of the chapters as an example.

ABSTRACT FROM DOMENICO MANZONI'S BOOK

CAP. XIII.

Regole breuissime del giornal & quaderno.

Nota che la Regola del Giornale & Quaderno, in se contiene sei cose, cio e.

Dare, Havere, Qualita, Quantita, Tempo & Ordine.

Dare, significa douer dare, cio e il debitore, o uno o piu che siano.

Havere, uvol dir douer havere, cio e il creditore, o uno o piu che siano.

Qualita sono quelle cose che tu maneggi, & siano di che sorte si vogliono.

Quantita, e il numero, peso over misure, o piccioli, o grandi che si siano.

Tempo, si e il giorno, ilmese & lanno, sotto il quale tu fai la partida.

Ordine, e quello, che nella presente opera con facilita insegnamo.

Le due prime, sono affermative, e principali in ogi cosa.

La cosa debitrice, sempre va posta avanti a la creditrice.

Davanti a la cosa debitrice, vi si pone uno per a questo modo P.

Davanti a la cosa creditrice, vi si pone uno A cosi A.

Il P, in tal luogo significa la cosa debitrice.

E lo A in tal luogo significa la cosa creditrice.

Il giornale, si divide il debitore dal creditore, con due liniette a questo modo
lequali dinotano, che de una partida dalgiornale, sempre se ne convien
far due nel quaderno.

Il giorno, si nota nel giornal di sopra da la partida.

Et nel quaderno, si nota, dentro dalla partida.

Il numero de le carte del quaderno, nel giornale, si mette avanti la partida.

Et nel quaderno, il medesimo si mette dopo la partida.

Li nomi de le partide vive in l'alfabeto, vi si poneno a man destra.

Et quelli de le cose morte, si notano a man sinistra.

Per le cose vive, qui s intende ogni creaturi animata.

E per le morte, s intende robbe, over ogni altra cosa.

TRANSLATION OF THE ABOVE ABSTRACT FROM DOMENICO MANZONI'S BOOK.

CHAPTER XIII.

Very Short Rules for the Journal and the Ledger.
(In verse form.)

You should note that the rules for the Journal and the Ledger contain six things, namely:

Give, Have, Quality, Quantity, Time and Order.

Give (Debit), means as much as "shall give", that is, the debtor be it one or more.

Have (Credit), means as much as "shall have", this is, the creditor be it one or more.

Quality, by this we understand the things you handle of whichever nature they may be.

Quantity, by this we understand the number, the weight or the measure, be it big or little.

Time, means the day, the month and the year in which the transaction is made.

Order, means that which we can easily learn from the present book.

The first two are most important and refer particularly to all things.

The things made debtor should be placed before the creditor.

In front of that which is made debtor is placed "Per", in this way "P".

Before the creditor we place an "A" in this way "A".

The "P" signifies that in this spot the things were made debtor.

And the "A" signifies that in this spot the things were made creditor.

In the Journal one must divide the debtor from the creditor by means of two small lines in this way //, which denotes that from one entry in the Journal two entries should be made in the Ledger.

In the Journal, The day should be given above the entries.

In the Ledger, The same is carried into the body of the entry.

In the Journal, the number of the Ledger pages is placed in front of the entry.

And in the Ledger we place the same after the entry.

The name of the living account is written in the Index to the right.

And those of the dead things are written to the left.

With "living things" is understood every creature with a soul (ogni creatura animata).

And with "dead things" is understood merchandise and everything else.

In Chapter eleven Manzoni also gives eight rules for journalizing. The four principal things pertaining to buying, selling, receiving, paying, exchanging, loaning and gifts are

1. The one who gives.
2. The one who receives.
3. The thing which is given.
4. The thing which is received.

It should be noted that here are four conditions to each transaction. While Manzoni does not explain their use, as we will see later on, Stevin gives us the proper interpretation for this, somewhat as follows:

One transaction will always need a double-entry. If Peter pays £100 we must consider

1. The one who gives, i. e., Peter.
2. The one who receives, i. e., proprietor.
3. The thing which is given, i. e., cash by Peter.
4. The thing which is received, i. e., cash from the proprietor.

Hence proprietor debit to Peter and cash debit to proprietor, which combined by eliminating the quantities of similar name and value, or by cancelling (as in algebra a=b; b=c; hence a=c) makes cash debit to Peter.

Manzoni then follows with these eight rules:

1. Debit merchandise for purchase.
2. Credit merchandise for sales.
3. Debit cash for cash sales.
4. Credit cash for cash purchase.
5. Debit buyer for sales on credit.
6. Credit seller for purchase on credit.
7. Debit persons who promise to pay.
8. Credit persons to whom we promise to pay.

In order to give the reader some idea of the scope of Manzoni's work, we give here a translation of the Index to his book.

PART I. JOURNAL.

Chapter
1. Those things which the merchant needs and the system of keeping a Ledger and its Journal.
2. The inventory, what it is and how merchants make it up.
3. Form and example of inventory.
4. Last urging and good instruction for the merchant in connection with the inventory.
5. A certain book, which majority of people use and which is called Memorial, Strazze or Vachetta; what it is; how we must write it up and for whom.
6. Some special little books, which it is customary to use; what they are and how they are written up. (Separate day books for petty expenses, household expenses, salaries, repairs, rents, separate classes of merchandise.)
7. The manner in which in some places the books are authenticated by law.

8. The first book, which is called Journal; what it is and how it is started and kept. (Mentioning the five customary standing lines of a journal.)
9. The two terms which are used in the Journal and the Ledger, the one named ''Cash,'' the other ''Capital,'' and what they mean.
10. Two other terms which are used in the Journal and which are mixed quite often, and what they mean. (''Per'' and ''A''—Debits separated from Credits by //.)
11. The principles underlying the use and arrangement of the Ledger. (Author claims this is very difficult to understand; ''Per'' and ''A'' used to separate debit from credit, but does not say how to make debits and credits except that he gives in connection with the various methods of buying and selling, eight rules for Journal entry.)
12. The manner and system by which each entry in the Journal must be written under the proper terms. (Samples of Journal entries, with application of rules from Chapter 11.)
13. Short rules for the Journal and Ledger, and the six things each entry must contain.
14. Explanation of old abbreviations and what is meant by ''*Lire de grossi.*'' The kind of money used by merchants in bookkeeping and which really does not exist. Common people use: Lire=20 soldi; 1 soldi=12 Picioli.

(In Ducats.)

1 ducat = 24 grossi.
1 grosso = 32 Picioli in gold.
1 Piciolo in gold = 1-15/16 Picioli in money by common people.

(In Lire de grossi.)

1 lira = 10 ducats.	1 soldo = 12 grossi.
1 lira = 20 soldi.	1 grosso = 32 Picioli.
1 grosso in gold = 5 grossi common money.	

15. Explanation needed in order to understand the examples of journal and ledger entries.

PART II. LEDGER.

1. The second and last principal mercantile book, called Ledger; what it is; how it is opened and kept.
2. The manner in which the old year is written in this book and about the kind of money used in posting. (Year and usually also the money is written in Roman figures; Arabic too easy to change: 0 to 6 or 9. Do not repeat date, but put a line. Leave no open spaces for others to fill in.)
3. The reason for having two entries in the Ledger for each single entry in the Journal.
4. The manner in which we use both terms for each entry in the Ledger. (''A'' on debit of Ledger, ''Per'' on credit of Ledger; unlike the Journal, where ''A'' denotes credit and ''Per'' debit.)
5. The manner and system to be used in transferring entries from the Journal to the Ledger. (Crosses Journal entry off with one diagonal line, at the time he enters the Ledger page, but does not say where to put this line.)
6. The manner of marking entries in the Journal which have been posted to the Ledger.
7. The two numbers of the Ledger pages which are written in the margin of the Journal, when the entry is posted from the Journal to the Ledger, the one above the other and separated by a line.
8. Another number, which we write at the beginning of each entry, through which each entry can easily be located again. (Numbers each Journal entry consecutively.)
9. The manner in which the entries are carried to another place in the Ledger when one page is filled. (Cancel blank space on either side to lowest place of writing. Balance not entered in the Journal. Carries balance only, with an abbreviation which means ''Carried forward.'')
10. The manner and system which should be followed in the checking of the books in order to detect errors. (Gives Ledger to assistant and keeps Journal, thus reversing method of Pacioli. He does not use a dot but ''another mark than that used first.'' (See chapter 6 above and two lines before each entry in the reproduction.)
11. The manner in which a correction in the Ledger is made when we have posted an entry to the wrong page in the Ledger. (Never cross the wrong entry out or erase it, for you cannot prove what was there, and hence it will be construed as deceit. If an entry is posted to debit that should be credit, put another on the credit to offset it, for same amount, then proceed correctly. Mark erroneous and corrective entries with an X or H (*havere*); some make correction in one entry by using double the amount.)
12. How to prepare an account for a debtor or a creditor when he asks for a statement of his account.

PIETRA'S JOURNAL AND LEDGER REPRODUCED

As stated in the historical chapter, in 1586, or nearly 100 years after Pacioli wrote, Don Angelo Pietra published a work on bookkeeping, which was fully illustrated with numerous examples. Undoubtedly Pietra had both Pacioli and Manzoni before him when writing his book, because he describes matters which Manzoni omitted but Pacioli gave, and also some which Manzoni mentioned and Pacioli did not. This will be explained fully elsewhere.

Pietra was a monk who endeavored to give a system to be used for monasteries, but which he claimed was expedient for those who do not trade, or in other words, for corporations not for profit, and for capitalists. The first page is a reproduction of the title page, in which the reader will find the author's name just above, and the date of publication just below, the picture.

The next page gives a chart of the various methods of buying and of selling, of each of which Pacioli says there are nine. Pietra sets them up here in a far more systematic manner, showing fifteen in all.

We show next the first four lines of the title page to the journal, which are the dedication of the journal: "In the Name of the most holy and undivided Trinity, Father, Son, and Holy Ghost." Also note the cross in the sixth line which is the sign used for the first journal and the first ledger when beginning a new business. Such journal and ledger as we have seen in Pacioli, is called the "cross journal" and the "cross ledger."

Next we give a page of the journal. From this page, we note:

(1) That the first page of the journal carries the opening of "In the Name of God."

(2) That thereafter comes the date in the middle of the page. The date is not again given until it is changed and then only the day of the month is given, omitting the year and the name of the month; "a di detto," meaning "on the .... day of the aforesaid month."

(3) That each journal entry is divided by a line, not clear across the page, but from page column to money column.

(4) That as in Manzoni's journal, no standing division lines in money columns are given (probably due to lack of printing facilities).

(5) That the money consideration of each entry is not only mentioned in the money column but also in the explanation of the journal entry.

(6) That the name of the debit account is given first and the credit last; that they are divided by two small slanting strokes followed by the preposition "a" like this: //a.

(7) That the name of the debit account is not preceded by "P" or by "Per" as Pacioli and Manzoni require.

(8) That the pages of the ledger to which the entries are transferred or posted are divided by a horizontal line or dash between the figures, the debit being always on top and the credit below.

(9) That each entry has a brief but full explanation of the transaction represented by the entry.

(10) That each entry is carefully checked with a dot (not a check mark as we use and Pacioli described or a dash as Manzoni showed) on the left of the ledger pages in the journal. These dots also appear in front of each ledger entry.

(11) That Pietra shows no combination journal entry or entries with more than one debit or credit.

(12) That he does not show the diagonal cancellation lines in the journal as an evidence of posting to the ledger.

(13) That he does not give any other value sign than the "Lire," omitting the *soldi, denari,* and *picioli* signs.

(14) That he very carefully provides a dash in the money column in the place of the cyphers.

The illustrations of the journal are followed by those of the ledger. The title page contains the name of the ledger, in the fifth line *"Libro maestro"* (master book or principal book). The ledger has the same dedication as the journal.

Folio one of Pietra's ledger is the equivalent of an opening balance account, giving the name of the old and new account, the page in the old ledger and the page in the new ledger, it being posted from the closing balance account in the old ledger and not from the journal. The assets are on the credit side and the liabilities on the debit side of the ledger. The account shows a deficit of L 1706 - 10 - 3. The assets are divided in two: first, the accounts receivable and their total, then the merchandise and other specific accounts.

This page corresponds to the English form of a balance sheet. It is the proprietor's half of the opening inventory journal entry placed direct in the ledger instead of in the journal, and as such this represents a proprietor's account upon the theory that the proprietor is credited for furnishing or loaning to the personification of the asset accounts and charged with the negative assets or liabilities. As our modern capital account represents a net difference between assets and liabilities (leaving surplus out of consideration), it cannot be said that Pietra employed a modern capital account, although the result is the same.

Page 59 of this ledger also represents an account with the proprietor or owner, and is really a continuation of the account on page one. The first entry on the debit is the balance and deficit of L 1706 - 10 - 3, properly transferred from page one without the aid of a journal entry. The following five entries are entries corrective of the net capital, because they refer to transactions of previous years and are of little importance for our study except that they show that the principle of surplus adjustments then existed.

The seventh entry on the debit, of L 4 - 17 - 10, refers to the same ledger page as this selfsame account bears (namely, 59). We find, therefore, the credit end of the entry on the credit side of this page. This entry does not come from the journal, but is merely a "cross" or "wash" entry in the nature of a memorandum for the purpose of recording an omitted transaction. Note how carefully both entries are marked with a little circle (o) to set them off from the others, much the same as we use a cross (X) nowadays for the same purpose, and as Pacioli and Manzoni also mention.

The last entry on the debit side (L 3744 - 0 - 3) is made also without the aid of the journal. Its counterpart is on page 61 of the ledger. It represesents the net worth or capital invested at the end of the year, and balances on page 61 with the difference between assets and liabilities, and is merely a methodical closing entry in order that all accounts may be closed at the transfer of all open accounts to the new ledger.

On the credit side we find the first five entries to be surplus adjustment entries. The sixth one is the cross entry already explained, and the last one, L 5448 - 10 - 5, is the net profit balance transferred from ledger page 60 without the use of the journal. Here then we have an account named "Monastery," the proprietor for which these books are kept. It stands charged with a capital deficit, credited with the annual profits and closed with a debit balance representing present net worth, identical with our present day Capital account. The deficit in the opening entry, as would appear from the text, seems to be due to the low values given to the fixed assets in order to avoid heavier taxation by the church authorities. The account shows no definite ledger heading, although the first word on the left page *"Monastero"* (monastery) is the name of the proprietor and is not repeated in each entry. The same method Pacioli and Manzoni describe and therefore we have not approached closer to the definite ledger heading.

Page 60 represents what we call today an "Income and Expenses" account, sometimes misnamed but being similar to a "Profit or Loss" account. It is not so named here. The debit side is called *"Spesa Generale"* (General Expenses),—the credit side *"Entrata Generale"* (General Income).

It should be remembered that these books were not kept for a mercantile establishment, which operates with the object of a profit in view, but only for a monastery, an eleemosynary corporation, an institution or corporation not for profit, hence it could not use the words profit or loss.

The balance on the debit of L 5448 - 10 - 5 is the excess of general income over general expenses, and is transferred to page 59, which we have explained is the proprietor's account or equivalent to our present capital account.

Page 61 contains the last page of the ledger of Pietra's book. It is similar to page one, except that debits and credits are reversed. Here then we have the closing "Balance account," called *"Esito,"* which means final or exit. It accurately represents our modern balance sheet, but is placed in the ledger as a permanent record and used as a medium to close all accounts in the ledger. It usually was and quite often now is the custom to start a new ledger each year, hence all accounts should be closed when the ledger is laid away. Pacioli nor Manzoni describe this account. They transfer the open balances of the asset and liability accounts direct to the new ledger.

You will note that the closing entry of L 3744 - 0 - 3 on the credit is taken from page 59, the monastery or capital account. You will also note that it is on the credit side of the account, and a total of the liabilities is drawn before the final balance. This is not done anywhere else in the ledger, showing that this account is different and represents two purposes: one, that of a final trial balance (after Profit and Loss accounts are closed) and thus becomes a statement of assets and liabilities; and, further, that net worth or capital is not considered a liability, but an item distinct from liabilities, for the purpose of closing the capital account in the ledger, and transferring it in the new ledger.

Page 21 of the ledger is given to show how carefully all blank spaces are cancelled by slanting lines; how accounts are kept in two kinds of money with the aid of a double column; that no reference is made to the pages in the journal from which the entries were posted, for the reason stated in the text that the date was a close enough reference; that the journal entries are not numbered, as was done by Manzoni. Pages given immediately before the amounts refer to the ledger page on which the other side of the double-entry appears; note that on the debit the preposition "a" is used for our "to" and on the credit "per" for our "by;" following Manzoni in this respect, but entirely opposed to Pacioli's teachings, opening and closing entries do not carry these prepositions; because they do not constitute true debits and credits as those transferred from the journal; printers then, as now, make errors in figures, as the fourth figure from the bottom of the debit side should be 250 instead of 205, as per addition and the opening entry on page one; the explanation in the journal is repeated in the ledger and more than one line is used for an entry if needed; a single line is drawn under the figures only and then the total put in; the word *"somma"* (total) is used in front of the figures instead of the double line we now rule under the total; no totals or lines are drawn when the account contains only one item; every entry is carefully checked with a dot in the left margin; the name of the account is engrossed at the beginning of the first line on the left and thus approaches the definite ledger heading of the present day; the date belonging to each entry is not set out in a definite column, although the text mentions this; *"dee dare"* (should give or debit) and *"dee havere"* (should have or credit) is only stated once at the beginning of each account and not in every entry, as we would infer from Pacioli the custom was.

In order to give the reader a clear understanding of what is contained in Pietra's book and to show how much more polished, complete and advanced it is than the book of either Pacioli or Manzoni, and to indicate the many new features he introduces, we are giving here a brief description of each chapter in the nature of an index.

1. Day book or scrap book and similar books are necessary in order to get journal and ledger in good form.
2. Explains debit and credit as to "A" and "Per"—our "To" and "By," and the two little lines // which separate debits from credits.
3. Makes a distinction between bookkeeping for bankers, merchants, and capitalists.
4. Describes the three ledgers for these three methods.
5. Says some more about the ledger for capitalist and calls it the "Economic Ledger." Author uses this kind of ledger in his book of samples which he adapts to the business of a monastery.
6. The first part of the inventory covering immovable assets.
7. The second part of the inventory covering merchandise or goods for use in the house (not fixtures— they belong to movables).
8. The third part of the inventory of movable assets.
9. Gives tabulated detailed inventory of the movable assets of a monastery.
10. About qualifications of bookkeeper, namely, bright and of good character; good handwriting; also knowledge, ambition, and loyalty, and gives reasons for each of these.
11. Necessity for use of but one particular coin in the Ledger as the money used in Italy is of so many different varieties. Here is used
    1 Scuto = 4 Lire = 80 Soldi in gold.
12. Describes the measures and weights used by the author.
13. Put a value on those things which are harvested and manufactured, but this should be lower than current prices so that the proceeds will not fall below this value in case of sale. What has been used should be charged to the proper department at the end of the year.
14. About the figures to be used. The Roman figures are difficult to change, but because fraudulent changes are more to be feared by bankers and merchants, he used the easier and more commonly used Arabic figures. Changes can be easily prevented by putting the money sign for lire directly in front and separating the divisions of the lire by little dashes, thus L 18 - 8 - 2—very much the same as done at present in England.
15. About the fiscal year. It can begin when one chooses, but must be twelve months long and must keep the same figures for the same year, namely, from June 1, 1586, to May 31st, 1586, not 1587.
16. Day books or memoranda books are necessary because the journal and ledger, due to their legal authentication, can be used only by the one bookkeeper appointed therefor and whose signature appears therein. Furthermore, transactions must be written down at the time and the place where they occur, and that may not be where the books are kept. Therefore, there are several memoranda books concurrently used, the first one of which is marked with a cross and those which follow with a letter in the order of the alphabet.
17. There should be at least three of these day books or memorials used—one for the cash receipts and disbursements and the deposits in the bank; one for the petty cash disbursements and one for all other entries from which the journal is written up, the latter to be in greater detail than the others.
    Other day books can be kept with the sales and purchases, rents, taxes, etc. A book is needed for the library and information pertaining to contracts, leases, employes, due dates, etc. Receipts for money loaned should be kept in bound book form so that they may not be lost or stolen. Each department head should keep such a book with its transactions, such as the shoe maker, gardener, tailor, etc.
18. Describes a blotter or tickler which contains a sheet for each month, and a line for each day in which the duties of the storekeeper and butler are written, one for each day in the year.
19. Gives such a book in full detail.
20. About the journal and how to keep it. Journal is basis of the ledger and therefore it is essential that it is kept correctly.
21. The beginning of the journal, in the name of God. The value of prayer to success and the use of the little cross (†) as explained elsewhere.
22. Entries should be made in the journal from day to day and hour to hour, but some times this is not possible, especially in a monastery, where the memoranda or day books of the various departments are delivered only once a month.
23. About the manner and order in which the entries are made in the journal. A list of days on which entries are to be made is prepared by days from all the memoranda or day books, the cash entries always first.
24. Gives an example of this list.
25. Eight things always needed to make a proper journal entry: Debit—Credit—Time—Value—Quality —Quantity—Price—Arrangement;
    The first two being the most important.
26. The greatest difficulty is to find what to debit and what to credit. All entries can be reduced to three principles.

27. List of above three principles:
    1. (Receipt, sales, payment of an account due, borrowing.
       (Disbursement, purchase, payment of a debt, loaning.
    2. (Purchasing on credit or for cash.
       (Selling on credit or for cash.
       (Exchanging with money or without.
    3. (Assignment of a debt to settle with a creditor, or vice versa, called drafts.

28. About the six other things needed for a proper journal entry.

29. How the journal is arranged. (See reproduction of journal page and explanatory notes appended; omits the consecutive numbering of Journal entry, as so many do, because the date is a sufficient guide to locate the entry in the journal.)

30. About the ledger and its formation.
    Explains the opening account on page 1 of the ledger, and states it is the reverse of the closing account. Here he mentions debit as *debito* and credit as *credito,* although he usually states debit as *"dee dare"* and credit as *"dee havere."* Capital account is the key and the seal of the ledger.

31. Explains the use of the two ledger accounts—"Opening" and "Monastery." "Opening" is what the merchant calls "Capital" and practically he claims the same for "Monastery."

32. Explains what entries may be made in the capital account. Corrections of errors and profits or losses belonging to previous years. What we call surplus adjustments.

33. Gives a table of such capital account entries.

34. About the arrangement of accounts in the ledger, the capital account to be at the end of the book.

35. List of accounts in the ledger.

36. The ordinary index.

37. The special index.

38. Posting figures in the journal (one above the other).

39. How the entry is written in the ledger. ("A" on debit side of ledger, "Per" on credit side of ledger.)

40. Transfer to a new page is made by drawing the difference between the two sides and transferring this to the new page.

41. How to correct errors in the entries.

42. Entries which are written direct in the ledger without having been put in the journal.

43. About the income and expense account and the method of buying and selling. The author here states that merchants use this account for their profits or losses.

44. The vouchering by a signature of the principal disbursements.

45. About the difference in bookkeeping for land rented and that cultivated for one's own account.

46. Three principal reasons why the income should be divided over the same accounts in which the expenses and salaries are separated, namely to each departmental sub-division.

47. When the best time is to enter the rentals from lands. In the fall when the harvest is made, as at the end of the fiscal year is a busy enough time.

48. About personal accounts and the carrying of accounts with two different money values.

49. About the cash account in the ledger, and its peculiar uses.

50. About the acquisition and alienation of lands, for which separate accounts are provided.

51. About the accounts with partners or joint ventures.

52. When and how to check with dots.

53. A short method of checking with dots.

54. How to take a trial balance, which also constitutes the balance sheet. Divides the same in four: 1, expenses; 2, income; 3, assets; 4, liabilities.

55. How to find trial balance errors in a checked ledger.

56. How to refute a wrong opinion about the trial balance. Explains the fact that while debits and credits must equal, that such does not mean that the assets equal the liabilities.

57. How to compute the income and expense account. This he considers the most difficult, as some accounts will have three closing entries,—one for profit on sales; one for merchandise used by other departments of the business; and one for merchandise remaining on hand. Furthermore, measures and weights should also be brought in balance.

58. The manner in which the closing balance account is made up. Accounts are only ruled at the end of the year by a line under the figures or amounts; then entering the total, which must be the same on both sides. If an account is closed during the year, only a line is drawn, but the total is put inside the column and not under the line.

59. About other methods of closing the ledger and their shortcomings. Here the author describes several methods used at that time of closing a ledger and prefers his own because it gives finally in one account the status of the capital, whereas the other methods do not do so.

60. How an account is rendered to the church authorities at the end of the fiscal year.

In the comparative index we have given the items which are discussed by all the four authors there mentioned. There are, however, a number of items which some of the authors use and others do not. From among these, the following are taken as the most important.

Pietra discusses the following in his book, but Pacioli and Manzoni do not:

Chapter
3   distinction in bookkeeping for bankers, merchants, and capitalists.
4   describes three ledgers for these three businesses.
5   describes more in detail the ledger for capitalists—called "Economic Ledger."
7   inventory of merchandise in stores.
10 qualifications of bookkeepers.
12 description of measures and weights used in book.
13 put value on things harvested and used, and those not sold but used in other departments.
15 describes fiscal year—use same numerals, although calendar year changes.
17 separate daybooks for the following subjects: cash—bank—petty cash—library—contracts—leases—salaries—due dates—loans—and one for each department.
18 & 19 daily tickler for bookkeeper and storekeeper's duties.
22 journal written up once a month in a monastery, because all daybooks are in use.
23 the order in which transfers from daybook to journal are made—a list of this prepared beforehand—cash entries always first.
25 & 28 eight things always needed in any journal entry.
26 & 27 rules for journalizing.
29 arrangement of journal with five standing lines, but omits numbers of journal entries.
31 divides capital into two accounts—opening capital at beginning of year—closing capital at end of year.
32 interim entries in capital account or surplus adjustments.
33 table of such capital entries.
34 capital account always at end of the ledger.
37 special index.
39 apparent transposition of "A" and "Per" in ledger from its use in journal.
42 list of entries which do not go through journal.
43 vouchering of disbursements.
45 book for lands rented and cultivated for own account.
46 income divided in same accounts as expenses.
47 when to enter rentals—in fall or end of fiscal year.
48 personal accounts and accounts with two different values of moneys.
50 acquisition and alienation of lands.
53 a short method of checking the ledger.

Pietra mentions the following in his book, as does Manzoni, but Pacioli does not, proving by this that Pietra had apparently available both Manzoni and Pacioli:

more than one memoriale
five standing or "down" lines in journal
definite rules for journal entries
six things always needed in each journal entry
about transposition of "A" and "Per" in ledger from its use in the journal
    (Pietra does not explain definitely although his examples give it.)
numbering of journal entries.

Pietra's Chapter 33 explains all entries which may appear in the capital account and illustrates them with the following tabulation:

1. During the year
2. At the end of the year

1. During the year.

A. Profits.

a. omitted credits
    a. collected   Cash to capital
    b. uncollected   Debtor to capital

b. judgments obtained
    a. collected   Cash to capital
    b. uncollected   Debtor to capital

B. **Losses.**

a. omitted debts
    a. paid   Capital to cash
    b. to be paid   Capital to creditor

b. judgments lost
    a. paid   Capital to cash
    b. to be paid   Capital to creditor

2. **At the end of the year.**

A. **Extraordinary Accounts.**

a. balances of accounts
    a. what is due   Capital to creditor.
    b. what is owed   Creditor to capital

b. balance sheet adjustment
    a. what is owed   several kinds and without
    b. what is due   connection with the books

B. **Ordinary Accounts.**

    a. excess in expenses   Capital to income
    b. excess in income   Expenses to capital

Pietra's Chapter 42 explains about the many entries which are made in the ledger, without going through the journal, and classifies them as follows:

Refers to entries which we transfer from the old ledger into the new, partly daily, partly at the end of the year.

1. the introduction

2. the opening of capital account when it is transferred from the closing capital account and not from a new inventory.

3. balances transferred from one account to another.

4. contra entries to correct errors.

5. profit or loss due to inventory adjustments.

6. the balance of the income and expense account.

7. all closing entries at the end of the year.

8. the closing of the closing capital account.

INDRIZZO
DE GLI ECONOMI,
O SIA ORDINATISSIMA
INSTRVTTIONE DA REGOLATAMENTE
FORMARE QVALVNQVE SCRITTVRA
IN VN LIBRO DOPPIO;

AGGIVNTOVI L'ESSEMPLARE DI VN LIBRO
NOBILE, CO'L SVO GIORNALE, AD VSO DELLA
CONGREGATION CASSINESE, DELL'ORDINE
DIS BENEDETTO.

CON DVE TAVOLE, L'VNA DE'CAPITOLI, ET L'ALTRA
DELLE COSE PIV DEGNE, A PIENO
INTENDIMENTO DI CIASCVNO

Opera nuoua, non meno vtile che neceffaria, a Religiofi, che viuono delle proprie
Rendite, & ad ogni Padre di Famiglia, che fi diletti
del Libro Doppio

Compofta da Don Angelo Pietra Genouefe Monaco, & indegno feruo di Giefu Chrifto.

IN MANTOVA, Per Francefco Ofanna. Con licenza de' Superiori. MDLXXXVI

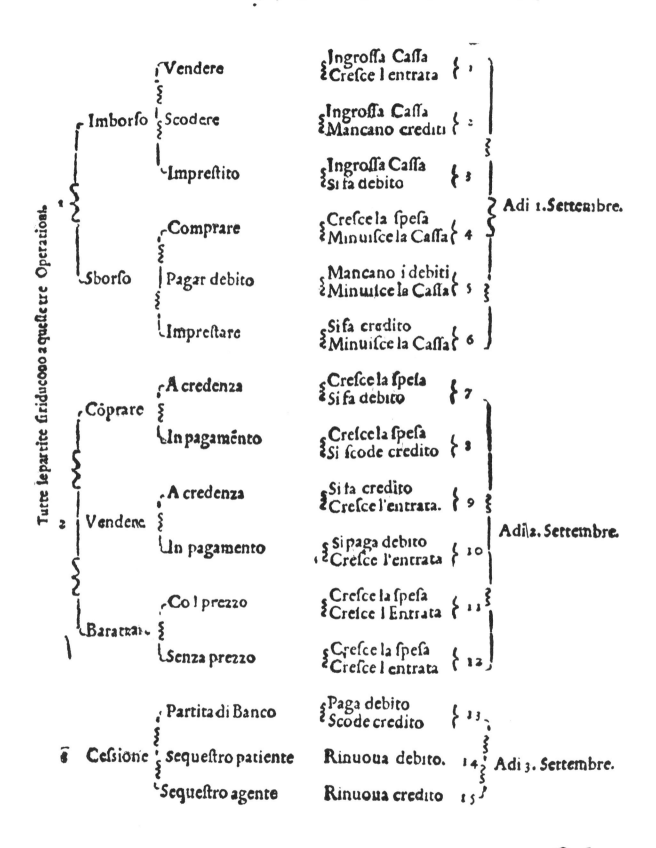

AL
NOME DELLA
SANTISSIMA ET
INDIVIDVA TRINITA'
PADRE, FIGLIO, E SPIRITO SANTO.

GIORNALE DEL LIBRO MAESTRO,
SEGNATO ✱ DEL MONASTERO,
DEL GLORIOSO PRECVRSOR
DI CHRISTO.
SAN GIO. BATTISTA D'ORIANA,
DELL'ANNO. 1586.

Cominciato adì primo Giugno. Scritto da me Don Gabriello da Parma,
Celleraro del detto Monaftero, di ordine del molto Reuerendo
Padre Don Romano Senefe Abate, della Congregation
Cafsinefe, dell'ordine del noftro Santifsimo
Padre Benedetto.

Adì primo di Giugno 1586.

Per Cartoleria / a Caſſa.lire venti β 10. ſpeſe in queſto libro doppio, col ſuo Giorna
le & Alfabeto , con altre due vacchette, e ſquarciafogli————————£ —20—10——
·32

Mutationi / a Caſſa,lire cinquantacinque β 10.date,cioe £ 22.al P.D.Benedet-
to da Bologna Decano, mutato queſto capitolo a Modona, per ſua mutatione di vn'anno, e buona mano. e £ 33— 10. date a Don Gio. Pietro da Salò,
mutato a Praglia,per ſua mutatione di vn'anno,ſpeſe fatte,e buona mano, co
me per loro riceuere appare diſtintamente nel libro di eſsi————————£ —55—10——
·32

Dette / a D.Mauro da Piacenza Concelleraro, lire diciſette β 12.conte a D.Va-
lentiniano da Napoli mutato a Roma,per ſua mutatione e buona mano,di me
ſi noue,ch'ei dimorò in queſto Monaſtero,come per ſuo riceuere————————£ —17—12——
·35

Adì 2.detto.

·32 **Caſſa** / a Federico barbaroſſa malgheſe,lire trecento quaranta otto β 12. con-
·53 temi per mano di Marco Solitario formaggiaro,a buó cóto del ſuo debito £ —348—12——

·35 **D. Mauro Concelleraro** / a Caſſa. lire cento trenta , contegli per ſpendere,
·32 come al mio libretto appare diſtintamente————————£ —130——

·38 **F.Thomaſo di Val camonica ſpenditore** // a Caſſa. lire nonantaſette β 14. 8. con
·32 tegli per ſpendere a minuto————————£ —97—14—8—

·58 **Cornelio Landino ſeruidore** / a D.Mauro Concelleraro, lire uenti,da lui ha-
·35 uute a buon conto del ſuo credito————————£ —20——

·32 **Caſſa** / ad Aleſſandro del Sole Affittuale,lire quattrocento ottantaſette β 10.
·51 da lui hauute a buon conto del ſuo debito————————£ —487—10——

·37 **P.D.Placido Mantouano Rettore di Badia** / a Caſſa,lire cento quaranta,conte-
·32 gli da ſpendere , come al mio libretto————————£ —140——

·39 **F.Manſueto Breſciano cuſtode al Priorato** // a Caſſa,lire ſettantacinque, con-
·32 tegli da ſpendere intorno alle poſſeſsioni————————£ —75——

·40 **P.Vigilantio Comaſco Oblato,cuſtode a Santi Martiri** / a Caſſa.lire cétouenti,
·32 mandategli da ſpendere,per mano di Fabritio Gallo noſtro fattore————£ —120——

·13 **Limoſine** / a D. Mauro,lire otto, date d'ordine del Reuerendo P.Abate, ad al-
·35 cuni hebrei fatti chriſtiani————————£ —8——

·58 **Berengario Serpentino camparo** // a F. Manſueto ,lire ſette β 10.da lui hauute
·39 a buon conto del ſuo ſalario————————£ —7—10——

Adì 3.detto.

·48 **m.Sigiſmondo Tranquillo** // a Gordiano Lampridio affittuale,lire dugento ot-
·51 tanta,contegli a noſtro nome in pagamento————————£ —280——

·16 **Badia** // al P.D.Placido,lire vndeci β 18.per dodici raſtelladori,& 24. forche di
·37 legno, compre per raſtellare & cuſtodire il fieno, come al ſuo libro————£ —11—18——

·19 **S. Martiri** //a F.Vigilantio, lire ſette β 15. 6. per diece pale compre per lo fru-
·40 mento , come al ſuo libro appare————————£ —7—15—6—

A 2

AL NOME DELLA SANTISSIMA ET

INDIVIDVA TRINITA

PADRE, FIGLIO, E SPIRITO SANTO.

LIBRO MAESTRO SEGNATO ✣, DEL
MONASTERO, DEL GLORIOSO
PRECVRSOR DI CHRISTO,
SAN GIO. BATTISTA D'ORIANA,
DELL'ANNO. 1586.

Cominciato al primo Giugno. Scritto da me Don Cefario da Cremona,
monaco del detto Monaftero; di ordine del molto Reuerendo
Padre Don Romano Senefe Abate, E del P. D. Gabriello
Parmiggiano Decano, e Celleraro del detto
Monaftero, della Congregation Cafsi-
nefe, dell'ordine del noftro
Santiffimo Padre
Benedetto.

1586.

INTROITO del presente libro + dee dare adi primo Giugno, per gl'infrascritti Creditori del Monaltero, qui tirati dall'Efito del libro dell'annopaffato, fegnato Z. carte 486. & a quello da i conti loro come appreffo. cioe.

.Alienationi dal libro Z.—	—car.429. Tirato in queſto libro. —	car. 15	ℒ 2750		
Ven. .Congregatione noſtra Caſsineſe —430	—Δ —96 — 4 7--6-	car. 42	ℒ -386 · 10		
R.D. .Clemente Aleni — — —431		car. 43	ℒ — 57 16 -·6		
m. .Ottauio Fortunato in Vinegia—436	—Δ 1200. a 5 per 100.	car. 45	ℒ 4800		
m. .Quintiliano Poeta in Vinegia—436	—Δ -600. a 4 per 100.	car. 45	ℒ 2400		
m. .Pompilio Defiderato in Vinegia — 436	—Δ -600 .a 4 per 100.	car. 45	ℒ 2400		
m. .Bartholo Saladino in Vinegia —437	—Δ 500. a 4 per 100.	car. 46	ℒ 2000		
m. .Zacheo Verace in Milano—437	—Δ -600. a 4 per 100.	car. 46	ℒ 2400		
.Mario Palmerino —438		car. 48	ℒ -547 -16 8.		
.Ramondo Pipino —438		car. 48	ℒ -493 10		
m. .Sabino Piſtoia —438		car. 48	ℒ -643 -18		
.Quintilio Purpurato —439		car. 48	ℒ -370-17-6.		
.Sigifmondo Tranquillo-—446		car. 48	ℒ -280		
m. .Torquato Rinieri —446		car. 49	ℒ -325		
.Enea Saiano —448		car. 49	ℒ -195 16		
.Illiano dalla Scala —449		car. 49	ℒ -485-10 8.		
m. .Liberio de'Mauri —449		car. 49	ℒ -893-15 5		
.Horatio Laureato —450		car. 49	ℒ -289-16-2		
m. .Seneca Valorofo affittuale—451		car. 52	ℒ -785 -18 4		
.Agolante de' Mori ferraro —463		car. 57	ℒ -127 12		
.Agrippa Tibullo marangone—464		car. 57	ℒ -68 - 7-8.		
.Pompeio Belcolore ciroico— —473		car. 57	ℒ -18 -10		
.Eugenio da Piſtoia barbero—474		car. 57	ℒ -12		
.Dante Congiurato barbero—474		car. 57	ℒ -10- 6.		
.Gerbino Ruſtico fornaro—476		car. 57	ℒ -37-12-10		
.Delfino Commodo camparo—477		car. 58	ℒ -78 12		
.Berengario Serpentino camparo—477		car. 58	ℒ -18 17 8.		
.Annibale Germano feruidore —480		car. 58	ℒ -130		
.Cornelio Landino feruidore—480		car. 58	ℒ - 30-15		
.Agapito Pagani feruidore —481		car. 58	ℒ -12 -17-9.		

.Somma ℒ 23052—16 · 2

.D Ee hauere adi primo Giugno, per gl' infrascritti Debitori del Monastero,
qui tirati dall'Esito del li b. dell'anno passato segnato Z.car. 436.& a quel
lo da i conti loro come appresso. cioè

R.D..Lorézo de'Simoni dal libro Z. carte 431	Tirato in questo libro	car. 45	£	--12	-6	
m. .Carlo Bianchino conto di tempo 450		car. 45	£	2750		
m. .Emanuelle Claudiano cóto di tepo 451		car. 55	£	1850		
.Aitolfo Corrado 455		car. 47	£	657	18	
.Maggio de' Popoli 455		car. 47	£	600		
.Costante Dragone 455		car. 47	£	150		
.Tiberio Stellato 456		car. 47	£	235	16	10
.Ottauiano Giordano 456		car. 47	£	258		
.Alessandro del Sole affittuale 457		car. 51	£	1370		
.Gordiano Lampridio affittuale 458		car. 51	£	1645	10	
.Federico Barbarossa malghese 459		car. 53	£	2248	10	
.Marino Orlando molinaro 461		car. 54	£	485	12	
.Ricardo Salomone molinaro 462	stara 30.Frumento	car. 54	£	372		
.Cassiano Amirante molinaro 463	stara 70.Misture	car. 55	£	348		
.Deodato Falcone massaro 465		car. 56	£	597	10	
.Demetrio Contestabile massaro 466		car. 56	£	642	14	
.Valerio Leoni massaro 467		car. 56	£	378	18	8
.Fabritio Gallo fattore 476		car. 57	£	25	15	
.Celestino Rosso seruidore 480		car. 58	£	16	14	7
m. .Zerbonio Quaranta gia affittuale 481		car. 58	£	947	16	
m. .Marco T.Villanuoua gia affittuale 482		car. 58	£	358	17	
.Fausto Giouiale gia nostro massaro 482		car. 58	£	588	18	6
.Innocentio Maiorano già fattore 483		car. 58	£	75	8	
.Leontio Manfredi gia nostro mol. 483		car. 58	£	18	7	6

Restanti di questo anno.   Somma £ 16634 - 12 - 1

.Ordinaria 323	Sale Pesi 70.	car. 2	£	70		
.Cascaria 324	Formaggio Pesi 50.	car. 3	£	225		
.Magazino d'Oglio 325	Oglio Pesi 30	car. 3	£	120		
.Forno di Farina 327	Farina Stara 45	car. 4	£	90		
.Vestieria 332	Rascie pezze cinque	car. 6	£	130		
.Calzoleria 333	Cordoani, & suole	car. 7	£	80		
.Barbaria 342	Sapone Pesi 10.	car. 9	£	30		
.Cantina di uino in Camerone 364	car.20.di uino per uso	car. 24	£	100		
.Cantina detta 364	car.20.da uendere a £ 15	car. 24	£	300		
.Cantina di uino diuersa 365	car.18. per uso	car. 25	£	90		
.Cantina di uino in Monastero 366	car.20. per uso	car. 25	£	100		
.Granaro di frumento in Camerone 367	stara 25.per uso	car. 26	£	50		
.Granaro detto 367	stara 155.da uendere a £3.18	car. 26	£	600		
.Granaro di Frumento diuerso 368	stara 45. per vso	car. 26	£	90		
.Granaro di Fruméto in Monastero 369	stara 20. per uso	car. 27	£	40		
.Granaro detto 369	stara 285.da uendere a £ 3.18	car. 27	£	800		
.Granaro di frumentata 370	stara 80 per uso	car. 27	£	120		
.Granaro di Vena, e Spelta 380	stara 60.per vso	car. 30	£	60		
.Magazino di Lino 381	Pesi 30.da uendere a £8.6.8.	car. 21	£	250		
.Cassa del P. Celleraro 412	In contanti	car. 32	£	1258	10	5
.D. Mauro Concelleraro 418	In contanti	car. 34	£	75	12	8
.F. Thomaso spenditore 422	In contanti	car. 38	£	32	10	6

.Monastero NOSTRO. 484

Somma £ 21346 - 5 - 9
------1706 10 - 5
Somma £ 23052 - 16 - 2

Dee hauere adi 23.Luglio   per Granaro del Monaſtero, per lo prezzo
commune a 2.di ſtara 196.frumento hauutcgli queſt'anno, come
al libro de' Granari appare diſtintamente———— ——— car. 27 ℒ—392———— -

.Et più   per Granaro di frumentata, hauuragli queſto anno, ragionata a β 30 prezzo commune ———————————— car. 27 ℒ—123———— -

.Et adi 26.Ottobre / per Cantina del Monaſtero, per carra 18. uino,
hauutogli come ſopra, ragionato a ℒ 5.prezzo commune —— car. 25 ℒ—90 ————

.Et più / per Granaro di Miglio, ſtara 46.ragionaro a β 30. ——— car. 28 ℒ—69 ————

.Et più / per Granaro di Melega, ſtara 48.ragionata a β 20. —— car. 29 ℒ—48

.Et adi 11.Maggio, per F.Vigilantio, hauuti da Piò 8.di prato affitta
to a ℒ 5.4.a Simone Guarnaccia ——————————————— car. 40 ℒ—41—12———

                                      .Somma ℒ—763—12———

.Dee hauere adi 23.Luglio / per Aquila Gradito affittuale ex parte r.per
lo prezzo commune a ℒ 2.di ſtara 250.frumento ne dee queſta raccol
ta, per lo fitto del primo anno——————————— car. 52 ℒ—500———

.Et più / per Aquila detto, per ſtara 40.di Vena, ne dee come ſopra,
ragionata a β 20.prezzo commune ————————— car. 52 ℒ—40———

.Et adi 26.Ottobre / per Aquila detto, per carra 18.uino ne dee co
me ſopra, ragionato al prezzo commune——————— car. 52 ℒ—90———

                                    .Somma ℒ—630———

.Dee hauere adi 23.Luglio / per Seuero Biondo maſſaro, & affittuale,
per ſtara 70.frumento ne dee per lo fitto di queſto 4. anno ——.car. 52 ℒ—140———

.Et adi 26.Ottobre / per Seuero detto per car 10.di uino ne dee co
me ſopra, ragionato a ℒ 5. prezzo commune—— car. 52 ℒ—50———

.Et adi 12.Nouembre / per Seuero detto, per lo fitto in denari di que.
ſto quarto anno finito a S.Martino, da pagarci come al ſuo còto car. 52 ℒ—400———

                                    .Somma ℒ—590———

.Dee hauere adi 27.Luglio / per Granaro di Faua, hauuragli queſto anno
in noſtra parte, ragionata a β 30.prezzo commune ———— car. 29 ℒ—52———

.Et più / per Granaro di Legumi, ſtara 8.hauuti, & ragionati utſ—car. 29 ℒ—12———

.Et adi 26.Ottobre / per Cantina del Monaſtero, per carra 12.uino ha
uutogli come ſopra, ragionato al prezzo commune di ℒ 5. — —car. 25 ℒ—60———

                                    .Somma ℒ—124—10———

.Dee hauere adi 14.Aprile / per Caſſa, uenduto a Gē
tile Maſſimino, a ℒ 10.il peſo, per mano del P.D.
Placido Rettore in Badia ———————— car. 34 peſi 102. 12. 6 ℒ 1025———

.Et per ſaldo di queſto conto, calato per quanto ſi e
ſtimato di più, in le due partite còtroſcritte car. 21 Peſi—2. 12. 6 ——————

                     .Somma peſi 105 ————ℒ 1025————

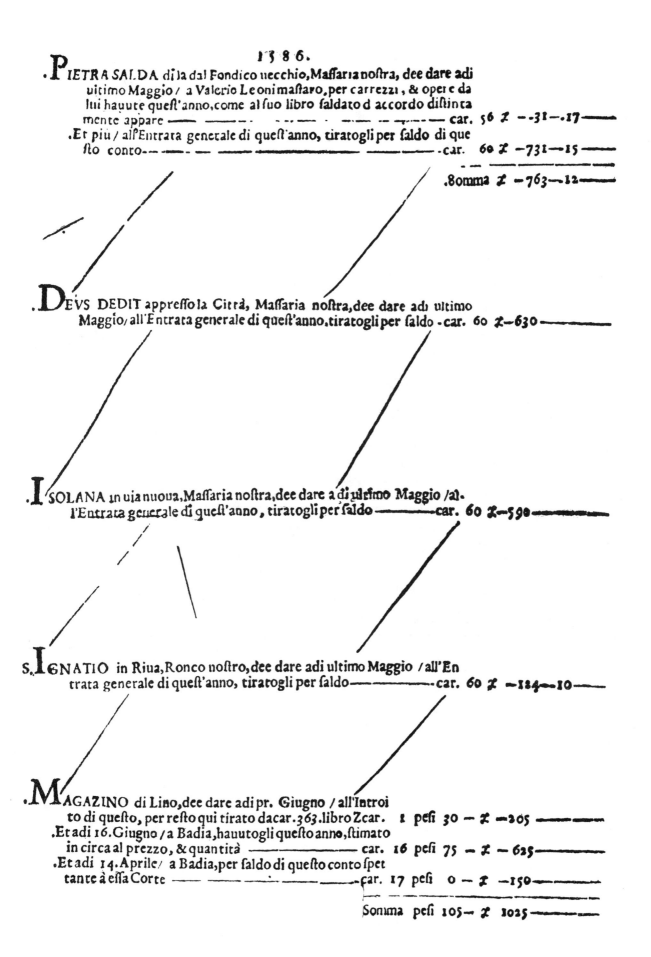

.**P**IETRA SALDA di la dal Fondico uecchio, Maffaria noftra, dee dare adi
ultimo Maggio / a Valerio Leoni maftaro, per carrezzi, & opere da
lui hauute queft'anno, come al fuo libro faldato d accordo diftinta
mente appare ——— · —— - ——— · —— ·—— car. 56 ℔ —-31—.17———

.Et piu / all'Entrata generale di queft'anno, tiratogli per faldo di que
fto conto— ——— —— ————— ———— .car. 60 ℔ —731—15———

.8omma ℔ —763—12———

.**D**EVS DEDIT appreffo la Citrà, Maffaria noftra, dee dare adi ultimo
Maggio / all'Entrata generale di queft'anno, tiratogli per faldo .car. 60 ℔—630———

.**I**SOLANA in uia nuoua, Maffaria noftra, dee dare a di ultimo Maggio / al.
l'Entrata generale di queft'anno, tiratogli per faldo ———— car. 60 ℔—590———

S..**I**GNATIO in Riua, Ronco noftro, dee dare adi ultimo Maggio / all'En
trata generale di queft'anno, tiratogli per faldo———— car. 60 ℔ —184—10———

.**M**AGAZINO di Lino, dee dare adi pr. Giugno / all'Introi
to di quefto, per refto qui tirato dacar.363.libro Zcar. 1 pefi 30 — ℔ —205 ———

.Et adi 16.Giugno / a Badia, hauutogli quefto anno, ftimato
in circa al prezzo, & quantità ———— car. 16 pefi 75 — ℔ — 625———

.Et adi 14.Aprile / a Badia, per faldo di quefto conto fpet
tante à effa Corte ——— · —— ———— .car. 17 pefi 0 — ℔ —150———

Somma pefi 105— ℔ 1025———

1586.

MONASTERO noſtro del glorioſo Precurſore , e degno Martire di Chriſto S.Gio: Battiſta d'Oriana,quale noſtro Sig. per ſua diuina bõ tà ſi degni diffendere,e proſperare,dee dare adi primo Giugno / all'Introito generale di queſt'anno, tiratogli da car.484.del libro Z. del l'anno paſſato ─────────────────────── car. 1 ₰ 1706─10─5─

1, .Et adi 7.Ottobre / a Caſſa,conti a Delio Peſcatore, in pagamento di quanto reſtaua ad hauere,per peſce da lui ha uuto queſta quareſima paſſata,come per ſua liſta in filza ──────────── car. 32 ₰ ─95─15─6─

6 .Et più / a Priſciano Volpe , p reſto di panno,raſcia,e tele da lui hauu te gli anni paſſati,come per ſua liſta in filza appare diſtintaméte,che per iſcordo non ſi ſcriſſero ───────────── car. 50 ₰ ─47─8.────

7 .Et più / a Caſſa,conti a m.Bartholomeo Calcinato,in uirtù di vna ſen tenza della Ruota,per acqua godutagli da noſtri di Badia gli anni paſſati,della ſua rata parte,come appare ne gli atti di m.Andrea Lo douici notaro diffulamente ───────── car. 32 ₰ ─135────

8 .Et piu / a Santo Squarcialupo,per tanti gli douemo pagare fra otto meſi,in uirtù di una ſentenza della Ruota,vſcita ne gli atti del detto notaro,per riſtoro di tempeſta patita l'anno 1582.che eſſo era Affit tuale a S.Remigio, con le ſpeſe ─────── car. 50 ₰ ─135─10─2─

9 .Et adi ultimo Maggio / a F.Thomaſo ſpenditore, per ſaldo di ſuo con to qui tirato,per ſuario occorſogli queſto anno ──── car. 39 ₰ ─0─18─1─

10 O .Et più / per Suario occorſo queſt'anno nel bilancio,come ſi uede car. 59 ₰ ─4─17─10─

.Et più / all'Eſito generale di queſt'anno,tiratogli per ſaldo di queſto conto ──────────────── car. 61 ₰ 3744─0─3─

.Somma ₰ 5870─0─3─

1   .**D**Ee hauere adi primo Ottobre / per Caſſa , contone dal R.P. F. Pietro
    Martire da Turino di S. Domenico, p̄ tāti hauuti da un penitete, in
    ſodisfattione di vno debito ſuo, che noi ſi haueuamo ſcordato-car. 32   _L_ —127—13 — 8 —

2   .Et più / per Riginaldo Campione, per la Boſchetta del Vallone, datta
    gli l'anno paſſato da tagliare, e da pagarne a S. Michele proſsimo
    paſſato, che non ſi ſcriſſe per iſcordo —————————— -car. 47   _L_ —50 ——————

3   .Et più / per Caſſa, contone da Donino Turchino già noſtro Affittuale,
    in virtù di una Sentēza di Ruota, per lo danno da lui hauuto in arbo
    ri tagliati, e non piantati in quel tempo, come ne gli atti di m. Vincē
    zo Roſſo notaro appare diſtintamente———————— car. 32   _L_ —146 ————

4   .Et più / per Naſtagio Calandra , per tanti ne dee in uirtù di una ſen
    tenza del Mag. Podeſtà. per l'interreſſe patito in uno paro di caual
    li da carrozza uendutine per ſani ——————————— car. 47   _L_ — 90 ——————

10   .Et adi ultimo Maggio / per D. Mauro ſecondo Celleraro , per ſaldo
    del ſuo conto, nel quale e ſeguito ſuario queſto anno ———— car. 36   _L_ —— 2—18— 4—

11   O   .Et più / per Cōtroſcrittione della conſimile partita per contro, poſta
    per eſſempio, eſſendo il bilancio uero, e reale ——— ———— car. 59   _L_ —— 4—17—10—

12   .Et piu / per la Speſa generale, per ſaldo di quel conto qui tirato, per
    quanto s'e ſpeſo meno queſto anno dell'Entrata hauuta.——— car. 60   _L_ 5448 —10—— 5—

                              .Somma   _L_ 5870 —0—— 3—

1586.

SPESA generale di queſt'anno , finito adi ultimo Maggio, dee dare, per ſal
do degli infraſcritti conti, qui tirati, & eſſinti dalle loro partite, co
me in eſsi conti diſtintamente appare cioè

.Ordinaria in danari	car.	4	ℒ 3372 — 13 — 11 —
.Caſciaria formaggio peſi 202.	car.	3	ℒ — 690 — 14 — 4 —
.Magazino d'Oglio peſi 168	car.	3	ℒ — 719 — 11 —
.Foreſteria	car.	3	ℒ — 205 — 16 — 5 —
.Forno, di Farina ſtara 438	car.	4	ℒ — 876 —
.Vino conſumato, carra 53	car.	4	ℒ — 265 —
.Infermeria	car.	4	ℒ — 402 — 17 — 5 —
.Spetieria	car.	5	ℒ — 262 — 17 —
.Straordinaria	car.	5	ℒ — 361 — 13 — 7 —
.Veſtieria	car.	6	ℒ 1892 — 5 — 8 —
.Calzoleria	car.	7	ℒ — 419 — 12 — 6 —
.Mutationi	car.	7	ℒ — 276 — 7 — 6 —
.Viaggi	car.	8	ℒ — 298 — 6 — 1 —
.Taſſe, & Annate	car.	8	ℒ 3337 — 4 —
.Datij, e Grauezze	car.	8	ℒ — 616 — 13 —
.Speſe Capitolari	car.	8	ℒ — 100 — 16 —
.Cartoleria	car.	9	ℒ — 156 — 6 — 3 —
.Libraria	car.	9	ℒ — 229 — 16 — 6 —
.Porti di lettere	car.	9	ℒ — 87 — 13 — 6 —
.Barbaria	car.	9	ℒ — 113 — 9 — 8 —
.Maſſeritie	car.	10	ℒ — 496 — 0 — 10 —
.Vtenſigli	car.	10	ℒ — 582 — 17 — 5 —
.Stalla	car.	11	ℒ 1028 — 4 — 8 —
.Fabrica	car.	11	ℒ 1131 — 9 — 6 —
.Reparationi	car.	11	ℒ — 210 — 9 — 10 —
.Liti, e Scritture	car.	12	ℒ — 411 — 10 — 3 —
.Salariati	car.	12	ℒ 1095 — 18 — 8 —
.Limoſine	car.	13	ℒ — 680 — 6 — 6 —
.Sagriſtia	car.	14	ℒ — 900 — 19 — 4 —
.Acquiſti fatti	car.	15	ℒ — 437 — 8 — 6 —

Somma ℒ 21660 — 19 — 10 —

.Speſo meno dell'Entrata di queſt'anno, che ſi tira al Monaſt. nꝛo. car. 59 ℒ 5448 — 10 — 5 —

.Somma ℒ 27109 — 10 — 3 —

ENTRATA generale di quest'anno finito adi ultimo Maggio, dee hauere,
per faldo degl'infrafcritti Conti qui tirati, & eftinti dalle loro parti
te, come in elsi conti diftintamente appare cioè

.Badia di S. Fulgentio in Camerone	car.	17	£ 4427--19 - 10
.Priorato di S. Remigio, Corte noftr'	car.	18	£ 1805 — 9 — 5
.S. Mauro Maffaria, e Corte noftra	car.	19	£ 1621 — 3
.S. Martiri, Maffaria, e Corte noftra	car.	19	£ -179 — 14 — 1
.Romea, Maffaria noftra	car.	20	£ 1010 — 18
.Acqua chiara, Maffaria noftra	car.	20	£ 2925 — 11
.S. Dionigi, Maffaria noftra	car.	20	£ -747 — 10
.Honorata, Maffaria noftra	car.	20	£ 1988
.Pietra Salda, Maffaria noftra	car.	21	£ -731 — 15
.Deusdedit, Maffaria noftra	car.	21	£ -636
.Ifolana, Maffaria noftra	car.	21	£ -590
.S. Ignatio, Ronco noftro	car.	21	£ -124 — 10
.Malgheria noftra	car.	22	£ -483 — 12
.Socida di Beftiami	car.	22	£ -. 52
.Razza di Caualli	car.	22	£ -.68
.Terratici diuerfi	car.	22	£ -227 -- 10
.Selue, e Bofchi	car.	22	£ -345
.Molina	car.	23	£ 1187 -- 15
.Cenfi, e Liuelli	car.	23	£ -126 — 19 — 11
.Fitti di Cafe, e Botteghe	car.	24	£ -980 — 4
.Horto del Monaftero	car.	24	£ -221 -- 18

Aumenti dal commun prezzo.

.Cantina di uino in Camerone, in carra 50. uenduto	car.	24	£ -444
.Cantina diuerfa, in carra 10. uenduto	car.	25	£ -84 — 3 — 4
.Cantina del Monaftero, in carra 16. uenduto	car.	25	£ -128 -- 12
.Granaro in Camerone, in ftara 937 Frumento uenduto	car.	26	£ 1825 — 16
.Granaro diuerfo — ftara 478	car.	26	£ 1074 - 15
.Granaro del Monaftero ftara 250	car.	27	£ -888 -- 16
.Granaro di Frumentata - ftara 220	car.	27	£ -320 -- 10
.Granaro di Segala ftara 618	car.	28	£ -900
.Granaro di Miglio — ftara 362	car.	28	£ -271 - 10
.Granaro di Panigo ftara 175	car.	28	£ -157 — 10
.Granaro di Faua — ftara 198	car.	29	£ -319 -- 10
.Granaro di Legumi ftara 15	car.	29	£ -22 — 8 — 8
.Granaro di Melega — ftara 230	car.	29	£ -172 -- 10
.Granaro d'Orgio ftara 30	car.	30	£ -.24

　　　　　　　　　　　　　　　.Somma £ 27109 -- 10 — 3

ESITO generale di queſt'anno, finito adi ultimo Maggio, dee dare, per li infraſcritti crediti del Monaſtero, qui tirati dai conti loro, cioe

	.Quilico Fedele, e fratelli	car. 50	₤ — 473	— 18	
m.	.Gordiano Lampridio affittuale	car. 51	₤ — 354	— 14	— 7
	.Eutitio Lanciano fornaſaro	car. 48	₤ — 824	— 10	
	.Henrico Lanfranco malgheſe	car. 54	₤ 2008	— 12	— 6
	.Oberro Baſiliſco molinaro	car. 55	₤ — 109	— 10	
	.Et piu Frumento ſtara 10.	car. 55	₤ 20		
	.Demetrio Conteſtabile maſſaro	car. 56	₤ — 414	— 18	
	.Valerio Leoni maſſaro	car. 56	₤ — 276	— 12	— 8
	.Vittorio, e Corteſe Palladini maſſari	car. 56	₤ — 153	— 15	— 6
	.Rinaldo Sanſone maſſaro	car. 56	₤ — 191	— 6	
	.Temiſtio Solimano maſſaro	car. 56	₤ — 67	— 13	
	.Dante Congiurato barbero	car. 57	₤ — 3	— 10	

Inesſigibili, & a lungo tempo

m.	.Marco Tullio Villanuoua gia affittuale	car. 58	₤ — 358	— 17	
	.Fauſto Giouiale gia maſſaro	car. 58	₤ — 588	— 18	— 6
	.Innocentio Maiorano gia fattore	car. 58	₤ — 75	— 8	
	.Leontio Manfredi gia molinaro	car. 58	₤ — 18	— 7	— 6

			Somma	₤ 5940 — 11 — 3

Reſtanti di queſto anno			car.	₤	
.Caſciaria formaggio, per uſo — peſi	50 a ₤ 2	car. 3	₤ — 100		
.Cantina di Camerone, per uſo — carra	12 a ₤ 5	car. 24	₤ — 60		
.Cantina diuerſa, per uſo — carra	20 a ₤ 5	car. 25	₤ — 100		
.Cantina del Monaſtero, per uſo — carra	16 a ₤ 5	car. 25	₤ — 80		
.Granaro di Camerone, per uſo — ſtara	10 a ₤ 2	car. 26	₤ — 20		
.Da uendere — ſtara	50 a ₤ 4. 10	car. 26	₤ — 225		
.Granaro diuerſo, per uſo — ſtara	10 a ₤ 2	car. 26	₤ — 20		
.Granaro del Monaſtero, per uſo — ſtara	82 a ₤ 2	car. 27	₤ — 164		
.Da uendere — ſtara	250 a ₤ 4. 10	car. 27	₤ 1125		
.Granaro di Vena, e Spelta — ſtara	50 a ₤ 1	car. 30	₤ — 50		
.Caſſa in contanti		car. 34	₤ — 596	— 19	— 6

.Somma ₤ 8481 — 1 — 9

IL FINE.

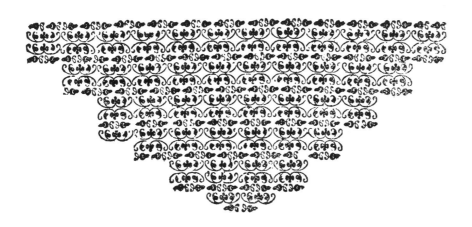

Esito generale di queſt'anno finito adi ultimo Maggio, dee hauere per gli
infraſcritti debiti del Monaſtero, qui tirati da i conti loro, cioè

m. .Bartholo Saladino in Vinegia, a Cenſo △ 500.		car. 46	ℒ	1000
m. .Aquila Gradito affittuale, conto di tempo		car. 52	ℒ	1500
R.D. Clemente Aleni noſtro Curato		car. 43	ℒ	37—16—6
.Fabritio Gallo noſtro fattore		car. 57	ℒ	24—5
.Delfino Commodo camparo		car. 58	ℒ	60
.Annibale Germano ſeruidore		car. 58	ℒ	115

Somma ℒ 4737—1—6

.Monaſtero noſtro reſta in credito, come ſi uede —— car. 59 ℒ 3744—0—8

.Somma ℒ 8481—1—9

I L   F I N E.

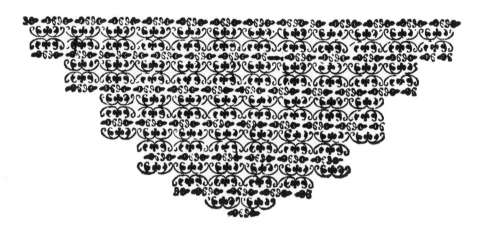

MAINARDI'S JOURNAL REPRODUCED

In 1632 there appeared in Bologna a work on bookkeeping, written by Matteo Mainardi. This book is of far later date than the ones heretofore mentioned, but as explained in the historical chapter it is remarkable in that it attempts to describe, besides the system for the merchants, one for the keeping of executors' and trustees' accounts. It follows Pietra and Manzoni closely in a good many instances.

The illustrations have small value for us except to indicate the little progress that was made in Italy with the shifting of the center of trade from Italy to Holland, as Simon Stevin's book hereinafter reproduced, which was published in 1604 in Holland, was far in advance of this of Mainardi's. We reproduce the title page of the second edition of this book, and a page which explains the purpose of the book as far as trustees' and executors' accounts are concerned. The two pages of the journal we give in order to show that each page is provided with the address to the Deity, that the dot is used for checking, and that we here find so-called combination journal entries, by which we mean entries in which are combined more than one credit or more than one debit in one entry. We do not, however, find the use of the word "sundries," as in Stevin's work and as we use it to this day. It will be noted that in such entries the debits are always named first and itemized before the credits are enumerated, and that the division between debits and credits is made with two horizontal lines or dashes, one below the last debit and one above the first credit. We also note the absence of the money signs, except the principal or the lire sign.

IL CAMBIO
REALE
PER
OGNI PIAZZA.
Formalmente Ragguagliato
DA
MATTEO MAINARDI.

Con diuersi altri Quesiti vtili, curiosi, e necessarij
alla Mercatura

In questa nuoua Impressione aggiòntoui il modo,
che hoggidì si pratica.

IN BOLOGNA. M. D. CC.

Per il Longhi. *Con licenza de' Superiori.*

M. DC. XXXIV.

Laude, e gloria della Santiſsima, & Indiui-
dua Trinità Padre, Figliuolo, e Spirito
Santo; della Glorioſiſsima Vergine Maria,
delli Santi Apoſtoli Pietro, e Paolo, e delli
Santi N. N. noſtri Protettori, come ancora
di tutta la Corte Celeſtiale. Amen.

Queſto preſente Libro chiamato Giornale, di forma
N. di carte N. coperto di N. di carte num. N. e ſegnato
N. è di Rutiglio figliuolo del già Sig. Leonido Fonga-
relli pupillo, d'età d'anni N. & erede (ò ab inteſtato, ò
teſtamentario) del ſudetto Sig Leonido, paſſato à mi-
glior vita li 16. Gennaro del preſente anno, ſotto la tu-
tela di N. ſopra del quale, per mano di N. ſarà notato
regolatamente, e formalmente, ogni qualità di beni
ſtabili, e mobili, beſtiami, debitori, e creditori del d.
già Sig. Leonido, e per conſeguenza hora ſpettante al
medeſimo Sig. Rutiglio ſuo figliuolo, & erede, come
ſopra; e ſuſſeguentemente tutte l'entrate, e ſpeſe,
che frà l'anno ſeguiteranno in queſta eredità, le quali
partite tutte ſaranno leuate da queſto Libro, e portate
per mano del ſudetto N. ſopra vn altro Libro chiamato
Libro Maeſtro di forma, carta, coperta, e ſegno come
queſto, di carte num. N. à ſuoi appartati luoghi, con-
forme è lo ſtile Mercantile, che però eſſo Pupillo (e per
eſſo il Sig. N. ſuo Commiſſario Teſtamentario) intende,
che li ſia data piena, & indubitata fede in giudicio, e
fuori.

In fede di che &c.

Io N. Commiſſario Teſt. &c. affermo quanto di ſopra.
Io N. Scriuano accetto, e giuro quanto di ſopra.

A

GIOR-

Laus Deo, & B. Virg. Rofarij M. DC. XXXIII.

Adì 31. Decembre Sabbato.

. 10   Alli, Manmini, &c. al banco lir. quattrocentotrè, fol. tredici, den. quattro quat li por-
     tò il noftro Caneuaro contanti , retratti fino à quefto giorno fudetto, di Faffi dieci-
     milla da cauazzatura venduti à minuto, à bolognini fette la carica, e numero fet-
     temilla di vite, à bolognini trentadue il cento, come fi vede per vna taglia .   L.{403. 13. 4

. 11   A credito Faffi da cauazzatura in cafa num. 10000.   L.291.13.4

. 11   A credito Faffi di vite in cafa num. 7000.   L.112,

. 9   A fpefe di fuoco lir. vintifei, fol. trè, den. due quat. per num. ottocentoquindici Faffi
     da cauazzatura, e num. quattrocent'ottantadue di vite ferbati per cafa.   L.{ 26. 3. 2

. 11   A credito Faffi da cauazzatura num. 815.   L.20. 7.6.

. 11   A credito Faffi di vite num 482.   L. 5.15.8.

. 7   A Luca Barbini noftro lauoratore alla Poffeffione di Pondi lir, centodiciafette quat,
     cioè lir. cento per li patti in denari contanti , e lir. diciafette per corbe quattro
     d'Orzo hauuto più mefi fono dal noftro Fattore, à lir. quattro, fol. cinque la corba,
     d' accordo .   L.{117. —

. 7   A credito alla Poffeffione di Pondi .   L. 100.

. 9   A credito Orzo à Montorio cor. 4.   L. 17,

. 7   A Domenico Manganella noftro Suozzo alla Poffeffione di Bella lir. centoquarant'
     vna, fol. cinque quat. cioè lir. centouinti per li patti, che deue pagare in denari
     lir. vent'vna, fol. 5. per corbe 5. d'orzo hauuta dal Fattore, d'accordo.   L.{141. 5. —

. 8   A credito alla Poffeffione di Bello.   L. 120.

. 9   A credito à Orzo in granaro di Montorio corbe 5.   L. 21.5.

. 7   A Liuio Carboni, e fratelli noftri mezzaiuoli à Montoria lir. centofeffantatrè , fol.
     due, den. fei quat. cioè lir. centoquaranta per li patti, che paga in denari, e lir.
     ventitrè, fol. due, den. fei per corbe cinque, e meza d'Orzo hauuto, d'accordo.   L.{163. 2. 6

. 8   A credito la Poffeffione di Montorio .   L.140.

. 9   A credito Orzo à Montorio corbe cinque, e meza .   L. 23.2.6.

. 7   A Angelo Sufa noftro Suozzo à Romanello lir centoquarantatrè , fol. due , den. fei
     quat. cioè lir. centouinti per li patti che paga in danari , e lir. vintitrè, fol. dieci,
     den. fei per corbe cinque, e meza d'Orzo hauuto, d'accordo, più dì fono.   L.{143. 2. 6

. 8   A credito la Poffeffione di Romanello .   L. 120.

. 9   A credito Orzo in granaro di Montorio corbe cinque, e meza.   L. 23.2.6.

A Mt.

Laus Deo, & B. Virg. Rosarij M. DC. XXXIII.

Adì 31. Decembre Sabbato.

. 14	A Michele Landinelli nostro bracente à Romanello lir. vintinoue, cioè lir. vinti per la pigione della casa, e lir. noue quat. per corbe due, quar. due d'orzo, bauuto più giorni sono dal Fattore, d'accordo. L. 29. —	
. 7	A credito Luogo di Romanello. L. 20.	
. 9	A credito Orzo in granaro cor. 2. quar. 2. L. 9.	

. 13	A spese d'Elemosine lir. centononanta, sol. otto, quat. dispensate il Natale passato à diuersi Luoghi Pij, & à poueri della nostra Parochia, per l'anima del Sig. Leonido, per noi dalli Mannini, &c. L. 190. 8. —
. 10	A credito alli Mannini, &c. al banco.

. 12	A Canape grezzo in Villa lir. cinquecentosessantanoue, sol. quattordici quat. per valuta di lib. duemillaottocentoquarant'otto, e meza di Canape, bauuta dalli nostri lauoratori, della sua parte, apprezzata senza pregiudicio lir. vinti il cento. L. 569. 14. —
. 7	A credito Luca Barbini per lib. 537. e meza. L. 107. 10.
. 7	A credito Domenico Manganelli per lib. 711. L. 142. 4.
. 7	A credito Liuio Carboni per lib. 837. e meza. L. 167. 10.
. 7	A credito Angelo Susa, per lib. 612. e meza. L. 122. 10.
. 7	A credito Michele Landinelli lib. 150. L. 30.
. 14	

. 7	A spese di reparationi, e fabriche lir. centotrentanoue, sol. sei, den. otto quat. pagati per mandato questo giorno sudetto à M. N. nostro Capelletto, e sona, cioè lir. cinquanta per la sua annua prouisione di coprire, e riuedere tutte le nostre case di Villa, e di Città, e il resto per spese, che dà conto bauere fatto in risarcire le case di Villa, come di tutto ne appare lista in filza di più somma, per mandato dalli Mannini, &c. al banco. L. 139. 6. 8
. 10	A credito li Mannini, &c. al banco.

. 7	Alla Possessione di Pondi lir. settantasette, sol. otto, den 8. quat. si fanno buoni à M. Sabadino Pazaglia di Mal'albergo, e sono per sei nauate di stramo, mandatoci li mesi passati, compresoui le condotte, così d'accordo insieme. L. 77. 8. 8
. 8	Alla Possessione di Bello lir. settantasette, sol. otto, den. otto quat. buoni al sudetto, come sopra, per sei nauate di stramo da letto, come sopra detto. L. 77. 8. 8
. 8	Alla Possessione di Montorio lir. centocinque, sol. tredici per otto nauate di stramo da letto mandatoli il sudetto, come sopra. L. 105. 13. —
. 8	Alla Possessione di Romanello lir. centocinque, sol. tredici quat. buoni al sudetto per altre otto nauate di stramo da letto bauute, come sopra. L. 105. 13. —
. 14	A credito Sabadino Pazaglia lir. 366. 3. 4.

A Sa-

❧ Nieuwe Instructie

Ende bewijs der looffelijcker Consten des
Rekenboecks/ende Rekeninghe te houdene
nae die Italiaensche maniere/allen Cooplie
den/Rentmeesteren/Tollenaren/Assijsmee
steren/ zeer nut ende profytelijck: Informe=
rende eenen yeghelijcken/hoe hy zekere ende
perfecte Rekeninghe houden sal met dobbel
boecken nae der manieren voors. Waer duer
elck by hem seluen lichtelijck in allen sinen sa
ken eñ affairē groote experientie crighen sal.

❡ Ghetranslateert met grooter diligentien/
wt die Italiaensche tale in onser spraken
duer Jan ympyn Christoffels (saligher
memorien) Coopman van Antwer=
pen: Ende nu ter liefden eñ profy
te des ghemeynen weluaerts
eerst wtghegeuen int Jaer
M.CCCCC.XLIIII.

❡ Cum Gratia ı Preuilegio/vier Jaren lanck
duerende/zoot blijct by der Copien van die
Keyserlijcke Maiesteyt verleent.

NOTES ON YMPYN

We are reproducing herewith the title page of Ympyn's book, which we have taken from Kheil's book, where a thorough comparative study is made between Ympyn and Pacioli. Ympyn, as we have seen, was the first Dutch writer who practically translated Pacioli into Dutch, French and English, and from him continental Europe has derived its subsequent texts on bookkeeping. The original of this book was not available to the writer, but we have taken from Kheil's book the most important subject-matters which we review in the following lines:

Ympyn, as stated heretofore, copied Pacioli practically verbatim. We find, however, here and there a few deviations which we think it important to mention at this place.

Pacioli speaks about the two divisions of his book, one covering inventory and the other "disposition." He is somewhat vague in explaining this latter term. Ympyn says that "disposition" is "the establishment, systematizing and execution of the current and customary as well as the extraordinary affairs of a business.

Ympyn suggests that the index should be bound in parchment and placed either at the beginning or the end of the ledger, but in such a manner that it can be taken out if necessary. He uses the Italian terms "Per" and "A" untranslated. In front of corrective ledger entries he uses a cross and does not mention any other distinguishing marks. The term "cash" is personified to cashier instead of pocket book, as used by Pacioli. He enlarges on the terms "Cash" and "Capital" more than Pacioli does. For branch stores the sales are entered into a sales journal, and totaled once a week for transfer to the ledger. Ympyn is more extensive in his explanations than Pacioli about *barrato* or trade, also about the draft and its use. We should remember, however, that Pacioli describes these more fully in the parts of his book not covered by the subject of bookkeeping.

Ympyn recommends a separate book for household expenses, and a petty expense book for the small expenses of the business. The totals are transferred from these books to the journal once a month. He mentions a special cash book for special kinds of species or for foreign money which is handled by the firm, very much as some banks today use a separate account with bank notes of large denominations. He advocates the use of separate books for statistics, or memoranda, in the nature of diaries; and suggests a shipping book. As to accounts, he mentions interest, building rents, ground rents, expenses, household expenses, merchandise expenses, building repair, garden expenses, salaries, loans, expenses of childbirths and an account for marriage gifts.

Like Pacioli and Manzoni, Ympyn uses a profit and loss account, very much the same as we do today. He also draws off a balance to prove the correctness of the ledger. Ympyn, however, puts the balance at the end of the ledger as an account, although he does not explain it as such in his text; in this he does not follow Pacioli. He balances the profit and loss account to capital account without passing it through the journal.

Ympyn specifically mentions that merchandise must be inventoried at cost and he uses a merchandise inventory account, to which all accounts showing an inventory of merchandise or goods on hand are closed and then this account in turn is closed to the balance account. He does not journalize these entries. However, we find that he does journalize his profit and loss items, as does Manzoni, but which Pacioli does not do.

Assets in the balance account are put on the credit side and liabilities on the debit side. He uses no opening balance account in the new ledger, but evidently posts from the old balance account in the old ledger in reverse order to the new ledger, because the closing balance account in the old ledger gives the folios to which the items are posted in the new ledger. We have seen that Pacioli says that you can transfer the capital account either as a balance in one item, or itemized; the latter having the advantage of then representing a summary of the inventory, and each new ledger then starts with an inventory.

The journal, profit and loss, capital, and balance accounts illustrated by Ympyn are printed in Kheil's German review of Ympyn, but we regret that he did not reproduce them actually, as with the modern printing much of the form and arrangement is lost.

Ympyn permits no erasures. He wishes a line drawn through the wrong amount or words the same as Pacioli does, in order to be able to prove of what the error consisted. He insists that explanations to the journal entries must be so clear that anybody can understand the transactions they record; that books kept in the Italian manner as described by him, with a journal and a ledger, "make everything as clear as daylight and will prevent swindles and defalcations, as occur now so frequently and almost daily."

He adds the freight to the merchandise and posts it to the merchandise account. He deprecates trading on long credit, and announces it as bad because "the wolf does not eat any days and the due date comes nearer not only by day but as well by night."

The two diagonal lines of which Pacioli speaks, are used in the journal when the posting is finished and in the ledger when the account is closed or transferred to the new ledger. Capital account Ymypn credits with the assets and debits with the liabilities, which agrees with the idea of the personifying of accounts and results in a net credit in this account, which net credit is the same as we use in the capital account to this day. Ympyn uses no ledger headings and shows but one column in the journal. He uses Roman figures in all money columns, both ledger and journal.

STEVIN'S JOURNAL ANDLEDGER REPRODUCED

The following pages, Nos. 119 to 136, represent reproductions of the journal and ledger and other interesting forms as given in the book of Simon Stevin, which appeared in the Dutch language in Amsterdam in 1604, was rewritten in The Hague in 1607, republished in Latin in 1608, and republished by Stevin's son Hendrick in 1650. As we have seen, Stevin was a tutor and adviser of Prince Maurits of Orange, then Governor of some of the Dutch provinces. Stevin first taught the Prince bookkeeping and then induced him to install a double-entry system of bookkeeping throughout his domains and government establishments.

Stevin apologizes for the use of terms in foreign languages, such as debit, credit, debitor, creditor, balance, journal, finance, etc., but says they are necessary because if he used Dutch terms the bookkeepers would not understand what he was writing about, and as bookkeepers only are supposed to profit by the regulations promulgated and ordered by Maurits, the Prince of Orange, for the double-entry municipal accounting system, he insists that he must use the foreign terms.

The objection of the Prince that government clerks would not understand Italian or double-entry bookkeeping, he overcomes by advising that he could hire and should hire clerks who did know it, for they undoubtedly would be better men.

The objections to the necessity of double-entry bookkeeping for municipalities and governments he reasons away by stating that a merchant has some direct personal supervision over his bookkeepers and cashiers, but the government must direct them through other persons. As this is not as safe as the merchant's personal supervision, it follows that if a merchant needs double-entry bookkeeping and finds it profitable, the government needs it that much more.

Stevin does not give rules for the making of journal entries, but he explains a difficulty which the Prince evidently met, when the latter asks: "If Peter pays me $100, there are two debits and two credits: I am his debtor and my cash is also a debtor; he is my creditor and his cash is also a creditor. Which two of these four must I select for my books?" Stevin answers: "Take always my creditor and my debtor because Peter keeps books with his creditor and his debtor."

Stevin urges upon the Prince that governmental treasurers invariably become rich, and when they die leave such a muddled state of affairs and records that there is nothing left but to forgive and forget, but that such is not the case with bookkeepers and cashiers of mercantile establishments; they invariably die poor. A merchant, he says, knows what his bookkeeper or his cashier or treasurer should have, but this is not so with a Prince, who has to take the cashier's word for it.

The Prince then asks if bookkeeping ever had been worthy of such consideration that books were published on it. Stevin replied that numerous writers had taken up the subject, and that while doubtless the double-entry system was originated in olden times, yet in Italy where it is said to have been executed first, it is considered an art of which no other is so honorable and worthy.

The Prince (apparently floored by Stevin's lucid arguments) thereupon agrees to take up the study with the view of installing double-entry bookkeeping in the governmental departments as soon as Stevin and he were through with their studies of algebra.

Stevin has a firm place in the heart of the writer, because he mentions in his book that one of his forbears was a treasurer of the city of Flissingen, thus supplying the missing data for the genealogy of his family.

Comparison of the journal and the ledger with the reproductions of the Italian writers heretofore given, will at once show that in printing as well as in arrangement the Dutch were far superior to the Italian. A comparison with Pietra and Mainardi will make this very plain. The examples must be pronounced as being excellent for their time. The journal entries are differently grouped than has been done by any previous writers, very much more systematic, and in many instances only totals from other records are used.

It will be noted that all religious terms at the top of pages or at the beginning of books, customarily used in the Italian method, have been omitted. The slightest reference to the Deity is absent in these books, due to the fight for religious freedom which then waged in Holland. Stevin was a great supporter of the Protestant party, so much so that Brown relates that when in 1645 a proposal was made to erect a statue at Bruges to his memory, a Catholic agitation was aroused in the House of Representatives to defeat the project. Even a clerical editor expunged his name from a Dutch dictionary of biography, where it had appeared in earlier editions. However that may be, the writer having been born in Holland and there having kept numerous sets of books, can vouch that twenty years ago the majority of books which came under his supervision were opened and closed in the name of the Diety.

Stevin's omission of the use of religious terms was followed in England, whereas Europe to this day follows Ympyn and others, which is corroborating evidence that Stevin through Dafforne has influenced English and American bookkeeping more than has Mellis, who followed Pacioli in the use of religious terms.

Through a peculiar coincidence the use of the terms "pepper" and "ginger" appear as frequently in his illustrations and examples, as they do in those of the Italian and other previous writers.

Stevin personifies the impersonal or economic accounts when he states that cash account is an account with the cashier and follows this idea throughout his work in connection with other accounts. He mentions the three methods of buying and selling theretofore described by the Italians, namely, on account, for cash, and in trade, and the combinations that can be made with these three. Like his predecessors, he states that in the beginning of every book two entries are necessary, which should cover merchandise, and cash on hand, as also the debts owing and accounts owning, and like Pacioli and Ympyn he explains fully that sometimes a business can be started on credit but he doubts the advisability.

Stevin is the first to use the system of controlling accounts, and as shown in the first page herewith reproduced, in the second line after the table, the same name for these accounts is retained today. He uses the word "contrerole," which comes from the French "controler," which in turn comes from the two Latin words "contra" and "rotulus" (our roll) and "rota" (our wheel). The definition of the word "control" is "to check by a duplicate register" or "verify an account." The total of his controlling account was obtained from the detailed monthly reports from the sub-treasurers or cashiers of the various places and departments, and were posted to these controlling accounts through the medium of journal entries. From these accounts tables were compiled showing the delinquencies for each year of each sub-treasury or of each place. He describes that an endless variety of these tables may be made in order to show the true status of the various operations at various places. He also states that if no tables are desired, then there should be a separate account for each column in these tables, and especially for each year. The table reproduced shows how particular and careful he was on this subject.

The ledger shows both the page of the journal and the page upon which the other part of the double-entry appears in the ledger. This is one of the first writers who enters the journal pages in the ledger. The pages of the journal are, however, put in the margin, on the left of the date in the ledger and not directly to the left of the amount, as we are accustomed to do at the present time. The explanations in the ledger will appear to you to be shorter and clearer and more to the point as to relevancy than was customary in the Italian method. It should also be noted that the term "per" is used on both sides of the ledger. Stevin says that many bookkeepers use "a" on the debit side where he uses "per." He suggests that his method is more reasonable, as can be learned by translating the entry in an ordinary sentence; thus, which is better language? "Peter is debit to me 'for' ('per') pepper sold to him," or "Peter is debtor to me 'to' ('a') pepper sold to him." He then states that it is not a matter of importance, that his readers can do as they like, but he wishes them to follow the better sentence.

In the journal he does not use the expression "per" before the debitor, nor "a" before the creditor, nor does he divide them with the two slanting lines // as do Pacioli, Manzoni, Pietra and Ympyn. Stevin simply used "debit per" between the names of the debtor and creditor thus coming closer to our present form of journal entry.

It is difficult to state what the two diagonal lines (//) between the debits and credits mean.

In the chapter entitled "Discursion in Theory" there has been set forth in detail Stevin's theory of a double entry with two debits and two credits, thus carrying the transaction through the proprietor's account but eliminating the same by algebraic formula.

The late Joseph Hardcastle, C.P.A., of New York, in 1903, in his "Accounts of Executors and Trustees," chapter on "The Personalistic Theory," very plainly sets forth the same idea elucidated by Stevin. He even goes so far as to state that Pacioli (he spells it with an "i") and Manzoni used the slanting lines between debits and credits to indicate the omission of the word "proprietor" twice.

Stevin explains that Roman figures in the ledger are not needed because they are never used in the journal, which is a book of more importance, and if they are not put in the book of more importance why should we put them in the book of less importance? He explains (as does Pacioli) that the ledger is not important because if the ledger is lost it can be written up entirely from the journal, whereas the reverse is not true, because the detail which the journal contains is lacking in the ledger. He further states that in the Italian books Roman figures are not used in the day book.

It will be noticed that each page of the ledger has a consecutive number (not as we number by giving two pages, the debit and the credit, one and the same number). Stevin explains that this is better because then all your debit pages will be uneven and the credit pages will be even numbers, which will aid in checking if an error is made in putting the little dividing line between figures representing the pages of the debit and the credit in the journal, as is customary in the Italian method. The fact that but one column is used in the journal, makes this little dividing line between the figures of the debit postings and those of the credit postings very important. Stevin further explains in this connection that it is still more confusing with a combination journal entry, where there are a number of debits and but one credit, or vice versa, when the word "sundries" is used. This because the debit of a combination journal entry comes first, and thereafter a number of credits, yet the total of the journal entry (which is the amount for the debit entry), stands at the last and therefore the debit is posted last, as will be seen from the illustration reproduced.

Stevin is the first of the writers mentioned in this book to use combination journal entries with the word "sundries." We have seen that Mainardi has combination journal entries or journal entries with more than one debit and more than one credit, but he does not use the word "sundries."

In the ledger it will be noted that the first entries, or the opening balances on some of the accounts, bear the date of "0 January." The use of the cipher at the beginning of the year, he says is absolutely necessary, because the books are opened on neither December 31st nor January 1st. It is a period in between these two. He explains this with the illustration that the first rung is not the beginning of the ladder.

The date in the ledger is repeated before each entry, instead of following the Italian method of using the words "a di detto," which mean "the..............day of the above month," because he says the date to which "ditto" refers may be several pages back and therefore hard to read at first sight.

115

Unlike Pacioli, Pietra and Ympyn, Stevin uses definite headings for his ledger accounts, and is the first one to use the terms "debit" and "credit" instead of "*dee dare*" and "*dee havere*." He puts the year on top of the page, and he balances his ledger accounts by making a sub-total. Closing entries do not go through the journal. Profit and loss account is written up at the end of the year, and also at the close of particular transactions, and while Stevin does not give a trial balance, in his descriptions he speaks very particularly of the same, and describes how to prepare it. While in his illustration he credits a legacy to the profit and loss account, in his text he admonishes the reader to put it to the capital account, giving his specific reasons for it. Cash entries are journalized in daily totals. He maintains a separate cash book in which the receipts are put on the debit and the disbursements on the credit, the same as they would be found in the ledger if it were a ledger account. He also explains that this looks as if it were double work but it is not, as it is not the bookkeeper's work to keep a cash book, but the cashier's. He further argues that because the bookkeeper is sometimes also the cashier, that fact should not alter the rule. He has a separate cash book for petty expenses, in which to enter small items which are posted to the ledger only once a month, in order to lessen the number of entries.

About the reconcilement of differences between bookkeepers, cashiers, treasurers and others, he claims that these variations are due to the different closing periods of accounts and reports by the various officials, and requires that they be preserved by writing their full detail in the journal and making a reference of the same on the ledger account affected. Stevin says that as the head bookkeepers through these reconcilements would discover entries which belonged to a period previous to the date of their discovery and their entry in the journal, that the current date on which the entry is made in the journal should be used in that book, but that in the explanation the original date should be used (we now use "as of date" so and so). But he warns his readers that when posting these entries to the ledger, the original date and not the journal entry date should be used. He advises that trial balances be taken in February, May, August, and November, which are customary mercantile due dates, which in turn will lead to a settlement of many accounts and will make this work easy and light. Furthermore, it will give data and statistics upon which the merchants can base their buying, selling, and credit budgets for the future. He advises that the Italian method of bookkeeping is so adapted to expansion that whereas before but one bookkeeper could be employed, under the double-entry system any number of bookkeepers can be used, for, if the work becomes too much for one man the system should be revised so as to provide for controlling accounts. This means to post in totals only, so that one sub-division can be given to a bookkeeper to be controlled by one head bookkeeper, who deals in totals only.

As to the cash book, it is used because it obviates the making of numerous journal entries every day, thus shortening the work greatly. He fully illustrates this, and transfers the totals of the cash book to the ledger by journal entries, preferably monthly.

Stevin provides a double column in the ledger account for merchandise. In one of these he puts the weights and measures, and insists that they be balanced also. He says that in his illustrations he made them come out even, although he admits that that very seldom happens. The result, however, would be the same, for the balance to be carried to the new ledger or to be used in "the statement of affairs" would be based upon the weight, and whatever is over or short, as far as weight and measure is concerned, would automatically adjust itself in the profit and loss.

He objects to the name of "*memorial*" as used in the Latin countries for the day book, stating that "*memorial*" is a book of memoranda (things to be remembered), whereas the day book is used to write in roughly the daily transactions preparatory to journalizing them. This he calls a blotter. He draws a line between each journal entry from one side of the book to the other side of the book, through all the standing lines and columns. He explains that this line is necessary, because some entries cover several pages. (How we accountants wish some bookkeepers would make journal entries with explanations pages long!)

Stevin says it is customary to ascertain once a year what the profit or the loss of the business has been. This is what he calls "balancing" or "making a statement of balance" or "ascertaining of capital." For this purpose, he advises to "add together cash and merchandise on hand and actual accounts receivable, deduct therefrom the accounts payable; the difference is net capital provided the accounts receivable are all good. The difference between the net capital of last year and this year is the profit or loss for the year." According to Stevin, the making of a statement of affairs was not done concurrently with the closing of the books, the latter being done only when a new ledger is opened or where the merchant retires from business or dies.

To prove his profit and loss arrived at through the making of a statement of affairs as above explained, he makes up a profit and loss account, which he calls "proof statement." Therefore, his profit or loss is ascertained first from the balance sheet, and in order to prove whether that is correct, he builds a profit and loss account. How few modern bookkeepers and young accountants understand this principle today!

It will be seen from the reproduction of his financial statement and profit and loss account, that the profit and loss statement is just as it would appear in the ledger account if these entries were really posted to a ledger account as we do today. The balance sheet therefore represents an unposted journal entry, whereas the profit and loss account shows the result of a posted journal entry. In this Stevin is of course inconsistent.

Stevin makes the statement of affairs a mathematical problem rather than the result of debits and credits. He adds and subtracts, but does not reason where "proprietorship begins and ends," as he does with all other journal entries. Hence, the entries comprising the closing of the ledger and the profit and loss account should not be in the journal (he reasons), as the making of such entries is only done when proprietorship is affected. They are merely the bringing together to a conclusion of net proprietorship or net capital.

He further explains that the ledger must always be in balance because of the mathematical rule of "equal amounts added to equal amounts must give equal totals."

In closing the ledger, Stevin transfers the balance of the various accounts direct to other accounts in the ledger without the aid of journal entries, and calls it often "by *slote*" the Dutch, and sometimes "*per solde*" the Italian for "in order to close." He puts his assets and liabilities into the capital account, and his profit and losses in the profit and loss account. He finally closes all accounts by closing the profit and loss account into the capital account. As the difference between present assets and liabilities or net proprietorship must be equal to the capital at the beginning of the year, plus or minus the current profits or losses, the entering of the present assets and liabilities in his capital account is an unnecessary duplication, except it be to effect a closing of all ledger accounts and using the capital account for this purpose as a clearing account.

Stevin explains this method by saying that other writers, and especially the Dutch writer Bertholomi de Rentergem, have in the rear of their ledgers a "balance account," (as Pietra and Ympyn) into which they close their ledger accounts. This, Stevin says, is built from a journal entry made in the old journal. This entry is also posted in reverse order in the new ledger from the journal entry in the old journal. This method Stevin does not like. He says these writers when opening their first journal and ledger, in the beginning of a new business, start with an inventory (see Pacioli and others), but in subsequent ledgers he says they do not do this, and there they call it a balance account. Why not be consistent, he pleads, and open each subsequent journal and ledger with an inventory? He dislikes the balance account method evidently so very much that he wants to get away from it as far as he can, and thus he dumps it all into the capital account, because, he adds, "the result is exactly the same."

Stevin gives an exhaustive chapter about the settlement of partnership affairs. He states that if all the partners are active and were conducting a portion of the business in various cities on the principle of branch stores, each partner should keep a separate set of books, very much the same as the method he explains for consignments or traveling agents, and at headquarters or at one of the branches there should be a joint bookkeeper, whose duty it is to deal in totals, so that each partner may know where he stands in relation to the others. If only one partner is active, this partner should keep the books.

He learned in one instance, as very likely modern accountants will learn from time to time, that a good merchant, no matter how illiterate he is or how ignorant he may be about bookkeeping, usually can tell very accurately whether the accountant's financial statement and bookkeeping results are correct. Stevin was called in to adjust the affairs between a number of partners, of a large partnership. The five active partners were residents of the cities of Venice, Augsburg, Cologne, Antwerp, and London, where they conducted branch establishments of the firm. One of these partners had not kept any books. Stevin was finally induced by this partner to visit him and to write up a full set of books of all the transactions of the partnership which he could find, and thus ascertain the financial settlement between the partners. This he did, after considerable labor. The particular partner who had kept no books, however, objected to the settlement, because it was £300 less than he figured was coming to him. To prove this, he stated that they had no assets or liabilities of any kind, having liquidated the business; therefore he said: "If I deduct my disbursements from my receipts, and add to the balance what is due me from the others, the total must be my portion of the profit." Stevin agreed with him that this was right, and the set of books was discarded and a settlement made upon the argument of the partner who was ignorant as far as bookkeeping was concerned. From this experience Stevin determined upon the following rule: when called in to make a partnership settlement, he would demand three things: first, the amount each partner has received more in cash than he paid, or what he paid more than he received; second, the difference between presently existing accounts receivable and accounts payable, to which he added the cash and merchandise on hand; third, what the agreement was between the partners as to divisions of profits and losses. He illustrates the application of this rule by the following example:

A paid more than he received by £2,000

B received more than he paid by 4,000

C paid more than he received by 3,000

The net assets, or the difference between accounts receivable and payable, added to the cash and merchandise on hand, amounted to £7,000

Each partner was to receive one-third of the profits or stand one-third of the losses. He then puts up the following account:

Partnership Debit.		Partnership Credit.	
Due A	£ 2,000	Due from B	£ 4,000
Due C	3,000	Net assets	7,000
Total due A and C	£ 5,000		£11,000
Net profit	6,000		
Total	£11,000		

As of above profit one-third is due to each of the partners, each partner's account would stand as follows:

Due A as per above	£2,000	
Plus one-third of the profits	2,000	
	——	£4,000
Due C as per above	£3,000	
Plus one-third of the profits	2,000	
	——	5,000
		9,000
Due from B as per above	£4,000	
Less one-third of the profits	2,000	
	——	2,000
Net assets		£7,000

Those of us who have read the numerous involved court cases on partnership settlement, certainly must admire Stevin's ingenuity.

Consignment accounts, which Pacioli calls traveling accounts, are more thoroughly described in this work. Stevin thinks it wrong to debit consignment account and credit merchandise, when the goods are shipped on consignment, because the test when to make an entry is "the beginning and the end of proprietorship." He says it would be foolish to debit a clerk and credit merchandise when a clerk takes goods from a cellar or warehouse to the store or from one part of the store to another. And he feels that consignment is a transaction of a similar nature, with only a greater distance between the places of storage. He states if we want to keep track of these consignment transactions, it should be by way of memoranda but not in the regular books. Like Pacioli, he wants the traveling man or consignee to keep books on the double-entry system and report sales at convenient times, these reports to be entered in a separate journal and ledger until there is "a beginning and an end of proprietorship." It is important to note that Stevin very seldom uses the word "capital," but substitutes the word "proprietorship" throughout.

All the way through, Stevin uses as a test for the making of a journal entry "the beginning and end of proprietorship." Thus, when goods arrive in the warehouse, that is the beginning of proprietorship, and that account is not touched again, as far as the journal and ledger are concerned, until the goods have left proprietorship through consumption. So, if a barrel of beer were received from the brewer, it would go into the warehouse account or the merchandise account, and there remain until finally the butler on one of the war vessels would distribute it to the sailors, when it would be charged out to them. In the interim, however, the warehouse has sent it to a small ship, which brings it to the ocean, there it is transferred onto a transport, and probably is transferred on the ocean two or three times from one steward's warehouse on one ship to another steward's warehouse on another, until it finally reaches the war vessel upon which it is consumed. While he urges the necessity of following this barrel of beer from place to place, he states that this should be done only in memorandum accounts and not in the general ledger.

Equally insistent he is on the reissue of tools used in the construction of fortifications, canals and buildings, or on the farms and in the field. He says that tools are first purchased, issued to one particular piece of work and then returned to the warehouse and used in other places and transferred from place to place until finally worn out. All of this he feels should be carefully recorded but not in the general ledger.

As to the wages, he very carefully explains that a wages or pay roll account avails one nothing. The wages he says should be carefully distributed to each department for which they are incurred, exactly the same as we have seen Pietra does. He first distributes his wages, as he distributes all his supplies, to definite departments. Thus he says we can arrive at true costs. This method he uses also in checking up the supply house and the cook, for he instructs the cook, as we have seen, to give a record of the daily meals served in order to check the pay roll, and he checks the cook by instructing the warehouse men to figure out the cost of the meals per man. Thus he says, if the cost per meal is considerably higher than the average, and the pay roll agrees with the meals served, then the warehouse man has either made an error or stolen some goods.

In this connection, he provides a perpetual inventory, in which each kind of merchandise has two columns, one for the receipts or "ins" and one for the disbursements or the "outs." He balances each column when new goods arrive, then counts what is left, and adjusts his books to the actual count.

Gifts of merchandise, he states, must be valued, for three reasons: first, in order to be able to ascertain actual expenses and consumption of merchandise for each department; second, the proprietor should know at all times for how much he is obligated to others; third, in order to know exactly the actual capital invested.

In municipal accounting, he urges that the ledger of any year be held open until at least the end of the next year, to prevent heavy transcribing, very much the same as is done now with some tax rolls.

Stevin in instructing his bookkeepers in the municipal department, tells them to use the words "debit" and "credit" in the explanation of each journal entry, thus making it a little plainer to the uninitiated in the terms of bookkeeping. From the illustrations it will be noted that he does not do so in mercantile bookkeeping, but only uses the term "debit."

What the writer has said in praise of Stevin should not be interpreted as meaning that he considers Stevin's system perfect or even as perfect as we have today, for in many respects, it is not. But the writer believes that Stevin has left his unmistakable stamp on modern American methods. It would be interesting to study the earliest American financial books and ledgers in order to establish that through the Dutch settlers of New Amsterdam (now New York) Stevin's ideas were brought to America, rather than by way of England through Dafforne, who we will see further on in the book, failed to translate to the English language many of Stevin's ideas.

VERRECHTING
VAN
DOMEINE

Mette CONTREROLLE en ander behouften vandien.
't Welck is

Verclaring van ghemeene Regel, waer deur ver-
boèt worden alle abuyſen mette ſwaricheden uytte ſelve ſpruytende, die-
men tot noch toe uyt geen Rekencamers van Domeine en Finance
heeƭ connen weren.

Weſende Oeffeninghen des Doorluchtichſten Hoogſtghe-
boren Vorſt en Heere MAVRITS by Gods Ghe-
nade Prince van Orange, &c. Ho: Loff: Memorie.

Beſchreven deur SIMON STEVIN van Brugghe, in ſijn leven des Hooghghemelten Heere
PRINCEN Superintendent vande Finance, &c. En uyt ſijn naghelaten
Hantſchriften by een gheſtelt deur ſijn Soon HENDRICK
STEVIN Ambachtsheere van Alphen.

TOT LEYDEN,
Ter Druckerye van IVSTVS LIVIVS,
In 't tweede Iaer des Vredes.

STAET VAN MY DIERICK

Roofe gemaeckt op den laetften December 1600.

Staet of capitael debet.		Staet of capitael credit.	
Per *Aernout Iacobs fol.* 14	51. 8. 0.	Per *noten fol.* 7 - 173 ℔ 5 onc. tot	
Reft debet hier geftelt by flote		7. ß 't pont, comt - - 60. 15. 2	
van defen - - -	3140. 9. 1.	Per *peper fol.* 7 - 120 ℔ tot 40 ß	
		't pont, comt - - - - 20. 0. 0.	
Somme 3191. 17. 1.		Per *Omaer de Svvarte fol.* 9 - 513. 12. 0.	
		Per *Adriaen de VVinter fol.* 11 - 150. 6. 0.	
		Per *Pieter de VVitte fol.* 11 - - 448. 0. 0.	
		Per *Iacques de Somer fol.* 13 - 54. 18. 6.	
		Per *caffe fol.* 19 - - - 1944. 7. 5.	
		Somme 3191. 17. 1.	

Sulcx dat Debiteurs, met gereet gelt en vvaren, hier
meer bedragen dan Crediteurs voor vveerde des
capitaels op den laetften van December 1600 - 3140. 9. 1.

Maer op den laetften December 1599, of 't begin
des jaers 1600 dat een felve is, vvas het capitael
van 2153 ℔ 3 ß 8 ß, vvant treckende den debet
514 ℔ 6 ß, vanden credit 2667 ℔ 9 ß 8 ß, blijft
als vooren - - - - - 2153. 3. 8.

VVelcke getrocken vande 3140 ℔ 9 ß 1 ß, blijft
voor 't gene datter op dit jaer verovert is, ende in
defe ftaet gefocht vviert - - - 987. 5. 5.

STAET PROEF.

MAer om nu te fien of het bovefchreven vaft gaet, fo dient
dit tot een proef: Ick vergaer al de reften der poften van
vermeerderende of verminderende capitael, 't vvelck fyn de reften der poften die inde voorgaende ftaetmaking niet en qua-
men,

men, als totte vvefentlicke ftaet niet behoorende : Ende vvant
de felve fyn partyen van vvinft en verlies voorgevallen inden tijt
defer bouckhouding, dats federt o Ianuarius 1600, vvelcke by
aldienmen het bouck flote (gelijck int volgende 10 Hooftftick
gedaen fal vvorden) op rekening van vvinft en verlies fouden
commen, foo moet dan daer deur oock verovering bevonden
vvorden van 987 $\mathcal{L}$ 5 β 5 $\S$. Tot defen einde begin ick het
Schultbouck te overloopen van vooren aen, ende ontmoet my
eerft de pofte der nagelen fol. 5, vvaer op ick vvinft bevinde van
75. 4. 7. daer na ontmoeten my noten en ander goeden, als hier
na volght. Doch ftaet noch te gedencken, dat overfchietende
goeden hier berekent vvorden ten felven prijfe als inden voor-
gaenden ftaet, om dat vvy nemen haer vveerde foo te vvefen,
vvildemen in d'een en d'ander nemen den prijs verandert te zijn,
men foudet oock meugen doen.

VVinft en verlies debet.	VVinft en verlies credit.
Per oncoften van coomfchap fol. 16 - 57. 7.0.	Per vvinft op nagelen fol. 5 - - 75.4.7.
Per oncoften vanden huyfe fol. 16 - 107. 10.0.	Per vvinft op noten fol. 7 - - 109. 7. 2.
	Per vvinft op peper fol. 7 - - 18.19. 0.
Somme 164. 17.0.	Per vvinft op gimber fol. 9. - - 41. 8.4.
	Per rekening van vvinft en verlies
Reft credit als prouffijt overeencom-	(vviens pofte te gedencken is dat
mende mette voorgaende reke-	ten tijde defer vvercking in debet
ning hier geftelt per folde - - 987.5.5.	alleenelick hadde tyvee partyen, te
	vveten van 100 $\mathcal{L}$ en 12 $\mathcal{L}$,
Somme 1152.2.5.	maer in credit drie partien als 4
	$\mathcal{L}$ 3. 4. en 15 $\mathcal{L}$ met 1000
	$\mathcal{L}$) fol. 19 - - - 907. 3. 4.
	Somme 1152. 2. 5.

Nu dan het prouffijt deur defe vvyfe oock bevonden fijnde
van 987 $\mathcal{L}$ 5 β 5 $\S$, als te vooren int flot des ftaets, foo mach
dit tot proef des vvercx verftrecken.

MERCKT

			't Iaer 1600.	ℒ	ß	₰
	o	Ianua.	Verscheyden partien debet per Capitael van my Dierick Roose			
			2667 ℔ 9 ß 8 ₰, deur dat ick ten voornoemden da-			
			ge staet van goet makende, my bevonden hebbe toe te be-			
			hooren de navolgende partien van gelt, vvaren en schulden:			
			Ende eerst :			
4			Casse in zereden gelde - - - -	880	0	0
4			Nagelen 4 balen vvegende			
			n° 3 - 87 - tar 1.2. ⎫			
			5 - 90¼ tar 1.4. ⎪			
			4 - 86½ tar 1.2. ⎬ Net 350 ℔ 8 onc. tot 10 ß 't pont, comt	175	5	0
			7 - 91¼ tar 1.0 ⎭			
			———————			
			355 tar 4: 8.			
6			Noten 4 balen vvegende			
			n° 9 - 79 tar 1.4. ⎫			
			7 - 82 tar 1.4. ⎪			
			6 - 84 tar 1.2. ⎬ Net 320 ℔ tot 9 ß 't pont, comt	144	0	0
			8 - 80 tar 1.6. ⎭			
			———————			
			325 tar 5.0.			
6			Peper 3 balen vvegende			
			n° 9 - 250 tar 2.0. ⎫			
			10 - 260 tar 2.0. ⎬ Net 758 ℔ tot 30 ₰ 't pont, comt	94	15	0
			11 - 254 tar 2.0. ⎭			
			———————			
			764 tar 6.0.			
8			Gimber 5 balen vvegende			
			n° 4 - 266 tar 2.0. ⎫			
			5 - 260 tar 2.0. ⎪			
			6 - 258 tar 2.0. ⎬ Net 1294 ℔ tot 32 ₰ 't pont, comt	172	10	8
			7 - 264 tar 2.0. ⎪			
			8 - 256 tar 2.0. ⎭			
			———————			
			1304 tar 10.0.			

Het navolgende syn Debiteurs getrocken uyt de voorschreven staet.

				ℒ	ß	₰
8	-	- -	Omaer de Svvarte verschynende 6 Meye 1600. - -	200	0	0
10	-	- -	Adriaen de VVinter verschynende 8 Iunius 1600. -	350	6	0
10	-	- -	Pieter de VVitte verschynende 20 Iunius 1600. -	360	8	0
12	-	- -	Iacques de Somer verschynende 1 Martius 1600. -	290	5	0
3			Somme	2667	9	8
2	o	Ianua.	Capitael van my Dierick Roose debet per verscheyden Krediteu-			
			ren, an de vvelcke ik my ten voornoemde dage deur de voor-			
			schreven staetmaking bevinde schuldich te syne als volght :			
13	-	- -	Ioos Noirot verschynende den 7 Maerte 1600. - -	100	0	0
15	-	- -	Davit Roels verschynende den 2 Meye 1600,	150	0	0
15	-	- -	Aernout Iacobs verschynende den 10 April 1600. -	264	6	0
			Somme	514	6	0

D 3   Onc often

			't Iaer 1600.	ℓ	ß	ᵍ
16/5	28	Februa.	Oncosten van coomschap debet per casse, deur betaelt in dese maent van Februarius blijckende by 't memoriael van dien	3	0	0
16/5	28	Februa.	Oncosten vanden huyse debet per casse, deur betaelt in dese maent van Februarius blijckende by 't memoriael van dien	3	4	0
12/5	7	Maerte.	Iacques de Somer debet per nagelen, deur dat ick an hem vercocht heb 2 balen te betalen binnen 2 maenden, vvegende n° 3 - 87 - tar 1.2. / 5 - 90$\frac{1}{4}$ tar 1.4. } Net 174 ℔ 14 onc. tot 12 ß 't pont / 177$\frac{1}{4}$ tar 2.6.	104	18	6
6/15	28	Maerte.	Noten debet per Davit Roels, deur dat ick van hem gecocht heb 3 balen te betalen binnen 3 maenden, vvegende n° 4 - 79 tar 1.0. / 5 - 80 tar 1.0. / 6 - 82 tar 1.0. } Net 238 ℔ tot 8 ß 't pont, comt - / 241 tar 3.0.	95	4	0
16/5	31	Maerte.	Oncosten van Coomschap debet per casse, deur betaelt in dese maent van Maerte blijckende by 't memoriael van dien	4	2	0
16/5	31	Maerte.	Oncosten vandē huyse dzbet per casse, deur betaelt in dese maent van Maerte blijckende by 't memoriael van dien - -	6	6	0
4/5	6	April.	Casse debet per nagelen, deur dat ick contant vercocht heb 1 balen an Iosep Sanders vvegende n° 4 - 86$\frac{1}{2}$ tar 1.2. / 7 - 91$\frac{1}{4}$ tar 1.0. } Net 175 ℔ 10 onc. tot 13 ß 't pont / 177$\frac{3}{4}$ tar 2.2.	114	3	1
8/5	20	April.	Gimber debet per casse, deur dat ick contant gecocht heb 3 balen van Louys Ianß, vvegende n° 14 - 264 tar 2.0. / 15 - 270 tar 2.0. / 16 - 266 tar 2.0. } Net 794 ℔ tot 30 g 't pont - / 800 tar 6.0.	99	5	0
16/5	30	April.	Oncosten van coomschap debet per casse, deur betaelt in dese maent April blijckende by 't memoriael van dien - -	3	10	0
16/5	30	April.	Oncosten van den huyse debet per casse, deur betaelt in dese maent van April blijckende by 't memoriael van dien	6	0	0
14/9	12	Meye.	Davit Roels debet per Omaer de Svvarte, deur dat ick Davit geaßigneert heb van Omaer t'ontfangen in volle betalingh van dies ick Davit schuldich ben, vervallende den 2 Maerte 1600, en in mindering van dies my Omaer schuldich is, vervallende 6 Meye 1600	150	0	0

Verschey-

				ℒ	ß	¾
	30	Meye.	**'t Iaet 1600.** Verscheyden partien debet per Aernout Iacobs, van hem gecocht de navolgende partien te betalen binnen een maent, en eerst :			
4	-	- -	Nagelen 2 balen vvegende n° 11 - 90 tar 1. 0. 12 - 88 tar 1. 0. } Net 176 ℔ tot 10 ß 't pont -	83	0	0
			178 tar 2. 0.			
6	-	- -	Noten 2 balen vvegende n° 13 - 86 tar 1. 8. 14 - 88 tar 1. 8. } Net 171 ℔ tot 8 ß 't pont -	68	8	⅃
15			174 tar 3. 0. Somme	151	8	0
10	30	Meye.	Pieter de VVitte debet per verscheyden partien, an hem vercocht te betalen binnen 5 vveken, en eerst :			
9	-	- -	Gimber 8 balen vvegende n° 4 - 266 tar 2. 0. 5 - 260 tar 2. 0. 6 - 258 tar 2. 0. 7 - 264 tar 3. 0. 8 - 256 tar 2. 0. 14 - 264 tar 2. 0. 15 - 270 tar 2. 0. 16 - 266 tar 2. 0. } Net 2088 ℔ tot 36. ß 't pont -	313	4	0
			2104 tar 16. 0.			
7	-	- -	Noten 7 balen vvegende n° 4 - 79 tar 1. 0. 5 - 80 tar 1. 0. 6 - 82 tar 1. 0. 9 - 79 tar 1. 4. 7 - 81 tar 1. 4. 3 - 84 tar 1. 2. 8 - 80 tar 1. 6. } Net 558 ℔ tot 12 ß 't pont -	331	16	0
			566 tar 8. 0. Somme	648	0	0
4 / 9	31	Meye.	Casse debet per Omaer de Svvarte, van hem ontfaen in mindering van 't verschenen den 6 Meye 1600	30	0	0
12 / 5	31	Meye.	Ioos Noirot debet per casse, an hem betaelt in mindering van 't verschenen den 7 Maerte 1600	50	0	0
14 / 5	31	Meye.	Aernout Iacobs debet per casse, an hem betaelt in minderingh van 't verschenen den 10 April 1600 - - -	200	0	0
16 / 5	31	Meye.	Oncosten van coomschap debet per casse, deur betaelt in dese maent van Meye blijckende by 't memoriael van dien - - -	4	5	0
16 / 5	.31	Meye.	Oncosten vanden huyse debet per casse, deur betaelt in dese maent van Meye blijckende by 't memoriael van dien - - -	7	0	0
4 / 13	20	Iunius.	Casse debet per Iacques de Somer, van hem ontfaen in minderingh van 't verschenen den 1 Maerte 1600	200	0	0

Aernout

					₤	ß	§
14 / 5	28	Iunius.	Aernout Iacobs debet per casse, an hem betaelt in voldoeningh van 't verschenen den 10 April 1600 - - -		64	6	0
16 / 5	30	Iunius.	Oncosten van Coomschap debet per casse deur betaelt in dese maent van Iunius blijckende by 't memoriael van dien - -		2	10	0
16 / 5	30	Iunius.	Oncosten vanden huyse debet per casse, deur betaelt in dese maent van Iunius blijckende by 't memoriael van dien -		5	0	0
8	4	Iulius.	Omaer de Svvarte debet per verscheyden partien, an hem vercocht te betalen binnen 2 maenden, die gelevert zijn in handen van Andries Corffyn Facteur. En dat deur last vanden voorschreven Omaer, blijckende by syn missive vanden 16 Iunius 1600 : En ten eersten				
7	-	-	Peper 3 balen vvegende n° 9 - 250 tar. 2. 0. 10 - 260 tar. 2. 0. } Net 758 ℔ tot 36 § 't pont. 11 - 254 tar. 2. 0. ——— 764 tar. 6. 0.		113	14	0
7	-	-	Noten 2 balen vvegende n° 13 - 86 tar. 1. 8. 14 - 88 tar. 1. 8. } Net 171 ℔ tot 10 ß 't pont - ——— 147 tar. 3. 0.		85	10	0
5	-	-	Nagelen 2 balen vvegende n° 11 - 90 tar. 1. 0. 12 - 88 tar. 1. 0. } Net 176 ℔ tot 13 ß 't pont - ——— 178 tar. 2. 0. Somme		114 / 313	8 / 12	0 / 0
4	8	Iulius.	Casse debet per verscheyden persoonen, van hemlien ontfaen gereet gelt als volght.				
11	-	-	Adriaen de VVinter in mindering van verschenen 8 Iunius 1600		200	0	0
11	-	-	Pieter de VVitte in volle betaling vant verschenen 20 Iulius 1600		360	8	0
11	-	-	Pieter de VVitte in mindering van 't verschenen den 5 Iulius 1600		200	0	0
13	-	-	Iacques de Somer in volle betaling vant verschenen 1 Mart. 1600		90	5	0
13	-	-	Iacques de Somer in mindering vant verschenen 7 Meye 1600		50	0	0
			Somme		900	13	0
	16	Iulius.	Verscheyden persoonen debet per casse, an hemlien betaelt gereet gelt als volght :				5
12	-	-	Ioos Noirot in volle betaling van 't verschenen 7 Maerte 1600 -		50	0	0
14	-	-	Davit Roels opt verschenen den 28 Iunius 1600 -		60	0	0
14	-	-	Aernout Iacobs opt verschenen den 30 Iunius 1600 -		100	0	0
5			Somme		210	0	0
14 / 5	20	Iulius.	Davit Roels debet per casse, an hem betaelt in voldoeningh van 't verschenen den 28 Iunius 1600		35	4	0
6 / 19	28	Iulius.	Noten debet per casse, deur dat ick gecocht heb 3 balen gereet gelt vvegende net 240 ℔ tot 7 ß 't pont - - -		84	0	0
			Peper				

			't Iaer 1600.	$\mathcal{L}$	β	
	4	Aug.	Peper debet per noten, deur dat ick gemangelt heb tegen Andries Claeß. als volcht :			
6	-	- -	Peper 120 ℔ tot 40 ℈ 't pont by Andries Claeß. an my gelevert, comt	20	0	0
7	-	- -	Noten 66 ℔ 11 oncen tot 6 β 't pont , die ick an Andries Claeß. gelevert heb, comt	20	0	0
18 / 19	18	Aug.	Rekening van vvinst en verlies debet per casse , deur dat ick met Catrine mijn dienstmaecht ten huvvelicke gegeven hebbe	100	0	0
	21	Aug.	Verscheyden partien debet per Aernout Iacobsz. deur dat ick van hem gelicht hebbe 1000 $\mathcal{L}$ op intrest tegen 12 ten hondert t'siaers , en dit voor een maent, vvaer af de verscheyden partien dusdanich zijn:			
18	-	- -	Casse deur dat ick van hem ontfaen hebbe de boveschreven hooftsomme van	1000	0	0
18	-	- -	Rekening van vvinst en verlies deur dien den intrest der boveschreven hooftsomme op een maent bedraecht	12	0	0
15			Somme	1012	0	0
12	10	Sept.	Iacques de Somer debet per verscheyden partien , deur dat ick hem gegeven heb 500 $\mathcal{L}$ op intrest tegen 10 ten hondert s'siaers , en dit voor een maent, vvaer af de verscheyden partien dusdanich zijn :			
19	-	- -	Casse deur dat ick hem getelt hebbe de boveschreven hooftsomme van	500	0	0
19	-	- -	Rekening van vvinst en verlies , deur dien den interest der boveschreven hooftsomme op een maent bedraecht	4	3	4
			Somme	504	3	4
10	18	Sept.	Adriaen de VVinter debet per verscheyden partien 180 $\mathcal{L}$, deur dat hy van my ontfaen heeft op vvissel 100 $\mathcal{L}$ steerlinx tot 33 β het pont, bedragende 165 $\mathcal{L}$, om die vveerom te betalen an Omaer de Svvarte binnen Lonnen op tvvee maenden na sicht, het pont steerlinx gerekent op 36 β, vvaer af de verscheyden partien dusdanich zijn :			
19	-	- -	Casse deur dat hy van my ontfaen heeft de boveschreven somme van	65	0	0
19	-	- -	Rekening van vvinst en verlies, deur dien de vvissel van 3 β te punde op de 100 $\mathcal{L}$ steerlincx bedraecht	15	0	0
			Somme	180	0	0
14 / 19	23	Sept.	Aernout Iacobsz debet per casse, an hem betaelt datter verschenen vvas den 21 September 1600	1012	0	0
18 / 19	21	Sept.	Casse debet per rekening van vvinst en verlies, deur geerst te hebben het gaet mijns Ooms	1000	0	0
18 / 13	12	Octob.	Casse debet per Iacques de Somer , van hem ontfaen datter verschenin vvas den 10 October 1600	504	3	4

E   Omaer

			't Iaer 1600.	ℒ	ℬ	⅋
8	14	Decem.	Omaer de Svvarte tot Lonnen debet per Adriaen de VVinter, deur dat hy voor my ontfaen heeft op vrissel vanden selven Adriaen, blijckende by syn schryven. - - -	180	0	0
11						
16	31	Decem.	Oncosten van coomschap debet per casse, deur betaelt inde maenden van Iulius, Augustus, September, October, November, en December, blijckende by 't memoriael van dien - - -	40	0	0
19						
16	31	Decem.	Oncosten vanden huyse debet per casse deur betaelt inde maenden van Iulius, Augustus, September, October, November, en December, blijckende by 't memoriael van dien - - -	80	0	0
19						

Merckt dat dese tvvee laetste pattien van oncosten souden na 't gemeen gebruyck verdeelt behooren te vvorden ten einde van yder maent, soo veel op elcke viel : Doch alsoot vergeten vvas, ick en hebt niet vvillen verschryven, te meer dattet inde daet somvvylen soo toegaet.

			Capitael debet.　　　't Iaer 1600.	ℒ	ß	g
1	0	Ianua.	Per verscheyden partien	515	6	0
	31	Decem.	Per noten fol. 7, deur datter inde ftaetmaking bevonden zyn 173 ℔ 5 oncen, nu vveerdich 7 ß 't pont, comt	60	13	1
	31	Decem.	Per peper fol. 7, deur datter inde flaetmaking bevonden zijn 120 ℔, nu vveerdich 40 g 't pont, comt	20	0	0
	31	Decem.	Per Omaer de Svvarte verfchynende den 4 September en 14 December 1600 fol. 9	513	12	0
	31	Decem.	Per Adriaen de VVinter verfchynende den 8 Iunius 1600 fol. 11	150	6	0
	31	Decem.	Per Pieter de VVitte verfchynende den 5 Iulius 1600 fol. 11	448	0	0
	31	Decem.	Per Iacques de Somer verfchynende den 7 Meye 1600 fol. 13	54	18	6
	31	Decem.	Per caffe fol. 19　-　　-　　-　　-　　-	1941	7	5
			Somme	3706	3	

4 Fol.			Caffe debet.　　　't Iaer 1600.	ℒ	ß	g
1	0	Ianua.	Per capitael fol. 3　-　　-　　-	880	0	0
2	6	April.	Per nagelen fol. 5	114	3	1
3	31	Meye.	Per Omaer de Svvarte fol. 9	30	0	0
3	20	Iunius.	Per Iacques de Somer fol. 13	200	0	0
4	8	Iuliue.	Per verfchryden partien	500	13	0
			Somme	2124	16	1

			Nagelen debet.　　't Iaer 1600.	℔	onc.	ℒ	ß	g
1	0	Ianua.	Per capitael fol. 3　-　　-	350	8	175	5	0
3	30	Meye.	Per Aernout Iacobs fol. 15　-　　-　　-	176	0	83	0	0
			Somme	526	8	258	5	0
	31	Decem.	Per rekening van vvinft en verlies fol. 19 hier geftelt, by flote van defen, vvefende prouffyt op nagelen　-　-			75	4	7
			Somme	526	8	333	9	7

Fol.			Noten debet.　　't Iaer 1600.	℔	onc.	ℒ	ß	g
1	0	Ianua.	Per capitael fol. 3　-　　-　　-	320	0	144	0	0
2	28	Maerto	Per Davit Roels fol. 15	238	0	95	4	0
3	30	Meye.	Per Aernout Iacobs fol. 15　-　　-　　-	171	0	68	8	0
4	28	Iulius.	Per caffe fol. 19　-　　-	240	0	84	0	0
			Somme	969	0	391	12	0
	31	Decem.	Per rekening van vvinft en verlies fol. 19, hier geftelt by flote van defen, vvefende prouffyt op noten　-			109	7	2
			Somme	969	0	500	19	2

Capitael credit. 't Iaer 1600.

				$\mathcal{L}$	ß	3/4
0	Ianua.	Per verscheyden partien	- - - -	2667	9	8
31	Decem.	Per Aernout Iacobs verschynende den 30 Iunius 1600 fol. 14	-	51	8	5
31	Decem.	Per rekening van winst en verlies fol. 18	- -	987	5	5
		Somme		3706		1

Caſſe credit. 't Iaer 1600.

Fol.					$\mathcal{L}$	ß	
2	28	Februa.	Per oncoſten van coomſchap fol. 16	- - -	3	0	0
2	28	Februa.	Per oncoſten vanden huyſe fol. 16	- -	3	4	0
3	31	Maerte	Per oncoſten van coomſchap fol. 16	- -	4	2	0
2	31	Maerte	Per oncoſten vanden huyſe fol. 16	-	1	6	0
2	20	April.	Per gimber fol. 8	- -	99	8	0
2	30	April.	Per oncoſten van coomſchap fol. 16	-	3	10	0
2	30	April.	Per oncoſten vanden huyſe fol. 16	-	6	0	0
3	31	Meye.	Per Ioos Noirot fol. 12	-	50	0	0
3	31	Meye.	Per Aernout Iacobs fol. 14	-	200	0	0
3	31	Meye.	Per oncoſten van coomſchap fol. 16	-	4	5	0
3	31	Meye.	Per oncoſten vanden huyſe fol. 16	-	7	0	0
4	28	Iunius.	Per Aernout Iacobs fol. 14	-	64	6	0
4	30	Iunius	Per oncoſten van coomſchap fol. 16	-	2	10	0
4	30	Iunius.	Per oncoſten vanden huyſe fol. 16	-	5	0	0
4	16	Iulius.	Per verſcheyden partien	- -	210	0	0
4	20	Iulius.	Per Davit Roels fol. 14	-	35	4	0
			Somme		703	12	0
			Per ſlot van deſen, en overgedragen in debet fol. 48	-	1421	4	1
			Somme		2124	16	1

Nagelen credit. 't Iaer 1600.

				℔	onc.	$\mathcal{L}$	ß	
2	7	Maerte	Per Iacques de Somer fol. 12	- -	174	14	110	18	6
2	6	April.	Per caſſe fol. 4	-	175	10	114	3	1
4	4	Iulius.	Per Omaer de Svvarte fol. 8	- -	176	0	114	8	0
			Somme		526	8	333	9	7

Noten credit. 't Iaer 1600.

				℔	onc.	$\mathcal{L}$	ß	
3	30	Meye.	Per Pieter de Vvitt fol. 10	- -	558	0	334	16	0
4	4	Iulius.	Per Omaer de Svvarte fol. 8	-	171	0	85	10	0
4	4	Aug.	Per peper fol. 6	-	66	11	20	0	0
			Somme		795	11	440	6	0
	31	Decem.	Per capitael fol. 2 deur datter inde ſtaetmaking bevonden zijn 173 ℔ 5 oncen noten, nu vveerdich 7 ß 't pont, comt - - -		173	5	60	13	2
			Somme		969	0	500	19	2

			Peper debet.　　　't Iaer 1600.					
1	0	Ianua.	Peper capitael fol. 3	758	0	91	15	0
5	4	Aug.	Per noten fol. 7	120	0	20	0	0
			Somme	878	0	114	15	0
	31	Decem.	Per rekening van vvinst en verlies fol. 19, hier gestelt by slote van desen, vvesende prouffijt op peper			18	19	0
			Somme	878	0	133	14	0

			Gimber debet.　　't Iaer 1600.	℔ onc.		ℒ	ℬ	ℊ
1	0	Ianua.	Per capitael fol. 3	1294	0	172	10	8
2	20	April.	Per caffe fol. 5	794	0	99	5	0
			Somme	2088	0	271	15	8
	31	Decem.	Per rekening van vvinst en verlies fol. 19. hier gestelt by slote van desen vvesende prouffijt op gimber			41	8	4
			Somme	2088	0	313	4	0

			Omaer de svvarte debet.　　t Iaer 1600.		ℒ	ℬ	ℊ
1	0	Ianua.	Per capitael verschynende 6 Meye 1600 fol. 3		200	0	0
4	4	Iuliu.	Per verschyden partien verschynende 4 Sept. 1600		313	12	0
6	14	Decem.	Per Adriaen de VVinter op vvissel fol. 11		180	0	0
			Somme		693	12	0

10

			Adriaen de VVinter debet.　　't Iaer 1600.	ℒ	ℬ	ℊ
1	0	Ianua.	Per capitael verschynende 8 Iunius 1600 fol. 3	350	6	0
5	18	Sept.	Per verscheyden partien verschynende 2 maenden na sicht des vvissel briefs	180	0	0
			Somme	530	6	0

Peper credit.   't Iaer 1600.

Fol.								
4	4	Iulius.	Per Omaer de Svvarte fol. 8	758	0	113	14	
	31	Decem.	Per capitael fol. 2 deur datter inde staetmaking bevonden zijn 120 ℔ peper, nu vveerdich 40 ℔ 't pont, comt	120	0	20	0	0
			Somme	878	0	133	14	0

Gimber credit.   't Iaer 1600.

Fol.				℔ one.		£	ß	
3	30	Meye.	Per Pieter de VVitte fol. 10	2088	0	313	4	0

Omaer de Svvarte credit.   't Iaer 1600.

2	12	Meye.	Per Davit Roels opt verschenen 6 Meye 1600 fol. 14	150	0	0
3	31	Meye.	Per casse opt verschenen 6 Meye 1600 fol. 4	30	0	0
			Somme	180	0	0
	31	Decem.	Per capitael fol. 2 hier gestelt by slote van desen	513	12	
			Somme	693	12	0

Adriaen de VVinter credit.   't Iaer 1600.

Fol.				£	ß	
4	8	Iulius.	Per casse opt verschenen 8 Iunius 1600 fol. 4	200	0	0
6	14	Decem.	Per Omaer de Svvarte opt verschenen hier neven fol. 8	180	0	0
			Somme	380	0	0
	31	Decem.	Per capitael fol. 2 hier gestelt by slote van desen	150	6	0
			Somme	530	6	0

Pieter de VVitte debit. 't Iaer 1600.

							ℒ	ß	§
1	0	Ianua.	Per capitael verschynende 20 Iunius 1600 fol. 3	-	-		360	8	0
3	30	Meye.	Per verscheyden partien verschynende 5 Iulius 1600	-	-		648	0	0
					Somme		1008	8	0

12

Iacques de Somer debet. t Iaer 1600.

							ℒ	ß	§
1	0	Ianua.	Per capitael verschynende 1 Maerte 1600 fol. 3.	-	-		290	5	0
2	7	Maerte	Per nagelen verschynende 7 Meye 1600 fol. 5				104	18	6
5	10	Sept.	Per verscheyden partien te betalen 10 Octob. 1600		-		504	3	4
					Somme		899	6	10

Ioos Noirot debet. 't Iaer 1600.

							ℒ	ß	§
3	31	Meye.	Per casse opt verschenen 7 Maerte 1600 fol. 5	-	-		50	0	0
4	16	Iulius.	Per casse opt verschenen 7 Maerte 1600 fol. 5	-	-		50	0	0
					Somme		100	0	0

14

Davit Roels debit. t Iaer 1600.

							ℒ	ß	§
2	12	Meye.	Per Omaer de Svvarte opt verschenen 2 Meye 1600 fol. 9		-		150	0	0
4	16	Iulius.	Per casse opt verschenen 28 Iunius 1600 fol. 5	-	-		60	0	0
4	20	Iulius.	Per casse opt verschenen 28 Iunius 1600 fol. 5	-	-		35	4	0
					Somme		215	4	9

Aernout Iacobs credit. Iaer 1600.

							ℒ	ß	§
3	31	Meye.	Per casse opt verschenen 10 April 1600 fol. 5	-	-		200	0	0
4	28	Iunius.	Per casse opt verschenen 10 April 1600 fol. 5	-	-		64	6	0
4	16	Iulius.	Per casse op 't verschenen 30 Iunius 1600 fol. 5	-	-		100	0	0
5	23	Sept.	Per casse op 't verschenen 21 Sept. 1600 fol. 19	-	-		1012	0	0
					Somme		1376	6	0
	31	Decem.	Per capitael fol. 3 hier gestelt by slote van desen	-	-		51	8	0
					Somme		1427	14	0

Pieter de VVitte credit.   't Iaer 1600.

				£	ß	₰
4	8	Iulius.	Per casse opt verschenen 20 Iunius 1600 fol. 4	360	8	0
4	8	Iulius.	Per casse opt verschenen 5 Iulius 1600 fol. 4	200	0	0
			Somme	560	8	0
	31	Decem.	Per capitael fol. 2 hier gestelt by slote van desen	448	0	0
			Somme	1008	8	0

Iacques de Somer credit.   t Iaer 1600.

13

				£	ß	₰
3	20	Iunius.	Per casse opt verschenen 1 Maerte 1600 fol. 4	200	0	0
4	8	Iulius.	Per casse opt verschenen 1 Maerte 1600 fol. 4	90	5	0
4	8	Iulius.	Per casse opt verschenen 7 Meye 1600 fol. 4	50	0	0
5	12	Octob.	Per casse opt verschenen 10 Octobris 1600 fol. 18	504	3	4
			Somme	841	8	4
	31	Decem.	Per capitael fol. 2 hier gestelt by slote van desen	54	18	6
			Somme	899	6	10

Ioos Noirot credit.   t Iaer 1600.

1	0	Ianua.	Per capitael verschynende 7 Maerte 1600 fol. 2	100	0	0

Davit Roels credit.   't Iaer 1600.

				£	ß	₰
1	0	Ianua.	Per capitael verschynende 2 Meye 1600 fol. 2	150	0	0
2	23	Maerte	Per noten verschynende 18 Iunius 1600 fol. 6	95	4	0
			Somme	215	4	0

Aernout Iacobs credit.   t Iaer 1600.

				£	ß	₰
1	0	Ianua.	Per capitael verschynende 10 April 1600 fol. 2	264	6	0
3	30	Meye	Per verscheyden partien verschynende 30 Iunius 1600	151	8	0
5	21	Aug.	Per verscheyden partien verschynende 21 Sept. 1600	1012	0	0
			Somme	1427	14	0

Oncosten van Coomschap debet. 't Iaer 1600.

			£	β	g
4	28 Februa	Per casse fol. 5	3	0	0
1	31 Maerte	Per casse fol. 5	4	2	0
1	30 April.	Per casse fol. 5	3	10	0
3	31 Meye.	Per casse fol. 5	4	5	0
4	30 Iunius.	Per casse fol. 5	2	10	0
6	31 Decem.	Per casse fol. 19	40	0	0
		Somme	57	7	0

Oncosten vanden huyse debet. 't Iaer 1600.

			£	β	g
2	28 Februa.	Per casse fol. 5	3	4	0
2	31 Maerte	Per casse fol. 5	6	6	0
1	30 April.	Per casse fol. 5	6	0	0
3	31 Meye.	Per casse fol. 5	7	0	0
4	30 Iunius.	Per casse fol. 5	5	0	0
6	31 Decem.	Per casse fol. 19	80	0	0
		Somme	107	10	0

Casse debet.   t Iaer 1600.

			£	β	g
	20 Iulius.	Per slot van casse fol. 5, 't vvelck daer in credit gebrocht vvas	1421	4	1
5	21 Aug.	Per Aernout Iacobsen fol. 15	1060	0	0
5	24 Sept.	Per rekening van vvinst en verlies fol. 19	1060	0	0
5	12 Octob.	Per Iacques de Somer fol. 13	504	3	4
		Somme	3925	7	5

Rekening van vvinst en verlies debet. 1600.

			£	β	g
5	18 Aug.	Per casse fol. 19	100	0	0
5	21 Aug.	Per Aernout Iacobsen fol. 15	12	0	0
	31 Decem.	Per oncosten van coomschap fol. 17	57	7	0
	31 Decem.	Per oncosten vanden huyse fol. 17	107	10	0
		Somme	276	17	0
	31 Decem.	Per capitael fol. 3 hier gestelt by slote van desen	987	5	5
		Somme	1264	2	5

Oncoſten van Coomſchap credit. 't Iaer 1600.

				ℒ	ℬ	⅁
31	Decem.	Per rekening van vvinſt en verlies fol. 18 hier geſtelt by ſlote van deſen		57	7	

Oncoſten vanden huyſe credit. 't Iaer 1600.

				ℒ	ℬ	⅁
31	Decem.	Per rekening van vvinſt en verlies fol. 18 hier geſtelt by ſlote van deſen		107	10	

Caſſe credit. 't Iaer 1600.

Fol				ℒ	ℬ	⅁
4	28	Iulius.	Per noten fol. 6	84	0	
5	18	Aug.	Per rekening van vvinſt en verlies fol. 18	100	0	0
5	10	Sept.	Per Iacques de Somer fol. 12	500	0	0
5	18	Sept.	Per Adriaen de VVinter fol. 10	163	0	0
5	23	Sept.	Per Aernout Iacobs fol. 14	1012	0	0
6	31	Decem.	Per Oncoſten van coomſchap fol. 16	40	0	0
6	31	Decem.	Per Oncoſten vanden huyſe fol. 16	80	0	0
			Somme	1981	0	0
	31	Decem.	Per capitael fol. 2, hier geſtelt by ſlote van deſen	1944	7	5
			Somme	3925	7	5

Rekening van vvinſt en verlies credit. 1600.

				ℒ	ℬ	⅁
5	10	Sept.	Per Iacques de Somer fol. 12	4	3	4
5	18	Sept.	Per Adriaen de VVinter fol. 10	15	0	0
5	24	Sept.	Per caſſe fol. 18	1000	0	0
	31	Decem.	Per vvinſt op nagelen fol. 4	75	4	7
	31	Decem.	Per vvinſt op noten fol. 6	109	7	2
	31	Decem.	Per vvinſt op peper fol. 6	18	19	0
	31	Decem.	Per vvinſt op gimber fol. 8	41	8	4
			Somme	1264	2	5

Reſtanten van Hoghenhuyſe.

	1611	1612	1613	1614	1615
1611	-800 - 0 - 0				
1612	500 - 0 - 0	900 - 0 - 0			
1613	370 - 0 - 0		600 - 0 - 0		
1614	150 - 0 - 0		330 - 0 - 0	930 - 0 - 0	
1615	70 - 0 - 0	0 - 0 - 0	300 - 0 - 0	700 - 0 - 0	590 - 0 - 0

Den ſin der voorſchreven tafel is duſdanich : Ghenomen d'eerſte vijf jaren van velen, dattet houden der contrerolle gheduert heeft, te weſen van 1611. 1612. 1613. 1614. 1615. Hier af ſijn vijf colommen, voor elck jaers beſonder contrerolle een : Noch ſijn op den cant gheſtelt derghelijcke vijf jaren, haer anwijſingh doende op elck der reſten daer nevens ſtaende, waer af 't ghebruyck duſdanich is.

Ghenomen datmen na het jaer 1615 wil weten de ſommen der Reſtanten dieder ſijn ten eynde van yder jaer, der jaren 1611. 1612. 1613. 1614. 1615. Om dat te vinden, ick ſie dat nevens het jaer 1615 op den cant ſtaen 70 - 0 - 0. onder het jaer 1611; Daer na 0 - 0 - 0. onder 1612, voorts 300 onder 1613. En ſo voorts 700 - 0 - 0. onder 1614. en 590 - 0 - 0. onder 1615. Angaende voorſchreven 0 - 0 - 0. ſtaende nevens het jaer 1615, en dat onder 1612, ſulcx beteyckent het jaer 1612 heel voldaen te weſen, ſonder daer na van dat jaers rekening eenighe Reſtanten meerte connen vallen.

O 2   Het

RICHARD DAFFORNE PARTLY REPRODUCED

In the Library of Congress and in the Library of Harvard College, we find a book by Gerard Malynes, printed in London in 1656, under the title of *"Consuetudo Vel Lex Mercatoira,"* or *"The Ancient Law Merchant."* This book is a voluminous work, written in the English language, one-half of which contains a digest of the law merchant as then existing; the other half of the volume is occupied by a reprint of Richard Dafforne's book on bookkeeping, "The Merchants' Mirrour." It also contains an introduction to merchants' accounts, by John Collins, together with a treatise by Abraham Liset of Ghent, called "Amphithalami or the Accomptants Closet."

We have seen that Richard Dafforne was really the first writer in the English language whose work went through several editions and therefore may be considered as having been more popular than that of his predecessors Ympyn, Oldcastle, Mellis, and Peele. Dafforne resided for a good many years in Holland, where he obtained his knowledge of bookkeeping. He was a teacher in the Dutch and English languages, and in bookkeeping. Part of his treatise called "The Merchants' Mirrour" was written in Amsterdam before he moved to London. The preface to his book indicates his familiarity with the then existing books on bookkeeping, as he names quite a number. Most of the authors of these books he discredits, but he seems to think highly of Simon Stevin, whom he copied in a number of instances. Simon Stevin, however, was a great scholar, whereas Dafforne evidently was but a shallow teacher, for while he quotes freely from Stevin on the most important points, yet he omits to bring home the force of the question as Stevin does. Thus through Dafforne's faulty transfer of the bookkeeping ideas of the Dutch authors into the English language, we have lost the very essence and foundation of the theory of bookkeeping. Any one reading Stevin first and then Dafforne, will have no trouble in arriving at this conclusion. It is like the reading of a letter from an experienced old man, followed by the treatment of the same subject by a high school student.

In the following pages we are giving a partial reproduction of Dafforne's book, consisting of the title page, the introduction, about half of the text, and a few pages of the journal and ledger, together with the entire trial balance. We are omitting part of the text, because it is simply a repetition of previously mentioned methods, applied to numerous mercantile transactions. All of the text in which he attempts to give some theory or explanations, we have reproduced. It will at once be seen that Dafforne was great at explaining HOW a thing should be done, but incapable of expressing clearly WHY a thing should be done. He has attempted this in one or two places, and failed signally. We are reproducing so much of his book, because, as explained before, we believe that in Pacioli, Manzoni, Ympyn, Stevin, and Dafforne we have the gradual steps of the transfer of bookkeeping knowledge, within a little over one hundred years, from the Italian through the Dutch into the English; unless, indeed, the Dutch transferred their knowledge to America, direct through the settlers of New Amsterdam (now New York).

At the time of Dafforne's writing, English mercantile customs and bookkeeping methods certainly were in a bad way, judging by Dafforne's own words and complaints. There is an entire absence in the journal and ledger of references to the Deity, although the text is full of them. Dafforne even quotes in the language in which it was written a Dutch dissertation on "God, the Giver of all good, all knowledge, and all wisdom."

He explains that a merchant in Amsterdam uses a cash book and a bank book, because his ledger and journal are always behind in posting, otherwise "the ledger might cause the avoidance of the use of these two books." He urges the use of a petty expense book, the totals of which are posted once a month or quarterly, in order to avoid numerous small entries.

What Pacioli calls the memorandum book he calls a waste book, because he says everything is transferred from it into the journal, and when this is done it is useless to preserve it. In Holland they do not preserve it. The inventory and the trial balance are not written in this waste book, because they contain information of a private nature. Blotting or erasures in the journal are improper. He puts his slanting lines (//) in the left-hand margin of the waste book, in order to indicate the transfer to another book, and he evidently prefers this method to the diagonal line drawn through the entries, because, as he says, "it obscures the writing and the figures." Checking of the journal and ledger he calls "re-pointing," using the translation of the old Italian expression of "lancing" or "pointing" as explained elsewhere under Pacioli. Dafforne, however, does not say how he does it.

He does not use the expressions "debit" or "credit" throughout his books, but names them debitor and creditor. He charges the one and discharges the other. He insists that nothing can be entered in the ledger unless it is first entered in the journal. This includes the forwarding of balances from a full page to a new page also the closing entries for profit or loss, and the balancing of the accounts.

Inventory he says consists of stock or estate or capital of the owner, which consists of "increasing improperly" and "decreasing improperly" of the stock or estate. He attempts to explain what the word "improperly" means by quoting from Stevin, but he missed entirely what Stevin meant, as he applies it wrongly.

He uses the word "stock" wherever Stevin uses the word "capital." As the word "stock" comes evidently from stick or stem, it really has the same origin as the word "capital," as through all the definitions and derivations of the word "stock" the thought of "main" or "principal" seems to appear. From this we might state that capital stock is really tautology, for the two words mean the same thing.

In explaining the first journal entry "cash debitor to stock," he personifies the cash account, because it "represents (to me) a man." He indicates the meaning of debitor by stating that by reason of giving the cash to the man, he is obliged to "render it back," or, as we have seen in Italian, "shall give." He indicates the meaning of creditor by mentioning the words "upon confidence," or, as we have seen in Italian "trusting." In spite of his quoting so freely from Stevin, and coming so near to what Stevin says, Dafforne has failed entirely to transfer to posterity the idea of the real reason for a double entry or two debits and two credits. The nearest he comes to it is by stating that cash, merchandise, and all we possess are but "members of that whole body (*stocke*), therefore by the joint meeting of all those members the body (*stocke*) is made compleat." Thus it goes through the entire book, always HOW but never WHY, the very opposite of Stevin.

Merchandise of large size and quantities is always kept in a separate account, designated by the name of the merchandise it deals in. If, however, the merchandise consists of small articles of which but a few are handled, the account is called a general merchandise account. He credits a legacy in one place to stock or capital account, and in several other places direct to the profit and loss account. Debitors he calls those "of whom we are to have," or in other words, as written in the Italian, those who "shall give." Creditors he calls "debt-demanders" and as far as inventory items are concerned, he says that *stocke* is debitor to these debt-demanders.

He says that through a personal or private ledger you can keep a secret of a person's present worth or estate. He is very emphatic in denouncing the use of the cash account for this purpose, as he states three Dutchmen do in their treatise, namely, Waninghen, Buingha, and Carpenter. Here he again barely rubs elbows with Stevin's ideas of proprietorship. He flays the three Dutchmen for promulgating ideas as "book deforming" instead of "book reforming," and he calls their ideas "indefendable errour," "forged imagineries," "forrain bred defects." He further says: "If we were as exact discussors as we are imitators, we had not been so besotted as to entertain those forrain defects, having better at home." It should be noted that elsewhere he praises Stevin, and nowhere does he flay him like the above three Dutchmen, yet had Dafforne been less of a discussor and more of an imitator, he would have presented Stevin's exact theories without fault, and thus preserved them for us in the English language as Stevin did for his Dutch countrymen.

He gives 15 rules each for journalizing debits and credits, but he personifies everything to debitor and creditor. In the ledger he uses a double column, one for money, the other for quantities and weights. Cash discounts he deducts from cost of merchandise, whereas rebates are credited to profit and loss. Thus he disagrees, as he says, with Passchier Goossens, Johannes Buingha, J. Carpenter, and Henry Waninghen. Dafforne succeeded here through his faulty reasoning, in mixing up things to such an extent that many minds today are still mixed up on this subject. Waninghen and Carpenter want to carry trades of merchandise through the cash account. Rightly he objects to this, for cash he says should have no entry unless money is really paid or received.

He does not call in his text the difference between the debits and the credits "the balance," as we do today. He says deduct the lesser from the greater, and make a journal entry for "the difference." In his ledger accounts, however, he does not call it, like the Italians do, "difference" but he calls it "balance to close." He uses the word "equalizing" where we now use "balancing," the same as we translated Pacioli's word "*saldo*" into "equalizing" or "closing." The closing of the ledger he calls "ballancing of the leager," or "leagers-conclusion." Like Stevin he claims that the ledger needs to be balanced when new books are started, or when the merchant ceases to trade or the owner dies. Balancing, he says, consists of three things, the equalizing of all open accounts, the entering of the difference and transferring of the same to the new account or to the balance account. He does not like the word "balancing," and prefers to call it "estate reckoning," the same as Stevin does, and in this connection he refers to Stevin by saying that Stevin carries his closing balances into his opening capital account, which he calls contradictory, and merely a mistake on Stevin's part. The balancing is divided into a trial balance and a true balance; the trial balance consists of debits and credits of the open ledger accounts before profit and loss entries are made. He published in Amsterdam a "three-fold-mony-ballance," which we have reproduced further on. The true balance he says consists of the "remainders" of the ledger accounts after profit and loss entries have been made.

It should be noted that he says "remainders," as does Pacioli, and not "balances," as we use today. The remainders of the accounts he puts in the true balance on the same side as they are in the ledger; namely if cash is debit in the ledger it should be debit in the true balance, for he says, balance is a debitor in the place of cash. He gives a detailed explanation of how to close accounts kept in foreign money, and to take care of the profit or loss in the exchange at the time of closing. While he exhibits a balance account and makes journal entries in order to close all accounts in this balance account, he is very particular in explaining that such a procedure is not needed if you desire to use the balance book in the nature of private information. In that case, he says, post direct from the old account in the old ledger to the new account in the new ledger.

The illustrations given of the journal will show that all entries are numbered, that he uses "debitor to" instead of "debit per," as Stevin uses. Neither does he use the slanting lines (//) so customary in the Italian method, for a division between the debit and the credit, although but one column is given. The ledger page references in the journal are written in the form of a fraction, as Pacioli mentions. Ledger headings, while not as used at this day, are more pronounced than the Italian method, and are almost identical to Stevin's ideas.

In the ledger accounts herewith reproduced, "to" is used on the debit side and "by" on the credit. The journal page is also given as well as the ledger folio of the relative entry in the other part of the ledger. Both sides of the ledger bear the same number of the page, and they are called folio. He does not use the word "sundries," in the journal nor in the ledger, nor does he use a sub-total in balancing his ledger accounts, as Stevin does, but uses in front of the total the Italian word *"summe."* Nowhere in his work does he use the term "assets and liabilities." He uses dots instead of check marks.

THE
MERCHANTS
MIRROUR.

OR,
DIRECTIONS
For the perfect Ordering and Keeping of his
ACCOUNTS.

Framed by way of DE.BITOR and CREDITOR, after the
(fo termed) *Italian Manner* : Containing 250 *Rare* Queftions,
With their Anfwers, in forme of a DIALOGUE.

AS LIKEWISE

A VVASTE-BOOK, with a complete JOURNAL and LEAGER thereunto appertaining;
Unto the which I have annexed two other *Wafte-Books* for exercife of the *Studious*: and at the
end of each is entred the brief Contents of the *Leagers* Accounts, arifing from thence.

AND ALSO

A MONETH-BOOK, very requifite for Merchants, and commodious for all other
SCIENCE-LOVERS of this Famous Art.

The Third Edition, Corrected and Amended.

Compiled by RICHARD DAFFORNE of *Northampton*, *Accountant*, and
Teacher of the fame, after an Exquifite Method, in the
Englifh and *Dutch* Language.

J. Vanden V.

Soo eenigh licht-berifpend Man,
Myn werk beracht, oft foeckt t'onteeren,
Die maecket beeter, Soo hy kan :
'Khebb groote luft noch meer te Leeren.

H. L. S.

Oordeelt iemant voor het Leezen;
Niet goet kan fyn Oordel weezen.

Leerende, leere ick.

The Contents are immediately prefixed before the Book.

LONDON,
Printed by *R. H.* and *J. G.* for *Nicholas Bourn*, at the South-entrance of the
Royall Exchange, 1660.

TO THE
RIGHT HONOURABLE
AND
RIGHT WORSHIPFULL
THE
GOVERNOURS,
AND
FELLOWSHIP

O F

- *Merchants Adventurers of England.*
- *English Merchants for the Discovery of New Trades.*
- *Merchants of East-land.*
- *Merchants of England, trading into the Levant Seas.*
- *Merchants of London, trading into the East-Indies.*
- *Adventurers of the City of London, for a Trade upon the Coasts and In-lands of divers parts of America.*

RICHARD DAFFORNE so wisheth your Understandings Illumination, in your Terrestriall Talents Administration, that with comfort you may hear the joyfull Sentence of your twice commended service; *Mat.* 25. Ver. 21, 23.

> *Well done thou good, and faithfull servant* true,
> *Thou hast been faithfull over things a few,*
> *Ile make thee Ruler over many things,*
> *Possesse the joy of thy Lord,* King of Kings.

RIGHT HONOURABLE, *&c.*

Fter many yeers residence at Amsterdam in Holland, I (upon the often Importunate Letters of some Merchants, my very good Friends) resolved to pitch the Tent of my abode in *London*, which being effected *in Anno* 1630. I then (after some rest) set my course unto severall Stationers Shops; there gazing about me (as one reviving from a Trance) to view what the Laborious Artist had acted and divulged in Print (as other Nations) for the Assistance of Merchandizing, wherewith (BLESSED BE THE GREAT ALL) this Renowned City is throughly Enterlaced, and Adorned.

But as a Shipper anchoring upon an unknown Ile, presently perceiveth those

a 2

parts

parts not to be inhabited, by the *Non-tillage,* or the like ; even ſo (contrary to my expectation)I perceiving the number of Writers to be few,feared that love to this Art was likewiſe ſmall : SEEING THAT GOOD ACCEPTANCE ENGENDERETH GOOD PERFORMANCE. The truth of this I can *averre* with many Inſtances in ſeverall Authors ; as *Foreſtain, John Impen, Cloot, Mennher, Savonne, Nicholas Pieterſon, Rentergem, Marten Vanden Dyck, Hoorbeck, van Damme, Wencelaus, Coutereels, Simon Stevin, Iohn Willemſon, Waninghen, Paſſchia, Gooſſen,* and divers others, whoſe Books are extant. By which may evidently be conjectured,that in thoſe times,and in their parts where they then publiſhed their Works, were found many *Science-lovers* that affected this Art ; by whoſe allurements thoſe worthy Writers were induced to ſet Pen to Paper, endeavouring with their beſt gifts to ſatisfie the deſire of thoſe Art-deſirers.

The Merchants of the Low-countries (of whom I can ſpeak in part) being generally enamoured of this Art;becauſe of its Utility,allure their Teachers to induſtry, by applauding their Vigilancy; encouraging them (with the preſence of their Children and Servants in the Schooles) daily to publiſh new Queſtions ; or at leaſt to revive the profitable Labours of ancient Authors, making them fit for our times.

But we,alas,the ſmall love (pardon my truth ſpeaking) that a great part of our Merchants bear to this Science, daunteth the Pen of Induſtry in our Teachers,making them with a ſuſpective fear to doubt(& not altogether groundleſs) that the profit will not countervail their pains ; by which means *Teachers, Merchants,* and therefore *Youth,* are linked in *Arts enemies ſhackles.*

What may be the cauſe of this Ignorance ? Are our *Teachers* ſo inſufficient ? Or both *dame Nature,* with her *Coadjute* or induſtry beſtowed her Benevolence more ſparingly upon our Nation than upon others? The laſt cannot be: for we can learn it exquiſitly abroad of other Nations(as multitudes can witneſs)why not at home?I anſwer,as before,becauſe at home(for want of love to this Art) many *Merchants* are inſufficient *Preſidents* to their Servants, who by their *Documents* can be but *Equivalent Imitators.* Want of love to this *Art,* is the cauſe why *James Peele,* and others that have written in Engliſh upon this ſubject,are knowne by *Name onely,* and not by *Imitation.* Yea, even the memory of their *Names* dieth, being there is no cauſe to commit their painfull Labours to the *Name-reviving* Preſs. How then ſhall our Youth attain unto this Art, but by frequenting abroad amongſt other *nations* ? And
> *They being then at Rome,*
> *VVill do as there is done.*

This ſtupidity cannot be imputed to our *Teachers* : for if at home (as other people do) we did by *Love* allure, and with *Reward* induce each other to Art by a competent Diſpenſation amongſt our ſelves, of that money which we beſtow abroad amongſt *Aliens,* then would our *Teachers* be vigilant, our *Land* adorned with this Knowledge, and our *Youth* ſhould not need to be tranſported into other Countries for *Arts documents.*

Againſt the foreſaid Ignorance I have emboldened *my ſelf* to prepare
this

this *Antidote*, being by *Nature* obliged to offer up part of the *Widowes Mite* of my knowledg unto the *Land* of my *Breaths firſt drawing*.

Divers are the humours of men : therefore there is but ſmall Probability to pleaſe all : yet to endeavour a generall ſatisfaction is unblameable.

My intent is not to preſcribe theſe *Principles* as fully ſufficient, though for their *Number* approveable: for time at preſent doth not yield permiſſion to impart what my Affections deſired, and *Will* determined to divulge, but theſe are *Allurements onely*, to ſtir up the *better experienced* to amend what I (through want of Art) have not ſo compleatly handled as I deſire, and it deſerves, being an *Art* (ſaith *Simon Stevin* in his Princely Book-keeping, *fol.* 7, *&* 12.) worthy to be numbred amongſt the *Liberall* Sciences. But I already hear Objections a-gainſt the *Firſt*, & *Second* Waſte-books ; that therein are exerciſed ſome accounts, which are altogether needleſſe here in *England* : as is the *Banck-Account*. I grant it to be an Account not uſefull in our Kingdome, but that the knowledge thereof ſhould be un-uſefull to this Arts-Learners, I deny. True it is, that by *Birth* we are *Circumferenced with the Ocean* ; but the *Great-All* hath not ſo ſtrictly limited us within the bounds thereof, that we are abridged from the *Converſation* and *En-tercourſe of Merchandizing* with forrain Nations, as well by their frequenting of our *Borders*, as we Commercing with them in the Body of their *Countries*. And when our Merchants (Old or Young) trade with them in their places, *muſt not they learn to be acquainted with their phraſes* uſed among them concerning *Commerce?* Of which BANCK is none of the leaſt in ſeverall places of Europe, unto which our Engliſh Merchants have their Concourſe. And muſt the advertiſement of the *Courſe* thereof (before we come to the Actuall exerciſe) be a *Blemiſh*, and ac-counted as a *needleſſe thing* in my Book ? *Right Worſhipfuls* behold the Rancor of black Envy, that endeavoureth to have us ignorant of Martiall affairs, untill we come to the point of Battail. The like Objection is alleaged againſt my entring of an Account of *Time* and *Ready-mony*. What if we have them not in uſe a-mongſt our ſelves ? Let us caſt up our accounts with other *Nations*, and (to our coſt) they will teach us how to frame an account of *Time* and *Ready-mony*, if our *Factor*, or *Correſpondent* be in disburſe for us any quantity of mony, and for Time worth the reckoning, as experience hath ſhewed me in many paſſages. And what then ? Muſt not we ſeek the aid of ſome experienced to aſſiſt us ? be-cauſe we regarded not the documents of them (at home) that endeavoured to inform us of the *Manner* and *Matter*. What *Amercement* doth not this *Diſdain-wor-thy* wilfull Ignorance merit ?

Again, the keeping of an account of *Time* and *Ready-mony* (ſay they) may be avoided with an *account Currant*, or a *General account*, upon which is entred matters *Bought, Sold, Drawn, Remitted, Given*, or *Taken* upon Depoſito, and the like: of which manner I am no way ignorant. But let us come to the Period, or Foot of that *General account*, and there the Concluſion ſheweth, that I am DEBITOR to another, or the *Contrary* : how ſhall I find *Ready-money* that at preſent I am to *receive* or *pay* upon that account ?

a 3

 Good Friend of mine (faith *Simon Steven*) being exerciſed in the Old *Hiſtories*, did ſee this forme of Book-keeping (meaning his owne) before it was perfected in the Preſſe ; he was of judgement that it had not been uſed in *Italy*, but about two hundred years : But that the ſame, or one in many parts very like this, was uſed in the time of *Julius Cæſar*, and in Rome long before ; and that ſome Reliques of Ancient time are come to the hands of them, that of late have received it again.

Which Opinion I thought not to be un-beſeeming, the rather, becauſe it ſeemeth ſtrange, that ſo exquiſite a Deep-diving-Science ſhould be invented ſo lately : But be it as it will, I will enter the Opinion of my above-ſaid Friend, who ſaith, that

In place of the proper words now uſed in the Italian-book-keeping, formerly other of the like ſignification were uſed : as theſe,

	Debt-book, Great-book, or Leager ———	*Tabulæ accepti & expenſi.*
	Debitor and Creditor —————————	*Acceptum & expenſum.*
For	Parcells tranſported into the Leager ———	*Nomina tranſlata in Tabulas.*
	Parcells not tranſported ———————	*Nomen jacens.*
	Waſte-book, or perhaps Journall ———	*Adverſaria.*

All which (ſaith he) is apparent in innumerable places of the Latine Writers ; but eſpecially *ex Oratione Ciceronis pro Roſcio Comœdo*. And that the one ſide of their Book was uſed for *Debitor*, the other for *Creditor*, is manifeſt (ſaith he) in a certain place, *Naturalis hiſtoriæ Plinii, lib. 2. cap. 7.* where he ſpeaking of Fortune, ſaith thus :

Huic omnia E X P E N S A.
Huic omnia F E R U N T U R A C C E P T A, *& in tota* R A T I O N E *Mortalium ſola* U T R A M Q U E P A G I N A M *facit.*

If others took regard unto this matter, perhaps further certainty might be found, and that this forme of Book-keeping, not onely by the Romans, but might have been in uſe before them amongſt the Grecians : for being the Romans were no great Inventors, but had their exquiſite Art from the Grecians, it is in reaſon moſt probable to come from them ; whereof further certainty might be found in reading the Greek Hiſtories. Thus much in *Simon Steven, fol.* 105, 106.   A   JUDICIOUS

Briefe CONTENTS of the chiefeft Points contained in this Book.

The Contents of the Book.

INTRODUCTION.

THE FIRST PLACE.

SPEAKERS,

Philo-Mathy. School-Partner.

Phil. HOw now School Partner? Whither away thus folitarye? it feems you are in fome ferious Meditation.

Sch. Surely you have judged aright : for I was mufing upon our Mafters Inftructions of Book-keeping, taught us by way of Queftions aud Anfwers; whereof I have forgotten much, becaufe I frequent not the daily examination,

2 *Phil.* Very likely : *For Exercife is the Preferver of Art*; therefore do I daily refort to the examination, which (you know) our Mafter continually ufeth : the which not onely confirmeth what we have, but it is likewife *an Augmenter of Knowledg*, according to the Motto of James Peel : *Practice procureth perfection*

Sch. Surely you fay truth : Therefore I intreat you (feeing we have time and opportunity) to queftion me in fuch things as at prefent are readieft in your mind; beginning with the firft grounds of our Mafters Inftructions, and fo in brief fort to wade through them all, for the refreshing of my memory.

3 *Phil.* Very gladly : for in queftioning of you I fhall be the better confirmed in that which already I have obteined. But feeing that all good gifts (even in mean Mechanical matters) proceed from the *All-giver*, as in *Exod.*31. Ver.2,3,4,6,7. appeareth, therefore do I humbly intreat my underftandings illumination from thee :

O! al-verbulleud' Een, die alles fcheppe zyt,
Self-ftandigh weezen, zonder Stof, of form, of Tyat,
Of yet dat ons begrip, vedenken kan, of vaten :
Al-fchoon, Almatigh, Wys, end Goedigh boven maten!
Onnoemelike-Alf, All-hærfchende Natuur !
Weet-wzaaks milde Bozn ! Stort ghy te dezer uur,
Of Strael, of Kracht, of Gheeft ! font my wifdom, and zeeghe,
Dat ick den grond uyt-vind', end' onder wyz' ter deeghe,
Dus weet maer ftuck-werk is, vol ougheft adigheeden,
Wy fluyten huyden a'ers vaak dan my ghiftren deeden,
Meeft als de Menfch hoogh vlieght (end'mift utw Hulp O Heer)
Hy fnevelt on-bewaand met Icarus ter neer !
Ach ! Laat zelf achtings Liefo, of waan my doe gheen fchennis,
Gheeft my een fcherp begrip, Goed wzdeel, ware kennis.
Der dinghen onder fcheid dozu, uyt my te Leezen,
Tefchiften Goed, end Quaad, valt dit ! wat mach my deeren ?

B 2   Taking

Taking now my beginning from our Mafters grounds, I intend in order (according to capacity) to paffe through them all: and being that Book-writing, by way of Debitor and Creditor, after the (fo termed) Italian manner, is renowned to be an exquifite knowledg, fhew me its event.

Sch. The Event or End is (faith one) that which moveth to *Action,* and the End finall is ever better then that which is for the End; yet this End cannot be attained, but by another thing intended, as a means thereunto: So, that all things which (as means) are for, and conduce to the End, are not intended, nor profecuted, but out of a deliberate and full intention of the End.

In like manner.

The End of Book-writing is to give contentment unto the Book-owner, and to fhew him (or them, whom they do concern) at all times, and in every degree, how his Eftate ftandeth in the fo written Books. For, the view of a well eftablifhed Eftate in a mans Books, procureth contentment unto the poffeffor; yet this contentment (for no reft without former labour) cannot be attained, but by another thing intended as a means thereunto: to wit, *Book-keeping knowledge:* and being known, profecuted, and affected; the fame being very Requifite, Ufefull, and Commodious for the writing.

Of {

    Princely Revenues, findings of Cuftomes, and the like duties; of which at prefent I intend not to treat, but may hereafter have fome occafion to fhew the neceffity thereof in Princely Courts, as well as in Merchants paffages Of the which there is a worthy work compiled in Dutch for Prince Maurice, Conte of Naffaw, which he learned of the Compiler, Simon Stevin h's Mathematician, and exercifed the fame in his Court, which ftill (as I have been informed) is there in ufe, as alfo in the Swethian Court, and elfewhere.

    Merchants-trading; being for *Proper, Factorage,* or *Company* accounts: of this I intend to fpeak at prefent.

And this Mirrour of Eftate is not to be feen in any Book, but onely in the Leager, whofe proper office it is to fhew the Eftate of the fame to the Book-owner.

Of needleffe Books.

This reproveth the keeping of a mans Eftate in many Books: as in a Book of Buying, another of Selling, another of Receipts, another of Shipping, and what not? All thefe Books cannot fhew a mans Eftate, nor Cafe of ftanding with any man, or in any Commodity, untill all matters are drawn to a head upon a paper in form of a Leager; fo that they have every way as much trouble in writing their imperfect form, as we in making our work compleat at once: but the generality want capacity to apprehend the manner, and rectifie their own defects: therefore they affect this form but with fmall affection.

Phil. Being that the tenor of our fpeech concerneth *Books,* I take it not unfitting that you rehearfe thofe Books that are moft requifite for Merchants ufe, to avoid all thofe needleffe Books.

Of the Cafh-Book, and Banck-Book.

Sch. A Merchant in Amfterdam ufeth a Cafh Book, and a Banck-Book, becaufe his Journall and Leager are (in pofting) behind-hand, elfe the Leager might caufe the avoiding for thofe two Books.

Of the Specie-Book.

A Merchant ufeth likewife a Specie-Book, More ufefull for the Low-Countries then for England, becaufe of the variety of Coines there in ufe; as likewife in times of controverfie to approve what Coins paffed in Receipt of Payment: whereof John Coutereels of Antwerp

werp hath fhewed a worthy example in his Book called 𝕯𝖊𝖓 𝕾𝖙𝖎𝖑𝖊 𝖛𝖆𝖓 𝕭𝖔𝖊𝖐-𝖍:𝖚𝖜𝖊𝖓,

Of the petty Expences-Book.

More, he ufeth a Book of petty Expences for houfe-keeping, and fmall disburfements upon Merchandizing ; the which are pofted once a moneth, or quarter of a year, into the Journall, of which the faid John Coutereels N°. B. *fol.9,*10, 11. hath lively inftances. Simon Stevin in his Princely Book-keeping, *fol.*52. writeth concerning this Book, thus :

This Book of Expences is likewife a kind of a Cafh-Book, and is onely for charges, which generally are pofted once a moneth in one fume into the Journall : partly, for brevity, to poft many petties into one fumme : partly, becaufe in great mens houfes, its the proper office of fome one man to adminiftrate thofe petty expences, rendring an account of each particular, as well for Muftard and Matches to kindle the fire, as of things of greater importance, unto which end there is kept a Particular-Book.

Copy Book of Letters.

More, he keepeth a Copy Book of Letters, which informeth his memory of what he hath written unto others ; and this Book is very requifite againft controverfies of advices, the Letters fometimes not being well underftood by the receiver.

Of the Memoriall.

A Merchant may ufe a Memoriall, there to note fome things that properly appertain to no other Book : as for inftance ; I lent unto a man a fhilling, or a pound, for a day or a week, its fufficient to note a word or two *per* memory, without making any Journall parcell of the fame : yea not in the Clad or Wafte-Book, for that hath another office. *Simon Stevin,* *fol.*21. Some enter fuch things in the Clad, but the fame is fo large, that by prolongation of time its hard to be found ; and caufeth likewife a doubt in the Accomptant whether it fhall be pofted, or not.

Copy Book for Accounts.

Some ufe likewife a Copy Book for Accounts, fent, or delivered to any man, becaufe the Leager agreeth not compleatly in each particular parcell in order, or day, with the fent Account ; elfe that Book, and the writing thereof might be avoided, Of which form, if any man defire an inftance, may have it in the Book of John Coutereels, *lit*.O.*fol*.6.*&*.7.

Four other principall Books doth a Merchant ufe in his Traffique, to wit:

A
{ *Wafte-book*, fore-runner of the Journall
{ *Journall*, or Day-book, fore-runner of the Leager.
{ *Leager*, or Gather-book, Mirrour of a mans Eftate.
{ *Factor-book*, for the entring of each particular received, pack or parcell of wares alone, that cometh into his hands to fell, either in Commiffion, or for Company Account. Of thefe laft four Books I intend to treat, and to explain their proper offices, as much as the *All-Comprizer* fhall pleafe to impart to my prefent memories apprehenfion.   For,

On thee, O God, I do depend,
Ever me with thy Shield depend,
That Jefus my Redeeming Lord
May Mercies fentence me offord :
And that the Illuminating Sp'rit
Grant that I may know my felf aright,
To put my confidence alone
In Trinity, but elfe-where none.
For none but thou didft wifdome give
Unto Bezaleel, Uri's fonne :   Anb

And even of love thou didſt relieve
Him with another choſen One.
L O R D, ſo infuſe thy gifts in me,
And aid me in this work of mine,
That it to many uſefull be,
The praiſe thereof ſhall all be thine.

WASTE BOOK:

So called, becauſe when the matter is written into the Journall, then is this book void, and of no eſteem ; eſpecially in Holland, where the buying people firme not the Waſte-book, as here our Nation do in England.

Phil. Explaine the office and dependances of the Waſte-book.
Sch. Two things are to be noted in the Waſte-book.

$$\text{The} \begin{Bmatrix} Form \\ Office \end{Bmatrix} \text{thereof.}$$

The *Forme* is, that this book is lined towards the left hand with one line (but ſome uſe two) and towards the right hand with three ; leaving towards the left hand a Margine or whiteneſs of an inch or leſſe, according to the books largeneſſe, to enter therein the Day, Moneth, Mark of the Commodity, or all : and between the three lines towards the right hand, there to enter the mony, as by ſeverall inſtances ſhall be made plain.

The *office* of this book is, that onely the Daily-trading ought to be written therein, e-ven as it is truly acted :

A S

Buying, Selling, Receiving, Paying, Drawing, Remitting, Aſſignments, Shipping, &c. and this muſt be entred immediately upon the action of the thing acted, to the end no paſ-ſing parcells be forgotten, according to the Dutch Proverb: Dat men ſchꝛyft, Dat blyft, That which is written, Remaineth. In this book ought neither Inventory nor Ballance of the Leager to be entred ; for that is againſt the office of this book : it being onely to write Traficking paſſages in. In this book may write Maſter, Accomptant, or any Servant of the houſe, by whom the thing is acted, or by advice and order of another. In this book muſt the matter be entred in plain ſincerity as it is acted, without Debitor, or Creditor forme ; for that is the proper office of the Journall : likewiſe many people underſtand the Waſte-book entrances, that apprehend not the Journall forme. In this book ought the parcels to be entred cloſe under each other as they were acted, without leaving of any emp-ty paper, to avoid ſuſpicion of *Forging* any parcells betwixt them, upon any omitted occaſi-on : and each parcell ought to be ſeparated with a line from the other before written, and enſuing parcel. In this book ought the acted matter to be firſt entred ; partly, becauſe it is a fore-runner of the Journal:eſpecially when the Merchant uſeth an Accomptant that dwel-leth without his houſe; for he may ſometime be abſent when ſuch matters are acted. Again, there may be an error committed in Weight, Meaſure, Quantity or Caſting. Again, be-cauſe the matter or condition may be changed, by diminiſhing or augmenting of any thing; or by wholly leaving out of any matter, the bargain being broken, and ſo that parcell can-celled there : for Blotching or Racing out of any parcell in the Journall is unbeſeeming.

Phil. What conſiderations elſe are to be obſerved in this Waſte-book ?
Sch. Five other things muſt be duely obſerved in this book:
1. The Year, Moneth, Day, Town or Place where ſuch matters are acted.
2. The Name and Surname of the Party with whom we trade : or, if it be Factorage, then unto the former name muſt be added the Owners name for whom the thing is effe-cted, as likewiſe the place of his Reſidence : and whether the Bargain be for Time or Ready mony, that's alike, in reſpect of Booking the ſame unto him whoſe Commodities they are.

3. The

3. The quantity or quality of the thing traded for : as, Ells, Pieces, Colours; Weight, Mark, Number, Exchanges, Affignments, or the like.

4. The value of price of the thing traded for : whether Wares, Exchanges, or the like.

5. The conditions or circumftances that were ufed about the matter : as Time, Suretifhip, Bonds given, or taken, Brokeridge, &c.

The Wafte Book parcells are of tenour, as the enfuing examples.

Anno 1630. the 25. of March, in London.

	£	s	d
Marmaduke Grimfton of Northampton, lendeth me 68. *l*. untill the firft of May next coming : which fumme(by his affignment)my Cafhier receiveth of *Arthur Manering*, in confideration whereof I am to allow him certain mony ; being, with principall————	69	15	.7
Affigned *Sybrant Johnfon* upon *Thomas Cofter*, for the accompt of *Seager Solt*, to receive, 495. *l*. the remainer hath my Cafhier received of *John Sybrantfon*, by affignment of the faid *Cofter*, with 7. *l*. 10. for fix weeks time forbearance : the whole being————	951		.9
Agreed with *Jacob Johnfon* of Marken, to let him have 3000. Florines for Franckford, at 81.ß. Flemifh, to be repayd to me, or Affignes, the firft of June next ; as the Exchange fhall then return from Franckford : this being mony for the Company of *Edward Denis* at Northampton and me, each one halfe, producing————	1012	10	
In part of payment of the fame, I deliver him 18.Lafts, 7. Mudde of Rye, being in Company ½ for *Edward Denis*, and ½ for me ; at 150. gl. each Laft ready-mony, is gl. 3834. 8. 12. The remainer have I made good in Banck (for him) upon the accompt of *John Johnfon* Vinck, abating 22.⅔ gl. for Banck-mony, at one *per Cent.* the whole produceth	1012	10	

Day. 27

1630. March 30.

Phil. What ufe have thofe flantling ftrokes that are drawn in the Margine ?

Sch. They have two ufes : 1. They fhew how far is pofted out of the Wafte-book into the Journall ; and they are a fure mark that a man omit no parcell, being called away from his pofting : neither to enter one thing twice upon the faid calling away. 2. They fhew how many Journal parcells are included in fuch a Wafte Book parcel : infomuch, that in re-pointing of the Wafte-Book, a man may the eafier fee the quantity of the included parcells, when the Wafte and Journall fhall be compared againft each other. Some draw thofe ftrokes on the right hand, where the mony is ; but that multitude of Strokes darkneth the mony fummes : *each his choice.* The Wafte-Book parcells ought with all convenient fpeed to be pofted into the Journall, and Leager, to the end the Book owner may the better difcern how his cafe ftandeth with each man, and matter. Thus much of the Wafte-Book in *Form, Office,* and *Circumftances* : Now,

OF THE JOURNALL.

It being the firft exquifite Book, wherein carefully muft be obferved, that each parcel have its Charge, and Difcharge : that is, the true *Debitor*, and *Creditor*, wherewith each Journal parcel ought to begin : which being well apprehended, and with fit words(according to the nature of the matter)expreffed, *is one of the chiefeft principles belonging*

7

belonging unto book-keeping. Mark well ; he that can difcern the true *Debitor* and *Creditor,* in any propounded propofition (concerning this Art) hath the right (Theorick) *inward-ground-knowledge* and contemplation of the matters : and he, and *onely* he (with the help of Arithmetick*)* goeth firm in his action, to give each man his due, and book his matters under due and true Titles. It is very requifite (if poffible it may be effected) that the Journall be written by one man : for in times of controverfie he can beft anfwer for his own poftings.

8   *Phil.* What things are moft requifite in the Journall to be noted ?
   Sch. Three Notable things are to noted in the Journall :

             1. The *Matter* whereof it is made.
             2. The *Form* thereof.
             3. The *Office* whereunto it is ufed.

OF THE JOURNALLS MATTER.

9   *Phil.* Proceed to the Explication of the firft member.
   Sch. The *Matter* whereof the Journall is made, may be drawn to five chief branches : for it

proceedeth
1. From the Inventary : as in the 10. and fo to 61. place.
2. From Traffickes continuall Exercife : as in **62.** place (including 205.)
3. From tranfporting of full accounts in the Leager unto a new leaf, See 206. place.
4. From the equalizing of Over, or Under-weights, Meafures, or the like. See 212. place.
5. From the Leagers Conclude, or Ballancing of the Leager. See 215. place

10   *Phil.* Go on with the firft branch.
   Sch. An ufuall Inventary generally confifteth in

Stocks,

1. Ready-mony, and that in Cafh, in Banck, or both.
2. Wares remaining unfould for proper accompt : under this fecond member is included Houfes, Lands, Rents, Ships-parts ; as alfo Wares unfould for Factorage, or Company-accompts, and thofe that were formerly fhipt unto another place, being as yet unfould for Proper, Factorage, or Company accompts.

Increafing : improperly by means of

3. Debi-tors : and them a-gaine in
1. People unto whom we formerly fould : or, that promifed us payment of exchanges, and the like.
2. Factors,
3. Partners, that have not as yet given us full fatisfaction.
4. Mafters,

Decreafing : improperly by means of

4. Debt-deman-ders : and them in
1. People of whom we have bought, or whofe Bills we have accepted.
2. Factors,
3. Partners, unto whom we as yet have not given full
4. Mafters, content.
5. Wares, partly fould for Factorage, of Company-account.

11   *Phil.* In the above-ftanding Table you fpeak of Stockes Increafing, and Decreafing Im-properly ; explain the word Improper.
   Sch. Simon Stevin, difcourfing of Merchants Book-keeping, *fol.* **55.** with *Prince Mau-rits.*

*rits,*concerning Stockes Increafing, and Decreafing : the Prince faith, that, *Monies, Wares,* and *Debitors,* Increafe Stock : for the more a man hath of them, the greater will his Stock be. Contrarily, *Debt-demanders* Decreafe Stock. Simon Stevin replyeth, to be of another Opinion; expreffing himfelf with the enfuing Inftance : If (faith he) in former Books I bought of Peter a Bale of Pepper upon Time; that Pepper augmenteth not my Stock: for Peter demandeth of me the value, time being expired. In like manner, my Stock decreafeth not, becaufe Peter is a *Debt-demander* : for its as much augmented by the Pepper. But if a Bale of Pepper be given me, that, truly augmenteth my Stock: for I enter, *Pepper-debitor* to Stock. And, *fol* 54. A Merchant giving certain hundreds to Marriage with his *Daughter,* that decreafeth Stock. By this may eafily be difcerned, what Stock Augmenter, and Diminifher properly is.

12 | *Phil.* Speaking of Stocks Increafing, and Decreafing, you rehearfed in how many parts the fubftance of an Inventary did confift; but let me now hear you *nominate* the true *Debitors* and *Creditors* of the fame *onely,* without any other Circumftances of Dictations.

Sch. To give you the better content, I will fpeake of each in order as they ftand: and firft,

OF THE READY MONY.

13 | *Phil.* How Book you the Ready-mony after the way of Debitor and Creditor ·
Sch. *Cafh* Debitor to *Stock.*

14 | *Phil.* Why make you *Cafh* Debitor ?
Sch. Becaufe *Cafh* (having received my mony into it) is obliged to reftore it again at my pleafure : for *Cafh* reprefenteth (to me) a man, to whom I (onely upon confidence) have put my mony into his keeping; the which by reafon is obliged to render it back, or, to give me an account what is become of it : even fo, if *Cafh* be broken open, it giveth me notice what's become of my mony, elfe it would redound it wholly back to me.

15 | *Phil.* Why do you ufe the word *Cafh,* being the word *Mony* is in ufe amongft our Nation ?
Sch. Simon Stevin treating of this word with *Prince Maurits* of *Naffau,* in the fift Head point of his Princely Book-keeping, *fol* 52. faith, that he could give none other reafon, *but onely,* that this word is in *Ufe,* which if it were not, I account it better (faith he) to have faid, *Mony is Debitor.*

Our Mafter ufually alledged the difference between private, and generall difcourfes, fhewing that many words are ufually among Dutch, French, and other Nations, with whom a Merchant doth trafficke: therefore he thought it fitteft to ufe generall words, as being generally known, and moft ufefull in Book-keeping; elfe (faid he) why fhould not *Mony* bear its *own Name* as well as other commodities ?

16 | *Phil.* One other Queftion I have to demand before you proceed, which is, Why is Stock made *Creditor* ?
Sch. Becaufe the word *Stock* containeth in it, all what a man poffeffeth; whether *Money, Wares, Debts* due to us, or the like : and (marke this well) *Cafh,* yea, each particular thing that I poffeffe, is but a member of that whole body *Stocke*; therefore by the joynt meeting of all thofe members, the body (*Stock*) is made compleat.

17 | *Phil.* Having paffed the firft part of Ready-mony, treat now fomewhat

OF THE MONY IN BANCKE.

For in the hands of the Honourable *Lords* of the Bancke, I have a certain fumme of money; how fhalll I Book that ?

C   *Sch.* Banck

NOTE.—*Pages 23 to 43, 10 to 14, 24 to 44, 48, 49 and 53 of the text are omitted, because they give questions and answers setting forth how journal entries under differing circumstances are made. They do not present any argumentation or theory, nor do they show why they are made, and therefore are practically nothing but repetitions of what has been said in other pages.*

40   *Phil.* Let me hear you enter this according to the nature of the Inventary.

Sch. They were fent before; and therefore I enter now.

Edward Denis of Northampton his account at Roan in France, in the Adminiftration of *P. D.* Debitor to Stock ; for the charges by me done at the firft fending. See **46.** place.

41   *Phil.* But fuppofe the charges that you did at the firft fending were writ off from his above-named Roan account, unto his account currant, being that I would have all disbut-fed money upon one account ; and therefore that account hath no charge now upon it.

Sch. *Edward Denis* of Northampton, his account at Roan in France, in the Adminiftra-tion of *P. D.* is Debitor to Stock: *Nota,* for a Blank fumme, both in Debit and Credit ; and muft be fo carried to each account *per Formam*, becaufe there muft not be a Debitor without a Creditor, nor the contrary.

42   *Phil.* Suppofe *P. D.* had in the former books made fale of part, or whole ; whereof you had advice then, but no Returns. See **46.** place.

Sch. *P. D.* at Roan, for the proper account of *E. D.* at *N. N.* Debitor to Stock ; for as much as the known fales import : and fo I pafs forward, according to the Tables tenour, unto.

Wares abroad, unfold, for Company-Account.

43   *Phil.* I perceive you cleave clofe to the Table.

Sch. School-men (as I have read) fay, that a good Difputant ought never to digreffe from the propounded Propofition, untill it be difcuffed. Neither ought any Writer to commit a digreffion from the grounds of his intended fubject, as is here the before-entred Table in the 10. place, as alfo the enfuing three Tables ; to wit, The Table of Accounts *Proper* in the **63.** place : the Table of *Factorage*-accounts in the **122.** place : and the Table of *Company*-accounts in the **174.** place. From thefe I intend not to ftray ; but in order will work upon them (as the Table fhall deliver matter thereunto :) the more, becaufe any one which fhall have occafion to feek a matter in any of thofe particular Tables, whether in the *Inventaries*, *Proper*, *Factorage*, or, *Company*-Tables, may prefently know what goeth before, or, followeth his defired matter.

44   *Phil.* But to our intended purpofe ; rehearfe fome Inftances of Company unfold Wares.

Sch.
{ Voyage to Roan, configned to *Pierre du Pont*, being in Company for *James Bartram*, and me, each ½ ——————————— } Debitor

Voyage to Lisborne, configned to *Pedro del Verdo*, being in to

Company, ½ for *Robert Clifton*, and Partner, ⅛ for *James Joyner* ; Stock.

and ½ for me. ————————————

45   *Phil.* Having in order waded through the fecond branch of the Inventary-Table, in the 10. place ; proceed to the third branch of Stocks increafing: being

DEBITORS, OF WHOM WE ARE TO HAVE.

Sch. Four in number are they comprehended under, in the third branch of the 10. place, and may all be joyned as under one ; yet in brief I will touch each apart : as

{ 1. *B. C.* to whom we formerly fold, or, that he had accepted our Exchanges, Debitor to Stock.

2. *C. D.* at Venice my account currant, Debitor to Stock.

                                                 3. Partner,

{ 3. Partner, { Who hath part of My estate in his hands, to be imployed, by him for the good of our Company: *N. N.* my account by him in Company, Debitor to Stock.
Whose part of Stock is in my hands to be by me imployed, and I am for him in disburse: *N.N.* his account by me in Company, Debitor to Stock.

4. *M.M.* at Colchester his account Currant, Debitor to Stock.

By the word *Currant*, do not I understand the account that is opposite to an account of *Time*, (for I distinguish them by the name of *Time*, and Ready-mony) but by *Currant*, I understand, a *Running* account, (*Conte-Courante*) upon the which all things may passe, as well for time, as Ready-mony.

46 *Phil.* Thus I see you have passed through the three branches of Stocks Increasing, with the dependances of the same in a briefe manner: what followeth next to treat of?

DEBT-DEMANDERS.

Sch. In the 10. place is shewed, that Stock hath (Improperly) a Decreasing part; and that again is divided into five Sub divisions: of these in briefe likewise, after a plain manner: as thus,

Stocke is Debitor to {

1. *D. E.* Of whom we formerly bought, or whose Bills in former Books we accepted, and presently Booked them, but not due to be paid in those Books.

2. *E. F.* at Constantinople, my account *Currant*; for that he hath made me more Returns then my sold Wares did import.

3. Partner, { My account by him in Company, he having paid out more then his part doth import.
His account by me in Company: I having received into my hands mony for sold Wares, and detain his part thereof, where he ought to have it.

4. *F. G.* His account *Currant*; the credit of which being heavier then his Debit: but whether it be in Ready-mony, or, for Wares sold upon time, thats not materiall, in respect of his *Running-accounts* form.

5. *G. H.* His account of Kersies, for so much as was sold upon that account in the former Book: See 36. place.

Durances in Company, $\frac{1}{2}$ for *A.B.* $\frac{1}{3}$ for *B.C.* and $\frac{1}{6}$ for me: for so much as in the former Book was sold upon that account: See 37. place, it being compared with this.

Edward Denis of Northampton, his account at *Roan in France*, in the Administration of *P. D.* for as much as the known Sales import. *Nota*, in the 42. place, the Factor was made Debitor to Stock, for the like summe: therefore our Stock standeth well in the like case with others. Again, we have our first charges done us good unto our Stock in the 40. place.

Stock Debitor to Voyage to Lisborne, consigned unto *Pedro del Vergo*, being in Company, $\frac{1}{3}$ for *Robert Clifton*, and Partner $\frac{1}{6}$ for *James Joyner*, and $\frac{1}{2}$ for me: for as much as the known Sales import. You must conceive, that *Pedro del Vergo*, our account, being in Company, $\frac{1}{3}$ for *Robert Clifton*, and Partner; $\frac{1}{6}$ for *I.I.* and $\frac{1}{2}$ for me: either *standeth*, or, *should stand* Debitor to Stock, for the like summe, that Stock standeth Debitor to the Voyage for the Sales; for the *Voyage* cannot have a Credit, but by one, or more Debitours that *even* Counter-poize that Credit.

47 *Phil.* I have seen your *Dxterity* in the handling of the Inventary-Table, as also in the Booking of a mans known estate; but if a Merchant will not have his estate known, how

how will you behave your felf therein? Ha! I think I have pos'd you now. Now you are ftall'd, I trow.

Sch. In fuch difficult Queftions you cannot debarre me, to take the aid of fome Renowned Authors : for in the firft place of our Dialogue I feared my weakneffe, becaufe I frequented not the daily Examination ; but although I frequeut not the School, I am yet not ignorant of what the Authors paffages are upon this Subject : and therefore I will decide your Queftion, with the Solution of Mafter *Henry Waninghen* in the firft Chapter, the 17. Queftions anfwer ; his words are thefe : *Cafh muft be entred in place of Stocke , making all that is due to us Debitor to Cafh : contrarily, Cafh Debitor to all them that are to have of us.*

With him (in the very fame words) agreeth his Difciple *Joannes Buingha,* who now at Amfterdam, after the death of his before-named Mafter, fucceedeth his place in Schoolmafterfhip. See the 38. page of his Book, printed 1627.

J. Carpenter Gent. in his *Moft Excellent Inftruction,* printed in London 1632. is a direct *Imitator* of both the former : *See fol.* 20.24. of his Book : and no mervaile ; for the greateft part of his publifhed Book, is nothing elfe but a generall copy of *Henry Waninghens* Book, both in words, and number of the Queftions. *J. C.* in his Epiftle to the Reader, pretendeth Ignorance, of not knowing the Author, who in the French Language many years agone was eafie to be found.

48   *Phil.* Shew me fome Iaftances how they would Book their paffages.
     Sch. In briefe I will : and firft,

OF THE WARES.

     Grograines,
     Kerfies   } Debitor to Cafh.
     Durances,

             Of the People that owe to us.

     Robin Good-fellow,
     Herman Hard-head, } Debitor to Cafh.
     John Gentleman,

             Of the People that we owe unto.

           Rowland Red-beard.
     Cafh Debitor to { *Ralph Would-well.*
           Reynft Reach-farre.

49   *Phil.* Suppofe a man at the making of his Inventary hath fome mony, how fhall he Book that?
     Sch. The before-named in the places of their Books mentioned, fay, *The Ready-mony is not to be entred, till you disburfe the fame.*

50   *Phil.* Suppofe with part of that concealed mony you bought *Wares,* and with other part, paid them unto whom you are indebted : how enter you that?

     Wares,
     People, } Debitor to Cafh.

51   *Phil.* This being thus rehearfed, what will you conclude ; have thefe (think you) digreffed?
     Sch. Suppofe they had, what's that to me? But becaufe you fhould not flout at me, thinking my capacity to be fo ftupid, that it is void of diftinction, I will in fome briefe notes onely touch the fame.
                                       Firftly,

First, let me consider whether the Book-owner be more indebted then his Estate is worth ; which if he be, then is their entrance good, for his Estates concealment : *for the Debit side of Cash ought to be heaviest, or, having no mony, it must be even, because all is paid out :* but if he have any Estate, then is the *Credit* of his Cash (who standeth in *Stocks* stead) heaviest : and therefore an *Errour*, being there is more paid, then was received.

Secondly, the commodities that we have at the making of our Inventary, were bought in *former* Books, and there made *Debitors* ; and that we now enter them again *Debitors* to *Cash*, is to re-buy them : and consequently, in place of *book-reforming, book-deforming,* and an *undefendable Errour.*

Thirdly, the People whom we now make *Debitors* to *Cash*, are *absolutely* our *Debitors* ; and do we *pay* them, who are to *pay* us ? many men would desire to be *our* Debitors.

Fourthly, As senselesse is it, to make Cash *Debitor* to People that are to have of us ; will they that are to have of us 100. P. for a Bill of Exchange by us accepted, say, *Come my Friend,* you have accepted an Exchange, to pay at time expired, which is now : send your man to my house, and the mony shall incontinently be paid to him ? *I think nothing lesse.*

☞Fifthly, Cash may never be ☞*named. Nota, not named,* but when *money* is either truly, and really paid, or, received, as in the 17.place is mentioned. But if these People enter *forged* Imaginaries in the *Fore-front* of their Books : what is not to be expected before the End ?

Sixthly, The *Stock* which they seek to *conceale,* is manifest in the *difference* of Cash it self. For let then transport their *Cash,* and they shall find (if as before is said, that their Estate stand well) that *Cash* is, and in transporting forward, always remaineth *Creditor.* Ballance that *Cash,* and tell me what shall be done with the *difference.* Carry it to a new account, what then ? there it will prove to be *Stock.* Carry it to Profit and Losse, there it will prove to be *Stockes Augmenter. Wonder is it,* that these and many other *Forrain bred-defects* must now be *cloathed in English Attire,* and passe for currant amongst us ! Surely, our Judgement is weak in the *discerning of this Art.*

Phil. I perceive their passages in Booking of their Matters, doth not digest with you ; is there a more plain way ? discover that.

Sch. If we were as *Exact Discussors,* as we are *Imitators* ; we had not been so *besotted,* as to entertain those Forrain defects, having *better at home.*

Look into *James Peele,* whose well-entrances, through neglecting Age (or disdain of Domestick Writers, and extolling of Forrain) are as strange to us, as though (as the saying is) they were written in Heathen Greek.. He sheweth us the fit ground-work, how to conceale a mans Estate, in the Booking of his private aceounts, and matters manifested for Merchandizing.

Phil. Instance some particulars, how to Book the manifested part.

Sch. You speak of *part* ; whether he bring in *part,* or, *All,* who can certainly know that ? being that we can but *Aime* at it, as the Blind at the *colour of Cloth.* And for that which he manifesteth, may be

entred
{
Cash,————————————
Banck,————————————
Perpetuanes,————————————
Marmaduke Man,————————————
John Knoll at Lisborn, my account Proper,—
}
Debitor unto the *Private* account.

Phil. How shall the Master, or Book-owner, enter into his *private* Books the things manifested for Merchandizing ?

Sch. Generall account for Traffick, Debi-tor to
{
Cash,
Banck,
Perpetuanes,
Marmaduke Man,
John Knoll at Lisborn, my account Proper.
}

D

Phil.

55   *Phil.* Suppose there is gained upon Wares sould.
Sch. Wares Debitor to Private account, for the Gaines ; do the like in Factor accounts, and all other, upon which Gaines ariseth.

56   *Phil.* Suppose I lose by Wares, or Exchanges.
Sch. Private account, Debitor to Wares, Exchanges, or, unto that account ; upon which Losse ariseth.

57   *Phil.* At the Conclude of my Book, I surrender *Monies, Debts,* and *Unsould-Wares.*
Sch. Private account Debitor to Cash, Men, and Wares, each *name* severally.

58   *Phil.* How shall the Book-owner enter back in his private Books the *surrendred* severall matters?
Phil. Cash, Men, Wares, each *name* severally, Debitor to Generall account for Traf-fick.

59   *Phil.* How shall the Book-owner enter into his Private Book, the Gaines that are found upon his Book of Traffick?
Sch. Generall account for Traffick, Debitor to Profit and Losse.

60   *Phil.* But if he lost in his Book for Traffick.
Sch. Profit, and Losse Debitor to Generall account for traffick ; because it hath *sur-rendred* back lesse, then formerly was confidented unto the same: Judge of the Gaines likewise, that the Generall account for Traffick yielded more, then the first in-laid Principall. Here you see the matter *plainly discussed.* Here you see the ground-work, by which they are *confuted,* gathered from *one* of our *own Nation ;* which to their mis-en-trings might rather have been

A worthy Refutation,
Then, by their Approbation
To bring them to our Nation.

But it seeemeth that this Absurdity (and many more, which upon due Examination of their works apparently *I can make* appear) was not *discerned,* or, being *discerned,* how to amend it, *Experience had not befriended them.*

61   *Phil.* Rehearse some other Instances of their Mis-entrances, that (for the Reader) they may be as *Buoyes* in this *Sea,* to keep him from Ignorances Ship-wrack.
Sch. Very loth am I to *pry* any further into their Books: for their *Adsurdities* are ma-ny in divers matters. And if I should dive into them all, it would be thought that I one-ly uttered *Satyricall Snarlings,* where my *plain meaning* is, to stirre them up to a more *serious study,* that the *silly* beginner be not frustrate of his Expectation: seeking in them (as one saith) *Sapientia,* but finding *Apedia:* therefore let me proceed towards our intended purpose.

62   *Phil.* Well ; for this time let us do as you desire : What followeth next to treat of, seeing the *Inventory,* with the Dependances (which is the *first matter* whereof the Jour-nall is made) are discussed?
Sch. The second matter whereof the *Journall* is made, is the next thing in order that we are to treat upon ; and proceedeth from

TRAFFICKES CONTINUALL EXERCISE,

as in the Ninth place is rehearsed : wherein is to be considered three Principall accounts, consisting

In

In {Proper / Factorage / Company} Accounts: and each of these again, in {

{ *Domestick-affaires:* for so I terme those things, which I in actuall Administration, administrate as chiefe Manager in the matter ; whether in *Proper, Factorage,* or, *Company* accounts.

Forraine-affaires: for so do I nominate those matters, that another administrateth as chiefe Actor in the matter, without hand-action of me, or, mine: and thus do my ——————————————————————

{ *Factor* / *Partner* } With the Wares, Bills, and Monies that I send to him, to be imployed for me.

Friend: unto whom I sent my Masters Wares, because they were not *Vendible* here, as in the 39. place is expressed : the said *Friend* is to be countable for the Sales thereof to me, and I to my Master, with whose order I sent them thither ; he not having any acquaintance with the man, nor Trading for that place. Of these I intend to treat in *Order,* as they are entred in the above-standing Table : but first I will Book some exquisite

Rules of aide, very requisite in Trades continuance, to be learned without Book.

1. Whatsoever commeth unto us (whether Mony, or Wares) for Proper, Factorage, or Company account, the same is ——*Debitor.*

2. Whosoever Promiseth, the Promiser is ——*Debitor.*

3. Unto whom we pay (whether with Mony, Wares, Exchanges, Assignations) being for his own account : that man is ——*Debitor.*

4. Unto whom we pay (as above) for another mans account :
The man for whose account we pay, is ——*Debitor.*

5. When we buy Wares for another mans account (whether we pay them presently, or not, that is all one in the entrance) and send them unto him, or unto another by his order.
The man for whose account we bought, and sent them, is for the Wares, and Charges, ——*Debitor.*

6. If we deliver an Assignation unto any man (whether it be our own, or anothers) that man for whose account we deliver that Assignation in payment, is ——*Debitor.*
N O T A,
This is much like the third Article, but this is here thus entred, because this Article is here more largely explained, for the better understanding of Assignation.

7. When we, or any other man for us, sendeth commodities unto another Land, or Towne, to be sould, for *Proper* or *Company* account, then is

1. Whatsoever goeth from us (whether Mony, or Wares) for Proper, Factorage, or Company account, the same is——*Creditor.*

2. Unto whom we Promise, the Promised man is——*Creditor.*

3. Of whom we receive (whether Mony, Wares, Exchanges, Assignations) being for his own account : that man is ——*Creditor.*

4. Of whom we receive (as above) for another mans account :
The man for whose account we receive, is——————*Creditor.*

5. When we buy for our selves, or for another man, and pay not presently,
The man of whom we bought those Wares, is——————*Creditor.*

6. Whosoever delivereth an Assignation unto us upon any man, for his own account : the man of whom we received it, is *Creditor.*
O R,
Upon whom I deliver mine Assignation, to be paid by him for his own account, that man is——————*Creditor.*
O R,
Whosoever (to pleasure, or accommodate me) payeth my Assignation, the accommodating man, is————*Creditor.*

7. When we receive advice from our Factor, that those sent commodities, or part of them are sould, or lost then is

Voyage

Voyage to such a place consigned to such a man————————————*Debitor.*	Voyage to such a place consigned to such a man————————*Creditor.*

8. When we pay Custome, Insurance, or other charges, upon the sending of those commodities, then is

Voyage (as above)————————*Debitor.*

8. Cash, or charges of Merchandizing is *Creditor. Nota,* divers Merchants keep such an account of charges of Merchandizing, especially those that have Cashiers within their own house.

9. When we cause the sent goods to be insured, but pay it not presently, then is

Voyage (as above)—————————*Debitor.*

9. The Insurer is——————————*Creditor.*

10. When we ensure any mans sent Wares, and receive the mony presently, then is Cash————————————*Debitor.*

10. Insurance-reckoning,
       Or   is *Creditor.*
     Profit, and Losse.——
Chuse of these which you please.

11. When we Insure any mans sent Wares, and receive not the mony presently, then is the man, for whose account we Insured those Wares,—————————*Debitor.*

11. As above————————————*Creditor.*
Nota,
Merchants that trade much in this kinde, use an account in their Books, called *Insurance-reckoning.*

12. When we receive advice, that the former sent Wares, or part of them are sold, then is
The Factor that sold them for our account————————————————*Debitor.*

12. When we receive *Returnes,* either in Mony or Wares, in lieu of those sould Wares, then is
The Factor that payeth us, or causeth us to be paid,——————————————*Creditor.*

13. If any man draw Exchanges upon us for himself, or for any other man, the man for whose account the same was drawn, is——————————————————*Debitor.*

13. If we draw Exchanges upon any man for himself, or for any other man, the man for whose account we draw, the same is————————————————*Creditor.*

14. If we remit Exchanges unto any man, for himself, for me, or any other man:
The Factor, *If for me,* or the man for whose account it was remitted, is——*Debitor.*

14. If any man remitteth Exchanges unto us for himself, for me, or for another man;
The Factor, if for me, or the man for whose account the same was remitted to me is——————————————————*Creditor.*

15. When we lose by gratuities given, whether great, or small, or howsoever, then is Profit and Losse————————*Debitor.*

15. When we gain by gratuities received, whether great, or small, or howsoever, then is Profit, and Losse———*Creditor.*

Phil. Having thus placed your *Rules of aide,* proceed (as was determined) to the first of your before-mentioned Principall accounts.

Sch. The first nominated Principall account (for plain apprehensions sake) I will *display* under the form of account

Prop̄er

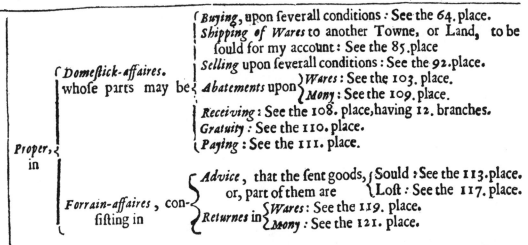

64   *Phil.* The Table being entred in briefe as above, requireth an explaining ; therefore let me see your Entrances upon each member apart.

Sch. The parts being divided into Affaires *Domestick,* and *Forraine,* I intend to treat first of the first ; and therein again of the branches orderly as they follow, whose beginning is with

BUYING.

65   *Phil.* I *buy* Wheat, and pay for the same presently, even upon the receit thereof: How shall I enter that ?

Sch. Wheat Debitor to Cash. *Nota,* Some will, that of the like Passages should be made a double Entrance, because upon all Occasions the mans name might be found upon the Alphabet : each do his pleasure ; I account this way clear, and evident. For afterward if any controversie should arise, that Book (from whence the Question ariseth) will shew the Year, and Moneth ; then is it upon my Book easie to be found. *Nota,* All accounts of *Commodities* must have lines *within,* to keep the quantity of *Ells, Measure, Weight,* and the like.

66   *Phil.* I Buy Rye *Contant,* but pay not instantly.

Sch. Rye Debitor to the *Man* of whom I bought it. *Nota,* the word *Contant* signifieth, *upon Demand* ; and that again, for 1.2.3. daies, or 1.2. or three weeks : generally, it is included under one moneths time ; for that which is contained under the *nomination of moneths,* is 1.2.3. or more moneths.

67   *Phil.* I buy upon two moneths time a little parcell of Pepper, Ginger, Cloves, or the like ; some one parcell to the value of 10. *l* and some lesse.

Sch. Groceries, Debitor to the *Man* of whom I bought them : understand my meaning, which is not, that I should make the Commodity Debitor to the *Mans servant,* because I bought it of him ; but unto the Principall, or Man, *to whom it belongeth,* in respect of my knowledge. *Nota,* the Entrance of that which I buy, upon 2. Daies, 2. Moneths, 2. Years, is all as one : for my acknowledged man must be known upon my Books, as well for 2. Daies, as for 2. Years.

68   *Phil.* I buy Latton-wyre upon 3. moneths paying $\frac{1}{67}$ part presently.

Sch. Latton-wyre Debitor to the *Man Principall,* from whence it came. And then, *Man Principall,* Debitor to Cash, for the $\frac{1}{67}$ part now paid. I enter this thus in $\frac{1}{67}$ parts, because some make the Bought Wares Debitor to the Selling man, for the part upon Time : and Wares Debitor to Cash, for the part paid. Here you see Wares are divided into two parts, (which is unseemly) and therefore must have two Journall parcells : so there is every way as much writing, as to make the Wares Debitor to the man for the whole ; and then, him Debitor to Cash for the paid part. But if I buy severall Wares to pay $\frac{1}{67}$ part in money, what brave divisions would then arise ? For each parcell must have two Debitors, and

Creditors,

Creditors, which will be no fmall trouble; or elfe they muft learn to place their parcels with more judgment.

69

Phil. I buy Cloth upon 9. moneths Time, which is to ride out ⅜, then to difcount for 6. moneths : paying for them in Banck, and *enjoy* Banck-monies allowance in hand.

Sch. Cloth Debitor to the *Man,* for the whole coft upon 9. Moneths : *and then,* the Man Debitor to Cloth for the Difcount; *and then,* the Man Debitor to Banck for the fumme writ in : *and then,* Cafh Debitor to Profit and Lofle; becaufe the mony by me written in Banck, and the Difcount, counter-vailed the firft Principall upon 9. moneths.

70

Phil. I buy Barly upon 8. moneths time, difcounting inftantly; paying part in Mony, part by Affignement, part with Rye : the remainer in Banck, *abating* fo much as the Banck-monies allowance is worth.

Sch. Barly Debitor to the *Man,* for the whole upon 8. moneths : 2. the Man Debitor to Cafh for the fumme payd : 3. the Man Debitor unto him, who was to pay my Affignation for his own account : 4. The Man Debitor to Rye, for the delivered value : 5. The Man Debitor to Banck for the fumme made good, either upon his account, or, upon the account of another, by his order : 6. The Man Debitor to Profit, and Lofle, for Banck-monies allowance; becaufe this, and the Banck-mony, make both but one compleat part of payment : but it I had writ in Banck his compleat part of payment, and he made good the mony for Banck allowance to me, by paying it in hand; then muft we enter, Cafh Debitor to Profit, and Lofle : 7. The Man Debitor to Barly for the 8. moneths difcount. *Nota, Henry Waninghen, Chapter* 2. *Queftion* 14. entereth the Man Debitor to Profit, and Lofle, for the difcount. *Paffchier Gooffens, zu Hamburgh,* printed 1594. *parcell* 44. 47. and others, entreth the like. *Johannes Buingha, folio* 39. *Queftion* 7. entreth the like. *J. Carpenter, fol.* 34. his Booking is with *Henry Waninghen* the 14. *parcell* alike; and .. nely an Imitator : and fo of other Authors. But *premeditation* fheweth, that the *Rebates* of commodities fhould *not be* carried unto Profit, and Lofle, as our printed Authors in generall do, without any further in-fight into the nature of the matter : For *Barly,* which before was *Barly* upon *Time,* is now become *Barly* for *Ready-mony;* which at the buying (in refpect of the Time I was to ftand out, and have the ufe of the mony in *mine own* hands) coft me *more* then it now will yield me *Ready mony;* the while then *Barly* upon 8. moneths was more charged at the buying, then it now is worth *Contant,* reafon requireth that *Barly* fhould be *difcharged,* becaufe I have disburfed my mony : *See Ralph Handfon upon Abatements in his Table.*

This muft be well regarded in *Rebates,* to the end, that each *Horfe* may bear his own Burthen; well *noting,* that the *Rebates* are not made good in *mony : See Ralph Handfon.*

☞ But if we buy fundry commodities, and have an allowance upon the whole buying, then muft we enter,

The man of whom I bought, Debitor to Profit, and Lofle Proper : for *no one* commodity may *enjoy the allowance* made upon the whole Cargo, or Parcell; and to make a divifion *pro rato,* of each commodities Capitall, would be a troublefome (but true) worke : therefore Profit and Lofle is the briefeft carriage in fuch matters, being the *Facis* after either of the wayes, redoundeth unto our finall advance for the Abatement. This in briefe.

Buying ⎰ For Ready-mony, and prefently pay : See the 65. place.
　　　 ⎱ Upon time, the conditions being feverall : See 66, 67, 68, 69, 70.

BARTER, OR TRUCKE.

71

Phil. I buy Wares, for other Wares; value being equall.

Sch. In bought Wares (what name foever) Debitor to the Deliverd Wares : this is feldome feen. ☞ But if writing be not tedious unto us, or we not paper-penurious, the beft, and moft uni-forme Booking (in refpect of the generall verieties) of giving, or receiving of diverfities (being Wares, and Mony, or feverall Wares) is to have the received Wares Debitor to the Trucking Man; and then, the Trucking Man Debitor to the Delivered Wares.

Phil.

72 *Phil.* You have related your minde in things of an Equall value ; but if I buy Wares paying with *other* Wares and Mony.

Sch. Henry Waninghen, Chapter 2. unto the *6. Queſtion,* anſwereth in Dutch ; *Tgoet oatmen kœpt Debit aen Caſſa, Daer naer, Caſſa Debitaen't goet oatmen toegheeſt, I Engliſh it :* The Wares that we buy, Debitor to Caſh ; *afterwards,* Caſh Debitor to the Wares that we deliver : *as thus,* The Wares that I buy are worth 100. l. and the Wares that I deliver are worth 90. l. Conſequently, *I paying the Man,* he muſt have 90. l. in Wares, and 10. l. in *Mony* ; ſo that *Caſh* is for the 10. l. paid, more *Credit* then *Debit ;* therefore Caſh hath its due. With *Henry Waninghen* agreeth *J. Carpenter, fol.* 2. *parcell* 8. as bove ; he writeth, the goods bought, owe unto Caſh for the whole ſumme : *and after,* Caſh oweth unto the goods, which you have delivered to the Seller, for the value of them.

73 *Phil.* Seeing you *Imitate* in entring of their words ; have they your *Approbation ?*

Sch. I have related their words, not as an *affectionate-Follower,* but as an *Admirer* of their *Imitation.* For as in the 17. and 51. place by this ☞ is ſaid ; Caſh may not be *named* (no not *Named*) but where *Mony* is either *Really paid,* or *received : Nota,* and the while that it is abſolutely falſe, that Caſh hath in the above-mentioned 72. place not *paid* out 100. l. but onely 10. l. nor hath it *received* any peny of the 90. l. therefore for the 90. l. on each ſide, I ſay *Caſh* is an *Aſſe.*

74 *Phil.* But in the concluſion, it cometh all to one purpoſe.

Sch. That is not meteriall : why many words, when few may ſuffice ? For *J. Carpenter fol.* 32. *parcell* 7. anſwereth *direct* to the number ; *The goods which you buy, owe to the Seller :* And contrarily, *He oweth to Caſh, and to the goods which you have delivered him.* This is ſomewhat like a mans mony : But as in the 71. place is ſaid ; Idleneſſe in writing, or Penuriouſneſſe in paper, is the cauſe of theſe *Folly entrances.* For not onely in this, but in Exchanges, and the like, becauſe we will not have (as ſome terme it) *a Book full of names,* we muſt have our paſſages ſmothered under the covert of *Imaginary obſcurity* ; whereas we may have them delectably Booked, if we were not ſparing in writing. Daer en is met, ſonder vero꜓iet, *Nothing without trouble.* But I have no time to diſcuſſe other mens works ; therefore let me proceed.

75 *Phil.* I buy Wares, delivering a great value ; and receiving the *Over-plus* back in Mony.

Sch. In-bought Wares Debitor to the Selling Man, for their value ; 2. The Man Debitor to Delivered Wares, for their value : 3. Caſh Debitor to the Man, for the Received mony, to equall the Truck. So, in brief ; if the Wares are of an equall value, *then enter* Bought Wares, Debitor to the Trading man : 2. Trading Man Debitor to Delivered Wares ; becauſe the value is equall. If un-equall, and Mony given ; *then enter,* In-bought Wares Debitor to the Trading Man : *and then,* Trading Man Debitor to Delivered Wares, and to Caſh. But if un-equall, and Mony *Received* ; In-bought Wares, and Caſh, Debitor to the Trading Man : *and then,* Trading Man Debitor to *Delivered* Wares. And ſo I proceed to Wares bought, which are to be

Delivered mee, 2. 3. Weekes, or Moneths after
the agreement.

76 *Phil.* I buy Wares, agreeing now for Quantity, and Price ; but am to receive them 2 moneths hence.

Sch. The *Promiſing Man* is Debitor to *Promiſe-reckoning.*

77 *Phil.* I have already by this one parcell conceived, that you digreſſe from divers Printed Aathors : for,

Paſſchier Goeſſens of Bruſſel, in the German Language.
Pieter Nicolaeſon Daventrienſis.
John Willemſon of Leuven.

John

Tranſporting of Accounts in the Leager from one
Leafe *unto* another.

207 | *Phil.* What are the *Motives?*
Sch. They may be *two*; the one, when the *Leaves* of the Leager are full written in the Debitor, or Creditor ſide, or both. The other, becauſe the *former* accounts are concluded, ſo that upon foot of that account, generally there remaineth a remainer due to me, or from me; and we will have the account begunne again upon a *New* Leafe.

208 | *Phil.* Is this all?
Sch. Herein again is to be obſerved, whether thoſe accounts that are to be Tranſported, be *Commodities-accounts*, which in *New* leaves are to be continued as upon the former: *or*, whether they are *Ships-parts*, Houſes, Rents, Lands, Intereſts, Inſurances, *Factor-accounts*, or the like: of which (for that time) we make no *eſtimation of Eſtate*, but onely a tranſport for Tradings further continuance, untill a Generall Ballance be made.

209 | *Phil.* How muſt Commodities-reckonings fitly be tranſported, to make *true Journall* parcells of them?
Sch. In all tranſports (if poſſible) muſt heedfully be heeded, that not any parcell be poſted with *Blinde-ſummes*, or Blancks, *as ſome tearme them*: that is, *Not without Mony-ſummes*. Many in their Books tranſport with *Blankes* in their Leager, yet have Mony to tranſport, if they had *Art* to carry them *handſomely* forwards; to which end obſerve the enſuing Documents.
Suppoſe the *Wares* were Cambrix-cloth, and the whole *Debitor-ſide* contained 400. Peeces, which coſt 765.*l'*.8.*s*. and that the whole ſale in the *Creditor-ſide* were 278. Peeces; producing in mony 789.*l'*.10.*s*. *Nota*, theſe cannot be ſubſtracted from each other to make Journall parcells, but in the one will be Wares without Mony; and in the other Mony without Wares: which kind of Tranſports are very abſurd, though uſed by many.

Their *forme is as this Inſtance.*

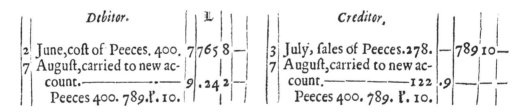

Debitor.		L			Creditor.			
2 June, coſt of Peeces. 400.	7	765	8	—	3 July, ſales of Peeces. 278.	—	789	10 —
7 Auguſt, carried to new account.———	9	.24	2	—	7 Auguſt, carried to new account.———122	.9	—	—
Peeces 400. 789.*l'*. 10.					Peeces 400. 789. *l'*. 10.			

To avoid the above-entred abſurdity of *Wares* in one Journall parcell, but *no Mony*; and *Mony* in the other Journall parcell, but *no Wares*: enter as the enſuing Journall inſtance inſtanceth.
Cambrix-cloth upon *folio* 30. Debitor to Cambrix-cloth upon *folio* 12. 765.*l'*. 8.*s*. for the preſent coſts of 400. Peeces, being the whole Debitor-ſide, in Wares, and Mony for want of place tranſported to a new leafe, the mony is 765.*l'*.8.*s*.

And then

Cambrix-cloth upon *folio* 12. Debitor to Cambrix-cloth upon *folio* 30. 789.*l'*. 10.*s*. for the ſales of 278. Peeces, being the whole Creditor-ſide, in Wares, and Mony, tranſported for want of place to a new leafe, the mony being————789.*l'*.10.*s*.

Thus ought each Journall parcell in Wares tranſporting truly to be Journalized, then the Leager will ſtand as this enſuing inſtance inſtanceth.

Fol. 12.

Fol. 12. Debitor.		£			12. Creditor.		£	
2	June, cofts of Peeces. 400.	7765	8	—	3	July, fales of Peeces. 278. —	789	10	—
7	Auguft, carried to new ac-				7	Auguft, carried to new ac-			
	count Peeces,————278	30789	10	—		count.————400	30765	.8	—
	Peeces 678. 1554. *l*. 18. $\tilde{s}$.					Peeces. 678. 1554. *l*. 18. $\tilde{s}$.			

And folio 30. will ftand

7. Aug. cofts of Peeces 400. 765. *l*. 8. $\tilde{s}$.   7. Aug. fales of Peeces 278. 789. *l*. 10. $\tilde{s}$.

    Here you fee the Leager ftand again as formerly it did, to be continued in writing, as before: here you fee each Journall parcell compleately carried: and thus ought Factor-accounts to be croffed: Forrain-mony, under Forrain-mony, as here Peeces under Peeces: and Inlandifh-mony under Inlandifh-mony, as before is inftanced. *Nota*, Do the like in Houfes, Lands, Rents, Legacies, Interefts, Ships-parts, Infurances, and the like: becaufe the principall (by Deduction) fhould not be Diminifhed untill the finall finifhing of thofe accounts.

210   *Phil.* Is this an ufuall courfe in the tranfporting of all kinds of accounts ?
    Sch. No: In your Generall accounts with Common-trading-people, as alfo in *Cafh,* Bank, Stock, Profit and Loffe, *or the like:* deduct the *Leffer* from the *Greater,* and make a Journall parcell for the *difference,* as thus:

    If the *Debitor-fide* of any of the above-named accounts (which are to be tranfported) be heavieft, then for the *difference* make the

    New account Debitor to the old.

    If the *Creditor-fide* be heavieft, then for the *difference* of any of thofe accounts, make the

    old account Debitor to the New.

211   *Phil.* What Obfervations arife from hence ?
    Sch. Hence is it manifeft, that in the Leager ought to be neither *Debitor,* nor *Creditor,* but fuch as have their

    Originall from the Journall,

whofe proper Office it is, to explain why the *one man,* or *thing* is Indebted unto the other, as hereafter in the Explication of the Journall Office fhall appear in the 244. place: and fo I end with the *Third Ground matter,* of which the Journall is made.

212   *Phil.* Explicate the *fourth Ground-matter,* of which the Journall is made.
    Sch. The *fourth Member* of the 9. place, faith, that it proceedeth from the

    Equalizing, or, even-making of over, or, under-meafures,
       Weight, Leackage, Pounds, Ells,
          or the like.

213   *Phil.* Inftance fome matters in *Proper-accounts.*
    Sch. When we find any *under-meafure* in Corn, or *Leakage* in Wine, or *Shortneffe* in Length. *then enter,* Profit and Loffe Debitor to the *wanting-matter;* rating it as you pleafe: for that rating neither augmenteth, nor diminifheth your Eftate ; but is onely done for decentneffe, to have mony in the Debit, and Credit of fuch Journall parcell:.

              Phil.

214 | *Phil.* Rehearſe ſome inſtances in *Factorage*-accounts.

Sch. If in weight I find in any commodity leſſe by ſales, becauſe of drineſs, or the like ; enter, *John Knoll* his account Currant, Debitor to *John Knoll* his account of Saffron : rating them as before, to bring them into the *true* form of *Debitor* and *Creditor*, in Journall and Leager. Hence may eaſily be gathered how to deal in Company-accounts ; which I now paſſe, and ſo proceed to the next matter in order.

215 | *Phil.* Whence ariſeth the *Fift Ground-matter*, that maketh a Member of the Journall ?

Sch. In the 9. place it is ſaid to ariſe from the

Leagers-Concluſion , or *Ballancing* of the Leager.

216 | *Phil.* What Cauſes may move a man to a Generall Ballance ?

Sch. The ſame may be either of theſe three :

1. When the Journall, and Leager are full written ; ſo that there muſt be New-Books :———

2. When a Merchant ceaſeth from Trading :———

3. When the book-Owner departeth this world:——— } Then is a Ballance requiſite.

217 | *Phil.* What underſtand you by the word *Ballance* ?

Sch. By *Ballance* I underſtand, An *Equall-making* in *Equivalent manner all the Open-ſtanding Leager-accounts* ; tranſporting all thoſe Open-ſtanding Leager differences under One laſt framed, accounts Title, whoſe name Generally we call *Ballance* : for being that that account *includeth* all the Leagers remaining differences ; ſo it *concludeth* with *One* ſolely it ſelf. *Nota,* the word *Ballance* ſeemeth to be borrowed from a pair of Scales : for as true Scales ought neither to be heavier then other ; ſo a true taked Generall Ballance ought not to differ the leaſt naming value : for the Generall Debitor and Creditor muſt juſtly counter-poize each other in even-monies nomination ; *elſe,* the Book is out of ſquare, the ſummes ill taken, or amiſſe added. In place of the word *Ballance,* I ſhould rather enter *Eſtate-reckoning* : for by drawing the whole Book to a head, I draw with *One* an account of my *Eſtate.* Simon Stevin in his *Princely Book-keeping,* carrieth the *Leagers* difference at the Years end, unto the *firſt begun* Stock when he *began* his Books : but he contradicteth himſelf. For he began well the *Firſt* day of January, in making all that owed to him *Debitors* to Stock ; and Stock *Debitor* to them who were *Debt-demanders* : but at his Leagers *concluding,* the 31. of December, he entreth Stock *Debitor* to his *Debitors* ; and he entreth his *Debt-demanders,* as *Augmentors* of his Stock. Such entrances made by him are but a *miſtake onely* ; in me they were *meer* Abſurdities.

Ballance is either a *Triall,* or *True-ballance.*

Of the *Tryall-ballance.*

218 | *Phil.* Relate the *manner* of making a Tryall-ballance.

Sch. Add the Debitor ſummes of all the Leager *Un-equall-open-ſtanding-accounts* upon a Paper together, or in a Book thereto prepared : *then* , add all the Creditor parcels in the whole Leager together by themſelves, becauſe the *Uniformity* of the *Generall Additions* ſhould be manifeſted ; if they be to each other *equivalent* , then (if no whole parcell be left out) are the Journall *mony-parcells* truely tranſported into the Leager.

219 | *Phil.* What more is to be ſaid of the Tryall-ballance .

Sch. The *Tryall-ballance* is of two ſorts : The firſt is a Survay (as above) of the Leager accounts.

accounts, fo foon as all the parcells are tranfported out of the *Wafte-book* into the Journall, and from thence into the Leager : *Nota,* before any *unfold wares,* or *Gain,* and *Loffe* of any accounts be meddled with. Of fuch matter is the firft ballance of the *three-fold-mony-bal-lance* in my Great Wafte-Book, printed 1621. at Amfterdam in Englifh, and Dutch ; and fhall be in this Book.

220   *Phil.* Inftance the fecond fort.
Sch. The fecond fort of the *Tryall-ballance* is feen, when all *unfould Wares,* and *Out-land-ifh monies* are rated : all *Abatements,* as likewife *Gaines* or *Loffes* are known. Of fuch matter is the fecond *Three-double-mony-ballance* in my Great Wafte-Book ; and fhall be in this. In this *fecond* ballance is alfo comprifed the parcells appertaining to the *true* ballance : *elfe,* that fecond ballance could not be even-weighty.

Of the *True-ballance.*

221   *Phil.* Proceed to the fame.
Sch. The *true-ballance* arifeth from the *Remainers* of Leager accounts ; as well in *Mony,* Unfold Wares, *Voyages* not wholly fold, *Houfes, Lands, People, &c.* not yet compleatly perfected : and are therefore tranfported to the New-Books ; to be there fully finifhed : Leaving the *Old-Books* to their perpetuall reft, except fome *Scrupulous* matter moleft them. Of fuch matter is the *Third* ballance of the *Three-double-mony-ballance* in my Great Wafte-Book, and fhall be in this.

Obfervations in ballancing of the Leager.

But for a preparative, firft *note,* that *even* as the Monies, Wares, Voyages, Houfes, Lands, and people were in their accounts (whether Debitors, or Creditors) even fo muft they ftand in your Ballance : and fo of each other matter. Reafon, for Ballance repre-fenteth in that onely account, all that the other reprefent through the whole Book : for if they were Debitors, Ballance is a Debitor in their place : if they were Creditors, Ballance is likewife a Creditor.

222   *Phil.* Go forwards in this matter.
Sch. There ought to be obferved *A Decent Order* in Leagers ballancing : *that is,* Which account ought *firft* to be concluded, and which laft ; both in *Debitor* and *Creditor* fide : this is not of Neceffity, but for Decentneffe in Order.

223   *Phil.* Profecute your opinion in the Order.
Sch. Firft, ballance the accounts of the People of whom you bought : or to whom you fould : *Reafon* : becaufe all Difcounts, Abatements, Mif-caftings, or Omiffions that have happened, may be rectified : to the end each account may bear its own burthen : take then the difference of each mans account (being found to agree) and enter them into your Ballance-Book (as in the 218. place is mentioned) untill the finall Ballance be found even-weighty.

224   *Phil.* Which next ?
Sch. Secondly, ballance the Peoples accounts with whom you had to deal for Ex-changes, Affignations, or the like : entring the differences into your Ballance-Book there-unto prepared.

225   *Phil.* What followeth ?
Sch. Thirdly, ballance your *Factors* accounts : firft for *Proper,* and then for *Company,* (but there is no neceffity in this Order, as it faid) the Remainers being well found, your Gain,

4. VOYAGE.

Debitor.	*Creditor.*
For 100. Pieces of Cambrix shipt at 3. l. each Piece, is——300.l.——	For Sales of 80. Pieces, at 2.l.16.s̄. is ——————224.l.—— Unfold, 20. Pieces, at 3.l. *per* Piece,—————60.l.— Loſt by Sales,————16.l.— Summe—300.l. ——

235   *Phil.* Go forward in the order of your Leagers Ballancing.
   Sch. Fifthly, ballance your *Commodities-accounts*; firſt for *Proper :* then, for *Company.*

236   *Phil.* Suppoſe them all ſold; and there is Gaines.
   Sch. The firſt Voyage is a Preſident.

237   *Phil.* Suppoſe your Commodities to be ſold in part.
   Sch. The ſecond Voyage is an Inſtance.

238   *Phil.* Suppoſe that none of your Commodities are ſold.
   Sch. The third Voyage ſheweth the form.

239   *Phil.* Suppoſe loſſe upon the Sale of part of your Commodities, or upon the whole.
   Sch. If loſſe upon part Sales, the Fourth Voyage is an Inſtance : If loſſe upon the Sale of a whole parcell : See

THE FORME.

Debitor.	*Creditor.*
For 16. Butts of Sack coſt with charges. ————134. l.8.	For Sale of 16. Butts, at 8. l. 6. is ——————132.l.16, Loſt by the Sale——————1. l. 12. Summe 134.l.8.

Under the name of *Commodities* in the ſecond branch of the 10. place, is included *Houſes, Lands, Ships-parts*; upon which if you will ſee the yearly Gain, or Loſſe, *then* rate them as they coſt; entring them in Credit as in the ſecond Voyage : *then*, in your Houſe, and Land will appear what is gained by the Rents, above reparation, and maintaining of them; and in your Ships parts will be made plain what is advanced by their Voyages, more then her victualling : carrying your Proper Gains or Loſs, to Profit and Loſs proper; and Companies Gain, or Loſs, to Profit and Loſs in Company. But if you will let them run on un-till the finall ending of them; then *croſs* them, as is ſhewed in the ſecond Inſtance of Cambrix-cloth, in the 209. place.

240   *Phil.* What followeth next in the Ballance order ?
   Sch. Sixthly, ballance your Company Profit and Loſs, imparting to each Partner his due upon fit account : and your part upon Profit and Loſs proper.
   Seventhly, ballance your Partners account, tranſporting the difference unto your Bal-lance-book (as in the 218. place is mentioned) untill the finall ballance be found Eaven-weighty.
   Eighthly, ballance Caſh, and Bank, carrying their differences to your Ballance-book.
   Ninthly, conclude your Profit and Loſs proper, carrying the difference to your Stock-account.
   Tenthly, conclude your Stock-account, tranſporting that difference (which is the
ſumme

ſumme of your Eſtate) unto your Ballance-book: then ought your Ballance account to be equall-weighty.

NOTA,

Having drawn all your Leager to a head in your Ballance-Book, and found it to b eright taken: then may you take your Journall in hand, and poſt them as they in order follow upon your Ballance-book, unto your Ballance-account in the Leager.

Or if you will not make a Ballance-account in your Leager, you may let your Ballance-book be your private contentment; and tranſport each Ballance-parcell out of the Old Leager into the New: avoiding your Ballance-writing into the Journall, both at the End of the Old Leager, or beginning of the New: entring into the Old Leager the *folio* whither carried into the New; and in the New Leager the *leaf* from whence that remainer is brought out of the Old Leager; and ſo avoid (perhaps) the writing of two or three hundred Journall-parcels in both Leagers.

Particular Obſervations upon each ſide of the true-ballance in Debit,
and Credit, for the Memories refreſhing.

241   *Phil.* Rehearſe firſt the Obſervations that ariſe upon the *Debitor-ſide* of the *True-bal-lance.*

Sch. In a much-Trafficking-Merchants-Books are five things to be regarded:

Firſtly, of De-bitors, and them in

> *People*—unto whom we ſold, or that have promiſed us payment of Exchanges, or Aſſignations, and the like.
> *Partners*—unto whom we have delivered Mony or Wares, to be by them imployed for the Companies good.
> *Factors*—that ſerve us in Commiſſion,— who as yet have not given
> *Maſters*—whom we ſerve in Commiſ-fion, — us full ſatisfaction: Again, the firſt of theſe two may
> ariſe from Proper, Factorage, or Company-accounts.

Secondly, of the Unſold Wares, formerly ſhipt to another Town, or Land, there to be ſold for *Proper, Factorage,* or *Company-account.*

Thirdly, of Matters as yet remaining *Unſold* under our own Adminiſtration: conſiſting again in *Wares, Houſes, Lands, Jewels, Ships-parts,* and the like: whereof ſome of thoſe *Wares* may be for *Proper, Factorage,* or *Company-accounts:* and thoſe *Ships-parts* for Proper, or Company-accounts.

Fourthly, of the *Ready-mony* in Caſh, in Bank, or in both.

Laſtly, of Company Gain, and Loſſe; of the which we ſtill keep an open-ſtanding-account, becauſe the Company continueth in Trading, upon unchangeable terms. And theſe in ſubſtance are all that concern the Contents of Ballances-Debitor-ſide.

242   *Phil.* Proceed to the obſervations in the Creditor-ſide of the *True ballance.*
Sch. Four things are heedfully to be regarded.

Firſtly,
Debt-demandırs;
and them in

> *People*—of whom we bought, as alſo, whoſe Exchanges we accepted; or whoſe Aſſignments we promiſed unto their Creditor, having entred their Creditor into my book in place of them.
> *Partners*—of whom we have received Mony, or Wares, to imploy for Company-account, unto whom (as yet) we
> *Maſters*-whom we ſerve in Commiſ-fion, — have not given full conſent: The laſt of theſe
> *Factors*-that ſerve us in Commiſſion, may ariſe, either from
> Proper, Factorage, or Company-accounts.

H 2   *Secondly,*

Secondly, Unfold-*Wares, Houfes, Lands, Iewels, Rents, Voyages,* and the like : upon which accounts the Gains or Lofs (at prefent) is not defired to be known ; but are deferred untill the finall finifhing of that account, then to know the Generall *Gain,* or *Lofs* upon the fame: and thefe for *Proper,* fome for *Faftorage,* and fome for *Company-accounts.*

Thirdly, in Companies Profit and Lofs Reckonings, becaufe the divifion is not made in thefe Old-books, but profecuted untill the Companies finall finifhing.

Laftly, in *Stock-account,* whofe difference muft be carried to *Ballance* ; for that difference muft make your Ballance-account *Eaven-weighty* in the *Generall* Addition: *Nota,* for in it is contained the *true* difference between the *Ready-mony, Wares, Houfes, &c. Debitors* in your Ballance-debit-fide, and the *Debt-demanders* in the Creditor fide of your Ballance-account. Or more plain ; take the whole Debit-fide of your *Ballance,* deduct from that all that you owe : and the differing mony will be *Equall-weighty,* with the difference brought from your *Stock-account.* And thus much of the *fifth matter,* of which the Journal is made.

Of the Journalls Form.

243   *Phil.* This is the *fecond branch* in the Eight place : of which let me heare your Explication.

Sch. The *Form* is generally in folio, or the full bignefs of the Paper, be it fmall, or large: Ruled towards the *left-hand* with *one line,* and towards the *right-hand* with *three :* entring between them l'. ß. ȡ. as in the Wafte-book is, and in the Journals Inftances fha'l be made plain.

Some ufe two lines towards the *left-hand,* as doth Simon Stevin in his *Princely-book-keeping-Iournall* ufe three : entring therein the *Day,* and *Moneth:* but that maketh the Journall between line, and line, too narrow. My manner of my *day,* and *Moneths* entrances fhall be fhewed in the Explication of the Journals Office.

This Book is by *fome* numbred on each leaves-fide : the beginning-fide with **1.** the fecond with **2.** and fo through all the Book: of which I approve, and ufe it. For in a Great-trafficking-book (as an *Eaft, Weft, Turky,* or the like Company) feverall fides are oft-times filled in one day : fo that the Margin of the Leager quoteth *direftly* to the fide of that Journall-leaf, where the defired parcell is : and fo avoideth the perufall of needleffe fides.

Of the Journalls Office.

244   *Phil.* Let me know that : for that is the third *Notable* matter mentioned in the Eighth place.

Sch. The Journalls *Proper Office* is, to have the *Matter* (thereunto appertaining) entred in *Book-keepings true method,* with *words* fuitable to the *Aftion* ; plainly expreffing what ever was obfcurely booked in other books.

Book-keepings Office is, to book the acted matter in the true *Nomination* of *Debitor* and *Creditor,* with the *brief* (yet plain) Circumftances of the Action. Heedfully in this Journall muft be obferved, that the *Debitor,* that is, the *Man,* or *Thing,* that ought to be *charged,* be firft named, and placed towards the *left-hand,* as thus :

          Iames Mirth is Debitor.

Then enter the Creditor, Man, or Thing, that ought to be difcharged, as thus

          Iames Mirth is Debitor to *Iohn Melody.*

Unto them annex the quantity of Mony, as thus :

          Iames Mirth is Debitor to *Iohn Melody* 300.l'.12.ß.8.ȡ.

There-unto adde the reafon why the One Man, or Thing is indebted to the other : and this is gathered from the acted matter.

245   *Phil.* As how :

Sch. Compare the Waftebook parcels in the 6. place, with the enfuing Journall parcels framed out of them, and the *Reafons* may appear by the Circumftances.

                                                 Anno

		£	ȡ	ȿ
5 / 6	*Dito* is Debitor to Bank 369. £. 13. 10. ½ ȡ. written by his order upon the account of *John Johnson Vinck*, being the full of the before-mentioned exchange, the summe written in, is————————	369	13	10½
5 / 3	*Dito* is Debitor to Profit and Loss 3. £.14.8.ȡ. for Bank-mony of ℔ 2240.11.4. pen. at one *per centum*, is———————————————	.3	14	.8
6 / 5	*Edward Denis* of Northampton,*his* account by me in Company, is Debitor to Dito *Edward his* account of *Ready-mony*, 213.£.—5 ⅛ ȡ. for his ⅓ of ℔ 3834.8.12.pen. product of 18. Last, 7. Mudde of Company Rye, sold to *Iacob Iohnson*, as above; ⅓ thereof is———————————	213	—	.5

246   *Phil.* What signifie those Fractions ½ ⅔, and the like, in the Margine?
     Sch. Fractions they are none: but signifying-figures concerning the Leager: for the Figures above the stroke, shew upon what Leager-Leafe the Debitors are to be found; and the Figures under the stroke, point unto the Creditors in the said Leager.

247   *Phil.* Why are some pointed, and not other some?
     Sch. Those that are pointed, are transported into the Leager, the other not.

248   *Phil.* Some do not point at all.
     Sch. They are subject to mistake, or they must enter each figure above, and under, when they have entred the parcell into their Leager, and that is tedious. The points are very requisite to avoid Omissions, or not to charge one summe twice, if a man should be called from his posting.

249   *Phil.* When do you enter the figures above, or under the stroke?
     Sch. I lay the Journall open before me, making first the straight strokes that are between the figures against each parcell, on both sides of the Journall: then do I enter the folio, or leaves, or those figures, before I touch the Leager.

250   *Phil.* How then?
     Sch. Then setting my Journall before me, I transport all the *Debitors* and *Creditors* (that correspond upon one Leager-leafe) one after another into the Leager; then *removing* my hand from the Leager, immediately I set point by that Debitor, or Creditor, that is posted into the Leager, without removing of my Journall.

Thus much in brief of the Matter, Form, and Office of the Journall mentioned in the ninth place.

	£	ß	d
fent payment for Company-ufe, being——————— ——	146	11	—

117. *Thomas Truſt* at Antwerp for company of *Randoll Rice* ⅓, and ⅔ for me, our account of Time, debitor to Voyage to Antwerp, conſigned to dito *Thomas* for our company ⅓, and ⅔ l'. 1515. 7. ß. for the enſuing Wares ſold by him: the particulars are, *viz.*

8. Bales of Pepper, producing clear Ready-mony, as by the account —————— ——— gl. 2753.9.4.

30. Butts of Serreſe to *Iaques Gerritſon*; part at 2. moneths, producing (whereof ⅔ is received) as by the account, clear mony——— ——gl. 12400.-

gl. 15153.9.4. pen. reduced at 10. gl, or 33.ß.4.d. are—— —— | 1515 | .7 | |

118. *Dito Thomas* for our company, as above, our account of Ready-mony, debitor to the ſaid *Thomas* for company R.R. ⅓, and ⅔ me our account of Time l'.1102.—4.d. for gl.11020.3.9. pen. by him received of the before entred mony, is here——— | 1162 | — | .4 |

The 15. day of June. 1634.

119. *Debitors* to *Iacob Symonſon* his account of Cambrix-cloth, l.405. for 60. Pieces ſold joyntly to the enſuing parties, at 6 l'. 15. ß. upon an equall ſhare, at 4. moneths time, *viz.*
James Wilkinſon 20. Pieces——— l'.135.
George Pinchback 20. Pieces——— l'.135.
Andrew Hitchcock 20.Pieces —— l'.135.
The Rule in the 244. place is *contra-dicted*. | 405 | — | — |

120. *Jacob Symonſon* his account of Cambrix-cloth, debitor to Caſh l'.1.7.ß. for Brokage of l'.405. at ⅓ *per centum*, is—— | .1 | 7 | — |

121. *Dito* to Profit and Loſs l'.8.12.ß. for the enſuing particulars, *viz.*
For Ware-houſe-room at 2.d. *per Piece* l'.—10. ⎰
For Proviſion of Sales at 2. *per* C.———l'.8.2. ⎱ | .8 | 12 | —⌉ |

122. *Dito* to *Jacob Symonſon* his account Currant l'.390.14.ß. for the neat proceed made good there, without my prejudice of debts, yet ſtanding out upon 4. moneths time: the ſum now tranſported, is | 390 | 14 | — |

123. *Jean du Boys* for company *Randoll Rice* ⅓, and ⅔ for me, our account Currant, debitor to *Thomas Truſt* for dito company ⅓, and ⅔ our account of Ready-mony l'.1092.17.10 .d. for gl.11020.remitted in his own Bills, dated their 2. preſent: payable by, and unto himſelf, exchange at 121.d. are ᴹ∕ᵥᵥ.3642. 58.6.d. and here at 72.d. ——— | 1092 | 17 | 10 |

The 23. day of Iune 1624.

124. *Randoll Rice* his account Currant, debitor to *Diego del Varino* his account of Fruits l'. 541. 4. ß. 9.d. for ſeverall forts

M

		L	s	d
6.	185. *Randoll Rice* his account by me in company debitor to Ballance l.991.7.6.d. for so much due to him upon this account———	991	.7	.6
10.	186. *Hendrick vander Linden* ½, *John van Does* ⅙, *Jaques Reinst* ⅓, their account of commodities, debitor to *Ballance* l.194.12. 1.d. for 160. Pieces of Figs, and 4. Bales of Pepper sold, being the whole Wares in Credit, transported thus to have the account compleat in new books, as it here standeth: the mony is———	194	12	.1
10.	187. *Dito Company* their account of Ready-mony debitor to *Ballance* l 99.7.7.d. for conclude due to them———	99	.7	.7
13. 13.	188. *Dito Company* their account of Time, debitor to *Ballance* l.93.19.8.d. due to them for conclude of this account, being———	93	19	.8
13. 1.	189. *Ballance* debitor to Cash l.947.2.1.d. and is for so much by conclude remaining therein, and transported, being———	947	2	.1
7. 1.	190. *Profit and Loss* debitor to Stock l.1046.8.10.d. for gaines in this handle, transported to conclude this account, being———	1046	.8	10
1. 13.	191. *Stock* debitor to Ballance l.2902.12.7.d. for the difference of that account, being my present Estate; and transported thither to conclude this, being———	2902	12	.7

End of the Journall
A.
1634.

OF
THE LEAGER.

HAving (in form as is inftanced) entred all the trading-parcels of Merchandizing into the Journall in fuch after-following manner as they daily happened; then hath the *Book owner* his whole Trading, with all the Circumftances in writing: but not in fuch fort, that he is able to confer with any man about his accounts: for each mans feverall Parcels are difperfed through the whole Journall; neither doth it (in drawing an account to a Head upon a Paper) content the mind, fearing that any Parcels might be mif-taken or omitted. Upon the like Reafon we may conjecture the Obfcurity in knowing what mony is in Cafh, what weight, meafure, and quantity of any Commodity might be in the Ware-houfe; what Profit or Loffe there is upon any fort of Wares, or Matter; what Weekly, or Monethly debts are to be received, or payd for Wares, or Exchanges: and many fuch like.

For the avoyding of all fuch diffidences, the Journall Parcels muft be tranfported into the *Leager* in fuch manner, that all what doth concern one mans particular, muft (under one accounts Title) be gathered together, *to wit*, all his *Debit* parcels upon the Left-hand; and all his *Credit* parcels upon the Right-hand of the *Open lying Leager*; of the which many inftances follow in the Leager: the like manner muft be ufed in each fort, as *Mony, Wares, People,* or what ever elfe; each muft be gathered together in an Exquifite form, with few words.

The thing charged, or *Debitor*, muft have its difcharge, or *Creditor*, even oppofice againft it felfe when the Leager lieth open. In this Leager, where *Fol.* ftandeth between the lines before the L, both upon the Right and Left-hand, are many Arithmetical Characters. The Character, Characters, or Figures that ftand between the two lines upon the *Debitor* fide, point (as with a finger) unto the Folio where each feverall lines *Creditor* ftandeth in the faid Book, whether it be upon the fame Leafe, or elfe where: Contrarily, the Figures that ftand between the two lines upon the *Creditor*-fide, point at the Folio where each feverall lines

Debitor

174

Debitor ſtandeth in the ſaid Book, whether upon the ſame Leafe or elſe-where.

In Brief,

The Owner, *or the* Owing thing,
Or what-ſo-ever comes to thee :
Upon the Left-hand ſee thou bring ;
For there the ſame muſt placed be.

But

they unto whom thou doeſt owe,
Upon the Right let them be ſet ;
Or what-ſo-ere doth from thee go,
To place them there do not forget.

T H I S

Book ſheweth our *true Eſtate* in each particular account ; whether Bought, Sold, Sent, or Received, Commodity: People with-in, or without the Land ; Exchanges which way-ſo-ever, and the Coynes of theſe ſeve-rall places ; *Factorage*, *Company*, or what account elſe belongeth to *Traffick*: So that the *Leager* is the *Mirrour* by which onely the Eſtate can *truly*, and *plainly* be diſcerned.

O 2

Cash is Debitor.

Jour.	Day		Fol	L	s	d
1	1	Janu. To Stock, for severall coynes of mony —— —	. 1	1000	15	. 7
5	27	Febr. To *Iacob Symonson* his account Currant— —	2	. 328	10	11
9	22	April To *George Pinchback*, received in full. —	3	. . 9	11	. 2
10	. 8	May To Figs ⅓ *R. R.* ⅔ for me—	9	525	—	
12	22	Dito to *Iames Wilkinson*, received to clear a truck—	4	102	16	. 1
14	23	June To *Diego del Varino* his account of Cash —	12	. 25	10	. 7
14	—	Dito To Profit and Losse, gained by *Diego's* fruits —	7	. 13	. 4	
14	2	July To *George-Pinchback* received by his Assignment—	3	485	. 6	. 5
16	11	Dito To *Iacob Symonson* his account Currant—	2	. 28	. 1	7
16	20	Dito To *Randoll Rice* his account Currant— —	6	284	16	8
16	20	Dito To *Andrew Hitchcock* received in part—	11	100	—	
		Summe—	L	2903	13	—

1634.

Stock is Debitor.

Jour.	Day		Fol	L	s	d
1	1	Janu. To *Iacob Symonson* his account Carrant— —	. 2	150	—	
19	20	July To *Ballance*, for conclude carried thither— —	13	2902	12	7
		Summe—	L	3052	12	7

1633.
1634.

Wares are Debitors.

Jour.	Day		L	R	Fol	L	s	d
. 1	. 1	Janu. To Stock, resting unsold—— —	60	90	. 1	477	10	—
20	20	July To Profit and Losse gained			. 7	92	10	—
		Summe—	60	90	L	570	—	—

1633.
1634.

Cash is Creditor.

Jour	Dy		Fol	£	s	d
2	4	Janu. By *George Pinchback*, paid in part——— —	3	144	—	—
2	9	Dito By *James Wilkinson*, paid in part——— —	4	120	—	—
3	30	Dito By *George Pinchback*, paid him——— —	3	135	16	8
4	9	Febr. By *Iac. Symonson*. his account of Couchaneille, payd	3	.. 5	.5	4
4	21	Dito by voyage to Lisborn, consigned to *Diego del Varino* for company ⅓, and ⅔ paid———	5	594	—	—
5	13	March by Dansick-exchange for *Arthur Mump.* and me ½	8	200	—	—
5	—	Dito By Kersies in Company ⅓ *Iacob Symonson*, ⅔ for me	4	.. 2	.8	6
9	—	Dito By *Iacob Symonson* his Cambrix cloth———	8	.. 4	.7	—
6	22	Dito By *Iacob Symonson* his account Currant——— —	2	.. 9	.7	9
6	—	Dito By Figs in company ⅓ *R. R.* ⅔ for me——— —	9	.. 8	.7	6
6	29	Dito By *Hendrick vander Linden*, and Company their account of commodities, for charges——— —	10	...	12	5
7	7	April By Silver, for charges of 8. Barrs——— —	10	.. 4	.7	2
10	8	May By *Randoll Rice* his account Currant——— —	.6	.99	19	1
11	13	Dito By Amsterdam-exchange ½ for *Iacob Symonson*—	11	504	19	6
12	7	June By *Diego del varino* his account of Cash——— —	12	25	10	7
12	7	Dito By Figs in Company ⅓ *R. R.* ⅔ for me———	.9	23	.8	9
12	7	Dito By *Andrew Hitchcock* paid him———	11	.73	16	8
13	15	Dito By *Iacob Symonson* his account of Cambrix-cloth--	.8	.. 1	.7	—
19	20	July By *Ballance*, transported thither to conclude this--	13	947	.2	1

1634. (beside 6|29 row)

		Summe———	£	2903	13	—

Stock is Debitor.

Jour	Dy		Fol	£	s	d
1	1	Janu. By Cash, for severall coynes of mony——— —	.1	1000	15	7
1	—	Dito By Wares for sundry sorts unsold——— —	1	477	10	—
1	—	Dito By Kettles for 5. Barrels unsold——— —	2	.55	—	6
1	—	Dito By *Iean du Boys* at Roan my account Currant—	2	240	—	—
1	—	Dito By *Iacob Symonson* my account by him in company	2	229	—	—
1	—	Dito By *Iacob Symonson* his account of Couchaneille—	3	.. 3	17	8
19	20	July By Profit and Losse, gained by this handle——— —	7	1046	.8	10

1633. (beside first rows)   *1634.* (beside July row)

		Summe———	£	3052	12	7

Wares are Creditors.

Jour	Dy		£	1	Fol	£	s	d
2	13	Janua. By Kersies in company, by me layd in--	..	90	4	270	—	—
6	21	March By *Iacob Symonson*, sold to him———	60	..	2	300	—	—

1633. (beside March row)

		Summe—	60	90	£	570	—	—

Profit and Loſſe in company ⅓ for *Randoll Rice*, and ⅔ for me, Debitor.

Year		Day	Description	Fol	L	s	d
	3	23	Janu. To Profit and Loſſe for charges of a Remiſe ——	7	2	11	11
1634.	7	29	March. To *Iean du Boys*, for his Proviſion, and Brokage—	6	2	11	3
	17	20	July To *Thomas Truſt*, our account of Ready-mony, loſt--	13	9	2	6
	18	—	Dito To *Ran. Rice*, his account by me in comp. for ⅓ gains	6	444	9	8
	18	—	Dito To Profit and Loſſe, for my part gains ——————	7	296	6	5
			Summe—	L	755	1	9

Profit and Loſſe, Debitor.

Year		Day	Description	Fol	L	s	d
1633.	4	17	Febru. To *Iacob Symonſon* my account of Ready-mony, for his charges, being Brokage, and Proviſion——— —	3	—	10	1
1634.	17	20	July To *Iac. Symonſon* my account of Ready-mony, loſt-	3	25	—	11
	17	20	Dito To Silver, loſt by the ſale of 8. Barres_____	10	3	9	1
	19	20	Dito To Stock, gained by this handle._____----	1	1046	8	10
			Summe—	L	1075	8	11

Ballance, Debitor.

Year		Day	Description	Fol	L	s	d
1634.	18	20	July To *Jacob Symonſon* my account by him in company	2	301	—	8
	18	20	Dito To *Jean du Boys*, for company *R. R.* ⅓, me ⅔ Currant-	6	1092	17	10
	18	20	Dito To *Hen. van. Linden*, and comp. their commodies-	10	194	12	1
	18	20	Dito To Voyage to Antw. in comp. *R. R.* ⅓, and ⅔ me——	10	189	12	—
	18	20	Dito To *Andrew Hitchcock* due to me by conclude———	11	446	12	9
	18	20	Dito To *Arthur Mumperſon* my account by him in comp.	12	402	12	1
	18	20	Dito To *Tho. Truſt*, for comp. *R. R.* ⅓, me ⅔ our Time acco.	12	413	6	8
	18	20	Dito To Figs in comp. for *Iacob Symonſon* ⅔, and ⅓ for me-	13	806	6	11
	19	20	Dito To Caſh, reſting therein, and brought hither———	1	947	2	1
			Summe———	L	4794	3	1

Day		Fol	L	s	d
	Contra, Creditor.				
17 20	July By Voyage to Lisborn for dito company gained——	5	14	2	8
17 20	Dito By *Iean du Boys*, for dito company, gained——	6	80	11	7
17 20	Dito By *Iacob Symonfon*, for dito company, gained——	9	60	—	6
17 20	Dito By Voyage to Antwerp, for dito company, gained-	10	600	7	
	Summe——	L	75	1	9

	Day		Fol	L	s	d
		contra, Creditor.				
1633.	3 23	Janu. By Profit and Loffe in company ⅓ *R.R.* ⅔ me——	7	2	11	11
	4 9	Febru. By *Iacob Symonfon* his Couchaneille, for provifion	3	31	12	2
	5 13	March By Kerfies in comp. ⅓ and ⅔ for provifion & gains	4	128	5	—
1634.	8 15	April By *Iaccb Symonfon* my acco. by him in comp. gained	2	50		
	9 22	Dito By Danfick-exchange, gained by the fame——	8	10	19	9
	11 22	May By *George Pinchback* upon Sugar gained—— —		36	5	—
	13 15	June By *Iacob Symonfon* his Cambrix for provifion——	8	8	12	
	14 23	Dito By Cafh, for provifion of *Piego* his Fruits—— —	1	13	4	
	15 2	July By Amfterdam-exchange in company, gained——	11	23		8
	15 11	Dito By Figs ⅓, and ⅔ in comp. for provifion and gaines—	9	114	15	5
	17 20	Dito By Wares gained thereby—— — —	1	92	10	
	17 —	Dito By Kettles, gained thereby—— — —	2	20		2
	17 20	Dito By *Iean du Boys* my account Currant gained——	2	56	5	6
	17 20	Dito By Voyage to Amfterdam configned to *I.S.* gained	4	111	17	
	17 20	Dito By Intereft-reckoning, gained thereby—— —	5	16	6	2
	17 20	Dito By Voyage to Lisborn ⅔, and ⅓ for my gaines——	8	63	17	9
	18 —	Dito By Profit and Loffe ⅓, and ⅔ for my ⅔ gaines——	7	296	6	5
		Summe——	L	1075	8	11

	Day		Fol	L	s	d
		Ballance, Creditor.				
1634.	18 20	July By *Iacob Symonfon* his account by me in company-	5	512	3	8
	19 20	Dito By *Randoll Rice* his account by me in company——	6	991	7	6
	19 20	Dito By *Hend. vander Lind.* and comp. their commodities	10	194	12	1
	19 20	Dito By *Hend. vand. Linden*, and comp. their ready-mony	10	99	7	7
	19 20	Dito By *Hend. vand. Lind.* and comp. their Time account-	13	93	19	8
	19 20	Dito By Stock, for difference there, being my pref. eftate-	1	2901	12	7
		Summe——	L	4794	3	1

SURVEY OF THE Generall Ballance, or Estate-reckoning.	Thus ought your accounts to stand at the firſt view of the Bookes, when every thing is tranſported out of the Waſte-Book into the Leager.			Thus ought your *Second,* or *Triall-Ballance* to stand with the Loſſes.			Thus ought your True-Ballance to stand, which you tranſport into your New-Books.		
Debitor	Guil.	ſti.	p.	Guil.	ſti.	p.	Guil.	ſti.	p.
23 Dito. To Banck, as in fol. 1. appeareth	13688	17	8	5555	2	—	5555	2	—
Dito. To Houſe King *David,* fol. 2	6213	15	—						
Dito. To *Suſanna Peeters Orphans*	5573	16	8	713	14	8	713	14	8
Dito. To *Jack Pudding* my account Currant	11328	6	8	2648	6	8	2648	6	8
Dito. To Wines, for 15. Butts unfold	1260	—	—	1260	—	—	1260	—	—
Dito. To French Aquavitæ, for 58. Hogſheads	5568	—	—						
Dito. To Rye, for 18. Laſt, 7. Mudde, fol. 3.	2877	15	8	1533	15	8	1533	15	8
Dito. To Couchaneille, as in fol. 4.	10080	—	—	36	—	—			
Dito. To Braſil, as in fol.	10888	3	—	70	11	—			
Dito. To Intereſt-reckoning, fol.	44	14	—						
Dito. To Profit and Loſſe, fol.	320	2	8						
Dito. To Voyage to London, conſigned to *Jack Pudding,* fol.	7810	—	—	2600	—	—	2600	—	—
Dito. To Voyage to Hambrough, fol.	2353	3	—						
Dito. To Voyage to Danſick, fol.	1967	1	—						
Dito. To Inſurance-reckoning, fol.	3463	2	8						
Dito. To Caſh, as appeareth in fol.	29561	11	—	27153	8	—	27153	8	—
Dito. To Cambrix, 11. Peeces unfold	8900	—	—	440	—	—	440	—	—
Dito. To Ship the Rain-bow, fol.	1043	12	8						
Dito. *To Hans van Eſſen* at Hambrough, my account Currant, fol.	3780	—	—	60	—	—			
Dito. To *Peeter Braſſeur* at Danſick, my account Currant, fol.	3805	14	8	53	12	8			
Dito. To *Jack Pudding* at London, his account Currant, fol.	917	—	—						
Summe **gl.**	130544	15	—	42124	10	—	41904	6	8

180

SURVEY OF THE Generall-Ballance, or Estate-reckoning.	Thus ought your accounts to stand at the first view of your Books, when each parcel is transported out of the Waste-Book into the Journall and Leager.			Thus ought your Second, or Tryall-Ballance td stand with the Gains.			Thus ought your True Ballince to stand, which you transport to New-Books.		
Creditor.	Guil.	sti.	p.	Guil.	sti.	p.	Guil.	sti.	p.
23 Dito. By Banck, as in fol. 1. appeareth—	8133	15	8				')		
— Dito. By House King *David*, fol. 2. —	7538	15	—	1325	—	—			
— Dito. By *Susanna Peeters Orphans* —	4860	. 2	—						
— Dito. By *Jack Pudding* my account Currant ———	9145	—	—	. 465	—	—			
— Dito. By French Aqua-vitæ 58. Hogs-heads sold —— ——	6960	—	—	1392	—	—			
— Dito. By Rye, for 16. Last sold, fol. 3.	1788	12	8	444	12	8			
— Dito. By Couchaneille, as in fol. 4. —	13950	—	—	3906	—	—			
— Dito. By Brasil, as in fol. 4. ——	10817	12	—						
— Dito. By Interest-reckoning, fol. ——	102	16	8	58	2	8			
— Dito. By Profit and Losse, fol. ——	394	. 7	8	74	5	—			
— Dito. By Voyage to London, fol. ——	8350	—	—	3140	—	—			
— Dito. By Voyage to Hambrough —	3816	. 6	—	1463	. 3	—			
— Dito. By Voyage to Dansick, fol. ——	3805	14	8	1838	13	8			
— Dito. By Insurance-reckoning, fol. —	3576	6	—	113	3	8			
— Dito. By Cash, as appeareth in fol. —	2408	3	—						
— Dito. By Cambrix-Cloth, fol. ——	8105	12	—	545	12	—			
— Dito. By Ship the Rain-bow, fol. —	1432	12	8	389	—	—			
— Dito. By *Hans van Essen* my account—	3720	—	—						
— Dito. By *Peeter Brasseur* my account—	3752	2	—						
— Dito. By *Jack Pudding* at London, his account Currant —— —— ——	3294	18	—	2377	18	—	2377	18	—
— Dito. By Stock, for my just Estate —	24592	—	—	24592	—	—	39526	. 8	8
Summe gl. ———	130544	15	—	42124	10	—	41904	6	8

Afterword

To the reader's own judgment have been left the many conclusions that are to be drawn from these reproductions of bookkeeping's earliest exponents.

The author in no sense desired to intrude too strongly his own ideas upon his reader. It has been his intent to show clearly how the ideas expressed by Pacioli in the early Italian vernacular came down through many translations into German, into Dutch, into French and lastly into English, withstanding all the many changes of language, surviving the "Dark Ages" of history and retaining unchanged through the centuries their clarity of thought and purpose until today the modern bookkeeper and the professional accountant are to be found trudging faithfully in the footsteps of the Franciscan Friar of medieval times.

Natural prejudice or partiality toward heralding abroad the imprint left by the early authors of his mother country on his own profession in its making is to be expected from the writer as an Hollander-born and for this reason, if no other, he has been diffident to drive home the conclusions he himself has formed. It is devoutly to be hoped that the reader will experience the same pleasure in the reading that the author has taken in the making of this contribution to his fellows.